Aurora Floyd. A Novel

AURORA FLOYD.

A Novel.

BY M. E. BRADDON,

AUTHOR OF

"LADY AUDLEY'S SECRET."

RICHMOND:
WEST & JOHNSTON, 145 MAIN STREET.
1863.

Evans & Cogswell, Printers,
No. 3 Broad street, Charleston, S. C.

AURORA FLOYD.

CHAPTER I.

HOW A RICH BANKER MARRIED AN ACTRESS.

Faint streaks of crimson glimmer here and there amid the rich darkness of the Kentish woods. Autumn's red finger has been lightly laid upon the foliage—sparingly, as the artist puts the brighter tints into his picture; but the grandeur of an August sunset blazes upon the peaceful landscape, and lights all into glory.

The encircling woods and wide lawn-like meadows, the still ponds of limpid water, the trim hedges, and the smooth winding roads; undulating hill-tops, melting into the purple distance; laboring-men's cottages, gleaming white from the surrounding foliage; solitary roadside inns with brown thatched roofs and moss-grown stacks of lop-sided chimneys; noble mansions hiding behind ancestral oaks; tiny Gothic edifices; Swiss and rustic lodges; pillared gates surmounted by escutcheons hewn in stone, and festooned with green wreaths of clustering ivy; village churches and prim school-houses—every object in the fair English prospect is steeped in a luminous haze, as the twilight shadows steal slowly upward from the dim recesses of shady woodland and winding lane, and every outline of the landscape darkens against the deepening crimson of the sky.

Upon the broad *façade* of a mighty red-brick mansion, built in the favorite style of the early Georgian era, the sinking sun lingers long, making gorgeous illumination. The long rows of narrow windows are all aflame with the red light, and an honest homeward-tramping villager pauses once or twice in the roadway to glance across the smooth width of dewy lawn and tranquil lake, half fearful that there must be something more than natural in the glitter of those windows, and that maybe Maister Floyd's house is afire.

The stately red-built mansion belongs to Maister Floyd, as he is called in the honest *patois* of the Kentish rustics; to Archibald Martin Floyd, of the great banking-house of Floyd, Floyd, and Floyd, Lombard street, City.

The Kentish rustics knew very little of this city banking-house, for Archibald Martin, the senior partner, has long retired from any active share in the business, which is carried on entirely by his nephews, Andrew and Alexander Floyd, both steady, middle-aged men, with families and country-houses; both owing their fortune to the rich uncle, who had found places in his counting-house for them some thirty years before, when they were tall, raw-boned, sandy-haired, red-complexioned Scottish youths, fresh from some unpronounceable village north of Aberdeen.

The young gentlemen signed their names M'Floyd when they first entered their uncle's counting-house; but they very soon followed that wise relative's example, and dropped the formidable prefix. "We've nae need to tell these Southeran bodies that we're Scotche," Alick remarked to his brother as he wrote his name for the first time A. Floyd, all short.

The Scottish banking-house had thriven wonderfully in the hospitable English capital. Unprecedented success had waited upon every enterprise undertaken by the old-established and respected firm of Floyd, Floyd, and Floyd. It had been Floyd, Floyd, and Floyd for upward of a century; for, as one member of the house dropped off, some greener branch shot out from the old tree; and there had never yet been any need to alter the treble repetition of the well-known name upon the brass plates that adorned the swinging mahogany doors of the banking-house. To this brass plate Archibald Martin Floyd pointed when, some thirty years before the August evening of which I write, he took his raw-boned nephews for the first time across the threshold of his house of business.

"See there, boys," he said: "look at the three names upon that brass plate. Your uncle George is over fifty, and a bachelor—that's the first name; our first cousin, Stephen Floyd, of Calcutta, is going to sell out of the business before long—that's the second name; the third is mine, and I'm thirty-seven years of age, remember, boys, and not likely to make a fool of myself by marrying. Your names will be wanted by and by to fill the blanks; see that you keep them bright in the meantime; for, let so much as one speck rest upon them, and they 'll never be fit for that brass plate."

Perhaps the rugged Scottish youths took this lesson to heart, or perhaps honesty was a natural and inborn virtue in the house of Floyd. Be it as it might, neither Alick nor Andrew disgraced their ancestry; and when Stephen Floyd, the East-Indian merchant, sold out, and Uncle George grew tired of business, and took to building, as an elderly, bachelor-like hobby, the young men stepped into their relatives' shoes, and took the conduct of the business upon their broad Northern shoulders. Upon one point only Archibald Martin Floyd had misled his nephews, and that point regarded himself. Ten years after his address to the young men, at the sober age of seven-and-forty, the banker not only made a fool of himself by marrying, but, if indeed such things are foolish, sank still farther from the proud elevation of worldly wisdom by falling desperately in love with a beautiful but penniless woman, whom he brought home with him after a business tour through the manufacturing districts, and with but little ceremony introduced to his relations and the county families round his Kentish estate as his newly-wedded wife.

The whole affair was so sudden, that these very county families had scarcely recovered from their surprise at reading a certain paragraph in the left-hand column of the *Times*, announcing the marriage of "Archibald Martin Floyd, Banker, of Lombard street and Felden Woods, to Eliza, only surviving daughter of Captain Prodder," when the bridegroom's travelling carriage dashed past the Gothic lodge at the gates, along the avenue and under the great stone portico at the side of the house, and Eliza Floyd entered the banker's mansion, nodding good-naturedly to the bewildered servants, marshalled into the hall to receive their new mistress.

The banker's wife was a tall young woman of about thirty, with a dark complexion, and great flashing black eyes that lit up a face which might otherwise have been unnoticeable into the splendor of absolute beauty.

Let the reader recall one of those faces whose sole loveliness lies in the glorious light of a pair of magnificent eyes, and remember how far they surpass all others in their power of fascination. The same amount of beauty frittered away upon a well-shaped nose, rosy, pouting lips, symmetrical forehead, and delicate complexion, would make an ordinarily lovely woman; but concentrated in one nucleus, in the wondrous lustre of the eyes, it makes a divinity, a Circe. You may meet the first any day of your life; the second, once in a lifetime.

Mr. Floyd introduced his wife to the neighboring gentry at a dinner-party, which he gave soon after the lady's arrival at Felden Woods, as his country seat was called; and this ceremony very briefly despatched, he said no more about his choice either to his neighbors or his relations, who would have been very glad to hear how this unlooked-for marriage had come about, and who hinted the same to the happy bridegroom, but without effect.

Of course this very reticence on the part of Archibald Floyd himself only set the thousand tongues of rumor more busily to work. Round Beckenham and West Wickham, near which villages Felden Woods was situated, there was scarcely any one debased and degraded station of life from which Mrs. Floyd was not reported to have sprung. She was a factory-girl, and the silly old banker had seen her in the streets of Manchester, with a colored handkerchief on her head, a coral necklace round her throat, and shoeless and stockingless feet tramping in the mud: he had seen her thus, and had fallen incontinently in love with her, and offered to marry her there and then. She was an actress, and he had seen her on the Manchester stage; nay, lower still, she was some poor performer, decked in dirty white muslin, red cotton velvet, and spangles, who acted in a canvas booth, with a pitiful set of wandering vagabonds and a learned pig. Sometimes they said she was an equestrian, and it was at Astley's, and not in the manufacturing districts, that the banker had first seen her; nay, some there were ready to swear that they themselves had beheld her leaping through gilded hoops, and dancing the cachuca upon six barebacked steeds in that sawdust-strewn arena. There were whispered rumors that went even farther than these —rumors which I dare not even set down here, for the busy tongues that dealt so mercilessly with the name and fame of Eliza Floyd were not unbarbed by malice. It may be that some of the ladies had personal reasons for their spite against the bride, and that many a waning beauty, in those pleasant Kentish mansions, had speculated upon the banker's income, and the advantages attendant upon a union with the owner of Felden Woods.

The daring, disreputable creature, with not even beauty to recommend her—for the Kentish damsels scrupulously ignored Eliza's wonderful eyes, and were sternly critical with her low forehead, doubtful nose, and rather wide mouth — the artful, designing minx, who, at the mature age of nine-and-twenty, with her hair growing nearly down to her eyebrows, had contrived to secure to herself the hand and fortune of the richest man in Kent—the man who had been hitherto so impregnable to every assault from bright eyes and rosy lips, that the most indefatigable of manœuvring mothers had given him up in despair, and ceased to make visionary and Alnaschar-like arrangements of the furniture in Mr. Floyd's great red-brick palace.

The female portion of the community wondered indignantly at the supineness of the two Scotch nephews, and the old bachelor brother, George Floyd. Why did not these people show a little spirit — institute a commission of lunacy, and shut their crazy relative in a mad-house? He deserved it.

The ruined *noblesse* of the Faubourg St. Germain, the faded *duchesses* and wornout *vidames*, could not have abused a wealthy Bonapartist with more vigorous rancor than these people employed in their ceaseless babble about the banker's wife. Whatever she did was a new subject for criticism; even at that first dinner-party, though Eliza had no more ventured to interfere with the arrangements of the man-cook and housekeeper than if she had been a visitor at Buckingham Palace, the angry guests found that everything had degenerated since "that woman" had entered the house. They hated the successful adventuress — hated her for her beautiful eyes and her gorgeous jewels, the extravagant gifts of an adoring husband — hated her for her stately figure and graceful movements, which never betrayed the rumored obscurity of her origin — hated her, above all, for her insolence in not appearing in the least afraid of the lofty members of that new circle in which she found herself.

If she had meekly eaten the ample dish of humble-pie which these county families were prepared to set before her — if she had licked the dust from their aristocratic shoes, courted their patronage, and submitted to be "taken up" by them — they might, perhaps, in time, have forgiven her. But she did none of this. If they called upon her, well and good; she was frankly and cheerfully glad to see them. They might find her in her gardening-gloves, with rumpled hair and a watering-pot in her hands, busy among her conservatories; and she would receive them as serenely as if she had been born in a palace, and used to homage from her very babyhood. Let them be as frigidly polite as they pleased, she was always easy, candid, gay, and good-natured. She would rattle away about her "dear old Archy," as she presumed to call her benefactor and husband; or she would show her guests some new picture he had bought, and would dare — the impudent, ignorant, pretentious creature! — to talk about Art, as if all the high-sounding jargon with which they tried to crush her was as familiar to her as to a Royal Academician. When etiquette demanded her returning these stately visits, she would drive boldly up to her neighbors' doors in a tiny basket-carriage, drawn by one rough pony; for it was an affectation of this designing woman to affect simplicity in her tastes, and to abjure all display. She would take all the grandeur she met with as a thing of course, and chatter and laugh, with her flaunting theatrical animation, much to the admiration of mis-

guided young men, who could not see the high-bred charms of her detractors, but who were never tired of talking of Mrs. Floyd's jolly manners and glorious eyes.

I wonder whether poor Eliza Floyd knew all or half the cruel things that were said of her. I shrewdly suspect that she contrived somehow or other to hear them all, and that she rather enjoyed the fun. She had been used to a life of excitement, and Felden Woods might have seemed dull to her but for these ever-fresh scandals. She took a malicious delight in the discomfiture of her enemies.

"How badly they must have wanted you for a husband, Archy," she said, "when they hate me so ferociously. Poor, portionless old maids, to think I should snatch their prey from them! I know they think it a hard thing that they can't have me hung for marrying a rich man."

But the banker was so deeply wounded when his adored wife repeated to him the gossip which she had heard from her maid, who was a stanch adherent to a kind, easy mistress, that Eliza ever after withheld these reports from him. They amused her, but they stung him to the quick. Proud and sensitive, like almost all very honest and conscientious men, he could not endure that any creature should dare to befoul the name of the woman he loved so tenderly. What was the obscurity from which he had taken her to him? Is a star less bright because it shines on a gutter as well as upon the purple bosom of the midnight sea? Is a virtuous and generous-hearted woman less worthy because you find her making a scanty living out of the only industry she can exercise, and acting Juliet to an audience of factory hands, who gave threepence apiece for the privilege of admiring and applauding her?

Yes, the murder must out; the malicious were not altogether wrong in their conjectures: Eliza Prodder was an actress; and it was on the dirty boards of a second-rate theatre in Lancashire that the wealthy banker had first beheld her. Archibald Floyd nourished a traditional, passive, but sincere admiration for the British Drama. Yes, the *British* Drama; for he had lived in a day when the drama was British, and when *George Barnwell* and *Jane Shore* were among the favorite works of art of a play-going public. How sad that we should have degenerated since those classic days, and that the graceful story of Milwood and her apprentice-admirer is now so rarely set before us! Imbued, therefore, with the solemnity of Shakespeare and the drama, Mr. Floyd, stopping for a night at this second-rate Lancashire town, dropped into the dusty boxes of the theatre to witness the performance of *Romeo and Juliet* — the heiress of the Capulets being represented by Miss Eliza Percival, *alias* Prodder.

I do not believe that Miss Percival was a

good actress, or that she would ever become distinguished in her profession; but she had a deep, melodious voice, which rolled out the words of her author in a certain rich though rather monotonous music, pleasant to hear; and upon the stage she was very beautiful to look at, for her face lighted up the little theatre better than all the gas that the manager grudged to his scanty audiences.

It was not the fashion in those days to make "sensation" dramas of Shakespeare's plays. There was no *Hamlet* with the celebrated water-scene, and the Danish prince taking a "header" to save poor weak-witted Ophelia. In the little Lancashire theatre it would have been thought a terrible sin against all canons of dramatic art had Othello or his Ancient attempted to sit down during any part of the solemn performance. The hope of Denmark was no long-robed Norseman with flowing flaxen hair, but an individual who wore a short, rusty black cotton velvet garment, shaped like a child's frock and trimmed with bugles, which dropped off and were trodden upon at intervals throughout the performance. The simple actors held that tragedy, to be tragedy, must be utterly unlike anything that ever happened beneath the sun. And Eliza Prodder patiently trod the old and beaten track, far too good-natured, light-hearted, and easy-going a creature to attempt any foolish interference with the crookedness of the times, which she was not born to set right.

What can I say, then, about her performance of the impassioned Italian girl? She wore white satin and spangles, the spangles sewn upon the dirty hem of her dress, in the firm belief, common to all provincial actresses, that spangles are an antidote to dirt. She was laughing and talking in the whitewashed little green-room the very minute before she ran on to the stage to wail for her murdered kinsman and her banished lover. They tell us that Macready began to be Richelieu at three o'clock in the afternoon, and that it was dangerous to approach or to speak to him between that hour and the close of the performance. So dangerous, indeed, that surely none but the daring and misguided gentleman who once met the great tragedian in a dark passage, and gave him " Good-morrow, 'Mac,' " would have had the temerity to attempt it. But Miss Percival did not take her profession very deeply to heart; the Lancashire salaries barely paid for the physical wear and tear of early rehearsals and long performances; how, then, for that mental exhaustion of the true artist who lives in the character he represents?

The easy-going comedians with whom Eliza acted made friendly remarks to each other on their private affairs in the intervals of the most vengeful discourse; speculated upon the amount of money in the house in audible un-

dertones during the pauses of the scene; and when Hamlet wanted Horatio down at the foot-lights to ask him if he "marked that," it was likely enough that the prince's confidant was up the stage telling Polonius of the shameful way in which his landlady stole the tea and sugar.

It was not, therefore, Miss Percival's acting that fascinated the banker. Archibald Floyd knew that she was as bad an actress as ever played the leading tragedy and comedy for five-and-twenty shillings a week. He had seen Miss O'Neil in that very character, and it moved him to a pitying smile as the factory hands applauded poor Eliza's poison-scene. But, for all this, he fell in love with her. It was a repetition of the old story. It was Arthur Pendennis at the little Chatteris Theatre bewitched and bewildered by Miss Fotheringay all over again — only that instead of a feeble, impressionable boy, it was a sober, steady-going business-man of seven-and-forty, who had never felt one thrill of emotion in looking on a woman's face until that night — until that night — and from that night to him the world only held one being, and life only had one object. He went the next evening, and the next, and then contrived to scrape acquaintance with some of the actors at a tavern next the theatre. They sponged upon him cruelly, these seedy comedians, and allowed him to pay for unlimited glasses of brandy and water, and flattered and cajoled him, and plucked out the heart of his mystery; and then went back to Eliza Percival, and told her that she had dropped into a good thing, for that an old chap with no end of money had fallen over head and ears in love with her, and that if she played her cards well, he would marry her to-morrow. They pointed him out to her through a hole in the green curtain, sitting almost alone in the shabby boxes, waiting for the play to begin and her black eyes to shine upon him once more.

Eliza laughed at her conquest; it was only one among many such, which had all ended alike—leading to nothing better than the purchase of a box on her benefit night, or a bouquet left for her at the stage-door. She did not know the power of "first love upon a man of seven-and-forty. Before the week was out, Archibald Floyd had made her a solemn offer of his hand and fortune.

He had heard a great deal about her from her fellow-performers, and had heard nothing but good. Temptations resisted; diamond bracelets indignantly declined; graceful acts of gentle womanly charity done in secret; independence preserved through all poverty and trial — they told him a hundred stories of her goodness, that brought the blood to his face with proud and generous emotion. And she herself told him the simple history of her life—told him that she was the daughter of a merchant-captain called Prodder; that she was born at Liverpool; that she remembered little of her father, who was almost always at sea; nor of a brother, three years older than herself, who quarrelled with his father, the merchant-captain, and ran away, and was never heard of again; nor of her mother, who died when she, Eliza, was ten years old. The rest was told in a few words. She was taken into the family of an aunt who kept a grocer's shop in Miss Prodder's native town. She learned artificial flower-making, and did not take to the business. She went often to the Liverpool theatres, and thought she would like to go upon the stage. Being a daring and energetic young person, she left her aunt's house one day, walked straight to the stage-manager of one of the minor theatres, and asked him to let her appear as Lady Macbeth. The man laughed at her, but told her that, in consideration of her fine figure and black eyes, he would give her fifteen shillings a week to "walk on," as he technically called the business of the ladies who wander on to the stage, sometimes dressed as villagers, sometimes in court costume of calico trimmed with gold, and stare vaguely at whatever may be taking place in the scene. From "walking on" Eliza came to play minor parts, indignantly refused by her superiors; from these she plunged ambitiously into the tragic lead, and thus, for nine years, pursued the even tenor of her way, until, close upon her nine-and-twentieth birthday, Fate threw the wealthy banker across her pathway, and in the parish church of a small town in the Potteries the black-eyed actress exchanged the name of Prodder for that of Floyd.

She had accepted the rich man partly because, moved by a sentiment of gratitude for the generous ardor of his affection, she was inclined to like him better than any one else she knew, and partly in accordance with the advice of her theatrical friends, who told her, with more candor than elegance, that she would be a jolly fool to let such a chance escape her; but at the time she gave her hand to Archibald Martin Floyd she had no idea whatever of the magnitude of the fortune he had invited her to share. He told her that he was a banker, and her active mind immediately evoked the image of the only banker's wife she had ever known—a portly lady, who wore silk gowns, lived in a square, stuccoed house with green blinds, kept a cook and house-maid, and took three box tickets for Miss Percival's benefit.

When, therefore, the doting husband loaded his handsome bride with diamond bracelets and necklaces, and with silks and brocades that were stiff and unmanageable from their very richness—when he carried her straight from the Potteries to the Isle of Wight, and lodged her in spacious apartments at the best hotel in Ryde, and flung his money here and there as if he had carried the lamp of Aladdin

in his coat-pocket—Eliza remonstrated with her new master, fearing that his love had driven him mad, and that this alarming extravagance was the first outburst of insanity.

It seemed a repetition of the dear old Burleigh story when Archibald Floyd took his wife into the long picture-gallery at Felden Woods. She clasped her hands for frank, womanly joy, as she looked at the magnificence about her. She compared herself to the humble bride of the marquis, and fell on her knees, and did theatrical homage to her lord. "Oh, Archy," she said, "it is all too good for me. I am afraid I shall die of my grandeur, as the poor girl pined away at Burleigh House."

In the full maturity of womanly loveliness, rich in health, freshness, and high spirits, how little could Eliza dream that she would hold even a briefer lease of these costly splendors than the Bride of Burleigh had done before her.

Now the reader, being acquainted with Eliza's antecedents, may perhaps find in them some clew to the insolent ease and well-bred audacity with which Mrs. Floyd treated the second-rate county families who were bent upon putting her to confusion. She was an actress; for nine years she had lived in that ideal world in which dukes and marquises are as common as butchers and bakers in work-a-day life, in which, indeed, a nobleman is generally a poor, mean-spirited individual, who gets the worst of it on every hand, and is contemptuously entreated by the audience on account of his rank. How should she be abashed on entering the drawing-rooms of these Kentish mansions, when for nine years she had walked nightly on to a stage to be the focus for every eye, and to entertain her guests the evening through? Was it likely she was to be overawed by the Lenfields, who were coach-builders in Park Lane, or the Miss Manderlys, whose father had made his money by a patent for starch—she, who had received King Duncan at the gates of her castle, and had sat on her throne dispensing condescending hospitality to the obsequious Thanes at Dunsinane? So, do what they would, they were unable to subdue this base intruder; while, to add to their mortification, it every day became more obvious that Mr. and Mrs. Floyd made one of the happiest couples who had ever worn the bonds of matrimony, and changed them into garlands of roses. If this were a very romantic story, it would be perhaps only proper for Eliza Floyd to pine in her gilded bower, and misapply her energies in weeping for some abandoned lover, deserted in an evil hour of ambitious madness. But as my story is a true one—not only true in a general sense, but strictly true as to the leading facts which I am about to relate—and as I could point out, in a certain county, far northward of the lovely Kentish woods, the very house in which the events I shall describe took place, I am bound also to be truthful here, and to set down as a fact that the love which Eliza Floyd bore for her husband was as pure and sincere an affection as ever man need hope to win from the generous heart of a good woman. What share gratitude may have had in that love I can not tell. If she lived in a handsome house, and was waited on by attentive and deferential servants; if she ate of delicate dishes, and drank costly wines; if she wore rich dresses and splendid jewels, and lolled on the downy cushions of a carriage, drawn by high-mettled horses, and driven by a coachman with powdered hair; if, wherever she went, all outward semblance of homage was paid to her; if she had but to utter a wish, and, swift as the stroke of some enchanter's wand, that wish was gratified, she knew that she owed all to her husband, Archibald Floyd; and it may be that she grew, not unnaturally, to associate him with every advantage she enjoyed, and to love him for the sake of these things. Such a love as this may appear a low and despicable affection when compared to the noble sentiment entertained by the Nancys of modern romance for the Bill Sykeses of their choice; and no doubt Eliza Floyd ought to have felt a sovereign contempt for the man who watched her every whim, who gratified her every caprice, and who loved and honored her as much, *ci-devant* provincial actress as she was, as he could have done had she descended the steps of the loftiest throne in Christendom to give him her hand.

She was grateful to him, she loved him, she made him perfectly happy — so happy that the strong-hearted Scotchman was sometimes almost panic stricken at the contemplation of his own prosperity, and would fall down on his knees and pray that this blessing might not be taken from him; that, if it pleased Providence to afflict him, he might be stripped of every shilling of his wealth, and left penniless, to begin the world anew — but with her. Alas! it was this blessing, of all others, that he was to lose.

For a year Eliza and her husband lived this happy life at Felden Woods. He wished to take her on the Continent, or to London for the season; but she could not bear to leave her lovely Kentish home. She was happier than the day was long among her gardens, and pineries, and graperies, her dogs and horses, and her poor. To these last she seemed an angel, descended from the skies to comfort them. There were cottages from which the prim daughters of the second-rate county families fled, tract in hand, discomfited and abashed by the black looks of the half-starved inmates, but upon whose doorways the shadow of Mrs. Floyd was as the shadow of a priest in a Catholic country — always sacred, yet ever welcome and familiar. She had the trick of making these people like her before she set to work to reform their evil habits. At an early stage of her acquaintance with them, she was as blind to the dirt and disorder of their cottages as she would have been to a shabby carpet in the drawing-room of a poor duchess; but by and by she would artfully hint at this and that little improvement in the *ménages* of her pensioners, until, in less than a month, without having either lectured or offended, she had worked an entire transformation. Mrs. Floyd was frightfully artful in her dealings with these erring peasants. Instead of telling them at once in a candid and Christian-like manner that they were all dirty, degraded, ungrateful, and irreligious, she diplomatized and finessed with them as if she had been canvassing the county. She made the girls regular in their attendance at church by means of new bonnets; she kept married men out of the public houses by bribes of tobacco to smoke at home, and once (oh, horror!) by the gift of a bottle of gin. She cured a dirty chimney-piece by the present of a gaudy china vase to its proprietress, and a slovenly hearth by means of a brass fender. She repaired a shrewish temper with a new gown, and patched up a family breach of long standing with a chintz waistcoat. But one brief year after her marriage — while busy landscape-gardeners were working at the improvements she had planned; while the steady process of reformation was slowly but surely progressing among the grateful recipients of her bounty; while the eager tongues of her detractors were still waging war upon her fair fame; while Archibald Floyd rejoiced as he held a baby-daughter in his arms—without one forewarning symptom to break the force of the blow, the light slowly faded out of those glorious eyes, never to shine again on this side of eternity, and Archibald Martin Floyd was a widower.

CHAPTER II.

AURORA.

The child which Eliza Floyd left behind her, when she was so suddenly taken away from all earthly prosperity and happiness, was christened Aurora. The romantic-sounding name had been a fancy of poor Eliza's; and there was no caprice of hers, however trifling, that had not always been sacred with her adoring husband, and that was not doubly sacred now. The actual intensity of the widower's grief was known to no creature in this lower world. His nephews and his nephews' wives paid him pertinacious visits of condolence; nay, one of these nieces by marriage, a good, motherly creature, devoted to her husband, insisted on seeing and comforting the stricken man. Heaven knows whether her tenderness did convey any comfort to that shipwrecked soul. She found him like a man who had suffered from a stroke of paralysis, torpid, almost imbecile. Perhaps she took the wisest course that could possibly be taken. She said little to him upon the subject of his affliction, but visited him frequently, patiently sitting opposite to him for hours at a time, he and she talking of all manner of easy conventional topics — the state of the country, the weather, a change in the ministry, and such subjects as were so far remote from the grief of his life that a less careful hand than Mrs. Alexander Floyd's could have scarcely touched upon the broken chords of that ruined instrument, the widower's heart.

It was not until six months after Eliza's death that Mrs. Alexander ventured to utter her name; but when she did speak of her, it was with no solemn hesitation, but tenderly and familiarly, as if she had been accustomed to talk of the dead. She saw at once that she had done right. The time had come for the widower to feel relief in speaking of the lost one; and from that hour Mrs. Alexander became a favorite with her uncle. Years after, he told her that, even in the sullen torpor of his grief, he had had a dim consciousness that she pitied him, and that she was "a good woman." This good woman came that very evening into the big room, where the banker sat by his lonely hearth, with a baby in her arms—a pale-faced child, with great wondering black eyes, which stared at the rich man in sombre astonishment; a solemn-faced, ugly baby, which was to grow by and by into Aurora Floyd, the heroine of my story.

That pale, black-eyed baby became henceforth the idol of Archibald Martin Floyd, the one object in all this wide universe for which it seemed worth his while to endure life. From the day of his wife's death he had abandoned all active share in the Lombard-street business, and he had now neither occupation nor delight save in waiting upon the prattlings and humoring the caprices of this infant daughter. His love for her was a weakness, almost verging upon a madness. Had his nephews been very designing men, they might perhaps have entertained some vague ideas of that commission of lunacy for which the outraged neighbors were so anxious. He grudged the hired nurses their offices of love about the person of his child. He watched them furtively, fearful lest they should be harsh with her. All the ponderous doors in the great house at Felden Woods could not drown the feeblest murmur of that infant voice to those ever-anxious, loving ears.

He watched her growth as a child watches an acorn it hopes to rear to an oak. He repeated her broken baby-syllables till people grew weary of his babble about the child. Of course the end of all this was, that, in the common acceptation of the term, Aurora was spoiled. We do not say a flower is spoiled because it is reared in a hot-house where no breath of heaven can visit it too roughly; but then, certainly, the bright exotic is trimmed and pruned by the gardener's merciless hand, while Aurora shot whither she would, and there was none to lop the wandering branches of that luxuriant nature. She said what she pleased; thought, spoke, acted as she pleased; learned what she pleased; and she grew into a bright, impetuous being, affectionate and generous-hearted as her mother, but with some touch of native fire blended in her mould that stamped her as original. It is the common habit of ugly babies to grow into handsome women, and so it was with Aurora Floyd. At seventeen she was twice as beautiful as her mother had been at nine-and-twenty, but with much the same irregular features, lighted up by a pair of eyes that were like the stars of heaven, and by two rows of peerlessly white teeth. You rarely, in looking at her face, could get beyond these eyes and teeth; for they so dazzled and blinded you that they defied you to criticise the doubtful little nose, or the width of the smiling mouth. What if those masses of blue-black hair were brushed away from a forehead too low for the common standard of beauty? A phrenologist would have told you that the head was a noble one; and a sculptor would have added that it was set upon the throat of a Cleopatra.

Miss Floyd knew very little of her poor mother's history. There was a picture in crayons hanging in the banker's *sanctum sanctorum* which represented Eliza in the full flush of her beauty and prosperity, but the portrait told nothing of the history of the original, and Aurora had never heard of the merchant-captain, the poor Liverpool lodging, the grim aunt who kept a chandler's shop, the artificial flower-making, and the provincial stage. She had never been told that her maternal grandfather's name was Prodder, and that her mother had played Juliet to an audience of factory hands for the moderate and sometimes uncertain stipend of four and twopence a night. The county families accepted and made much of the rich banker's heiress; but they were not slow to say that Aurora was her mother's own daughter, and had the taint of the play-acting and horse-riding, the spangles and the sawdust, strong in her nature. The truth of the matter is, that before Miss Floyd emerged from the nursery she evinced a very decided tendency to become what is called "fast." At six years of age she rejected a doll and asked for a rocking-horse. At ten she could converse fluently upon the subject of point-ers, setters, fox-hounds, harriers, and beagles, though she drove her governess to the verge of despair by persistently forgetting under what Roman emperor Jerusalem was destroy-ed, and who was legate to the Pope at the time of Catharine of Aragon's divorce. At eleven she talked unreservedly of the horses in the Lenfield stables as a pack of screws; at twelve she contributed her half-crown to a Derby sweepstakes among her father's ser-vants, and triumphantly drew the winning horse; and at thirteen she rode across coun-try with her uncle Andrew, who was a mem-ber of the Croydon hunt. It was not without grief that the banker watched his daughter's progress in these doubtful accomplishments; but she was so beautiful, so frank and fear-less, so generous, affectionate, and true, that he could not bring himself to tell her that she was not all he could desire her to be. If he could have governed or directed that im-petuous nature, he would have had her the most refined and elegant, the most perfect and accomplished of her sex; but he could not do this, and he was fain to thank God for her as she was, and to indulge her every whim.

Alexander Floyd's eldest daughter, Lucy, first cousin, once removed to Aurora, was that young lady's friend and confidante, and came now and then from her father's villa at Fulham to spend a month at Felden Woods. But Lucy Floyd had half a dozen brothers and sisters, and was brought up in a very different manner from the heiress. She was a fair-faced, blue-eyed, rosy-lipped, golden-haired little girl, who thought Felden Woods a paradise upon earth, and Aurora more for-tunate than the Princess Royal of England, or Titania, Queen of the Fairies. She was direfully afraid of her cousin's ponies and Newfoundland dogs, and had a firm convic-tion that sudden death held his throne within a certain radius of a horse's heels; but she loved and admired Aurora, after the manner common to these weaker natures, and ac-cepted Miss Floyd's superb patronage and protection as a thing of course.

The day came when some dark but unde-fined cloud hovered about the narrow home circle at Felden Woods. There was a cool-ness between the banker and his beloved child. The young lady spent half her time on horseback, scouring the shady lanes round Beckenham, attended only by her groom — a dashing young fellow, chosen by Mr. Floyd on account of his good looks for Aurora's especial service. She dined in her own room after these long, lonely rides, leaving her father to eat his solitary meal in the vast dining-room, which seemed to be fully oc-cupied when she sat in it, and desolately empty without her. The household at Fel-den Woods long remembered one particular June evening on which the storm burst forth between the father and daughter.

Aurora had been absent from two o'clock in the afternoon until sunset, and the banker paced the long stone terrace with his watch in his hand, the figures on the dial-plate barely distinguishable in the twilight, waiting for his daughter's coming home. He had sent his dinner away untouched; his news-papers lay uncut upon the table, and the household spies we call servants told each other how his hand had shaken so violently that he had spilled half a decanter of wine over the polished mahogany in attempting to fill his glass. The housekeeper and her satel-lites crept into the hall, and looked through the half-glass doors at the anxious watcher on the terrace. The men in the stables talked of "the row," as they called this ter-rible breach between father and child; and when at last horses' hoofs were heard in the long avenue, and Miss Floyd reined in her thorough-bred chestnut at the foot of the terrace-steps, there was a lurking audience hidden here and there in the evening shadow eager to hear and see.

But there was very little to gratify these prying eyes and ears. Aurora sprang lightly to the ground before the groom could dis-mount to assist her, and the chestnut, with heaving and foam-flecked sides, was led off to the stable.

Mr. Floyd watched the groom and the two horses as they disappeared through the great gates leading to the stable-yard, and then said very quietly, "You don't use that animal well, Aurora. A six hours' ride is neither good for her nor for you. Your groom should have known better than to allow it." He led the way into his study, telling his daughter to follow him, and they were closeted together for upward of an hour.

Early the next morning Miss Floyd's gov-erness departed from Felden Woods, and between breakfast and luncheon the banker paid a visit to the stables, and examined his daughter's favorite chestnut mare, a beautiful filly, all bone and muscle, that had been trained for a racer. The animal had strained a sinew, and walked lame. Mr. Floyd sent for his daughter's groom, and paid and dis-missed him on the spot. The young fellow made no remonstrance, but went quietly to his quarters, took off his livery, packed a carpet-bag, and walked away from the house without bidding good-by to his fellow-ser-vants, who resented the affront, and pro-nounced him a surly brute, whose absence was no loss to the household.

Three days after this, upon the 14th of June, 1856, Mr. Floyd and his daughter left Felden Woods for Paris, where Aurora was placed at a very expensive and exclusive Protestant finishing school, kept by the Demoiselles Lespard, in a stately mansion *entre cour et jardin* in the Rue Saint Dominique, there to complete her very imperfect education.

For a year and two months Miss Floyd has been away at this Parisian finishing school; it is late in the August of 1857, and again the banker walks upon the long stone terrace in front of the narrow windows of his red-brick mansion, this time waiting for Aurora's arrival from Paris. The servants have expressed considerable wonder at his not crossing the Channel to fetch his daughter, and they think the dignity of the house somewhat lowered by Miss Floyd's travelling unattended.

"A poor, dear young thing, that knows no more of this wicked world than a blessed baby," said the housekeeper, "all alone among a pack of mustached Frenchmen."

Archibald Martin Floyd had grown an old man in one day — that terrible and unexpected day of his wife's death; but even the grief of that bereavement had scarcely seemed to affect him so strongly as the loss of his Aurora during the fourteen months of her absence from Felden Woods.

Perhaps it was that at sixty-five years of age he was less able to bear even a lesser grief; but those who watched him closely declared that he seemed as much dejected by his daughter's absence as he could well have been by her death. Even now, that he paces up and down the broad terrace, with the landscape stretching wide before him, and melting vaguely away under that veil of crimson glory shed upon all things by the sinking sun — even now that he hourly, nay, almost momentarily, expects to clasp his only child in his arms, Archibald Floyd seems rather nervously anxious than joyfully expectant.

He looks again and again at his watch, and pauses in his walk to listen to Beckenham church-clock striking eight; his ears are preternaturally alert to every sound, and give him instant warning of carriage-wheels far off upon the wide high-road. All the agitation and anxiety he has felt for the last week has been less than the concentrated fever of this moment. Will it pass on, that carriage, or stop at the lodge-gates? Surely his heart could never beat so loud save by some wondrous magnetism of fatherly love and hope. The carriage stops. He hears the clanking of the gates; the crimson-tinted landscape grows dim and blurred before his eyes, and he knows no more till a pair of impetuous arms are twined about his neck, and Aurora's face is hidden on his shoulder.

It was a paltry hired carriage which Miss Floyd arrived in, and it drove away as soon as she had alighted, and the small amount of luggage she brought had been handed to the eager servants. The banker led his child into the study, where they had held that long conference fourteen months before. A lamp burned upon the library table, and it was to this light that Archibald Floyd led his daughter.

A year had changed the girl to a woman — a woman with great hollow black eyes, and pale, haggard cheeks. The course of study at the Parisian finishing school had evidently been too hard for the spoiled heiress.

"Aurora, Aurora," the old man cried piteously, "how ill you look! how altered, how —"

She laid her hand lightly yet imperiously upon his lips.

"Don't speak of me," she said, "I shall recover; but you — you, father — you too are changed."

She was as tall as her father, and, resting her hands upon his shoulders, she looked at him long and earnestly. As she looked, the tears welled slowly up to her eyes, which had been dry before, and poured silently down her haggard cheeks.

"My father, my devoted father," she said, in a broken voice, "if my heart was made of adamant I think it might break when I see the change in this beloved face."

The old man checked her with a nervous gesture—a gesture almost of terror.

"Not one word — not one word, Aurora," he said, hurriedly; "at least, only one. That person—he is dead?"

"He is."

CHAPTER III.

WHAT BECAME OF THE DIAMOND BRACELET.

Aurora's aunts, uncles, and cousins were not slow to exclaim upon the change for the worse which a twelvemonth in Paris had made in their young kinswoman. I fear that the Demoiselles Lespard suffered considerably in reputation among the circle round Felden Woods from Miss Floyd's impaired good looks. She was out of spirits too, had no appetite, slept badly, was nervous and hysterical, no longer took any interest in her dogs and horses, and was altogether an altered creature. Mrs. Alexander Floyd declared it was perfectly clear that these cruel Frenchwomen had worked poor Aurora to a shadow: the girl was not used to study, she said; she had been accustomed to exercise and open air, and no doubt pined sadly in the close atmosphere of a school-room.

But Aurora's was one of those impressionable natures which quickly recover from any depressing influence. Early in September Lucy Floyd came to Felden Woods, and found her handsome cousin almost entirely recovered from the drudgery of the Parisian *pension*, but still very loath to talk much of that seminary. She answered Lucy's eager questions very curtly; said that she hated the Demoiselles Lespard and the Rue Saint Dominique, and that the very memory of Paris was disagreeable to her. Like most young ladies with black eyes and blue-black hair, Miss Floyd was a good hater; so Lucy forbore to ask for more information upon what was so evidently an unpleasant subject to her cousin. Poor Lucy had been mercilessly well educated; she spoke half a dozen languages, knew all about the natural sciences, had read Gibbon, Niebuhr, and Arnold from the title-page to the printer's name, and looked upon the heiress as a big brilliant dunce; so she quietly set down Aurora's dislike to Paris to that young lady's distaste for tuition, and thought little more about it. Any other reasons for Miss Floyd's almost shuddering horror of her Parisian associations lay far beyond Lucy's simple power of penetration.

The fifteenth of September was Aurora's birthday, and Archibald Floyd determined, upon this, the nineteenth anniversary of his daughter's first appearance on this mortal scene, to give an entertainment, whereat his country neighbors and town acquaintance might alike behold and admire the beautiful heiress.

Mrs. Alexander came to Felden Woods to superintend the preparations for this birthday ball. She drove Aurora and Lucy into town to order the supper and the band, and to choose dresses and wreaths for the young ladies. The banker's heiress was sadly out of place in a milliner's show-room; but she had that rapid judgment as to color, and that perfect taste in form, which bespeak the soul of an artist; and while poor mild Lucy was giving endless trouble, and tumbling innumerable boxes of flowers, before she could find any head-dress in harmony with her rosy cheeks and golden hair, Aurora, after one brief glance at the bright *parterres* of painted cambric, pounced upon a crown-shaped garland of vivid scarlet berries, with drooping and tangled leaves of dark shining green, that looked as if they had been just plucked from a running streamlet. She watched Lucy's perplexities with a half compassionate, half contemptuous smile.

"Look at that poor child, Aunt Lizzie," she said; "I know that she would like to put pink and yellow against her golden hair. Why, you silly Lucy, don't you know that yours is the beauty which really does *not* want adornment? A few pearls or forget-me-not blossoms, or a crown of water lilies and a cloud of white areophane, would make you look a sylphide; but I dare say you would like to wear amber satin and cabbage-roses."

From the milliner's they drove to Mr. Gunter's in Berkeley Square, at which world-renowned establishment Mrs. Alexander commanded those preparations of turkeys preserved in jelly, hams cunningly embalmed in rich wines and broths, and other specimens of that sublime art of confectionery which hovers midway between sleight of hand and cookery, and in which the Berkeley Square professor is without a rival. When poor Thomas Babington Macaulay's New Zealander shall come to ponder over the ruins of St. Paul's, perhaps he will visit the remains of this humbler temple in Berkeley Square, and wonder at the ice-pails and jelly-moulds, and refrigerators and stewpans, the hot plates, long cold and unheeded, and all the mysterious paraphernalia of the dead art.

From the West End Mrs. Alexander drove to Charing Cross; she had a commission to execute at Dent's — the purchase of a watch for one of her boys, who was just off to Eton.

Aurora threw herself wearily back in the carriage while her aunt and Lucy stopped at the watchmaker's. It was to be observed that, although Miss Floyd had recovered much of her old brilliancy and gayety of temper, a certain gloomy shade would sometimes steal over her countenance when she was left to herself for a few minutes—a darkly reflective expression, quite foreign to her face. This shadow fell upon her beauty now as she looked out of the open window, moodily watching the passers-by. Mrs. Alexander was a long time making her purchase, and Aurora had sat nearly a quarter of an hour blankly staring at the shifting figures in the crowd, when a man hurrying by was attracted by her face at the carriage-window, and started, as if at some great surprise. He passed on, however, and walked rapidly toward the Horse Guards; but, before he turned the corner, came to a dead stop, stood still for two or three minutes scratching the back of his head reflectively with his big bare hand, and then walked slowly back toward Mr. Dent's emporium. He was a broad-shouldered, bull-necked, sandy-whiskered fellow, wearing a cut-away coat and a gaudy neckerchief, and smoking a huge cigar, the rank fumes of which struggled with a very powerful odor of rum and water recently imbibed. This gentleman's standing in society was betrayed by the smooth head of a bull-terrier, whose round eyes peeped out of the pocket of his cut-away coat, and by a Blenheim spaniel carried under his arm. He was the very last person, among all the souls between Cockspur street and the statue of King Charles, who seemed likely to have anything to say to Miss Aurora Floyd; nevertheless, he walked deliberately up to the carriage, and, planting his elbows upon the door, nodded to her with friendly familiarity.

"Well," he said, without inconveniencing himself by the removal of the rank cigar, "how do?"

After which brief salutation he relapsed into silence, and rolled his great brown eyes slowly here and there, in contemplative examination of Miss Floyd and the vehicle in which she sat — even carrying his powers of observation so far as to take particular notice of a plethoric morocco bag lying on the back seat, and to inquire casually whether there was "anythink wallable in the old party's redicule."

But Aurora did not allow him long for this leisurely employment; for, looking at him with her eyes flashing forked lightnings of womanly fury, and her face crimson with indignation, she asked him, in a sharp, spasmodic tone, whether he had anything to say to her.

He had a great deal to say to her; but as he put his head in at the carriage - window and made his communication, whatever it might be, in a rum and watery whisper, it reached no ears but those of Aurora herself. When he had done whispering, he took a greasy, leather-covered account-book, and a short stump of lead pencil, considerably the worse for chewing, from his waistcoat-pocket, and wrote two or three lines upon a leaf, which he tore out and handed to Aurora. "This is the address," he said; "you won't forget to send?"

She shook her head, and looked away from him — looked away with an irrepressible gesture of disgust and loathing.

"You wouldn't like to buy a spaniel dawg," said the man, holding the sleek, curly, black and tan animal up to the carriage-window, "or a French poodle what 'll balance a bit of bread on his nose while you count ten? Hey? You should have him a bargain — say fifteen pound the two."

"No!"

At this moment Mrs. Alexander emerged from the watchmaker's, just in time to catch a glimpse of the man's broad shoulders as he moved sulkily away from the carriage.

"Has that person been begging of you, Aurora?" she asked, as they drove off.

"No. I once bought a dog of him, and he recognized me."

"And wanted you to buy one to-day?"

"Yes."

Miss Floyd sat gloomily silent during the whole of the homeward drive, looking out of the carriage-window, and not deigning to take any notice whatever of her aunt and cousin. I do not know whether it was in submission to that palpable superiority of force and vitality in Aurora's nature which seemed to set her above her fellows, or simply in that inherent spirit of toadyism common to the best of us; but Mrs. Alexander and her fair - haired daughter always paid mute reverence to the banker's heiress, and were silent when it pleased her, or conversed at her royal will. I verily believe that it was Aurora's eyes rather than Archibald Martin Floyd's thousands that overawed all her kinsfolk; and that if she had been a street-sweeper dressed

in rags and begging for half-pence, people would have feared her and made way for her, and bated their breath when she was angry.

The trees in the long avenue of Felden Woods were hung with sparkling colored lamps, to light the guests who came to Aurora's birthday festival. The long range of windows on the ground-floor was ablaze with light; the crash of the band burst every now and then above the perpetual roll of carriagewheels, and the shouted repetition of visitors' names, and pealed across the silent woods; through the long vista of half a dozen rooms opening one into another, the waters of a fountain, sparkling with a hundred hues in the light, glittered amid the dark floral wealth of a conservatory filled with exotics. Great clusters of tropical plants were grouped in the spacious hall; festoons of flowers hung about the vapory curtains in the arched doorways. Light and splendor were everywhere around; and amid all, and more splendid than all, in the dark grandeur of her beauty, Aurora Floyd, crowned with scarlet and robed in white, stood by her father's side.

Among the guests who arrive latest at Mr. Floyd's ball are two officers from Windsor, who have driven across the country in a mail phaeton. The elder of these two, and the driver of the vehicle, has been very discontented and disagreeable throughout the journey.

"If I 'd had the remotest idea of the distance, Maldon," he said, "I 'd have seen you and your Kentish banker very considerably inconvenienced before I would have consented to victimize my horse for the sake of this snobbish party."

"But it won't be a snobbish party," answered the young man, impetuously. "Archibald Floyd is the best fellow in Christendom, and as for his daughter—"

"Oh, of course, a divinity, with fifty thousand pounds for her fortune, all of which will no doubt be very tightly settled upon herself if she is ever allowed to marry a penniless scapegrace like Francis Lewis Maldon, of her Majesty's 11th Hussars. However, I don't want to stand in your way, my boy. Go in and win, and my blessing be upon your virtuous endeavors. I can imagine the young Scotchwoman — red hair (of course you 'll call it auburn), large feet, and freckles!"

"Aurora Floyd — red hair and freckles!" The young officer laughed aloud at the stupendous joke. "You 'll see her in a quarter of an hour, Bulstrode," he said.

Talbot Bulstrode, Captain of her Majesty's 11th Hussars, had consented to drive his brother-officer from Windsor to Beckenham, and to array himself in his uniform, in order to adorn therewith the festival at Felden Woods, chiefly because, having at two-and-thirty years of age run through all the wealth of life's excitements and amusements, and finding himself a penniless spendthrift in this species of coin, though well enough off for mere sordid riches, he was too tired of himself and the world to care much whither his friends and comrades led him. He was the eldest son of a wealthy Cornish baronet, whose ancestor had received his title straight from the hands of Scottish King James, when baronetcies first came into fashion; the same fortunate ancestor being near akin to a certain noble, erratic, unfortunate, and injured gentleman called Walter Raleigh, and by no means too well used by the same Scottish James. Now, of all the pride which ever swelled the breasts of mankind, the pride of Cornishmen is perhaps the strongest; and the Bulstrode family was one of the proudest in Cornwall. Talbot was no alien son of this haughty house; from his very babyhood he had been the proudest of mankind. This pride had been the saving power that had presided over his prosperous career. Other men might have made a downhill road of that smooth pathway which wealth and grandeur made so pleasant, but not Talbot Bulstrode. The vices and follies of the common herd were perhaps retrievable, but vice or folly in a Bulstrode would have left a blot upon a hitherto unblemished escutcheon never to be erased by time or tears. That pride of birth, which was utterly unallied to pride of wealth or station, had a certain noble and chivalrous side, and Talbot Bulstrode was beloved by many a parvenu whom meaner men would have insulted. In the ordinary affairs of life he was as humble as a woman or a child; it was only when Honor was in question that the sleeping dragon of pride which had guarded the golden apples of his youth, purity, probity, and truth, awoke and bade defiance to the enemy. At two-and-thirty he was still a bachelor, not because he had never loved, but because he had never met with a woman whose stainless purity of soul fitted her in his eyes to become the mother of a noble race, and to rear sons who should do honor to the name of Bulstrode; he looked for more than ordinary every-day virtue in the woman of his choice; he demanded those grand and queenly qualities which are rarest in womankind. Fearless truth, a sense of honor keen as his own, loyalty of purpose, unselfishness, a soul untainted by the petty baseness of daily life—all these he sought in the being he loved; and at the first warning thrill of emotion caused by a pair of beautiful eyes, he grew critical and captious about their owner, and began to look for infinitesimal stains upon the shining robe of her virginity. He would have married a beggar's daughter if she had reached his almost impossible standard; he would have rejected the descendant of a race of kings if she had fallen one decimal part of an inch below it. Women feared Talbot Bulstrode; manœuvring mothers shrank abashed from the cold light of those watchful gray eyes; daughters to marry blushed and trembled, and felt their pretty affectations, their ballroom properties, drop away from them under the quiet gaze of the young officer, till, from fearing him, the lovely flutterers grew to shun and dislike him, and to leave Bulstrode Castle and the Bulstrode fortune unangled for in the great matrimonial fisheries. So at two-and-thirty Talbot walked serenely safe amid the meshes and pitfalls of Belgravia, secure in the popular belief that Captain Bulstrode, of the 11th Hussars, was not a marrying man. This belief was perhaps strengthened by the fact that the Cornishman was by no means the elegant ignoramus whose sole accomplishment consist in parting his hair, waxing his mustaches, and smoking a meerschaum that has been colored by his valet, and who has become the accepted type of the military man in time of peace.

Talbot Bulstrode was fond of scientific pursuits; he neither smoked, drank, nor gambled. He had only been to the Derby once in his life, and on that one occasion had walked quietly away from the stand while the great race was being run, and the white faces were turned toward the fatal corner, and men were sick with terror and anxiety, and frenzied with the madness of suspense. He never hunted, though he rode like Colonel Asheton Smith. He was a perfect swordsman, and one of Mr. Angelo's pet pupils, a favorite lounger in the gallery of that simple-hearted, honorable-minded gentleman; but he had never handled a billiard-cue in his life, nor had he touched a card since the days of his boyhood, when he took a hand at long whist with his father, and mother, and the parson of the parish, in the south drawing-room at Bulstrode Castle. He had a peculiar aversion to all games of chance and skill, contending that it was beneath a gentleman to employ, even for amusement, the implements of the sharper's pitiful trade. His rooms were as neatly kept as those of a woman. Cases of mathematical instruments took the place of cigar-boxes; proof impressions of Raphael adorned the walls ordinarily covered with French prints, and water-colored sporting sketches from Ackermann's emporium. He was familiar with every turn of expression in Descartes and Condillac, but would have been sorely puzzled to translate the argotic locutions of Monsieur de Kock, *père*. Those who spoke of him summed him up by saying that he wasn't a bit like an officer; but there was a certain regiment of foot, which he had commanded when the heights of Inkermann were won, whose ranks told another story of Captain Bulstrode. He had made an exchange into the 11th Hussars on his return from the Crimea, whence, among other distinctions, he had brought a stiff leg, which for a time disqualified him from dancing. It was from pure benevolence, therefore, or from that indifference to all things which is easily mistaken for unselfishness, that Talbot Bulstrode had consented to accept an invitation to the ball at Felden Woods.

The banker's guests were not of that charmed circle familiar to the Captain of Hussars; so Talbot, after a brief introduction to his host, fell back among the crowd assembled in one of the doorways, and quietly watched the dancers; not unobserved himself, however, for he was just one of those people who will not pass in a crowd. Tall and broad-chested, with a pale, whiskerless face, aquiline nose, clear, cold gray eyes, thick mustache, and black hair, worn as closely cropped as if he had lately emerged from Coldbath Fields or Millbank prison, he formed a striking contrast to the yellow-whiskered young ensign who had accompanied him. Even that stiff leg, which in others might have seemed a blemish, added to the distinction of his appearance, and, coupled with the glittering orders on the breast of his uniform, told of deeds of prowess lately done. He took very little delight in the gay assembly revolving before him to one of Charles d'Albert's waltzes. He had heard the same music before, executed by the same band; the faces, though unfamiliar to him, were not new: dark beauties in pink, fair beauties in blue; tall, dashing beauties in silks, and laces, and jewels, and splendor; modestly downcast beauties in white crape and rose-buds. They had all been spread for him, those familiar nets of gauze and areophane, and he had escaped them all: and the name of Bulstrode might drop out of the history of Cornish gentry to find no record save upon gravestones, but it would never be tarnished by an unworthy race, or dragged through the mire of a divorce court by a guilty woman. While he lounged against the pillar of a doorway, leaning on his cane, and resting his lame leg, and wondering lazily whether there was anything upon earth that repaid a man for the trouble of living, Ensign Maldon approached him with a woman's gloved hand lying lightly on his arm, and a divinity walking by his side. A divinity! imperiously beautiful in white and scarlet, painfully dazzling to look upon, intoxicatingly brilliant to behold. Captain Bulstrode had served in India, and had once tasted a horrible spirit called bang, which made the men who drank it half-mad; and he could not help fancying that the beauty of this woman was like the strength of that alcoholic preparation—barbarous, intoxicating, dangerous, and maddening.

His brother-officer presented him to this wonderful creature, and he found that her earthly name was Aurora Floyd, and that she was the heiress of Felden Woods.

Talbot Bulstrode recovered himself in a moment. This imperious creature, this Cleopatra in crinoline, had a low forehead, a nose that deviated from the line of beauty, and a wide mouth. What was she but another trap set in white muslin, and baited with artificial flowers, like the rest? She was to have fifty thousand pounds for her portion, so she didn't want a rich husband; but she was a nobody, so of course she wanted position, and had no doubt read up the Raleigh Bulstrodes in the sublime pages of Burke. The clear gray eyes grew cold as ever, therefore, as Talbot bowed to the heiress. Mr. Maldon found his partner a chair close to the pillar against which Captain Bulstrode had taken his stand; and Mrs. Alexander Floyd swooping down upon the ensign at this very moment, with the dire intent of carrying him off to dance with a lady who executed more of her steps upon the toes of her partner than on the floor of the ball-room, Aurora and Talbot were left to themselves.

Captain Bulstrode glanced downward at the banker's daughter. His gaze lingered upon the graceful head, with its coronal of shining scarlet berries encircling smooth masses of blue-black hair. He expected to see the modest drooping of the eyelids peculiar to young ladies with long lashes, but he was disappointed; for Aurora Floyd was looking straight before her, neither at him, nor at the lights, nor the flowers, nor the dancers, but far away into vacancy. She was so young, prosperous, admired, and beloved, that it was difficult to account for the dim shadow of trouble that clouded her glorious eyes.

While he was wondering what he should say to her, she lifted her eyes to his face, and asked him the strangest question he had ever heard from girlish lips.

"Do you know if Thunderbolt won the Leger?" she asked.

He was too much confounded to answer for a moment, and she continued rather impatiently, "They must have heard by six o'clock this evening in London; but I have asked half a dozen people here to-night, and no one seems to know anything about it."

Talbot's close-cropped hair seemed lifted from his head as he listened to this terrible address. Good heavens! what a horrible woman! The hussar's vivid imagination pictured the heir of all the Raleigh Bulstrodes receiving his infantine impressions from such a mother. She would teach him to read out of the Racing Calendar; she would invent a royal alphabet of the turf, and tell him that "D stands for Derby, old England's great race," and "E stands for Epsom, a crack meeting-place," etc. He told Miss Floyd that he had never been to Doncaster in his life, that he had never read a sporting paper, and that he knew no more of Thunderbolt than of King Cheops.

She looked at him rather contemptuously.

"Cheops wasn't much," she said ; "but he won the Liverpool Autumn Cup in Blink Bonny's year."

Talbot Bulstrode shuddered afresh; but a feeling of pity mingled with his horror. "If I had a sister," he thought, "I would get her to talk to this miserable girl, and bring her to a sense of her iniquity."

Aurora said no more to the Captain of Hussars, but relapsed into the old far-away gaze into vacancy, and sat twisting a bracelet round and round upon her finely-modelled wrist. It was a diamond bracelet, worth a couple of hundred pounds, which had been given her that day by her father. He would have invested all his fortune in Messrs. Hunt and Roskell's cunning handiwork if Aurora had sighed for gems and gewgaws. Miss Floyd's glance fell upon the glittering ornament, and she looked at it long and earnestly, rather as if she were calculating the value of the stones than admiring the taste of the workmanship.

While Talbot was watching her, full of wondering pity and horror, a young man hurried up to the spot where she was seated, and reminded her of an engagement for the quadrille that was forming. She looked at her tablets of ivory, gold, and turquoise, and with a certain disdainful weariness rose and took his arm. Talbot followed her receding form. Taller than most among the throng, her queenly head was not soon lost sight of.

"A Cleopatra with a snub nose two sizes too small for her face, and a taste for horseflesh!" said Talbot Bulstrode, ruminating upon the departed divinity. "She ought to carry a betting-book instead of those ivory tablets. How *distraite* she was all the time she sat here! I dare say she has made a book for the Leger, and was calculating how much she stands to lose. What will this poor old banker do with her? put her into a madhouse, or get her elected a member of the jockey club? With her black eyes and fifty thousand pounds, she might lead the sporting world. There has been a female pope, why should there not be a female 'Napoleon of the Turf?'"

Later, when the rustling leaves of the trees in Beckenham Woods were shivering in that cold gray hour which precedes the advent of the dawn, Talbot Bulstrode drove his friend away from the banker's lighted mansion. He talked of Aurora Floyd during the whole of that long cross-country drive. He was merciless to her follies; he ridiculed, he abused, he sneered at and condemned her questionable taste. He bade Francis Lewis Maldon marry her at his peril, and wished him joy of *such* a wife. He declared that if he had such a sister he would shoot her, unless she reformed and burnt her betting-book. He worked himself up into a savage humor about the young lady's delinquencies, and talked of her as if she had done him an un-

pardonable injury by entertaining a taste for the turf; till at last the poor meek young ensign plucked up a spirit, and told his superior officer that Aurora Floyd was a very jolly girl, and a good girl, and a perfect lady, and that if she did want to know who won the Leger, it was no business of Captain Bulstrode's, and that he, Bulstrode, needn't make such a howling about it.

While the two men are getting to high words about her, Aurora is seated in her dressing-room, listening to Lucy Floyd's babble about the ball.

"There was never such a delightful party," that young lady said; "and did Aurora see so-and-so, and so-and-so, and so-and-so? and above all, did she observe Captain Bulstrode, who had served all through the Crimean war, and who walked lame, and was the son of Sir John Walter Raleigh Bulstrode, of Bulstrode Castle, near Camelford?"

Aurora shook her head with a weary gesture. No, she hadn't noticed any of these people. Poor Lucy's childish talk was stopped in a moment.

"You are tired, Aurora dear," she said; "how cruel I am to worry you!"

Aurora threw her arms about her cousin's neck, and hid her face upon Lucy's white shoulder.

"I am tired," she said, "very, very tired."

She spoke with such an utterly despairing weariness in her tone, that her gentle cousin was alarmed by her words.

"You are not unhappy, dear Aurora?" she asked, anxiously.

"No, no, only tired. There, go, Lucy. Good-night, good-night."

She gently pushed her cousin from the room, rejected the services of her maid, and dismissed her also. Then, tired as she was, she removed the candle from the dressing-table to a desk on the other side of the room, and, seating herself at this desk, unlocked it, and took from one of its inmost recesses the soiled pencil scrawl which had been given her a week before by the man who tried to sell her a dog in Cockspur street.

The diamond bracelet, Archibald Floyd's birthday gift to his daughter, lay in its nest of satin and velvet upon Aurora's dressing-table. She took the morocco case in her hand, looked for a few moments at the jewel, and then shut the lid of the little casket with a sharp metallic snap.

"The tears were in my father's eyes when he clasped the bracelet on my arm," she said, as she reseated herself at the desk. "If he could see me now!"

She wrapped the case in a sheet of foolscap, secured the parcel in several places with red wax and a plain seal, and directed it thus:

"J. C.,
Care of Mr. Joseph Green,
Bell Inn,
Doncaster."

Early the next morning Miss Floyd drove her aunt and cousin into Croydon, and, leaving them at a Berlin wool-shop, went alone to the post-office, where she registered and posted this valuable parcel.

CHAPTER IV.

AFTER THE BALL.

Two days after Aurora's birthnight festival, Talbot Bulstrode's phaeton dashed once more into the avenue at Felden Woods. Again the captain made a sacrifice on the shrine of friendship, and drove Francis Maldon from Windsor to Beckenham, in order that the young cornet might make those anxious inquiries about the health of the ladies of Mr. Floyd's household, which, by a pleasant social fiction, are supposed to be necessary after an evening of intermittent waltzes and quadrilles.

The junior officer was very grateful for this kindness; for Talbot, though the best of fellows, was not much given to putting himself out of the way for the pleasure of other people. It would have been far pleasanter to the captain to dawdle away the day in his own rooms, lolling over those erudite works which his brother officers described by the generic title of "heavy reading," or, according to the popular belief of those hare-brained young men, employed in squaring the circle in the solitude of his chamber.

Talbot Bulstrode was altogether an inscrutable personage to his comrades of the 11th Hussars. His black-letter folios, his polished mahogany cases of mathematical instruments, his proof-before-letters engravings, were the fopperies of a young Oxonian rather than an officer who had fought and bled at Inkermann. The young men who breakfasted with him in his rooms trembled as they read the titles of the big books on the shelves, and stared helplessly at the grim saints and angular angels in the pre-Raphaelite prints upon the walls. They dared not even propose to smoke in those sacred chambers, and were ashamed of the wet impressions of the rims of the Moselle bottles which they left upon the mahogany cases.

It seemed natural to people to be afraid of Talbot Bulstrode, just as little boys are frightened of a beadle, a policeman, and a school-master, even before they have been told the attributes of these terrible beings. The colonel of the 11th Hussars, a portly gentleman, who rode fifteen stone, and wrote his name high in the peerage, was frightened of Talbot. That cold gray eye struck a silent awe into the hearts of men and women with its straight, penetrating gaze, that always seemed to be telling them they were found out. The colonel was afraid to tell his best stories when Talbot was at the mess-table, for he had a dim consciousness that the captain was aware of the discrepancies in those brilliant anecdotes, though that officer had never implied a doubt by either look or gesture. The Irish adjutant forgot to brag about his conquests among the fair sex; the younger men dropped their voices when they talked to each other of the side-scenes at Her Majesty's Theatre; and the corks flew faster, and the laughter grew louder, when Talbot left the room.

The captain knew that he was more respected than beloved, and, like all proud men who repel the warm feelings of others in utter despite of themselves, he was grieved and wounded because his comrades did not become attached to him.

"Will anybody, out of all the millions on this wide earth, ever love me!" he thought. "No one ever has as yet—not even my father and mother. They have been proud of me, but they have never loved me. How many a young profligate has brought his parents' gray hairs with sorrow to the grave, and has been beloved with the last heart-beat of those he destroyed as I have never been in my life! Perhaps my mother would have loved me better if I had given her more trouble; if I had scattered the name of Bulstrode all over London upon post-obits and dishonored acceptances; if I had been drummed out of my regiment, and had walked down to Cornwall without shoes or stockings, to fall at her feet, and sob out my sins and sorrows in her lap, and ask her to mortgage her jointure for the payment of my debts. But I have never asked anything of her, dear soul, except her love, and that she has been unable to give me. I suppose it is because I do not know how to ask. How often have I sat by her side at Bulstrode, talking of all sorts of indifferent subjects, yet with a vague yearning at my heart to throw myself upon her breast, and implore of her to love and bless her son, but held aloof by some icy barrier that I have been powerless all my life to break down. What woman has ever loved me? Not one. They have tried to marry me because I shall be Sir Talbot Bulstrode of Bulstrode Castle; but how soon they have left off angling for the prize, and shrunk away from me chilled and disheartened! I shudder when I remember that I shall be three-and-thirty next March, and that I have never been beloved. I shall sell out, now the fighting is over, for I am of no use among the fellows here; and, if any good little thing would fall in love with me, I would marry her and take her down to Bulstrode, to my mother and father, and turn country gentleman."

Talbot Bulstrode made this declaration in all sincerity. He wished that some good and pure creature would fall in love with him, in order that he might marry her. He wanted some spontaneous exhibition of innocent feeling which might justify him in saying "I am beloved!" He felt little capacity for loving on his own side, but he thought that he would be grateful to any good woman who would regard him with disinterested affection, and that he would devote his life to making her happy.

"It would be something to feel that if I were smashed in a railway accident, or dropped out of a balloon, some one creature in this world would think it a lonelier place for the lack of me. I wonder whether my children would love me? I dare say not. I should freeze their young affections with the Latin grammar, and they would tremble as they passed the door of my study, and hush their voices into a frightened whisper when papa was within hearing."

Talbot Bulstrode's ideal of woman was some gentle and feminine creature crowned with an aureole of pale auburn hair; some timid soul with downcast eyes, fringed with golden-tinted lashes; some shrinking being, as pale and prim as the mediæval saints in his pre-Raphaelite engravings, spotless as her own white robes, excelling in all womanly graces and accomplishments, but only exhibiting them in the narrow circle of a home.

Perhaps Talbot thought that he had met with his ideal when he entered the long drawing-room at Felden Woods with Cornet Maldon, on the seventeenth of September, 1857.

Lucy Floyd was standing by an open piano, with her white dress and pale golden hair bathed in a flood of autumn sunlight. That sunlit figure came back to Talbot's memory long afterward, after a stormy interval, in which it had been blotted away and forgotten, and the long drawing-room stretched itself out like a picture before his eyes.

Yes, this was his ideal—this graceful girl, with the shimmering light for ever playing upon her hair, and the modest droop in her white eyelids. But, undemonstrative as usual, Captain Bulstrode seated himself near the piano, after the brief ceremony of greeting, and contemplated Lucy with grave eyes that betrayed no especial admiration.

He had not taken much notice of Lucy Floyd on the night of the ball; indeed, Lucy was scarcely a candle-light beauty; her hair wanted the sunshine gleaming through it to light up the golden halo about her face, and the delicate pink of her cheeks waxed pale in the glare of the great chandeliers.

While Captain Bulstrode was watching Lucy with that grave, contemplative gaze, trying to find out whether she was in any way different from other girls he had known, and whether the purity of her delicate beauty was more than skin deep, the window opposite to him was darkened, and Aurora Floyd stood between him and the sunshine.

The banker's daughter paused on the threshold of the open window, holding the collar of an immense mastiff in both her hands, and looking irresolutely into the room.

Miss Floyd hated morning callers, and she was debating within herself whether she had been seen, or whether it might be possible to steal away unperceived.

But the dog set up a big bark, and settled the question.

"Quiet, Bow-wow," she said; "quiet, quiet, boy."

"Yes, the dog was called Bow-wow. He was twelve years old, and Aurora had so christened him in her seventh year, when he was a blundering, big-headed puppy, that sprawled upon the table during the little girl's lessons, upset ink-bottles over her copy-books, and ate whole chapters of Pinnock's abridged histories.

The gentlemen rose at the sound of her voice, and Miss Floyd came into the room and sat down at a little distance from the captain and her cousin, twirling a straw hat in her hand and staring at her dog, who seated himself resolutely by her chair, knocking double knocks of good temper upon the carpet with his big tail.

Though she said very little, and seated herself in a careless attitude that bespoke complete indifference to her visitors, Aurora's beauty extinguished poor Lucy as the rising sun extinguishes the stars.

The thick plaits of her black hair made a great diadem upon her low forehead, and crowned her an Eastern empress—an empress with a doubtful nose, it is true, but an empress who reigned by right divine of her eyes and hair. For do not these wonderful black eyes, which perhaps shine upon us only once in a lifetime, in themselves constitute a royalty?

Talbot Bulstrode turned away from his ideal to look at this dark-haired goddess, with a coarse straw hat in her hand and a big mastiff's head lying on her lap. Again he perceived that abstraction in her manner which had puzzled him upon the night of the ball. She listened to her visitors politely, and she answered them when they spoke to her, but it seemed to Talbot as if she constrained herself to attend to them by an effort.

"She wishes me away, I dare say," he thought, "and no doubt considers me a 'slow party' because I don't talk to her of horses and dogs."

The captain resumed his conversation with Lucy. He found that she talked exactly as he had heard other young ladies talk, that she knew all they knew, and had been to the places they had visited. The ground they went over was very old indeed, but Lucy traversed it with charming propriety.

"She is a good little thing," Talbot thought, "and would make an admirable wife for a country gentleman. I wish she would fall in love with me."

Lucy told him of some excursion in Switzerland, where she had been during the preceding autumn with her father and mother.

"And your cousin," he asked, "was she with you?"

"No; Aurora was at school in Paris with the Demoiselles Lespard."

"Lespard — Lespard!" he repeated; "a Protestant pension in the Faubourg Saint Germain? Why, a cousin of mine is being educated there—a Miss Trevyllian. She has been there for three or four years. Do you remember Constance Trevyllian at the Demoiselles Lespard, Miss Floyd?" said Talbot, addressing himself to Aurora.

"Constance Trevyllian? Yes, I remember her," answered the banker's daughter.

She said nothing more, and for a few moments there was rather an awkward pause.

"Miss Trevyllian is my cousin," said the captain.

"Indeed!"

"I hope that you were very good friends."

"Oh, yes."

She bent over her dog, caressing his big head, and not even looking up as she spoke of Miss Trevyllian. It seemed as if the subject was utterly indifferent to her, and she disdained even to affect an interest in it.

Talbot Bulstrode bit his lip with offended pride. "I suppose this purse-proud heiress looks down upon the Trevyllians of Tredethlin," he thought, "because they can boast of nothing better than a few hundred acres of barren moorland, some exhausted tin mines, and a pedigree that dates from the days of King Arthur."

Archibald Floyd came into the drawing-room while the officers were seated there, and bade them welcome to Felden Woods.

"A long drive, gentlemen," said he; "your horses will want a rest. Of course you will dine with us. We shall have a full moon to-night, and you 'll have it as light as day for your drive back."

Talbot looked at Francis Lewis Maldon, who was sitting staring at Aurora with vacant, open-mouthed admiration. The young officer knew that the heiress and her fifty thousand pounds were not for him; but it was scarcely the less pleasant to look at her, and wish that, like Captain Bulstrode, he had been the eldest son of a rich baronet.

The invitation was accepted by Mr. Maldon as cordially as it had been given, and with less than his usual stiffness of manner on the part of Talbot.

The luncheon-bell rang while they were talking, and the little party adjourned to the dining-room, where they found Mrs. Alexander Floyd sitting at the bottom of the table.

Talbot sat next to Lucy, with Mr. Maldon opposite to them, while Aurora took her place beside her father.

The old man was attentive to his guests, but the shallowest observer could have scarcely failed to notice his watchfulness of Aurora. It was ever present in his care-worn face, that tender, anxious glance which turned to her at every pause in the conversation, and could scarcely withdraw itself from her for the common courtesies of life. If she spoke, he listened—listened as if every careless, half-disdainful word concealed a deeper meaning, which it was his task to discern and unravel. If she was silent, he watched her still more closely, seeking perhaps to penetrate that gloomy veil which sometimes spread itself over her handsome face.

Talbot Bulstrode was not so absorbed by his conversation with Lucy and Mrs. Alexander as to overlook this peculiarity in the father's manner toward his only child. He saw, too, that when Aurora addressed the banker, it was no longer with that listless indifference, half weariness, half disdain, which seemed natural to her on other occasions. The eager watchfulness of Archibald Floyd was in some measure reflected in his daughter; by fits and starts, it is true, for she generally sank back into that moody abstraction which Captain Bulstrode had observed on the night of the ball; but still it was there, the same feeling as her father's, though less constant and intense — a watchful, anxious, half-sorrowful affection, which could scarcely exist except under abnormal circumstances. Talbot Bulstrode was vexed to find himself wondering about this, and growing every moment less and less attentive to Lucy's simple talk.

"What does it mean?" he thought; "has she fallen in love with some man whom her father has forbidden her to marry, and is the old man trying to atone for his severity? That 's scarcely likely. A woman with a head and throat like hers could scarcely fail to be ambitious — ambitious and revengeful, rather than over-susceptible of any tender passion. Did she lose half her fortune upon that race she talked to me about? I 'll ask her presently. Perhaps they have taken away her betting-book, or lamed her favorite horse, or shot some pet dog, to cure him of distemper. She is a spoiled child, of course, this heiress, and I dare say her father would try to get a copy of the moon made for her if she cried for that planet."

After luncheon, the banker took his guests into the gardens that stretched far away upon two sides of the house — the gardens which poor Eliza Floyd had helped to plan nineteen years before.

Talbot Bulstrode walked rather stiffly from his Crimean wound, but Mrs. Alexander and

her daughter suited their pace to his, while
Aurora walked before them with her father
and Mr. Maldon, and with the mastiff close at
her side.

"Your cousin is rather proud, is she not?"
Talbot asked Lucy, after they had been talking of Aurora.

"Aurora proud! oh no, indeed! perhaps,
if she has any fault at all (for she is the dearest girl that ever lived), it is that she has not
sufficient pride — I mean with regard to servants, and that sort of people. She would
as soon talk to one of those gardeners as to
you or me; and you would see no difference
in her manner, except that perhaps it would
be a little more cordial to them than to us.
The poor people round Felden idolize her."

"Aurora takes after her mother," said Mrs.
Alexander; "she is the living image of poor
Eliza Floyd."

"Was Mrs. Floyd a countrywoman of her
husband's?" Talbot asked. He was wondering how Aurora came to have those great,
brilliant black eyes, and so much of the south
in her beauty.

"No; my uncle's wife belonged to a Lancashire family."

A Lancashire family! If Talbot Raleigh
Bulstrode could have known that the family
name was Prodder; that one member of the
haughty house had employed his youth in the
pleasing occupations of a cabin-boy, making
thick coffee and toasting greasy herrings for
the matutinal meal of a surly captain, and
receiving more corporal correction from the
sturdy toe of his master's boot than sterling
copper coin of the realm — if he could have
known that the great aunt of this disdainful
creature, walking before him in all the majesty of her beauty, had once kept a chandler's shop in an obscure street in Liverpool,
and, for aught any one but the banker knew,
kept it still! But this was a knowledge
which had wisely been kept even from Aurora herself, who knew little, except that,
despite of having been born with that alle-
gorical silver spoon in her mouth, she was
poorer than other girls, inasmuch as she was
motherless.

Mrs. Alexander, Lucy, and the captain
overtook the others upon a rustic bridge,
where Talbot stopped to rest. Aurora was
leaning over the rough wooden balustrade,
looking lazily at the water.

"Did your favorite win the race, Miss
Floyd?" he asked, as he watched the effect
of her profile against the sunlight; not a
very beautiful profile certainly, but for the
long black eyelashes, and the radiance under
them, which their darkest shadows could
never hide.

"Which favorite?" she said.

"The horse you spoke to me about the
other night — Thunderbolt; did he win?"

"No."

"I am very sorry to hear it."

Aurora looked up at him, reddening angrily. "Why so?" she asked.

"Because I thought you were interested in
his success."

As Talbot said this, he observed, for the
first time, that Archibald Floyd was near
enough to hear their conversation, and, fur-
thermore, that he was regarding his daughter
with even more than his usual watchfulness.

"Do not talk to me of racing; it annoys
papa," Aurora said to the captain, dropping
her voice. Talbot bowed. "I was right,
then," he thought; "the turf is the skeleton.
I dare say Miss Floyd has been doing her
best to drag her father's name into the Gazette, and yet he evidently loves her to distraction; while I —" There was something
so very pharisaical in the speech that Captain Bulstrode would not even finish it mentally. He was thinking, "This girl, who,
perhaps, has been the cause of nights of
sleepless anxiety and days of devouring care,
is tenderly beloved by her father, while I,
who am a model to all the elder sons of England, have never been loved in my life."

At half-past six the great bell at Felden
Woods rang a clamorous peal that went shivering above the trees, to tell the country-side
that the family were going to dress for dinner; and another peal at seven to tell the
villagers round Beckenham and West Wickham that Maister Floyd and his household
were going to dine; but not altogether an
empty or discordant peal, for it told the hungry poor of broken victuals and rich and
delicate meats to be had almost for asking in
the servants' offices — shreds of fricandeaux
and patches of dainty preparations, quarters
of chickens and carcasses of pheasants, which
would have gone to fatten the pigs for Christmas but for Archibald Floyd's strict com-
mands that all should be given to those who
chose to come for it.

Mr. Floyd and his visitors did not leave the
gardens till after the ladies had retired to
dress. The dinner-party was very animated,
for Alexander Floyd drove down from the
city to join his wife and daughter, bringing
with him the noisy boy who was just going to
Eton, and who was passionately attached to
his cousin Aurora; and whether it was owing
to the influence of this young gentleman, or
to that fitfulness which seemed a part of her
nature, Talbot Bulstrode could not discover,
but certain it was that the dark cloud melted
away from Miss Floyd's face, and she abandoned herself to the joyousness of the hour
with a radiant grace that reminded her
father of the night when Eliza Percival
played Lady Tenzel for the last time, and
took her farewell of the stage in the little
Lancashire theatre.

It needed but this change in his daughter
to make Archibald Floyd thoroughly happy.

Aurora's smiles seemed to shed a revivifying influence upon the whole circle. The ice melted away, for the sun had broken out, and the winter was gone at last. Talbot Bulstrode bewildered his brain by trying to discover why it was that this woman was such a peerless and fascinating creature. Why it was that, argue as he would against the fact, he was nevertheless allowing himself to be bewitched by this black-eyed siren — freely drinking of that cup of *bang* which she presented to him, and rapidly becoming intoxicated.

"I could almost fall in love with my fairhaired ideal," he thought, "but I can not help admiring this extraordinary girl. She is like Mrs. Nisbett in her zenith of fame and beauty; she is like Cleopatra sailing down the Cydnus; she is like Nell Gwynne selling oranges; she is like Lola Montez giving battle to the Bavarian students; she is like Charlotte Corday with the knife in her hand, standing behind the friend of the people in his bath; she is like everything that is beautiful, and strange, and wicked, and unwomanly, and bewitching; and she is just the sort of creature that many a fool would fall in love with."

He put the length of the room between himself and the enchantress, and took his seat by the grand piano, at which Lucy Floyd was playing slow harmonious symphonies of Beethoven. The drawing-room at Felden Woods was so long that, seated by this piano, Captain Bulstrode seemed to look back at the merry group about the heiress as he might have looked at a scene on the stage from the back of the boxes. He almost wished for an opera-glass as he watched Aurora's graceful gestures and the play of her sparkling eyes; and then, turning to the piano, he listened to the drowsy music, and contemplated Lucy's face, marvellously fair in the light of that full moon of which Archibald Floyd had spoken, the glory of which, streaming in from an open window, put out the dim wax candles on the piano.

All that Aurora's beauty most lacked was richly possessed by Lucy. Delicacy of outline, perfection of feature, purity of tint, all were there; but, while one face dazzled you by its shining splendor, the other impressed you only with a feeble sense of its charms, slow to come, and quick to pass away. There are so many Lucys, but so few Auroras; and while you never could be critical with the one, you were merciless in your scrutiny of the other. Talbot Bulstrode was attracted to Lucy by a vague notion that she was just the good and timid creature who was destined to make him happy; but he looked at her as calmly as if she had been a statue, and was as fully aware of her defects as a sculptor who criticises the work of a rival.

But she was exactly the sort of woman to make a good wife. She had been educated to that end by a careful mother. Purity and goodness had watched over her and hemmed her in from the cradle. She had never seen unseemly sights, or heard unseemly sounds. She was as ignorant as a baby of all the vices and horrors of this big world. She was ladylike, accomplished, well-informed; and if there were a great many others of precisely the same type of graceful womanhood, it was certainly the highest type, and the holiest, and the best.

Later in the evening, when Captain Bulstrode's phaeton was brought round to the flight of steps in front of the great doors, the little party assembled on the terrace to see the two officers depart, and the banker told his guests how he hoped this visit to Felden would be the beginning of a lasting acquaintance.

"I am going to take Aurora and my niece to Brighton for a month or so," he said, as he shook hands with the captain, "but on our return you must let us see you as often as possible."

Talbot bowed, and stammered his thanks for the banker's cordiality. Aurora and her cousin, Percy Floyd, the young Etonian, had gone down the steps, and were admiring Captain Bulstrode's thorough-bred bays, and the captain was not a little distracted by the picture the group made in the moonlight.

He never forgot that picture. Aurora, with her coronet of plaits dead black against the purple air, and her silk dress shimmering in the uncertain light, the delicate head of the bay horse visible above her shoulder, and her ringed white hands caressing the animal's slender ears, while the purblind old mastiff, vaguely jealous, whined complainingly at her side.

How marvellous is the sympathy which exists between some people and the brute creation! I think that horses and dogs understood every word that Aurora said to them — that they worshipped her from the dim depths of their inarticulate souls, and would have willingly gone to death to do her service. Talbot observed all this with an uneasy sense of bewilderment.

"I wonder whether these creatures are wiser than we?" he thought; "do they recognize some higher attributes in this girl than we can perceive, and worship their sublime presence? If this terrible woman, with her unfeminine tastes and mysterious propensities, were mean, or cowardly, or false, or impure, I do not think that mastiff would love her as he does; I do not think my thorough-breds would let her hands meddle with their bridles; the dog would snarl, and the horses would bite, as such animals used to do in those remote old days when they recognized witchcraft and evil spirits, and were convulsed by the presence of the uncanny. I dare say this Miss Floyd is a good, generous-hearted creature — the sort of person fast men would call a glorious girl — but as well-read in the *Racing Calendar* and *Ruff's Guide* as other ladies in Miss Yonge's novels. I 'm really sorry for her."

CHAPTER V.

JOHN MELLISH.

The house which the banker hired at Brighton for the month of October was perched high up on the East Cliff, towering loftily above the wind - driven waves; the rugged coast of Dieppe was dimly visible from the upper windows in the clear autumn mornings, and the Chain Pier looked like a strip of ribbon below the cliff—a pleasanter situation, to my mind, than those level terraces toward the west, from the windows of which the sea appears of small extent, and the horizon within half a mile or so of the Parade.

Before Mr. Floyd took his daughter and her cousin to Brighton, he entered into an arrangement which he thought, no doubt, a very great evidence of his wisdom; this was the engagement of a lady, who was to be a compound governess, companion, and chaperon to Aurora, who, as her aunt said, was sadly in need of some accomplished and watchful person, whose care it would be to train and prune those exuberant branches of her nature which had been suffered to grow as they would from her infancy. The beautiful shrub was no longer to trail its wild stems along the ground, or shoot upward to the blue skies at its own sweet will; it was to be trimmed, and clipped, and fastened primly to the stony wall of society with cruel nails and galling strips of cloth. In other words, an advertisement was inserted in the *Times* newspaper, setting forth that a lady by birth and education was required as finishing governess and companion in the household of a gentleman to whom salary was no object, provided the aforesaid lady was perfect mistress of all the accomplishments under the sun, and was altogether such an exceptional and extraordinary being as could only exist in the advertising columns of a popular journal.

But if the world had been filled with exceptional beings, Mr. Floyd could scarcely have received more answers to his advertisement than came pelting in upon the unhappy little postmaster at Beckenham. The man had serious thoughts of hiring a cart in which to convey the letters to Felden. If the banker had advertised for a wife, and had stated the amount of his income, he could scarcely have had more answers. It seemed as if the female population of London, with one accord, was seized with the desire to improve the mind

and form the manners of the daughter of the gentleman to whom terms were no object. Officers' widows, clergymen's widows, lawyers' and merchants' widows, daughters of gentlemen of high family but reduced means, orphan daughters of all sorts of noble and distinguished people, declared themselves each and every one to be the person who, out of all living creatures upon this earth, was best adapted for the post. Mrs. Alexander Floyd selected six letters, threw the rest into the waste-paper basket, ordered the banker's carriage, and drove into town to see the six writers thereof. She was a practical and energetic woman, and she put the six applicants through their facings so severely that when she returned to Mr. Floyd it was to announce that only one of them was good for anything, and that she was coming down to Felden Woods the next day.

The chosen lady was the widow of an ensign who had died within six months of his marriage, and about an hour and a half before he would have succeeded to some enormous property, the particulars of which were never rightly understood by the friends of his unfortunate relict. But, vague as the story might be, it was quite clear enough to establish Mrs. Walter Powell in life as a disappointed woman. She was a woman with straight light hair, and a lady-like droop of the head — a woman who had left school to marry, and, after six months wedded life, had gone back to the same school as instructress of the junior pupils — a woman whose whole existence had been spent in teaching and being taught; who had exercised in her earlier years a species of hand-to-mouth tuition, teaching in the morning that which she learned over night; who had never lost an opportunity of improving herself; who had grown mechanically proficient as a musician and an artist, who had a certain parrot-like skill in foreign languages, who had read all the books incumbent upon her to read, and who knew all things imperative for her to know, and who, beyond all this, and outside the boundary of the school-room wall, was ignorant, and soulless, and low-minded, and vulgar. Aurora swallowed the bitter pill as best she might, and accepted Mrs. Powell as the person chartered for her improvement — a kind of ballast to be flung into the wandering bark, to steady its erratic course, and keep it off rocks and quicksands.

"I must put up with her, Lucy, I suppose," she said, "and I must consent to be improved and formed by the poor, faded creature. I wonder whether she will be like Miss Drummond, who used to let me off from my lessons and read novels while I ran wild in the gardens and stables. I can put up with her, Lucy, as long as I have you with me; but I think I should go mad if I were to be chained up alone with that grim, pale-faced watch-dog."

Mr. Floyd and his family drove from Felden to Brighton in the banker's roomy travelling carriage, with Aurora's maid in the rumble, a pile of imperials upon the roof, and Mrs. Powell, with her young charges, in the interior of the vehicle. Mrs. Alexander had gone back to Fulham, having done her duty, as she considered, in securing a protectress for Aurora; but Lucy was to stay with her cousin at Brighton, and to ride with her on the downs. The saddle-horses had gone down the day before with Aurora's groom, a gray-haired and rather surly old fellow who had served Archibald Floyd for thirty years; and the mastiff called Bow-wow travelled in the carriage with his mistress.

About a week after the arrival at Brighton, Aurora and her cousin were walking together on the West Cliff, when a gentleman with a stiff leg rose from a bench upon which he had been seated listening to the band, and slowly advanced to them. Lucy dropped her eyelids with a faint blush, but Aurora held out her hand in answer to Captain Bulstrode's salute.

"I thought I should be sure to meet you down here, Miss Floyd," he said. "I only came this morning, and I was going to call at Folthorpe's for your papa's address. Is he quite well?"

"Quite — yes, that is — pretty well." A shadow stole over her face as she spoke. It was a wonderful face for fitful lights and shades. "But we did not expect to see you at Brighton, Captain Bulstrode; we thought your regiment was still quartered at Windsor."

"Yes, my regiment—that is, the Eleventh is still at Windsor; but I have sold out."

"Sold out!" Both Aurora and her cousin opened their eyes at this intelligence.

"Yes; I was tired of the army. It's dull work now the fighting is all over. I might have exchanged and gone to India, certainly," he added, as if in answer to some argument of his own; "but I'm getting middle-aged, and I am tired of roaming about the world."

"I should like to go to India," said Aurora, looking seaward as she spoke.

"You, Aurora! but why?" exclaimed Lucy.

"Because I hate England."

"I thought it was France you disliked?"

"I hate them both. What is the use of this big world if we are to stop for ever in one place, chained to one set of ideas, fettered to one narrow circle of people, seeing and hearing of the persons we hate for ever and ever, and unable to get away from the odious sound of their names?. I should like to turn female missionary, and go to the centre of Africa with Dr. Livingstone and his family — and I would go if it was n't for papa."

Poor Lucy stared at her cousin in helpless amazement. Talbot Bulstrode found himself falling back into that state of bewilderment in which this girl always threw him. What did she mean, this heiress of nineteen years of age, by her fits of despondency and outbursts of bitterness? Was it not perhaps, after all, only an affectation of singularity?

Aurora looked at him with her brightest smile while he was asking himself this question. "You will come and see papa?" she said.

Captain Bulstrode declared that he desired no greater happiness than to pay his respects to Mr. Floyd, in token whereof he walked with the young ladies toward the East Cliff.

From that morning the officer became a constant visitor at the banker's. He played chess with Lucy, accompanied her on the piano when she sang, assisted her with valuable hints when she painted in water-colors, put in lights here, and glimpses of sky there, deepened autumnal browns, and intensified horizon purples, and made himself altogether useful to the young lady, who was, as we know, accomplished in all lady-like arts. Mrs. Powell, seated in one of the windows of the pleasant drawing-room, shed the benignant light of her faded countenance and pale blue eyes upon the two young people, and represented all the proprieties in her own person. Aurora, when the weather prevented her riding, occupied herself more restlessly than profitably by taking up books and tossing them down, pulling Bow-wow's ears, staring out of the windows, drawing caricatures of the promenaders on the cliff, and dragging out a wonderful little watch, with a bunch of dangling inexplicable golden absurdities, to see what o'clock it was.

Talbot Bulstrode, while leaning over Lucy's piano or drawing-board, or pondering about the next move of his queen, had ample leisure to watch the movements of Miss Floyd, and to be shocked at the purposeless manner in which that young lady spent the rainy mornings. Sometimes he saw her poring over *Bell's Life*, much to the horror of Mrs. Walter Powell, who had a vague idea of the iniquitous proceedings recited in that terrible journal, but who was afraid to stretch her authority so far as to forbid its perusal.

Mrs. Powell looked with silent approbation upon the growing familiarity between gentle Lucy Floyd and the captain. She had feared at first that Talbot was an admirer of Aurora's; but the manner of the two soon dispelled her alarm. Nothing could be more cordial than Miss Floyd's treatment of the officer; but she displayed the same indifference to him that she did to everything else except her dog and her father. Was it possible that wellnigh perfect face and those haughty graces had no charm for the banker's daughter? Could it be that she could spend hour after hour in the society of the handsomest and most aristocratic man she had ever met, and yet be as heart-whole as when the acquaintance began? There was one person in the little party who was for ever asking that question, and never able to answer it to her own satisfaction, and that person was Lucy Floyd. Poor Lucy Floyd, who was engaged, night and day, in mentally playing that old German game which Faust and Margaret played together with the full-blown rose in the garden—"He loves me — loves me not!" Mrs. Walter Powell's shallow-sighted blue eyes might behold in Lucy Captain Bulstrode's attraction to the East Cliff, but Lucy herself knew better—bitterly, cruelly better.

"Captain Bulstrode's attentions to Miss Lucy Floyd were most evident," Mrs. Powell said one day when the captain left, after a long morning's music, and singing, and chess. How Lucy hated the prim phrase! None knew so well as she the value of those "attentions." They had been at Brighton six weeks, and for the last five the captain had been with them nearly every morning. He had ridden with them on the downs, and driven with them to the Dike, and lounged beside them listening to the band, and stood behind them in their box at the pretty little theatre, and crushed with them into the Pavilion to hear Grisi, and Mario, and Alboni, and poor Bosio. He had attended them through the whole round of Brighton amusements, and had never seemed weary of their companionship. But for all this, Lucy knew what the last leaf upon the rose would tell her when the many petals should be plucked away, and the poor stem be left bare. She knew how often he forgot to turn over the leaf in the Beethoven sonatas, how often he put streaks of green into a horizon that should have been purple, and touched up the trees in her foreground with rose-pink, and suffered himself to be ignominiously checkmated from sheer inattention; and gave her wandering, random answers when she spoke to him. She knew how restless he was when Aurora read *Bell's Life*, and how the very crackle of the newspaper made him wince with nervous pain. She knew how tender he was of the purblind mastiff, how eager to be friends with him, how almost sycophantic in his attentions to the big, stately animal. Lucy knew, in short, that which Talbot as yet did not know himself — she knew that he was fast falling head over heels in love with her cousin, and she had, at the same time, a vague idea that he would much rather have fallen in love with herself, and that he was blindly struggling with the growing passion.

It was so; he was falling in love with Aurora. The more he protested against her, the more determinedly he exaggerated her follies, and argued with himself upon the folly of loving her, so much the more surely did he love her. The very battle he was fighting kept her for ever in his mind, until he grew the veriest slave of the lovely vision which he only evoked in order to endeavor to exorcise.

"How could he take her down to Bulstrode, and introduce her to his father and mother?" he thought; and at the thought she appeared to him illuminating the old Cornish mansion by the radiance of her beauty, fascinating his father, bewitching his mother, riding across the moorland on her thorough-bred mare, and driving all the parish mad with admiration of her.

He felt that his visits to Mr. Floyd's house were fast compromising him in the eyes of its inmates. Sometimes he felt himself bound in honor to make Lucy an offer of his hand; sometimes he argued that no one had any right to consider his attentions more particular to one than to the other of the young ladies. If he had known of that weary game which Lucy was for ever mentally playing with the imaginary rose, I am sure he would not have lost an hour in proposing to her; but Mrs. Alexander's daughter had been far too well educated to betray one emotion of her heart, and she bore her girlish agonies, and concealed her hourly tortures, with the quiet patience common to these simple, womanly martyrs. She knew that the last leaf must soon be plucked, and the sweet pain of uncertainty be for ever ended.

Heaven knows how long Talbot Bulstrode might have done battle with his growing passion had it not been for an event which put an end to his indecision, and made him desperate. This event was the appearance of a rival.

He was walking with Aurora and Lucy upon the West Cliff one afternoon in November, when a mail phaeton and pair suddenly drew up against the railings that separated them from the road, and a big man, with huge masses of Scotch plaid twisted about his waist and shoulders, sprang out of the vehicle, splashing the mud upon his legs, and rushed up to Talbot, taking off his hat as he approached, and bowing apologetically to the ladies.

"Why, Bulstrode," he said, "who on earth would have thought of seeing you here? I heard you were in India, man; but what have you done to your leg?"

He was so breathless with hurry and excitement that he was utterly indifferent to punctuation, and it seemed as much as he could do to keep silence while Talbot introduced him to the ladies as Mr. Mellish, an old friend and school-fellow. The stranger stared with such open-mouthed admiration at Miss Floyd's black eyes that the captain turned round upon him almost savagely as he asked what had brought *him* to Brighton.

"The hunting-season, my boy. Tired of Yorkshire; know every field, ditch, hedge, pond, sunk fence, and scrap of timber in the three Ridings. I 'm staying at the Bedford;

I 've got my stud with me—give you a mount to-morrow morning if you like. Harriers meet at eleven — Dike Road. I 've a gray that 'll suit you to a nicety—carry my weight, and as easy to sit as your arm-chair."

Talbot hated his friend for talking of horses; he felt a jealous terror of him. This, perhaps, was the sort of man whose society would be agreeable to Aurora — this big, empty-headed Yorkshireman, with his babble about his stud and hunting-appointments. But, turning sharply round to scrutinize Miss Floyd, he was gratified to find that young lady looking vacantly upon the gathering mists upon the sea, and apparently unconscious of Mr. John Mellish, of Mellish Park, Yorkshire.

This John Mellish was, as I have said, a big man, looking even bigger than he was by reason of about eight yards length of thick shepherd's plaid twisted scientifically about his shoulders. He was a man of thirty years of age at least, but having withal such a boyish exuberance in his manner, such a youthful and innocent joyousness in his face, that he might have been a youngster of eighteen just let loose from some public academy of the muscular Christianity school. I think the Rev. Charles Kingsley would have delighted in this big, hearty, broad-chested young Englishman, with brown hair brushed away from an open forehead, and a thick, brown mustache, bordering a mouth for ever ready to expand into a laugh. Such a laugh, too! such a hearty and sonorous peal, that the people on the Parade turned round to look at the owner of those sturdy lungs, and smiled good-naturedly for very sympathy with his honest merriment.

Talbot Bulstrode would have given a hundred pounds to get rid of the noisy Yorkshireman. What business had he at Brighton? Was n't the biggest county in England big enough to hold him, that he must needs bring his North-country bluster to Sussex for the annoyance of Talbot's friends?

Captain Bulstrode was not any better pleased when, strolling a little farther on, the party met with Archibald Floyd, who had come out to look for his daughter. The old man begged to be introduced to Mr. Mellish, and invited the honest Yorkshireman to dine at the East Cliff that very evening, much to the aggravation of Talbot, who fell sulkily back, and allowed John to make the acquaintance of the ladies. The familiar brute ingratiated himself into their good graces in about ten minutes, and by the time they reached the banker's house was more at his ease with Aurora than the heir of Bulstrode after two months acquaintance. He accompanied them to the door-step, shook hands with the ladies and Mr. Floyd, patted the mastiff Bow-wow, gave Talbot a playful sledge-hammer-like slap upon the shoulder, and ran back to the Bedford to dress for dinner. His spirits were so high that he knocked over little boys and tumbled against fashionable young men, who drew themselves up in stiff amazement as the big fellow dashed past them. He sang a scrap of a hunting-song as he ran up the great staircase to his eyry at the Bedford, and chattered to his valet as he dressed. He seemed a creature especially created to be prosperous — to be the owner and dispenser of wealth, the distributor of good things. People who were strangers to him ran after him and served him on speculation, knowing instinctively that they would get an ample reward for their trouble. Waiters in a coffee-room deserted other tables to attend upon that at which he was seated. Box-keepers would leave parties of six shivering in the dreary corridors while they found a seat for John Mellish. Mendicants picked him out from the crowd in a busy thoroughfare, and hung about him, and would not be driven away without a dole from the pocket of his roomy waistcoat. He was always spending his money for the convenience of other people. He had an army of old servants at Mellish Park, who adored him, and tyrannized over him after the manner of their kind. His stables were crowded with horses that were lame, or wall-eyed, or otherwise disqualified for service, but that lived on his bounty like a set of jolly equine paupers, and consumed as much corn as would have supplied a racing-stud. He was perpetually paying for things he neither ordered nor had, and was for ever being cheated by the dear honest creatures about him, who, for all they did their best to ruin him, would have gone through typical fire and water to serve him, and would have clung to him, and worked for him, and supported him out of those very savings for which they had robbed him, when the ruin came. If "Muster John" had a headache, every creature in that disorderly household was unhappy and uneasy till the ailment was cured; every lad in the stables, every servant-maid in the house, was eager that his or her remedy should be tried for his restoration. If you had said at Mellish Park that John's fair face and broad shoulders were not the highest forms of manly beauty and grace, you would have been set down as a creature devoid of all taste and judgment. To the mind of that household, John Mellish in "pink" and pipe-clayed tops was more beautiful than the Apollo Belvidere whose bronze image in little adorned a niche in the hall. If you had told them that fourteen-stone weight was not indispensable to manly perfection, or that it was possible there were more lofty accomplishments than driving unicorns, or shooting forty-seven head of game in a morning, or pulling the bay mare's shoulder into joint that time she got a sprain in the hunting-field, or vanquishing Joe Millings, the East Riding smasher, without so much as losing breath, those simple-hearted

Yorkshire servants would have fairly laughed in your face. Talbot Bulstrode complained that everybody respected him, and nobody loved him. John Mellish might have uttered the reverse of this complaint, had he been so minded. Who could help loving the honest, generous squire, whose house and purse were open to all the country-side? Who could feel any chilling amount of respect for the friendly and familiar master who sat upon the table in the big kitchen at Mellish Park, with his dogs and servants round him, and gave them the history of the day's adventures in the hunting-field, till the old blind fox-hound at his feet lifted his big head and set up a feeble music? No; John Mellish was well content to be beloved, and never questioned the quality of the affection bestowed upon him. To him it was all the purest virgin gold; and you might have talked to him for twelve hours at a sitting without convincing him that men and women were vile and mercenary creatures, and that if his servants, and his tenantry, and the poor about his estate, loved him, it was for the sake of the temporal benefits they received of him. He was as unsuspicious as a child, who believes that the fairies in a pantomime are fairies for ever and ever, and that the harlequin is born in patches and a mask. He was as open to flattery as a school-girl who distributes the contents of her hamper among a circle of toadies. When people told him he was a fine fellow, he believed them, and agreed with them, and thought that the world was altogether a hearty, honest place, and that everybody was a fine fellow. Never having an *arrière pensée* himself, he looked for none in the words of other people, but thought that every one blurted out their real opinions, and offended or pleased their fellows as frankly and blunderingly as himself. If he had been a vicious young man, he would no doubt have gone altogether to the bad, and fallen among thieves; but, being blessed with a nature that was inherently pure and innocent, his greatest follies were no worse than those of a big school-boy who errs from very exuberance of spirit. He had lost his mother in the first year of his infancy, and his father had died some time before his majority; so there had been none to restrain his actions, and it was something at thirty years of age to be able to look back upon a stainless boyhood and youth, which might have been befouled with the slime of the gutters, and infected with the odor of villanous haunts? Had he not reason to be proud of this?

Is there anything, after all, so grand as a pure and unsullied life — a fair picture, with no ugly shadows lurking in the background — a smooth poem, with no crooked, halting line to mar the verse — a noble book, with no unholy page — a simple story, such as our children may read? Can any greatness be greater? can any nobility be more truly noble? When a whole nation mourned with one voice but a few weeks since; when we drew down our blinds, and shut out the dull light of the December day, and listened sadly to the far booming of the guns; when the poorest put aside their work-a-day troubles to weep for a widowed queen and orphaned children in a desolate palace; when rough omnibus-drivers forgot to blaspheme at each other, and•tied decent scraps of crape upon their whips, and went sorrowfully about their common business, thinking of that great sorrow at Windsor, the words that rose simultaneously to every lip dwelt most upon the spotless character of him who was lost — the tender husband, the watchful father, the kindly master, the liberal patron, the temperate adviser, the stainless gentleman.

It is many years since England mourned for another royal personage who was called a "gentleman" — a gentleman who played practical jokes, and held infamous orgies, and persecuted a wretched foreign woman, whose chief sin and misfortune it was to be his wife — a gentleman who cut out his own nether garments, and left the companion of his gayest revels, the genius whose brightness had flung a spurious lustre upon the dreary saturnalia of vice, to die destitute and despairing. Surely there is some hope that we have changed for the better within the last thirty years, inasmuch as we attach a new meaning to-day to this simple title of "gentleman." I take some pride, therefore, in the two young men of whom I write, for the simple reason that I have no dark patches to gloss over in the history of either of them. I may fail in making you like them, but I can promise that you shall have no cause to be ashamed of them. Talbot Bulstrode may offend you with his sulky pride, John Mellish may simply impress you as a blundering, countrified ignoramus, but neither of them shall ever shock you by an ugly word or an unholy thought.

CHAPTER VI.

REJECTED AND ACCEPTED.

The dinner-party at Mr. Floyd's was a very merry one; and when John Mellish and Talbot Bulstrode left the East Cliff to walk westward at eleven o'clock at night, the Yorkshireman told his friend that he had never enjoyed himself so much in his life. This declaration must, however, be taken with some reserve, for it was one which John was in the habit of making about three times a week; but he really had been very happy in the society of the banker's family, and, what was more, he was ready to adore Aurora Floyd without any further preparation whatever.

A few bright smiles and sparkling glances, a little animated conversation about the hunting-field and the race-course, combined with a few glasses of those effervescent wines which Archibald Floyd imported from the fair Moselle country, had been quite enough to turn the head of John Mellish, and to cause him to hold wildly forth in the moonlight upon the merits of the beautiful heiress.

"I verily believe I shall die a bachelor, Talbot," he said, "unless I can get that girl to marry me. I've only known her half a dozen hours, and I 'm head over heels in love with her already. What is it that has knocked me over like this, Bulstrode? I 've seen other girls with black eyes and hair, and she knows no more of horses than half the women in Yorkshire; so it is n't that. What is it, then, hey?"

He came to a full stop against a lamp-post, and stared fiercely at his friend as he asked this question.

Talbot gnashed his teeth in silence.

It was no use battling with his fate, then, he thought; the fascination of this woman had the same effect upon others as upon himself; and while he was arguing with, and protesting against, his passion, some brainless fellow, like this Mellish, would step in and win the prize.

He wished his friend good-night upon the steps of the Old Ship Hotel, and walked straight to his room, where he sat with his window open to the mild November night, staring out at the moonlit sea. He determined to propose to Aurora Floyd before twelve o'clock the next day.

Why should he hesitate?

He had asked himself that question a hundred times before, and had always been unable to answer it; and yet he had hesitated. He could not dispossess himself of a vague idea that there was some mystery in this girl's life; some secret known only to herself and her father; some one spot upon the history of the past which cast a shadow on the present. And yet, how could that be? How could that be, he asked himself, when her whole life only amounted to nineteen years, and he had heard the history of those years over and over again? How often he had artfully led Lucy to tell him the simple story of her cousin's girlhood—the governesses and masters that had come and gone at Felden Woods—the ponies and dogs, and puppies and kittens, and petted foals; the little scarlet riding-habit that had been made for the heiress when she rode after the hounds with her cousin Andrew Floyd. The worst blots that the officer could discover in those early years were a few broken china vases, and a great deal of ink spilled over badly-written French exercises; and, after being educated at home until she was nearly eighteen, Aurora had been transferred to a Parisian finishing school—and that was all. Her life had been the every-day life of other girls of her own position, and she differed from them only in being a great deal more fascinating, and a little more wilful, than the majority.

Talbot laughed at himself for his doubts and hesitations. "What a suspicious brute I must be," he said, "when I imagine I have fallen upon the clew to some mystery simply because there is a mournful tenderness in the old man's voice when he speaks to his only child! If I were sixty-seven years of age, and had such a daughter as Aurora, would there not always be a shuddering terror mingled with my love—a horrible dread that something would happen to take her away from me? I will propose to Miss Floyd to-morrow."

Had Talbot been thoroughly candid with himself, he would perhaps have added, "Or John Mellish will make her an offer the day after."

Captain Bulstrode presented himself at the house on the East Cliff some time before noon on the next day, but he found Mr. Mellish on the door-step talking to Miss Floyd's groom and inspecting the horses, which were waiting for the young ladies; for the young ladies were going to ride, and John Mellish was going to ride with them.

"But if you 'll join us, Bulstrode," the Yorkshireman said, good-naturedly, "you can ride the gray I spoke of yesterday.—Saunders shall go back and fetch him."

Talbot rejected this offer rather sulkily. "I've my own horses here, thank you," he answered. "But if you 'll let your groom ride down to the stables and tell my man to bring them up, I shall be obliged to you."

After which condescending request Captain Bulstrode turned his back upon his friend, crossed the road, and, folding his arms upon the railings, stared resolutely at the sea. But in five minutes more the ladies appeared upon the door-step, and Talbot, turning at the sound of their voices, was fain to cross the road once more for the chance of taking Aurora's foot in his hand as she sprang into her saddle; but John Mellish was before him again, and Miss Floyd's mare was curveting under the touch of her right hand before the captain could interfere. He allowed the groom to attend to Lucy, and, mounting as quickly as his stiff leg would allow him, he prepared to take his place by Aurora's side. Again he was too late; Miss Floyd had cantered down the hill attended by Mellish, and it was impossible for Talbot to leave poor Lucy, who was a timid horsewoman.

The captain never admired Lucy so little as on horseback. His pale saint with the halo of golden hair seemed to him sadly out of place in a side-saddle. He looked back at the day of his morning visit to Felden, and remembered how he had admired her, and how exactly she corresponded with his ideal, and how determined he was to be bewitched with her rather than by Aurora. "If she had fallen in love with me," he thought, "I would have snapped my fingers at the black-browed heiress, and married this fair-haired angel out of hand. I meant to do that when I sold my commission. It was not for Aurora's sake I left the army, it was not Aurora whom I followed down here. Which did I follow? What did I follow, I wonder? My destiny, I suppose, which is leading me through such a witch's dance as I never thought to tread at the sober age of three-and-thirty. If Lucy had only loved me, it might have been all different."

He was so angry with himself that he was half inclined to be angry with poor Lucy for not extracting him from the snares of Aurora. If he could have read that innocent heart as he rode in sulky silence across the stunted turf on the wide downs — if he could have known the slow, sick pain in that gentle breast, as the quiet girl by his side lifted her blue eyes every now and then to steal a glance at his hard profile and moody brow — if he could have read her secret later, when, talking of Aurora, he for the first time clearly betrayed the mystery of his own heart — if he could have known how the landscape grew dim before her eyes, and how the brown moorland reeled beneath her horse's hoofs until they seemed going down, down, down into some fathomless depth of sorrow and despair! But he knew nothing of this, and he thought Lucy Floyd a pretty, inanimate girl, who would no doubt be delighted to wear a becoming dress as bridesmaid at her cousin's wedding.

There was a dinner-party that evening upon the East Cliff, at which both John Mellish and Talbot were to assist, and the captain savagely determined to bring matters to an issue before the night was out.

Talbot Raleigh Bulstrode would have been very angry with you had you watched him too closely that evening as he fastened the golden solitaire in his narrow cravat before his looking-glass in the bow-window at the Old Ship. He was ashamed of himself for being causelessly savage with his valet, whom he dismissed abruptly before he began to dress, and had not the courage to call the man back again when his own hot hands refused to do their office. He spilled half a bottleful of perfume upon his varnished boots, and smeared his face with a terrible waxy compound which promised to *lisser sans grais-ser* his mustache. He broke one of the crystal boxes in his dressing-case, and put the bits of broken glass in his waistcoat-pocket from sheer absence of mind. He underwent semi-strangulation with the unbending circular collar in which, as a gentleman, it was his duty to invest himself; and he could have

beaten the ivory backs of his brushes upon his head in blind execration of that short, stubborn black hair, which only curled at the *other ends;* and, when at last he emerged from his room, it was with a spiteful sensation that every waiter in the place knew his secret, and had a perfect knowledge of every emotion in his breast, and that the very Newfoundland dog lying on the door-step had an inkling of the truth, as he lifted up his big head to look at the captain, and then dropped it again with a contemptuously lazy yawn.

Captain Bulstrode offered a handful of broken glass to the man who drove him to the East Cliff, and then confusedly substituted about fifteen shillings worth of silver coin for that abnormal species of payment. There must have been two or three earthquakes and an eclipse or so going on in some part of the globe, he thought, for this jog-trot planet seemed all tumult and confusion to Talbot Bulstrode. The world was all Brighton, and Brighton was all blue moonlight, and steel-colored sea, and glancing, dazzling gas-light, and hare-soup, and cod and oysters, and Aurora Floyd — yes; Aurora Floyd, who wore a white silk dress, and a thick circlet of dull gold upon her hair, who looked more like Cleopatra to-night than ever, and who suffered Mr. John Mellish to take her down to dinner. How Talbot hated the Yorkshireman's big fair face, and blue eyes, and white teeth, as he watched the two young people across a phalanx of glass and silver, and flowers and wax candles, and pickles, and other Fortnum and Mason ware! Here was a golden opportunity lost, thought the discontented captain, forgetful that he could scarcely have proposed to Miss Floyd at the dinner-table, amid the jingle of glasses and popping of corks, and with a big powdered footman charging at him with a side-dish or a sauce-tureen while he put the fatal question. The desired moment came a few hours afterward, and Talbot had no longer any excuse for delay.

The November evening was mild, and the three windows in the drawing-room were open from floor to ceiling. It was pleasant to look out from the hot gas-light upon that wide sweep of moonlit ocean, with a white sail glimmering here and there against the purple night. Captain Bulstrode sat near one of the open windows, watching that tranquil scene, with, I fear, very little appreciation of its beauty. He was wishing that the people would drop off and leave him alone with Aurora. It was close upon eleven o'clock, and high time they went. John Mellish would of course insist upon waiting for Talbot; this was what a man had to endure on account of some old school-boy acquaintance. All Rugby might turn up against him in a day or two, and dispute with him for Aurora's smiles. But John Mellish was engaged in a very animated conversation with Archibald Floyd, having contrived, with consummate artifice, to ingratiate himself in the old man's favor, and, the visitors having one by one dropped off, Aurora, with a listless yawn that she took little pains to conceal, strolled out into the broad iron balcony. Lucy was sitting at a table at the other end of the room, looking at a book of beauty. Oh, my poor Lucy! how much did you see of the Honorable Miss Brownsmith's high forehead and Roman nose? Did not that young lady's handsome face stare up at you dimly through a blinding mist of tears that you were a great deal too well educated to shed? The chance had come at last. If life had been a Haymarket comedy, and the entrances and exits arranged by Mr. Buckstone himself, it could not have fallen out no better than this. Talbot Bulstrode followed Aurora on to the balcony; John Mellish went on with his story about the Beverly fox-hounds; and Lucy, holding her breath at the other end of the room, knew as well what was going to happen as the captain himself.

Is not life altogether a long comedy, with Fate for the stage-manager, and Passion, Inclination, Love, Hate, Revenge, Ambition, and Avarice, by turns, in the prompter's box? A tiresome comedy sometimes, with dreary, talkee, talkee front scenes which come to nothing, but only serve to make the audience more impatient as they wait while the stage is set and the great people change their dresses; or a "sensation" comedy, with unlooked-for tableaux and unexpected *dénoûments;* but a comedy to the end of the chapter, for the sorrows which seem tragic to us are very funny when seen from the other side of the foot-lights; and our friends in the pit are as much amused with our trumpery griefs as the Haymarket *habitués* when Mr. Box finds his gridiron empty, or Mr. Cox misses his rasher. What can be funnier than other people's anguish? Why do we enjoy Mr. Maddison Morton's farces, and laugh till the tears run down our cheeks at the comedian who enacts them? Because there is scarcely a farce upon the British stage which is not, from the rising to the dropping of the curtain, a record of human anguish and undeserved misery. Yes, undeserved and unnecessary torture — there is the special charm of the entertainment. If the man who was weak enough to send his wife to Camberwell *had* crushed a baby behind a chest of drawers, his sufferings would n't be half so delightful to an intellectual audience. If the gentleman who became embroiled with his laundress *had* murdered the young lady in the green boots, where would be the fun of that old Adelphi farce in which poor Wright was wont to delight us? And so it is with our friends on the other side of the foot-lights, who enjoy our troubles all the more because we have not always deserved them, and whose sorrows we shall gloat over by and by; when the bell for the next piece begins, and it is their turn to go on and act.

Talbot Bulstrode went out on to the balcony, and the earth stood still for ten minutes or so, and every steel-blue star in the sky glared watchfully down upon the young man in this the supreme crisis of his life.

Aurora was leaning against a slender iron pilaster, looking aslant into the town, and across the town into the sea. She was wrapped in an opera cloak; no stiff, embroidered, young ladified garment, but a voluminous drapery of soft scarlet woollen stuff, such as Semiramide herself might have worn. "She looks like Semiramide," Talbot thought. "How did this Scotch banker and his Lancashire wife come to have an Assyrian for their daughter?"

He began brilliantly, this young man, as lovers generally do.

"I am afraid you must have fatigued yourself this evening, Miss Floyd," he remarked.

Aurora stifled a yawn as she answered him. "I am rather tired," she said.

It was n't very encouraging. How was he to begin an eloquent speech, when she might fall asleep in the middle of it? But he did; he dashed at once into the heart of his subject, and he told her how he loved her; how he had done battle with this passion, which had been too strong for him; how he loved her as he never thought to love any creature upon this earth; and how he cast himself before her in all humility, to take his sentence of life or death from her dear lips.

She was silent for some moments, her profile sharply distinct to him in the moonlight, and those dear lips trembling visibly. Then, with a half-averted face, and in words that seemed to come slowly and painfully from a stifled throat, she gave him his answer.

That answer was a rejection!

Not a young lady's No, which means yes to-morrow, or which means perhaps that you have not been on your knees in a passion of despair, like Lord Edward Fitz Morkysh in Miss Oderose's last novel. Nothing of this kind; but a calm negative, carefully and tersely worded, as if she feared to mislead him by so much as one syllable that could leave a loop-hole through which hope might creep into his heart. He was rejected. For a moment it was quite as much as he could do to believe it. He was inclined to imagine that the signification of certain words had suddenly changed, or that he had been in the habit of mistaking them all his life, rather than that those words meant this hard fact, namely, that he, Talbot Raleigh Bulstrode, of Bulstrode Castle, and of Saxon extraction, had been rejected by the daughter of a Lombard-street banker.

He paused — for an hour and a half or so, as it seemed to him — in order to collect himself before he spoke again.

"May I — venture to inquire," he said — how horribly commonplace the phrase seemed; he could have used no worse had he been inquiring for furnished lodgings — "may I ask if any prior attachment — to one more worthy —"

"Oh no, no, no!"

The answer came upon him so suddenly that it almost startled him as much as her rejection.

"And yet your decision is irrevocable?"

"Quite irrevocable."

"Forgive me if I am intrusive; but, — but Mr. Floyd may perhaps have formed some higher views."

He was interrupted by a stifled sob as she clasped her hands over her averted face.

"Higher views!" she said; "poor, dear old man, no, no, indeed."

"It is scarcely strange that I bore you with those questions. It is so hard to think that, meeting you with your affections disengaged, I have yet been utterly unable to win one shadow of regard upon which I might build a hope for the future."

Poor Talbot! Talbot, the splitter of metaphysical straws and chopper of logic, talking of building hopes on shadows with a lover's delirious stupidity.

"It is so hard to resign every thought of your ever coming to alter your decision of to-night, Aurora" — he lingered on her name for a moment, first because it was so sweet to say it, and, secondly, in the hope that she would speak — "it is so hard to remember the fabric of happiness I had dared to build, and to lay it down here to-night for ever."

Talbot quite forgot that, up to the time of the arrival of John Mellish, he had been perpetually arguing against his passion, and had declared to himself over and over again that he would be a consummate fool if he was ever beguiled into making Aurora his wife. He reversed the parable of the fox; for he had been inclined to make faces at the grapes while he fancied them within his reach, and, now that they were removed from his grasp, he thought that such delicious fruit had never grown to tempt mankind.

"If — if," he said, "my fate had been happier. I know how proud my father, poor old Sir John, would have been of his eldest son's choice."

How ashamed he felt of the meanness of this speech! The artful sentence had been constructed in order to remind Aurora whom she was refusing. He was trying to bribe her with the baronetcy which was to be his in due time. But she made no answer to the pitiful appeal. Talbot was almost choked with mortification. "I see — I see," he said, "that it is hopeless. Good-night, Miss Floyd."

She did not even turn to look at him as he left the balcony; but, with her red drapery wrapped tightly round her, stood shivering in the moonlight, with the silent tears slowly stealing down her cheeks.

"Higher views!" she cried bitterly, repeating a phrase that Talbot used — "higher views! God help him!"

"I must wish you good-night and good-by at the same time," Captain Bulstrode said as he shook hands with Lucy.

"Good-by?"

"Yes; I leave Brighton early to-morrow."

"So suddenly?"

"Why not exactly suddenly. I always meant to travel this winter. Can I do anything for you — at Cairo?"

He was so pale, and cold, and wretched-looking that she almost pitied him in spite of the wild joy growing up in her heart. Aurora had refused him — it was perfectly clear — refused him! The soft blue eyes filled with tears at the thought that a demigod should have endured such humiliation. Talbot pressed her hand gently in his own clammy palm. He could read pity in that tender look, but possessed no lexicon by which he could translate its deeper meaning.

"You will wish your uncle good-by for me, Lucy," he said. He called her Lucy for the first time; but what did it matter now? His great affliction set him apart from his fellow-men, and gave him dismal privileges. "Good-night, Lucy; good-night and good-by. I — I — shall hope to see you again in a year or two."

The pavement of the East Cliff seemed so much air beneath Talbot Bulstrode's boots as he strode back to the Old Ship; for it is peculiar to us, in our moments of supreme trouble or joy, to lose all consciousness of the earth we tread, and to float upon the atmosphere of sublime egotism.

But the captain did not leave Brighton the next day on the first stage of his Egyptian journey. He staid at the fashionable watering-place; but he resolutely abjured the neighborhood of the East Cliff, and, the day being wet, took a pleasant walk to Shoreham through the rain; and Shoreham being such a pretty place, he was, no doubt, much enlivened by that exercise.

Returning through the fog at about four o'clock, the captain met Mr. John Mellish close against the turnpike outside Cliftonville.

The two men stared aghast at each other.

"Why, where on earth are you going?" asked Talbot.

"Back to Yorkshire by the first train that leaves Brighton."

"But this is n't the way to the station!"

"No; but they 're putting the horses in my portmanteau, and my shirts are going by the Leeds cattle-train, and —"

Talbot Bulstrode burst into a loud laugh, a

harsh and bitter cachinnation, but affording wondrous relief to that gentleman's overcharged breast.

"John Mellish," he said, "you have been proposing to Aurora Floyd."

The Yorkshireman turned scarlet. "It — it — was n't honorable of her to tell you," he stammered.

"Miss Floyd has never breathed a word to me upon the subject. I've just come from Shoreham, and you've only lately left the East Cliff. You've proposed, and you've been rejected."

"I have," roared John; "and it's doosed hard, when I promised her she should keep a racing-stud if she liked, and enter as many colts as she pleased for the Derby, and give her own orders to the trainer, and I'd never interfere; and — and — Mellish Park is one of the finest places in the county; and I'd have won her a bit of blue ribbon to tie up her bonny black hair."

"That old Frenchman was right," muttered Captain Bulstrode; "there is a great satisfaction in the misfortunes of others. If I go to my dentist, I like to have another wretch in the waiting-room; and I like to have my tooth extracted first, and to see him glare enviously at me as I come out of the torture-chamber, knowing that my troubles are over, while his are to come. Good-by, John Mellish, and God bless you. You're not such a bad fellow, after all."

Talbot felt almost cheerful as he walked back to the Ship, and he took a mutton cutlet and tomato sauce, and a pint of Moselle for his dinner; and the food and wine warmed him; and, not having slept a wink on the previous night, he fell into a heavy indigestible slumber, with his head hanging over the sofa-cushion, and dreamed that he was at Grand Cairo (or at a place which would have been that city had it not been now and then Bulstrode Castle, and occasionally chambers in the Albany), and that Aurora Floyd was with him, clad in imperial purple, with hieroglyphics on the hem of her robe, and wearing a clown's jacket of white satin and scarlet spots, such as he had once seen foremost in a great race. Captain Bulstrode arose early the next morning, with the full intention of departing from Sussex by the 8.45 express; but suddenly remembering that he had but poorly acknowledged Archibald Floyd's cordiality, he determined on sacrificing his inclinations on the shrine of courtesy, and calling once more at the East Cliff to take leave of the banker. Having once resolved upon this line of action, the captain would fain have hurried that moment to Mr. Floyd's house; but, finding that it was only half-past seven, he was compelled to restrain his impatience and await a more seasonable hour. Could he go at nine? Scarcely. At ten? Yes, surely, as he could then leave by the eleven o'clock train. He sent his breakfast away untouched, and sat looking at his watch in a mad hurry for the time to pass, yet growing hot and uncomfortable as the hour drew near.

At a quarter to ten he put on his hat and left the hotel. Mr. Floyd was at home, the servant told him—up stairs in the little study, he thought. Talbot waited for no more. "You need not announce me," he said; "I know where to find your master."

The study was on the same floor as the drawing-room, and close against the drawing-room door Talbot paused for a moment. The door was open; the room empty — no, not empty: Aurora Floyd was there, seated with her back toward him, and her head leaning on the cushions of her chair. He stopped for another moment to admire the back view of that small head, with its crown of lustrous raven hair, then took a step or two in the direction of the banker's study, then stopped again, then turned back, went into the drawing-room, and shut the door behind him.

She did not stir as he approached her, nor answer when he stammered her name. Her face was as white as the face of a dead woman, and her nerveless hands hung over the cushions of the arm-chair. A newspaper was lying at her feet. She had quietly swooned away sitting there by herself, with no one by to restore her to consciousness.

Talbot flung some flowers from a vase on the table, and dashed the water over Aurora's forehead; then, wheeling her chair close to the open window, he set her with her face to the wind. In two or three moments she began to shiver violently, and soon afterward opened her eyes and looked at him; as she did so, she put her hands to her head, as if trying to remember something. "Talbot!" she said, "Talbot!"

She called him by his Christian name, she who five-and-thirty hours before had coldly forbidden him to hope.

"Aurora," he cried. "Aurora, I thought I came here to wish your father good-by; but I deceived myself. I came to ask you once more, and once for all, if your decision of the night before last was irrevocable?"

"Heaven knows I thought it was when I uttered it."

"But it was not?"

"Do you wish me to revoke it?"

"Do I wish? do I—"

"Because, if you really do, I will revoke it: for you are a brave and honorable man, Captain Bulstrode, and I love you very dearly."

Heaven knows into what rhapsodies he might have fallen, but she put up her hand, as much as to say, "Forbear to-day, if you love me," and hurried from the room. He had accepted the cup of bang which the siren had offered, and had drained the very dregs thereof, and was drunken. He dropped into the chair in which Aurora had sat, and, absent-minded in his joyful intoxication, picked up the newspaper that had lain at her feet. He shuddered in spite of himself as he looked at the title of the journal; it was *Bell's Life*—a dirty copy, crumpled, and beer-stained, and emitting rank odors of inferior tobacco. It was directed to Miss Floyd, in such sprawling penmanship as might have disgraced the pot-boy of a sporting public house:

> "MISS FLOID,
>   fell dun wodes,
>   kent."

The newspaper had been redirected to Aurora by the housekeeper at Felden. Talbot ran his eye eagerly over the front page; it was almost entirely filled with advertisements (and such advertisements!), but in one column there was an account headed "FRIGHTFUL ACCIDENT IN GERMANY: AN ENGLISH JOCKEY KILLED."

Captain Bulstrode never knew why he read of this accident. It was in no way interesting to him, being an account of a steeple-chase in Prussia, in which a heavy English rider and a crack French horse had been killed. There was a great deal of regret expressed for the loss of the horse, and none for the man who had ridden him, who, the reporter stated, was very little known in sporting-circles; but in a paragraph lower down was added this information, evidently procured at the last moment: "The jockey's name was Conyers."

CHAPTER VII.

AURORA'S STRANGE PENSIONER.

Archibald Floyd received the news of his daughter's choice with evident pride and satisfaction. It seemed as if some heavy burden had been taken away, as if some cruel shadow had been lifted from the lives of father and daughter.

The banker took his family back to Felden Woods, with Talbot Bulstrode in his train; and the chintz rooms—pretty, cheerful chambers, with bow-windows that looked across the well-kept stable-yard into long glades of oak and beech—were prepared for the ex-Hussar, who was to spend his Christmas at Felden.

Mrs. Alexander and her husband were established with their family in the western wing; Mr. and Mrs. Andrew were located at the eastern angle; for it was the hospitable custom of the old banker to summon his kins-folk about him early in December, and to keep them with him till the bells of romantic Beckenham church had heralded in the New Year.

Lucy Floyd's cheeks had lost much of their delicate color when she returned to Felden, and it was pronounced by all who observed the change that the air of East Cliff, and the autumn winds drifting across the bleak downs, had been too much for the young lady's strength.

Aurora seemed to have burst forth into some new and more glorious beauty since the morning upon which she had accepted the hand of Talbot Bulstrode. There was a proud defiance in her manner, which became her better than gentleness becomes far lovelier women. There was a haughty *insouciance* about this young lady which gave new brilliancy to her great black eyes, and new music to her joyous laugh. She was like some beautiful, noisy, boisterous water-fall, for ever dancing, rushing, sparkling, scintillating, and utterly defying you to do anything but admire it. Talbot Bulstrode, having once abandoned himself to the spell of the siren, made no farther struggle, but fairly fell into the pitfalls of her eyes, and was entangled in the meshy net-work of her blue-black hair. The greater the tension of the bowstring, the stronger the rebound thereof; and Talbot Bulstrode was as weak to give way at last as he had long been powerful to resist. I must write his story in the commonest words. He could not help it! He loved her; not because he thought her better, or wiser, or lovelier, or more suited to him than many other women — indeed, he had grave doubts upon every one of these points — but because it was his destiny, and he loved her.

What is that hard word which M. Victor Hugo puts into the mouth of the priest in *The Hunchback of Notre Dame* as an excuse for the darkness of his sin? *Anakthe!* It was his fate. So he wrote to his mother, and told her that he had chosen a wife who was to sit in the halls of Bulstrode, and whose name was to be interwoven with the chronicles of the house; told her, moreover, that Miss Floyd was a banker's daughter, beautiful and fascinating, with big black eyes, and fifty thousand pounds for her dowry. Lady Raleigh Bulstrode answered her son's letter upon a quarter of a quire of note-paper, filled with fearful motherly prayers and suggestions; anxious hopes that he had chosen wisely; questionings as to the opinions and religious principles of the young lady — much, indeed, that Talbot would have been sorely puzzled to answer. Inclosed in this was a letter to Aurora, a womanly and tender epistle, in which pride was tempered with love, and which brought big tears welling up to Miss Floyd's eyes, until Lady Bulstrode's firm penmanship grew blotted and blurred beneath the reader's vision.

And whither went poor slaughtered John Mellish? He returned to Mellish Park, carrying with him his dogs, and horses, and grooms, and phaeton, and other paraphernalia; but his grief — having unluckily come upon him after the racing season — was too much for him, and he fled away from the roomy old mansion, with its pleasant surroundings of park and woodland: for Aurora Floyd was not for him, and it was all flat, stale, and unprofitable. So he went to Paris, or *Parry*, as he called that imperial city, and established himself in the biggest chambers at Meurice's, and went backward and forward between that establishment and Galignani's ten times a day in quest of the English papers. He dined drearily at Véfour's, the Trois Frères, and the Café de Paris. His big voice was heard at every expensive dining-place in Paris, ordering "*Toos killyar de mellyour: vous savez;*" but he sent the daintiest dishes away untasted, and would sit for a quarter of an hour counting the toothpicks in the tiny blue vases, and thinking of Aurora. He rode dismally in the Bois de Boulogne, and sat shivering in *cafés chantants*, listening to songs that always seemed set to the same melody. He haunted the circuses, and was wellnigh in love with a fair *manége* rider, who had black eyes, and reminded him of Aurora; till, upon buying the most powerful opera-glass that the Rue de Rivoli could afford, he discovered that the lady's face was an inch deep in a certain whitewash called *blanc rosati*, and that the chief glory of her eyes were the rings of Indian ink which surrounded them. He could have dashed that double-barrelled truth-revealer to the ground, and trodden the lenses to powder with his heel, in his passion of despair; better to have been for ever deceived, to have gone on believing that woman to be like Aurora, and to have gone to that circus every night until his hair grew white, but not with age, and until he pined away and died.

The party at Felden Woods was a very joyous one. The voices of children made the house pleasant; noisy lads from Eton and Westminster clambered about the balustrades of the staircases, and played battledoor and shuttlecock upon the long stone terrace. These young people were all cousins to Aurora Floyd, and loved the banker's daughter with a childish worship, which mild Lucy could never inspire. It was pleasant to Talbot Bulstrode to see that, wherever his future wife trod, love and admiration waited upon her footsteps. He was not singular in his passion for this glorious creature, and it could be, after all, no such terrible folly to love one who was beloved by all who knew her. So the proud Cornishman was happy, and gave himself up to his happiness without farther protest.

Did Aurora love him? Did she make him due return for the passionate devotion, the blind adoration? She admired and esteemed him; she was proud of him — proud of that

very pride in his nature which made him so different to herself, and she was too impulsive and truthful a creature to keep this sentiment a secret from her lover. She revealed, too, a constant desire to please her betrothed husband, suppressing, at least, all outward token of the tastes that were so unpleasant to him. No more copies of *Bell's Life* littered the ladies' morning-room at Felden; and when Andrew Floyd asked Aurora to ride to meet with him, his cousin refused the offer, which would once have been so welcome. Instead of following the Croydon hounds, Miss Floyd was content to drive Talbot and Lucy in a basket carriage through the frost-bespangled country-side. Lucy was always the companion and confidante of the lovers; it was hard for her to hear their happy talk of the bright future stretching far away before them — stretching down, down the shadowy aisles of Time, to an escutcheoned tomb at Bulstrode, where husband and wife would lie down, full of years and honors, in the days to come. It was hard to have to help them to plan a thousand schemes of pleasure, in which — Heaven pity her! — she was to join; but she bore her cross meekly, this pale Elaine of modern days, and she never told Talbot Bulstrode that she had gone mad and loved him, and was fain to die.

Talbot and Aurora were both concerned to see the pale cheeks of their gentle companion; but everybody was ready to ascribe them to a cold, or a cough, or constitutional debility, or some other bodily evil, which was to be cured by drugs and boluses; and no one for a moment imagined that anything could possibly be amiss with a young lady who lived in a luxurious house, went shopping in a carriage and pair, and had more pocket-money than she cared to spend. But the lily maid of Astolat lived in a lordly castle, and had doubtless ample pocket-money to buy gorgeous silks for her embroidery, and had little on earth to wish for, and nothing to do, whereby she fell sick for love of Sir Lancelot, and pined and died.

Surely the secret of many sorrows lies in this. How many a grief has been bred of idleness and leisure! How many a Spartan youth has nursed a bosom-devouring fox for very lack of better employment! Do the gentlemen who write the leaders in our daily journals ever die of grief? Do the barristers whose names appear in almost every case reported in those journals go mad for love unrequited? Did the LADY WITH THE LAMP cherish any foolish passion in those days and nights of ceaseless toil, in those long watches of patient devotion far away in the East? Do the curates of over-crowded parishes, the chaplains of jails and convict-ships, the great medical attendants in the wards of hospitals — do they make for themselves the griefs that kill? Surely not. With the

3

busiest of us there may be some holy moments, some sacred hour snatched from the
noise and confusion of the revolving wheel of
Life's machinery, and offered up as a sacrifice
to sorrow and care; but the interval is brief,
and the great wheel rolls on, and we have no
time to pine or die.

So Lucy Floyd, having nothing better to
do, nursed and made much of her hopeless
passion. She set up an altar for the skeleton,
and worshipped at the shrine of her grief;
and when people told her of her pale face,
and the family doctor wondered at the failure
of his quinine mixture, perhaps she nourished
a vague hope that before the spring-time came
back again, bringing with it the wedding-day
of Talbot and Aurora, she would have escaped
from all this demonstrative love and happiness, and be at rest.

Aurora answered Lady Raleigh Bulstrode's
letter with an epistle expressive of such gratitude and humility, such earnest hope of winning the love of Talbot's mother, mingled
with a dim fearfulness of never being worthy
of that affection, as won the Cornish lady's
regard for her future daughter. It was difficult to associate the impetuous girl with that
letter, and Lady Bulstrode made an image of
the writer that very much differed from the
fearless and dashing original. She wrote
Aurora a second letter, more affectionately
worded than the first, and promised the
motherless girl a daughter's welcome at Bulstrode.

"Will she ever let me call her 'mother,'
Talbot?" Aurora asked, as she read Lady
Bulstrode's second letter to her lover. "She
is very proud, is she not—proud of your ancient descent. My father comes from a Glasgow mercantile family, and I do not even
know anything about my mother's relations."

Talbot answered her with a grave smile.

"She will accept you for your native worth,
dearest Aurora," he said, "and will ask no
foolish questions about the pedigree of such a
man as Archibald Floyd — a man whom the
proudest aristocrat in England might be glad
to call his father-in-law. She will reverence
my Aurora's transparent soul and candid
nature, and will bless me for the choice I
have made."

"I shall love her very dearly if she will
only let me. Should I have ever cared about
horse-racing, and read sporting papers, if I
could have called a good woman 'mother?'"

She seemed to ask this question rather of
herself than of Talbot.

Complete as was Archibald Floyd's satisfaction at his daughter's disposal of her heart,
the old man could not calmly contemplate a
separation from this idolized daughter; so
Aurora told Talbot that she could never take
up her abode in Cornwall during her father's
lifetime; and it was finally arranged that the
young couple were to spend half the year in

London, and the other half at Felden Woods.
What need had the lonely widower of that
roomy mansion, with its long picture-gallery
and snug suites of apartments, each of them
large enough to accommodate a small family?
What need had one solitary old man of that
retinue of servants, the costly stud in the
stables, the new-fangled vehicles in the coach-
houses, the hot-house flowers, the pines, and
grapes, and peaches, cultivated by three
Scottish gardeners? What need had he of
these things? He lived principally in the
study, in which he had once had a stormy interview with his only child; the study in
which hung the crayon portrait of Eliza
Floyd; the room which contained an old-
fashioned desk he had bought for a guinea in
his boyhood, and in which there were certain
letters written by a hand that was dead, some
tresses of purple-black hair cut from the head
of a corpse, and a pasteboard ticket, printed
at a little town in Lancashire, calling upon
the friends and patrons of Miss Eliza Percival
to come to the theatre, for her especial benefit, upon the night of August 20, 1837.

It was decided, therefore, that Felden
Woods was to be the country residence of
Talbot and Aurora till such time as the young
man should succeed to the baronetcy and
Bulstrode Castle, and be required to live
upon his estate. In the meantime the ex-
Hussar was to go into Parliament, if the
electors of a certain little borough in Cornwall, which had always sent a Bulstrode to
Westminster, should be pleased to return
him.

The marriage was to take place early in
May, and the honeymoon was to be spent in
Switzerland and at Bulstrode Castle. Mrs.
Walter Powell thought that her doom was
sealed, and that she would have to quit those
pleasant pastures after the wedding-day; but
Aurora speedily set the mind of the ensign's
widow at rest by telling her that as she, Miss
Floyd, was utterly ignorant of housekeeping,
she would be happy to retain her services
after marriage as guide and adviser in such
matters.

The poor about Beckenham were not forgotten in Aurora Floyd's morning drives with
Lucy and Talbot. Parcels of grocery and
bottles of wine often lurked beneath the
crimson-lined leopard-skin carriage-rug; and
it was no uncommon thing for Talbot to find
himself making a footstool of a huge loaf of
bread. The poor were very hungry in that
bright December weather, and had all manner of complaints, which, however otherwise
dissimilar, were all to be benefited by one especial treatment; namely, half-sovereigns, old
brown sherry, French brandy, and gunpowder
tea. Whether the daughter was dying of
consumption, or the father laid up with the
rheumatics, or the husband in a raging fever,
or the youngest boy recovering from a fall

into a copper of boiling water, the above-named remedies seemed alike necessary, and were far more popular than the chicken-broths and cooling fever-drinks prepared by the Felden cook. It pleased Talbot to see his betrothed dispensing good things to the eager recipients of her bounty. It pleased him to think how even his mother must have admired this high-spirited girl, content to sit down in close cottage chambers and talk to rheumatic old women. Lucy distributed little parcels of tracts prepared by Mrs. Alexander, and flannel garments made by her own white hands; but Aurora gave the half-sovereigns and the old sherry; and I 'm afraid these simple cottagers liked the heiress best, although they were wise enough and just enough to know that each lady gave according to her means.

It was in returning from a round of these charitable visits that an adventure befell the little party which was by no means pleasing to Captain Bulstrode.

Aurora had driven farther than usual, and it was striking four as her ponies dashed past Beckenham church and down the hill toward Felden Woods. The afternoon was cold and cheerless; light flakes of snow drifted across the hard road, and hung here and there upon the leafless hedges, and there was that inky blackness in the sky which presages a heavy fall. The woman at the lodge ran out with her apron over her head to open the gates as Miss Floyd's ponies approached, and at the same moment a man rose from a bank by the roadside, and came close up to the little carriage.

He was a broad-shouldered, stout-built fellow, wearing a shabby velveteen cut-away coat, slashed about with abnormal pockets, and white and greasy at the seams and elbows. His chin was muffled in two or three yards of dirty woollen comforter, after the fashion of his kind; and the band of his low-crowned felt hat was ornamented with a short clay pipe, colored of a respectable blackness. A dingy white dog, with a brass collar, bow legs, a short nose, bloodshot eyes, one ear, a hanging jaw, and a generally supercilious expression of countenance, rose from the bank at the same moment with his master, and growled ominously at the elegant vehicle and the mastiff Bow-wow trotting by its side.

The stranger was the same individual who had accosted Miss Floyd in Cockspur street three months before.

I do not know whether Miss Floyd recognized this person; but I know that she touched her ponies' ears with the whip, and the spirited animals had dashed past the man, and through the gates of Felden, when he sprang forward, caught at their heads, and stopped the light basket carriage, which rocked under the force of his strong hand.

Talbot Bulstrode leaped from the vehicle, heedless of his stiff leg, and caught the man by the collar.

"Let go that bridle!" he cried, lifting his cane: "how dare you stop this lady's ponies?"

"Because I wanted to speak to her, that 's why. Let go my coat, will yer?"

The dog made at Talbot's legs, but the young man whirled round his cane and inflicted such a chastisement upon the snub nose of that animal as sent him into temporary retirement, howling dismally.

"You are an insolent scoundrel, and I 've a good mind to—"

"You 'd be hinserlent, p'raps, if yer was hungry," answered the man, with a pitiful whine, which was meant to be conciliating. "Such weather as this here 's all very well for young swells such as you, as has your dawgs, and guns, and 'untin'; but the winter 's tryin' to a poor man's temper when he 's industrious and willin', and can't get a stroke of honest work to do, or a mouthful of vittals. I only want to speak to the young lady: she knows me well enough."

"Which young lady?"

"Miss Floyd—the heiress."

They were standing a little way from the pony carriage. Aurora had risen from her seat and flung the reins to Lucy; she was looking toward the two men, pale and breathless, doubtless terrified for the result of the encounter.

Talbot released the man's collar, and went back to Miss Floyd.

"Do you know this person, Aurora?" he asked.

"Yes."

"He is one of your old pensioners, I suppose?"

"He is; do not say anything more to him, Talbot. His manner is rough, but he means no harm. Stop with Lucy while I speak to him."

Rapid and impetuous in all her movements, she sprang from the carriage, and joined the man beneath the bare branches of the trees before Talbot could remonstrate.

The dog, which had crawled slowly back to his master's side, fawned upon her as she approached, and was driven away by a fierce growl from Bow-wow, who was little likely to brook any such vulgar rivalry.

The man removed his felt hat, and tugged ceremoniously at a tuft of sandyish hair which ornamented his low forehead.

"You might have spoken to a cove without all this here row, Miss Floyd," he said, in an injured tone.

Aurora looked at him indignantly.

"Why did you stop me here?" she said; "why could n't you write to me?"

"Because writin 's never so much good as speakin', and because such young ladies as you are uncommon difficult to get at. How did I know that your pa might n't have put his hand upon my letter, and there 'd have been a pretty to do; though I dessay, as for that, if I was to go up to the house, and ask the old gent for a trifle, he would n't be back'ard in givin' it. I dessay he 'd be good for a fi-pun note, or a tenner, if it came to that."

Aurora's eyes flashed sparks of fire as she turned upon the speaker. "If ever you dare to annoy my father, you shall pay dearly for it, Matthew Harrison," she said; "not that I fear anything you can say, but I will not have him annoyed—I will not have him tormented. He has borne enough, and suffered enough, Heaven knows, without that. I will not have him harassed, and his best and tenderest feelings made a market of by such as you. I will not!"

She stamped her foot upon the frosty ground as she spoke. Talbot Bulstrode saw and wondered at the gesture. He had half a mind to leave the carriage and join Aurora and her petitioner; but the ponies were restless, and he knew it would not do to abandon the reins to poor timid Lucy.

"You need n't take on so, Miss Floyd," answered the man, whom Aurora had addressed as Matthew Harrison; "I 'm sure I want to make things pleasant to all parties. All I ask is, that you 'll act a little liberal to a cove wot 's come down in the world since you see him last. Lord, wot a world it is for ups and downs! If it had been the summer season, I 'd have had no needs to worrit you; but what 's the good of standin' at the top of Regent street such weather as this with tarrier pups and such likes? Old ladies has no eyes for dawgs in the winter; and even the gents as cares for rat-catchin' is gettin' uncommon scarce. There ain't nothink doin' on the turf whereby a chap can make an honest penny, nor won't be, come the Craven Meetin'. I 'd never have come anigh you, miss, if I had n't been hard up, and I know you 'll act liberal."

"Act liberally!" cried Aurora; "good Heavens! if every guinea I have, or ever hope to 'have, could blot out the business that you trade upon, I 'd open my hands and let the money run through them as freely as so much water."

"It was only good-natured of me to send you that 'ere paper, though, miss, eh?" said Mr. Matthew Harrison, plucking a dry twig from the tree nearest him, and chewing it for his delectation.

Aurora and the man had walked slowly onward as they spoke, and were by this time at some distance from the pony carriage.

Talbot Bulstrode was in a fever of restless impatience.

"Do you know this pensioner of your cousin's, Lucy?" he asked.

"No, I can't remember his face. I don't think he belongs to Beckenham."

"Why, if I had n't have sent you that 'ere *Life*, you would n't have know'd, would you, now?" said the man.

"No, no, perhaps not," answered Aurora. She had taken her porte-monnaie from her pocket, and Mr. Harrison was furtively regarding the little morocco receptacle with glistening eyes.

"You don't ask me about any of the particulars?" he said.

"No. What should I care to know of them?"

"No, certainly," answered the man, suppressing a chuckle; "you know enough, if it comes to that; and if you wanted to know any more, I could n't tell you, for them few lines in the paper is all I could ever got hold of about the business. But I always said it, and I always will, if a man as rides up'ard of eleven stone — "

It seemed as if he were in a fair way of rambling on for ever so long if Aurora had not checked him by an impatient frown. Perhaps he stopped all the more readily as she opened her purse at the same moment, and he caught sight of the glittering sovereigns lurking between leaves of crimson silk. He had no very acute sense of color; but I am sure that he thought gold and crimson made a pleasing contrast, as he looked at the yellow coin in Miss Floyd's porte-monnaie. She poured the sovereigns into her own gloved palm, and then dropped the golden shower into Mr. Harrison's hands, which were hollowed into a species of horny basin for the reception of her bounty. The great trunk of an oak screened them from the observation of Talbot and Lucy as Aurora gave the man the money.

"You have no claim upon me," she said, stopping him abruptly, as he began a declaration of his gratitude, "and I protest against your making a market of any past events which have come under your knowledge. Remember, once and for ever, that I am not afraid of you; and that if I consent to assist you, it is because I will not have my father annoyed. Let me have the address of some place where a letter may always find you — you can put it into an envelope and direct it to me here — and from time to time I promise to send you a moderate remittance, sufficient to enable you to lead an honest life, if you or any of your set are capable of doing so; but I repeat, if I give you this money as a bribe, it is only for my father's sake."

The man muttered some expression of thanks, looking at Aurora earnestly; but there was a stern shadow upon that dark face that forbade any hope of conciliation. She was turning from him, followed by the mastiff, when the bandy-legged dog ran forward, whining, and raising himself upon his hind legs to lick her hand.

The expression of her face underwent an immediate change. She shrank from the dog, and he looked at her for a moment with a dim uncertainty in his bloodshot eyes; then, as conviction stole upon the brute mind, he burst into a joyous bark, frisking and capering about Miss Floyd's silk dress, and imprinting dusty impressions of his fore paws upon the rich fabric

"The poor hammal knows yer, miss," said the man, deprecatingly, "you was never 'aughty to 'im"

The mastiff Bow-wow made as if he would have torn up every inch of ground in Felden Woods at this juncture, but Aurora quieted him with a look

"Poor Boxer!" she said, "poor Boxer! so you know me, Boxer!"

"Lord, miss, there's no knowin' the faithfulness of them animals."

"Poor Boxer! I think I should like to have you Would you sell him, Harrison?"

The man shook his head

"No, miss," he answered, "thank you kindly; there a'n't much in the way of dawgs as I'd refuse to make a bargain about If you wanted a mute spaniel, or a Russian setter, or a Isle of Skye, I'd get him for you and welcome, and ask you nothin' for my trouble, but this here bull-terrier's father, mother, and wife, and fambly to me, and there a'n't money enough in your pa's bank to buy him, miss."

"Well, well," said Aurora, relentingly, "I know how faithful he is Send me the address, and don't come to Felden again"

She returned to the carriage, and, taking the reins from Talbot's hand, gave the restless ponies their head, the vehicle dashed past Mr Matthew Harrison, who stood hat in hand, with his dog between his legs, until the party had gone by Miss Floyd stole a glance at her lover's face, and saw that Captain Bulstrode's countenance wore its darkest expression. The officer kept sulky silence till they reached the house, when he handed the two ladies from the carriage, and followed them across the hall Aurora was on the lowest step of the broad staircase before he spoke.

"Aurora," he said, "one word before you go up stairs."

She turned and looked at him a little defiantly, she was still very pale, and the fire with which her eyes had flashed upon Mr Matthew Harrison, dog-fancier and rat-catcher, had not yet died out of those dark orbs Talbot Bulstrode opened the door of a long chamber under the picture-gallery — half billiard-room, half library, and almost the pleasantest apartment in the house — and stood aside for Aurora to pass him

The young lady crossed the threshold as proudly as Marie Antoinette going to face her plebeian accusers The room was empty. Miss Floyd seated herself in a low easy-chair by one of the two great fireplaces, and looked straight at the blaze.

"I want to ask you about that man Aurora," Captain Bulstrode said, leaning over a

prie-dieu chair, and playing nervously with the carved arabesques of the walnut-wood frame-work

"About which man?"

This might have been prevarication in some; from Aurora it was simply defiance, as Talbot knew

"The man who spoke to you on the avenue just now. Who is he, and what was his business with you?" Here Captain Bulstrode fairly broke down. He loved her, reader, he loved her, remember, and he was a coward, a coward under the influence of that most cowardly of all passions, Love, — the passion that could leave a stain upon a Nelson's name; the passion which might have made a dastard of the bravest of the three hundred at Thermopylæ, or the six hundred at Balaklava He loved her, this unhappy young man, and he began to stammer, and hesitate, and apologize, shivering under the angry light in her wonderful eyes "Believe me, Aurora, that I would not for the world play the spy upon your actions, or dictate to you the objects of your bounty. No, Aurora, not if my right to do so were stronger than it is, and I were twenty times your husband, but that man, that disreputable-looking fellow who spoke to you just now — I don't think he is the sort of person you ought to assist"

"I dare say not," she said, "I have no doubt I assist many people who ought by rights to be in a workhouse or drop on the high-road, but, you see, if I stopped to question their deserts, they might die of starvation while I was making my inquiries; so perhaps it's better to throw away a few shillings upon some unhappy creature who is wicked enough to be hungry, and not good enough to deserve to have anything given him to eat"

There was a recklessness about this speech that jarred upon Talbot, but he could not very well take objection to it, besides, it was leading away from the subject upon which he was so eager to be satisfied

"But that man, Aurora, who is he?"

"A dog-fancier."

Talbot shuddered.

"I thought he was something horrible," he murmured; "but what, in Heaven's name, could he want of you, Aurora?"

"What most of my petitioners want,' she answered, "whether it's the curate of a new chapel with mediæval decorations, who wants to raise our Lady of Bons-Secours upon one of the hills about Norwood, or a laundress who has burnt a week's washing, and wants the means to make it good, or a lady of fashion, who is about to inaugurate a home for the children of indigent lucifer-match sellers; or a lecturer upon political economy, or Shelley and Byron, or Charles Dickens and the modern humorists, who is going to hold forth at Croydon; they all want the same thing — money! If I tell the curate that my principles are evangel-

ical, and that I can't pray sincerely if there
are candlesticks on the altar, he is not the
less glad of my hundred pounds. If I inform
the lady of fashion that I have peculiar opinions about the orphans of lucifer-match sellers, and cherish a theory of my own against
the education of the masses, she will shrug her
shoulders deprecatingly, but will take care to
let me know that any donation Miss Floyd
may be pleased to afford will be equally ac-
ceptable. If I told them that I had committed half a dozen murders, or that I had a silver statue of the winner of last year's Derby
erected on an altar in my dressing-room, and
did daily and nightly homage to it, they
would take my money and thank me kindly
for it, as that man did just now."

"But one word, Aurora — does the man
belong to this neighborhood?"

"No."

"How, then, did you come to know him?"

She looked at him for a moment steadily,
unflinchingly, with a thoughtful expression in
that ever-changing countenance — looked as
if she were mentally debating some point.
Then, rising suddenly, she gathered her shawl
about her and walked toward the door. She
paused upon the threshold and said,

"This cross-questioning is scarcely pleasant,
Captain Bulstrode. If I choose to give a five
pound note to any person who may ask me
for it, I expect full license to do so, and I will
not submit to be called to account for my actions — even by you."

"Aurora!"

The tenderly reproachful tone struck her to
the heart.

"You may believe, Talbot," she said, "you
must surely believe that I know too well the
value of your love to imperil it by word or
deed — you must believe this."

CHAPTER VIII.

POOR JOHN MELLISH COMES BACK AGAIN.

John Mellish grew weary of the great
City of Paris. Better love, and contentment,
and a crust in a *mansarde*, than stalled oxen
or other costly food in the loftiest saloons *au
premier*, and with the most obsequious waiters to do us homage, and repress so much as a
smile at our insular idiom. He grew heartily
weary of the Rue de Rivoli, the gilded railings of the Tuileries gardens, and the leafless
trees behind them. He was weary of the
Place de la Concorde, and the Champs Ely-
sées, and the rattle of the hoofs of the troop
about his imperial highness's carriage when
Napoleon the Third or the baby prince took
his airing. The plot was yet a hatching
which was to come so soon to a climax in the
Rue Lepelletier. He was tired of the broad
boulevards, and the theatres, and the cafés,

and the glove-shops — tired of staring at the
jewellers' windows in the Rue de la Paix, pic-
turing to himself the face of Aurora Floyd
under the diamond and emerald tiaras displayed therein. He had serious thoughts at
times of buying a stove and a basket of char-
coal, and asphyxiating himself quietly in the
great gilded saloon at Meurice's. What was
the use of his money, or his dogs, or his
horses, or his broad acres? All these put together would not purchase Aurora Floyd.
What was the good of life, if it came to that,
since the banker's daughter refused to share
it with him? Remember that this big, blue-
eyed, curly-haired John Mellish had been from
his cradle a spoiled child — spoiled by poor
relations and parasites, servants and toadies,
from the first hour to the thirtieth year of his
existence — and it seemed such a very hard
thing that this beautiful woman should be de-
nied to him. Had he been an Eastern potentate, he would have sent for his vizier, and
would have had that official bowstrung before
his eyes, and so made an end of it; but, being
merely a Yorkshire gentleman and land-owner, he had no more to do but to bear his burden quietly. As if he had ever borne anything quietly! He flung half the weight of
his grief upon his valet, until that functionary
dreaded the sound of Miss Floyd's name, and
told a fellow-servant in confidence that his
master "made such a howling about that
young woman as he offered marriage to at
Brighton that there was no bearing him."
The end of it all was, that one night John
Mellish gave sudden orders for the striking of
his tents, and early the next morning departed for the Great Northern Railway, leaving
only the ashes of his fires behind him.

It was only natural to suppose that Mr.
Mellish would have gone straight to his country residence, where there was much business
to be done by him: foals to be entered for
coming races, trainers and stable-boys to be
settled with, the planning and laying down
of a proposed tan-gallop to be carried out,
and a racing-stud awaiting the eye of the
master. But, instead of going from the Dover
Railway Station to the Great Northern Hotel, eating his dinner, and starting for Doncaster by the express, Mr. Mellish drove to
the Gloucester Coffee-house, and there took
up his quarters, for the purpose, as he said, of
seeing the Cattle-show. He made a melancholy pretence of driving to Baker street in
a Hansom cab, and roamed hither and thither
for a quarter of an hour, staring dismally
into the pens, and then fled away precipi-
tately from the Yorkshire gentlemen-farmers,
who gave him hearty greeting. He left the
Gloucester the next morning in a dog-cart,
and drove straight to Beckenham. Archibald Floyd, who knew nothing of this young
Yorkshireman's declaration and rejection, had
given him a hearty invitation to Felden

Woods Why should n't he go there? Only to make a morning call upon the hospitable banker, not to see Aurora, only to take a few long respirations of the air she breathed before he went back to Yorkshire

Of course he knew nothing of Talbot Bulstrode's happiness, and it had been one of the chief consolations of his exile to remember that that gentleman had put forth in the same vessel, and had been shipwrecked along with him

He was ushered into the billiard-room, where he found Aurora Floyd seated at a little table near the fire, making a pencil copy of a proof-engraving of one of Rosa Bonheur's pictures, while Talbot Bulstrode sat by her side preparing her pencils

We feel instinctively that the man who cuts lead-pencils, or holds a skein of silk upon his outstretched hands, or carries lap-dogs, opera-cloaks, camp-stools, or parasols, is "engaged" Even John Mellish had learned enough to know this He breathed a sigh so loud as to be heard by Lucy and her mother seated by the other fireplace — a sigh that was on the verge of a groan — and then held out his hand to Miss Floyd Not to Talbot Bulstrode He had vague memories of Roman legends floating in his brain, legends of superhuman generosity and classic self-abnegation, but he could not have shaken hands with that dark-haired young Cornishman, though the tenure of the Mellish estate had hung upon the sacrifice He could not do it He seated himself a few paces from Aurora and her lover, twisting his hat about in his hot, nervous hands until the brim was well-nigh limp, and was powerless to utter one sentence, even so much as some poor pitiful remark about the weather.

He was a great spoiled baby of thirty years of age; and I am afraid that, if the stern truth must be told, he saw Aurora Floyd across a mist that blurred and distorted the bright face before his eyes. Lucy Floyd came to his relief by carrying him off to introduce him to her mother, and kind-hearted Mrs Alexander was delighted with his frank, fair English face He had the good fortune to stand with his back to the light, so that neither of the ladies detected that foolish mist in his blue eyes

Archibald Floyd would not hear of his visitor's returning to town either that night or the next day

"You must spend Christmas with us,' he said, "and see the New Year in before you go back to Yorkshire. I have all my children about me at this season, and it is the only time that Felden seems like an old man's home Your friend Bulstrode stops with us" (Mellish winced as he received this intelligence), "and I shan't think it friendly if you refuse to join our party"

What a pitiful coward this John Mellish must have been to accept the banker's invitation, and send the Newton Pagnell back to the Gloucester, and suffer himself to be led away by Mr Floyd's own man to a pleasant chamber a few doors from the chintz rooms occupied by Talbot! But I have said before that love is a cowardly passion It is like the toothache, the bravest and strongest succumb to it, and howl aloud under the torture I don't suppose the Iron Duke would have been ashamed to own that he objected to having his teeth out I have heard of a great fighting man who could take punishment better than any other of the genii of the ring, but who fainted away at the first grip of the dentist's forceps John Mellish consented to stay at Felden, and he went between the lights into Talbot's dressing-room to expostulate with the captain upon his treachery.

Talbot did his best to console his doleful visitant.

"There are more women than one in the world," he said, after John had unbosomed himself of his grief—he did n't think this, the hypocrite, though he said it—" there are more women than one, my dear Mellish, and many very charming and estimable girls, who would be glad to win the affections of such a fellow as you"

"I hate estimable girls," said Mr Mellish, "bother my affections, nobody will ever win my affections, but I love her, I love that beautiful black-eyed creature down stairs, who looks at you with two flashes of lightning, and rides so well, I love her, Bulstrode, and you told me that she 'd refused you, and that you were going to leave Brighton by the eight o'clock express, and you did n't, and you sneaked back and made her a second offer, and she accepted you, and, damme, it was n't fair play"

Having said which, Mr. Mellish flung himself upon a chair, which creaked under his weight, and fell to poking the fire furiously

It was hard for poor Talbot to have to excuse himself for having won Aurora's hand He could not very well remind John Mellish that if Miss Floyd had accepted him, it was perhaps because she preferred him to the honest Yorkshireman. To John the matter never presented itself in this light The spoiled child had been cheated out of that toy above all other toys, upon the possession of which he had set his foolish heart It was as if he had bidden for some crack horse at Tattersall's, in fair and open competition with a friend, who had gone back after the sale to outbid him in some underhand fashion He could not understand that there had been no dishonesty in Talbot's conduct, and he was highly indignant when that gentleman ventured to hint to him that perhaps, on the whole, it would have been wiser to have kept away from Felden Woods

Talbot Bulstrode had avoided any further

allusion to Mr. Matthew Harrison, the dog-fancier, and this, the first dispute between the lovers, had ended in the triumph of Aurora.

Miss Floyd was not a little embarrassed by the presence of John Mellish, who roamed disconsolately about the big rooms, seating himself ever and anon at one of the tables to peer into the lenses of a stereoscope, or to take up some gorgeously bound volume and drop it on the carpet in gloomy absence of mind, and who sighed heavily when spoken to, and was altogether far from pleasant company. Aurora's warm heart was touched by the piteous spectacle of this rejected lover, and she sought him out once or twice, and talked to him about his racing-stud, and asked him how he liked the hunting in Surrey; but John changed from red to white, and from hot to cold, when she spoke to him, and fled away from her with a scared and ghastly aspect, which would have been grotesque had it not been so painfully real.

But by and by John found a more pitiful listener to his sorrows than ever Talbot Bulstrode had been, and this gentle and compassionate listener was no other than Lucy Floyd, to whom the big Yorkshireman turned in his trouble. Did he know, or did he guess, by some wondrous clairvoyance, that her griefs bore a common likeness to his own, and that she was just the one person, of all others, at Felden Woods to be pitiful to him and patient with him? He was by no means proud, this transparent, boyish, babyish good fellow. Two days after his arrival at Felden he told all to poor Lucy.

"I suppose you know, Miss Floyd," he said, "that your cousin rejected me? Yes, of course you do; I believe she rejected Bulstrode about the same time; but some men have n't a ha'porth of pride; I must say I think the captain acted like a sneak."

A sneak! Her idol, her adored, her demigod, her dark-haired and gray-eyed divinity, to be spoken of thus! She turned upon Mr. Mellish with her fair cheeks flushed into a pale glow of anger, and told him that Talbot had a right to do what he had done, and that whatever Talbot did was right.

Like most men whose reflective faculties are entirely undeveloped, John Mellish was blessed with a sufficiently rapid perception—a perception sharpened just then by that peculiar sympathetic prescience, that marvellous clairvoyance of which I have spoken; and in those few indignant words, and that angry flush, he read poor Lucy's secret; she loved Talbot Bulstrode as he loved Aurora—hopelessly.   .

How he admired this fragile girl, who was frightened of horses and dogs, and who shivered if a breath of the winter air blew across the heated hall, and who yet bore her burden with this quiet, uncomplaining patience;

while he, who weighed fourteen stone, and could ride forty miles across country with the bitterest blasts of December blowing on his face, was powerless to endure his affliction. It comforted him to watch Lucy, and to read in these faint signs and tokens, which had escaped even a mother's eye, the sad history of her unrequited affection.

Poor John was too good-natured and unselfish to hold out for ever in the dreary fortress of despair which he had built up for his habitation; and on Christmas eve, when there were certain rejoicings at Felden, held in especial honor of the younger visitors, he gave way, and joined in their merriment, and was more boyish than the youngest of them, burning his fingers with blazing raisins, suffering his eyes to be bandaged at the will of noisy little players at blind-man's-buff, undergoing ignominious penalties in their games of forfeits, performing alternately innkeepers, sheriff's officers, policemen, clergymen, and justices in the acted charades, lifting the little ones who wanted to see "de top of de Kitmat-tee" in his sturdy arms, and making himself otherwise agreeable and useful to young people of from three to fifteen years of age, until at last, under the influence of all this juvenile gayety, and perhaps two or three glasses of Moselle, he boldly kissed Aurora Floyd beneath the branch of mistletoe hanging, "for this night only," in the great hall at Felden Woods.

And having done this, Mr. Mellish fairly lost his wits, and was "off his head" for the rest of the evening, making speeches to the little ones at the supper-table, and proposing Mr. Archibald Floyd and the commercial interests of Great Britain with three times three; leading the chorus of those tiny treble voices with his own sonorous bass, and weeping freely — he never quite knew why — behind his table-napkin. It was through an atmosphere of tears, and sparkling wines, and gas, and hot-house flowers, that he saw Aurora Floyd, looking—ah! how lovely, in those simple robes of white which so much became her, and with a garland of artificial holly round her head. The spiked leaves and the scarlet berries formed themselves into a crown — I think, indeed, that a cheese-plate would have been transformed into a diadem if Miss Floyd has been pleased to put it on her head—and she looked like the genius of Christmas: something bright and beautiful—too beautiful to come more than once a year.

When the clocks were striking 2 A. M., long after the little ones had been carried away muffled up in opera-cloaks, terribly sleepy, and I 'm afraid, in some instances, under the influence of strong drink — when the elder guests had all retired to rest, and the lights, with a few exceptions, were fled, the garlands dead, and all but Talbot and John Mellish departed, the two young men walked up and down the long billiard-room, in the red glow of the two declining fires, and talked to each other confidentially. It was the morning of Christmas day, and it would have been strange to be unfriendly at such a time.

"If you'd fallen in love with the other one, Bulstrode," said John, clasping his old school-fellow by the hand, and staring at him pathetically, "I could have looked upon you as a brother; she's better suited to you, twenty thousand times better adapted to you than her cousin, and you ought to have married her — in common courtesy — I mean to say as an honorable — having very much compromised yourself by your attentions — Mrs. Whatsher-name—the companion—Mrs. Powell—said so —you ought to have married her."

"Married her! Married whom?" cried Talbot, rather savagely, shaking off his friend's hot grasp, and allowing Mr. Mellish to sway backward upon the heels of his varnished boots in rather an alarming manner. "Who do you mean?"

"The sweetest girl in Christendom—except one," exclaimed John, clasping his hot hands and elevating his dim blue eyes to the ceiling; "the loveliest girl in Christendom, except one —Lucy Floyd."

"Lucy Floyd!"

"Yes, Lucy; the sweetest girl in—"

"Who says that I ought to marry Lucy Floyd?"

"She says so—no, no, I don't mean that; I mean," said Mr. Mellish, sinking his voice to a solemn whisper, "I mean that Lucy Floyd loves you! She did n't tell me so—oh, no, bless your soul! she never uttered a word upon the subject: but she loves you. Yes," continued John, pushing his friend away from him with both hands, and staring at him as if mentally taking his pattern for a suit of clothes, "that girl loves you, and has loved you all along. I am not a fool, and I give you my word and honor that Lucy Floyd loves you."

"Not a fool!" cried Talbot; "you're worse than a fool, John Mellish—you're drunk!"

He turned upon his heel contemptuously, and, taking a candle from a table near the door, lighted it, and strode out of the room.

John stood rubbing his hands through his curly hair, and staring helplessly after the captain.

"This is the reward a fellow gets for doing a generous thing," he said, as he thrust his own candle into the burning coals, ignoring any easier mode of lighting it. "It's hard, but I suppose it's human nature."

Talbot Bulstrode went to bed in a very bad humor. Could it be true that Lucy loved him? Could this chattering Yorkshireman have discovered a secret which had escaped the captain's penetration? He remembered how, only a short time before, he had wished that this fair-haired girl might fall in love

with him, and now all was trouble and confusion. Guinevere was lady of his heart, and poor Elaine was sadly in the way. Mr. Tennyson's wondrous book had not been given to the world in the year fifty-seven, or no doubt poor Talbot would have compared himself to the knight whose "honor rooted in dishonor stood." Had he been dishonorable? Had he compromised himself by his attentions to Lucy? Had he deceived that fair and gentle creature? The down pillows in the chintz chamber gave no rest to his weary head that night; and when he fell asleep in the late daybreak, it was to dream of horrible dreams, and to see in a vision Aurora Floyd standing on the brink of a clear pool of water in a woody recess at Felden, and pointing down through its crystal surface to the corpse of Lucy, lying pale and still amid lilies and clustering aquatic plants, whose long tendrils entwined themselves with the fair golden hair.

He heard the splash of the water in that terrible dream, and awoke, to find his valet breaking the ice in his bath in the adjoining room. His perplexities about poor Lucy vanished in the broad daylight, and he laughed at a trouble which must have grown out of his own vanity. What was he, that young ladies should fall in love with him? What a weak fool he must have been to have believed for one moment in the drunken babble of John Mellish! So he dismissed the image of Aurora's cousin from his mind, and had eyes, ears, and thought only for Aurora herself, who drove him to Beckenham church in her basket carriage, and sat by his side in the banker's great square pew.

Alas! I fear he heard very little of the sermon that was preached that day; but, for all that, I declare that he was a good and devout man; a man whom God had blessed with the gift of earnest belief; a man who took all blessings from the hand of God reverently, almost fearfully; and as he bowed his head at the end of that Christmas service of rejoicing and thanksgiving, he thanked Heaven for his overflowing cup of gladness, and prayed that he might become worthy of so much happiness.

He had a vague fear that he was too happy — too much bound up heart and soul in the dark-eyed woman by his side. If she were to die! If she were to be false to him! He turned sick and dizzy at the thought; and even in that sacred temple the Devil whispered to him that there were still pools, loaded pistols, and other certain remedies for such calamities as those, so wicked as well as cowardly a passion is this terrible fever, Love!

The day was bright and clear, the light snow whitening the ground; every line of hedge-top and tree cut sharply out against the cold blue of the ⎯ ⎯ sky. The banker proposed that they should send home the carriages, and walk up the hill to Felden; so

Talbot Bulstrode offered Aurora his arm, only too glad of the chance of a *tête-à-tête* with his betrothed.

John Mellish walked with Archibald Floyd, with whom the Yorkshireman was an especial favorite; and Lucy was lost amid a group of brothers, sisters, cousins, aunts, and uncles.

"We were so busy all yesterday with the little people," said Talbot, "that I forgot to tell you, Aurora, that I had had a letter from my mother."

Miss Floyd looked up at him with her brightest glance. She was always pleased to hear anything about Lady Bulstrode.

"Of course there is very little news in the letter," added Talbot, "for there is rarely much to tell at Bulstrode. And yet — yes — there is one piece of news which concerns yourself."

"Which concerns me?"

"Yes. You remember my cousin, Constance Trevyllian?"

"Y-es—"

"She has returned from Paris, her education finished at last, and she, I believe, all-accomplished, and has gone to spend Christmas at Bulstrode. Good Heavens, Aurora, what is the matter?"

Nothing very much, apparently. Her face had grown as white as a sheet of letter-paper, but the hand upon his arm did not tremble. Perhaps, had he taken especial notice of it, he would have found it preternaturally still.

"Aurora, what is the matter?"

"Nothing. Why do you ask?"

"Your face is as pale as—"

"It is the cold, I suppose," she said, shivering. "Tell me about your cousin, this Miss Trevyllian; when did she go to Bulstrode Castle?"

"She was to arrive the day before yesterday. My mother was expecting her when she wrote."

"Is she a favorite of Lady Bulstrode?"

"No very especial favorite. My mother likes her well enough; but Constance is rather a frivolous girl."

"The day before yesterday," said Aurora; "Miss Trevyllian was to arrive the day before yesterday. The letters from Cornwall are delivered at Felden early in the afternoon, are they not?"

"Yes, dear."

"You will have a letter from your mother to-day, Talbot?"

"A letter to-day! oh, no, Aurora, she never writes two days running; seldom more than once a week."

Miss Floyd did not make any answer to this, nor did her face regain its natural hue during the whole of the homeward walk. She was very silent, only replying in the briefest manner to Talbot's inquiries.

"I am sure that you are ill, Aurora," he said, as they ascended the terrace-steps.

"I am ill."

"But, dearest, what is it? Let me tell Mrs. Alexander, or Mrs. Powell. Let me go back to Beckenham for the doctor."

She looked at him with a mournful earnestness in her eyes.

"My foolish Talbot," she said, "do you remember what Macbeth said to *his* doctor? There are diseases that can not be ministered to. Let me alone; you will know soon enough —you will know very soon, I dare say."

"But, Aurora, what do you mean by this? What can there be upon your mind?"

"Ah! what indeed! Let me alone, let me alone, Captain Bulstrode."

He had caught her hand, but she broke from him, and ran up the staircase in the direction of her own apartments.

Talbot hurried to Lucy with a pale, frightened face.

"Your cousin is ill, Lucy," he said; "go to her, for Heaven's sake, and see what is wrong."

Lucy obeyed immediately; but she found the door of Miss Floyd's room locked against her; and when she called to Aurora and implored to be admitted, that young lady cried out,

"Go away, Lucy Floyd; go away, and leave me to myself, unless you want to drive me mad!"

CHAPTER IX.

HOW TALBOT BULSTRODE SPENT HIS CHRISTMAS.

There was no more happiness for Talbot Bulstrode that day. He wandered from room to room till he was as weary of that exercise as the young lady in Monk Lewis's *Castle Spectre;* he roamed forlornly hither and thither, hoping to find Aurora, now in the billiard-room, now in the drawing-room. He loitered in the hall upon the shallow pretence of looking at barometers and thermometers, in order to listen for the opening and shutting of Aurora's door. All the doors at Felden Woods were perpetually opening and shutting that afternoon, as it seemed to Talbot Bulstrode. He had no excuse for passing the doors of Miss Floyd's apartments, for his own rooms lay at the opposite angle of the house; but he lingered on the broad staircase, looking at the furniture-pictures upon the walls, and not seeing one line in these Wardour-street productions. He had hoped that Aurora would appear at luncheon; but that dismal meal had been eaten without her; and the merry laughter and pleasant talk of the family assembly had sounded far away to Talbot's ears — far away across some wide ocean of doubt and confusion.

He passed the afternoon in this wretched

manner, unobserved by any one but Lucy, who watched him furtively from her distant seat, as he roamed in and out of the drawing-room. Ah! how many a man is watched by loving eyes whose light he never sees! how many a man is cared for by a tender heart whose secret he never learns! A little after dusk, Talbot Bulstrode went to his room to dress. It was some time before the bell would ring; but he would dress early, he thought, so as to make sure of being in the drawing-room when Aurora came down.

He took no light with him, for there were always wax candles upon the chimney-piece in his room.

It was almost dark in that pleasant chintz chamber, for the fire had been lately replenished, and there was no blaze; but he could just distinguish a white patch upon the green cloth cover of the writing-table. The white patch was a letter. He stirred the black mass of coal in the grate, and a bright flame went dancing up the chimney, making the room as light as day. He took the letter in one hand, while he lighted one of the candles on the chimney-piece with the other. The letter was from his mother. Aurora Floyd had told him that he would receive such a letter. What did it all mean? The gay flowers and birds upon the papered walls spun round him as he tore open the envelope. I firmly believe that we have a semi-supernatural prescience of the coming of all misfortune; a prophetic instinct, which tells us that such a letter, or such a messenger, carries evil tidings. Talbot Bulstrode had that prescience as he unfolded the paper in his hands. The horrible trouble was before him — a brooding shadow, with a veiled face, ghastly and undefined; but it was *there*.

"MY DEAR TALBOT—I know the letter I am about to write will distress and perplex you; but my duty lies not the less plainly before me. I fear that your heart is much involved in your engagement to Miss Floyd." The evil tidings concerned Aurora, then; the brooding shadow was slowly lifting its dark veil, and the face of her he loved best on earth appeared behind it. "But I know," continued that pitiless letter, "that the sense of honor is the strongest part of your nature, and that, however you may have loved this girl" (O God, she spoke of his love in the past!) "you will not suffer yourself to be entrapped into a false position through any weakness of affection. There is some mystery about the life of Aurora Floyd."

This sentence was at the bottom of the first page; and, before Talbot Bulstrode's shaking hand could turn the leaf, every doubt, every fear, every presentiment he had ever felt flashed back upon him with preternatural distinctness.

"Constance Trevyllian came here yesterday; and you may imagine that in the course

of the evening you were spoken of, and your engagement discussed."

A curse upon their frivolous women's gossip! Talbot crushed the letter in his hand, and was about to fling it from him; but, no, it *must* be read. The shadow of doubt must be faced, and wrestled with, and vanquished, or there was no more peace upon this earth for him. He went on reading the letter.

"I told Constance that Miss Floyd had been educated in the Rue St. Dominique, and asked if she remembered her. 'What!' she said, 'is it the Miss Floyd whom there was such a fuss about? the Miss Floyd who ran away from school?' And then she told me, Talbot, that a Miss Floyd was brought to the Demoiselles Lespard by her father last June twelvemonth, and that less than a fortnight after arriving at the school she disappeared; her disappearance, of course, causing a great sensation and an immense deal of talk among the other pupils, as it was said she had *run away*. The matter was hushed up as much as possible; but you know that girls will talk, and from what Constance tells me, I imagine that very unpleasant things were said about Miss Floyd. Now you say that the banker's daughter only returned to Felden Woods in September last. *Where was she in the interval?*"

He read no more. One glance told him that the rest of the letter consisted of motherly cautions and admonitions as to how he was to act in this perplexing business.

He thrust the crumpled paper into his bosom, and dropped into a chair by the hearth.

It was so, then! There was a mystery in the life of this woman. The doubts and suspicions, the undefined fears and perplexities, which had held him back at the first, and caused him to wrestle against his love, had not been unfounded. There was good reason for them all, ample reason for them, as there is for every instinct which Providence puts into our hearts. A black wall rose up round about him, and shut him for ever from the woman he loved; this woman whom he loved so far from wisely, so fearfully well; this woman, for whom he had thanked God in the church only a few hours before. And she was to have been his wife — the mother of his children perhaps. He clasped his cold hands over his face, and sobbed aloud. Do not despise him for those drops of anguish: they were the virgin tears of his manhood. Never since infancy had his eyes been wet before. God forbid that such tears as those should be shed more than once in a lifetime. The agony of that moment was not to be lived through twice. The hoarse sobs rent and tore his breast as if his flesh had been hacked by a rusty sword; and, when he took his wet hands from his face, he wondered that they were not red, for it seemed to him as if he had been weeping blood. What should he do?

Go to Aurora, and ask her the meaning of that letter? Yes; the course was plain enough. A tumult of hope rushed back upon him, and swept away his terror. Why was he so ready to doubt her? What a pitiful coward he was to suspect her—to suspect this girl, whose transparent soul had been so freely unveiled to him; whose every accent was truth! For, in his intercourse with Aurora, the quality which he had learned most to reverence in her nature was its sublime candor. He almost laughed at the recollection of his mother's solemn letter. It was so like these simple country people, whose lives had been bounded by the narrow limits of a Cornish village — it was so like them to make mountains out of the veriest mole-hills. What was there so wonderful in that which had occurred? The spoiled child, the wilful heiress, had grown tired of a foreign school, and had run away. Her father, not wishing the girlish escapade to be known, had placed her somewhere else, and had kept her folly a secret. What was there from first to last in the whole affair that was not perfectly natural and probable, the exceptional circumstances of the case duly considered?

He could fancy Aurora, with her cheeks in a flame, and her eyes flashing lightning, flinging a page of blotted exercises into the face of her French master, and running out of the school-room amid a tumult of ejaculatory babble. The beautiful, impetuous creature! There is nothing a man can not admire in the woman he loves, and Talbot was half inclined to admire Aurora for having run away from school.

The first dinner-bell had rung during Captain Bulstrode's agony; so the corridors and rooms were deserted when he went to look for Aurora, with his mother's letter in his breast.

She was not in the billiard-room nor the drawing-room, but he found her at last in a little inner chamber at the end of the house, with a bay-window looking out over the park. The room was dimly lighted by a shaded lamp, and Miss Floyd was seated in the uncurtained window, with her elbow resting on a cushioned ledge, looking out at the steel-cold wintry sky and the whitened landscape. She was dressed in black, her face, neck, and arms gleaming marble-white against the sombre hue of her dress, and her attitude was as still as that of a statue.

She neither stirred nor looked round when Talbot entered the room.

"My dear Aurora," he said, "I have been looking for you everywhere."

She shivered at the sound of his voice.

"You wanted to see me?"

"Yes, dearest. I want you to explain something to me. A foolish business enough, no doubt, my darling, and, of course, very easily explained; but, as your future husband, I

have a right to ask for an explanation; and I know, I know, Aurora, that you will give it in all candor."

She did not speak, although Talbot paused for some moments, awaiting her answer. He could only see her profile, dimly lighted by the wintry sky. He could not see the mute pain, the white anguish in that youthful face.

"I have had a letter from my mother, and there is something in that letter which I wish you to explain. Shall I read it to you, dearest?"

His voice faltered upon the endearing expression, and he remembered afterward that it was the last time he had ever addressed her with a lover's tenderness. The day came when she had need of his compassion, and when he gave it freely; but that moment sounded the death-knell of Love. In that moment the gulf yawned, and the cliffs were rent asunder.

"Shall I read you the letter, Aurora?"

"If you please."

He took the crumpled epistle from his bosom, and, bending over the lamp, read it aloud to Aurora. He fully expected at every sentence that she would interrupt him with some eager explanation; but she was silent until he had finished, and even then she did not speak.

"Aurora, Aurora, is this true?"

"Perfectly true."

"But why did you run away from the Rue St. Dominique?"

"I can not tell you."

"And where were you between the month of June in the year fifty-six and last September?"

"I can not tell you, Talbot Bulstrode. This is my secret, which I can not tell you."

"You can not tell me! There is upward of a year missing from your life, and you can not tell me, your betrothed husband, what you did with that year?"

"I can not."

"Then, Aurora Floyd, you can never be my wife."

He thought that she would turn upon him, sublime in her indignation and fury, and that the explanation he longed for would burst from her lips in a passionate torrent of angry words; but she rose from her chair, and, tottering toward him, fell upon her knees at his feet. No other action could have struck such terror to his heart. It seemed to him a confession of guilt. But what guilt? what guilt? What was the dark secret of this young creature's brief life?

"Talbot Bulstrode," she said in a tremulous voice, which cut him to the soul, "Talbot Bulstrode, Heaven knows how often I have foreseen and dreaded this hour. Had I not been a coward, I should have anticipated this explanation. But I thought — I thought the occasion might never come, or that, when it did come, you would be generous—and—trust me. If you can trust me, Talbot—if you can believe that this secret is not utterly shameful—"

"Not utterly shameful!" he cried. "O God, Aurora, that I should ever hear you talk like this! Do you think there are any degrees in these things? There must be no secret between my wife and me; and the day that a secret, or the shadow of one, arises between us, must see us part for ever. Rise from your knees, Aurora; you are killing me with this shame and humiliation. Rise from your knees; and if we are to part this moment, tell me, tell me, for pity's sake, that I have no need to despise myself for having loved you with an intensity which has scarcely been manly."

She did not obey him, but sank lower in her half kneeling, half crouching attitude, her face buried in her hands, and only the coils of her black hair visible to Captain Bulstrode.

"I was motherless from my cradle, Talbot," she said, in a half stifled voice. "Have pity upon me."

"Pity!" echoed the captain; "pity! Why do you not ask me for justice? One question, Aurora Floyd, one more question, perhaps the last I ever may ask of you—Does your father know why you left that school, and where you were during that twelvemonth?"

"He does."

"Thank God, at least, for that! Tell me, Aurora, then, only tell me this, and I will believe your simple word as I would the oath of another woman—tell me if he approved of your motive in leaving that school — if he approved of the manner in which your life was spent during that twelvemonth. If you can say yes, Aurora, there shall be no more questions between us, and I can make you, without fear, my loved and honored wife."

"I can not," she answered. "I am only nineteen, but within the two last years of my life I have done enough to break my father's heart — to break the heart of the dearest father that ever breathed the breath of life."

"Then all is over between us. God forgive you, Aurora Floyd; but, by your own confession, you are no fit wife for an honorable man. I shut my mind against all foul suspicions; but the past life of my wife must be a white, unblemished page, which all the world may be free to read."

He walked toward the door, and then, returning, assisted the wretched girl to rise, and led her back to her seat by the window, courteously, as if she had been his partner at a ball. Their hands met with as icy a touch as the hands of two corpses. Ah! how much there was of death in that touch! How much had died between those two within the last

few hours — hope, confidence, security, love, happiness, all that makes life worth the holding.

Talbot Bulstrode paused upon the threshold of the little chamber, and spoke once more.

"I shall have left Felden in half an hour, Miss Floyd," he said: "it will be better to allow your father to suppose that the disagreement between us has arisen from something of a trifling nature, and that my dismissal has come from you. I shall write to Mr. Floyd from London, and, if you please, I will so word my letter as to lead him to think this."

"You are very good," she answered. "Yes, I would rather that he should think that. It may spare him pain. Heaven knows I have cause to be grateful for anything that will do that."

Talbot bowed, and left the room, closing the door behind him. The closing of that door had a dismal sound to his ear. He thought of some frail young creature abandoned by her sister-nuns in a living tomb. He thought that he would rather have left Aurora lying rigidly beautiful in her coffin than as he was leaving her to-day.

The jangling, jarring sound of the second dinner-bell clanged out as he went from the semi-obscurity of the corridor into the glaring gas-light of the billiard-room. He met Lucy Floyd coming toward him in her rustling silk dinner-dress, with fringes, and laces, and ribbons, and jewels fluttering and sparkling about her, and he almost hated her for looking so bright and radiant, remembering, as he did, the ghastly face of the stricken creature he had just left. We are apt to be horribly unjust in the hour of supreme trouble, and I fear that if any one had had the temerity to ask Talbot Bulstrode's opinion of Lucy Floyd just at that moment, the captain would have declared her to be a mass of frivolity and affectation. If you discover the worthlessness of the only woman you love upon earth, you will perhaps be apt to feel maliciously disposed toward the many estimable people about you. You are savagely inclined when you remember that they for whom you care nothing are so good, while she on whom you set your soul is so wicked. The vessel which you freighted with every hope of your heart has gone down, and you are angry at the very sight of those other ships riding so gallantly before the breeze. Lucy recoiled at the aspect of the young man's face.

"What is it?" she asked; "what has happened, Captain Bulstrode?"

"Nothing; I have received a letter from Cornwall which obliges me to —"

His hollow voice died away into a hoarse whisper before he could finish the sentence.

"Lady Bulstrode — or Sir John—is ill, perhaps?" hazarded Lucy.

Talbot pointed to his white lips and shook his head. The gesture might mean anything. He could not speak. The hall was full of visitors and children going into dinner. The little people were to dine with their seniors that day, as an especial treat and privilege of the season. The door of the dining-room was open, and Talbot saw the gray head of Archibald Floyd dimly visible at the end of a long vista of lights, and silver, and glass, and evergreens. The old man had his nephews and nieces, and their children grouped about him, but the place at his right hand, the place Aurora was meant to fill, was vacant. Captain Bulstrode turned away from that gayly-lighted scene and ran up the staircase to his room, where he found his servant waiting with his master's clothes laid out, wondering why he had not come to dress.

The man fell back at the sight of Talbot's face, ghastly in the light of the wax candles on the dressing-table.

"I am going away, Philman," said the captain, speaking very fast, and in a thick, indistinct voice. "I am going down to Cornwall by the express to-night, if I can get to town in time to catch the train. Pack my clothes and come after me. You can join me at the Paddington Station. I shall walk up to Beckenham, and take the first train for town. Here, give this to the servants for me, will you?"

He took a confused heap of gold and silver from his pocket, and dropped it into the man's hand.

"Nothing wrong at Bulstrode, I hope, sir?" said the servant. "Is Sir John ill?"

"No, no; I've had a letter from my mother—I—you'll find me at the Great Western."

He snatched up his hat, and was hurrying from the room; but the man followed him with his great-coat.

"You'll catch your death, sir, on such a night as this," the servant said, in a tone of respectful remonstrance.

The banker was standing at the door of the dining-room when Talbot crossed the hall. He was telling a servant to look for his daughter.

"We are all waiting for Miss Floyd," the old man said; "we can not begin dinner without Miss Floyd."

Unobserved in the confusion, Talbot opened the great door softly, and let himself out into the cold winter's night. The long terrace was all ablaze with the lights in the high, narrow windows, as upon the night when he had first come to Felden; and before him lay the park, the trees bare and leafless, the ground white with a thin coating of snow, the sky above gray and starless—a cold and desolate expanse, in dreary contrast with the warmth and brightness behind. All this was typical of the crisis of his life. He was leaving warm love and hope for cold resignation or icy despair. He went down the terrace-steps, across the trim garden-walks, and out into that wide, mysterious park. The long avenue was ghostly in the gray light, the tracery of the interlacing branches above his head making black shadows, that flickered to and fro upon the whitened ground beneath his feet. He walked for a quarter of a mile before he looked back at the lighted windows behind him. He did not turn until a wind in the avenue had brought him to a spot from which he could see the dimly-lighted bay-window of the room in which he had left Aurora. He stood for some time looking at this feeble glimmer, and thinking—thinking of all he had lost, or all he had perhaps escaped—thinking of what his life was to be henceforth without that woman—thinking that he would rather have been the poorest ploughboy in Beckenham parish than the heir of Bulstrode, if he could have taken the girl he loved to his heart, and believed in her truth.

CHAPTER X.

FIGHTING THE BATTLE.

The new year began in sadness at Felden Woods, for it found Archibald Floyd watching in the sick-room of his only daughter.

Aurora had taken her place at the long dinner-table upon the night of Talbot's departure, and, except for being perhaps a little more vivacious and brilliant than usual, her manner had in no way changed after that terrible interview in the bay-windowed room. She had talked to John Mellish, and had played and sung to her younger cousins; she had stood behind her father, looking over his cards through all the fluctuating fortunes of a rubber of long whist; and the next morning her maid had found her in a raging fever, with burning cheeks and bloodshot eyes, her long purple-black hair all tumbled and tossed about the pillows, and her dry hands scorching to the touch. The telegraph brought two grave London physicians to Felden before noon, and the house was clear of visitors by nightfall, only Mrs. Alexander and Lucy remaining to assist in nursing the invalid. The West-End doctors said very little. This fever was as other fevers to them. The young lady had caught a cold, perhaps; she had been imprudent, as these young people will be, and had received some sudden chill. She had very likely overheated herself with dancing, or had sat in a draught, or eaten an ice. There was no immediate danger to be apprehended. The patient had a superb constitution; there was wonderful vitality in the system; and, with careful treatment she would soon come round. Careful treatment meant a two-guinea visit every day from each of these learned gentlemen, though, perhaps, had they given utterance to their inmost thoughts, they would have owned that, for all they could tell to the contrary, Aurora Floyd wanted nothing but to be let alone, and left in a darkened chamber to fight out the battle by herself. But the banker would have had all Saville Row summoned to the sick-bed of his child, if he could by such a measure have saved her a moment's pain; and he implored the two physicians to come to Felden twice a day if necessary, and to call in other physicians if they had the least fear for their patient. Aurora was delirious; but she revealed very little in that delirium. I do not quite believe that people often make the pretty, sentimental, consecutive confessions under the influence of fever which are so freely attributed to them by the writers of romances. We rave about foolish things in those cruel moments of feverish madness. We are wretched because there is a man with a white hat on in the room, or a black cat upon the counterpane, or spiders crawling about the bed-curtains, or a coal-heaver who *will* put a sack of coals on our chest. Our delirious fancies are like our dreams, and have very little connection with the sorrows or joys which make up the sum of our lives.

So Aurora Floyd talked of horses and dogs, and masters and governesses; of childish troubles that had afflicted her years before, and of girlish pleasures, which, in her normal state of mind, had been utterly forgotten. She seldom recognized Lucy or Mrs. Alexander, mistaking them for all kinds of unlikely people; but she never entirely forgot her father, and, indeed, always seemed to be conscious of his presence, and was perpetually appealing to him, imploring him to forgive her for some act of childish disobedience committed in those departed years of which she talked so much.

John Mellish had taken up his abode at the Grayhound Inn, in Croydon High street, and drove every day to Felden Woods, leaving his phaeton at the park-gates, and walking up to the house to make his inquiries. The servants took notice of the Yorkshireman's pale face, and set him down at once as "sweet" upon their young lady. They liked him a great deal better than Captain Bulstrode, who had been too "'igh" and "'aughty" for them. John flung his half-sovereigns right and left when he came to the hushed mansion in which Aurora lay, with loving friends about her. He held the footman who answered the door by the button-hole, and would have gladly paid the man half a crown a minute for his time while he asked anxious questions about Miss Floyd's health. Mr. Mellish was warmly sympathized with, therefore, in the servants' hall at Felden. If man had informed the banker's household how he was the best master in England, and

how Mellish Park was a species of terrestrial paradise, maintained for the benefit of trustworthy retainers; and Mr. Floyd's servants expressed a wish that their young lady might get well, and marry the "fair one," as they called John. They came to the conclusion that there had been what they called "a split" between Miss Floyd and the captain, and that he had gone off in a huff, which was like his impudence, seeing that their young lady would have hundreds of thousands of pounds by and by, and was good enough for a duke, instead of a beggarly officer.

Talbot's letter to Mr. Floyd reached Felden Woods on the 27th of December, but it lay for some time unopened upon the library table. Archibald had scarcely heeded his intended son-in-law's disappearance in his anxiety about Aurora. When he did open the letter, Captain Bulstrode's words were almost meaningless to him, though he was just able to gather that the engagement had been broken—by his daughter's wish, as Talbot seemed to infer.

The banker's reply to this communication was very brief; he wrote:

"MY DEAR SIR—Your letter arrived here some days since, but has only been opened by me this morning. I have laid it aside, to be replied to, D. V., at a future time. At present I am unable to attend to anything. My daughter is seriously ill.

"Yours obediently,
"ARCHIBALD FLOYD."

"Seriously ill!" Talbot Bulstrode sat for nearly an hour with the banker's letter in his hand, looking at these two words. How much or how little might the sentence mean? At one moment, remembering Archibald Floyd's devotion to his daughter, he thought that this serious illness was doubtless some very trifling business—some feminine nervous attack, common to young ladies upon any hitch in their love-affairs; but five minutes afterward he fancied that those words had an awful meaning—that Aurora was dying—dying of the shame and anguish of that interview in the little chamber at Felden.

Heaven above! what had he done? Had he murdered this beautiful creature, whom he loved a million times better than himself? Had he killed her with those impalpable weapons, those sharp and cruel words which he had spoken on the 25th of December? He acted the scene over again and again, until the sense of outraged honor, then so strong upon him, seemed to grow dim and confused, and he began almost to wonder why he had quarrelled with Aurora. What if, after all, this secret involved only some school-girl's folly? No; the crouching figure and ghastly face gave the lie to that hope. The secret, whatever it might be, was a matter of life and death to Aurora Floyd. He dared not try to guess what it was. He tried to close his mind against the surmises that would arise to him. In the first days that succeeded that terrible Christmas he determined to leave England. He would try to get some government appointment that would take him away to the other end of the world, where he could never hear Aurora's name — never be enlightened as to the mystery that had separated them. But now, now that she was ill — in danger, perhaps — how could he leave the country? How could he go away to some place where he might one day open the English newspapers and see her name among the list of deaths?

Talbot was a dreary guest at Bulstrode Castle. His mother and his cousin Constance respected his pale face, and held themselves aloof from him in fear and trembling; but his father asked what the deuce was the matter with the boy, that he looked so chapfallen, and why he didn't take his gun and go out on the moors, and get an appetite for his dinner like a Christian, instead of moping in his own rooms all day long, biting his fingers' ends.

Once, and once only, did Lady Bulstrode allude to Aurora Floyd.

"You asked Miss Floyd for an explanation, I suppose, Talbot?" she said.

"Yes, mother."

"And the result——"

"Was the termination of our engagement. I had rather you would not speak to me of this subject again, if you please, mother."

Talbot took his gun, and went out upon the moors, as his father advised; but it was not to slaughter the last of the pheasants, but to think in peace of Aurora Floyd, that the young man went out. The low-lying clouds upon the moorlands seemed to shut him in like prison-walls. How many miles of desolate country lay between the dark expanse on which he stood and the red-brick mansion at Felden! how many leafless hedge-rows! how many frozen streams! It was only a day's journey, certainly, by the Great Western; but there was something cruel in the knowledge that half the length of England lay between the Kentish woods and that far angle of the British Isles upon which Castle Bulstrode reared its weather-beaten walls. The wail of mourning voices might be loud in Kent, and not a whisper of death reach the listening ears in Cornwall. How he envied the lowest servant at Felden, who knew day by day and hour by hour of the progress of the battle between Death and Aurora Floyd! And yet, after all, what was she to him? What did it matter to him if she were well or ill? The grave could never separate them more utterly than they had been separated from the very moment in which he discovered that she was not worthy to be his wife. He had done her no wrong; he had given her a full and fair opportunity of clearing herself from the doubtful shadow on her name, and she had been unable to do so. Nay, more, she had given him every reason to suppose, by her manner, that the shadow was even a darker one than he had feared. Was he to blame, then? Was it his fault if she were ill? Were his days to be misery, and his nights a burden, because of her? He struck the stock of his gun violently upon the ground at the thought, and thrust the ramrod down the barrel, and loaded his fowling-piece furiously with nothing; and then, casting himself at full length upon the stunted turf, lay there till the early dusk closed in about him, and the soft evening dew saturated his shooting-coat, and he was in a fair way to be stricken with rheumatic fever.

I might fill chapters with the foolish sufferings of this young man; but I fear he must have become very wearisome to my afflicted readers — to those, at least, who have never suffered from this fever. The sharper the disease, the shorter its continuance; so Talbot will be better by and by, and will look back at his old self, and laugh at his old agonies. Surely this inconstancy of ours is the worst of all — this fickleness, by reason of which we cast off our former selves with no more compunction than we feel in flinging off a worn-out garment. Our poor, threadbare selves, the shadows of what we were! With what sublime, patronizing pity, with what scornful compassion, we look back upon the helpless dead and gone creatures, and wonder that anything so foolish could have been allowed to cumber the earth! Shall I feel the same contempt ten years hence for myself as I am to-day as I feel to-day for myself as I was ten years ago? Will the loves and aspirations, the beliefs and desires of to-day, appear as pitiful then as the dead loves and dreams of the by-gone decade? Shall I look back in pitying wonder, and think what a fool that young man was, although there was something candid and innocent in his very stupidity, after all? Who can wonder that the last visit to Paris killed Voltaire? Fancy the octogenarian looking round the national theatre, and seeing himself, through an endless vista of dim years, a young man again, paying his court to a "goat-faced cardinal," and being beaten by De Rohan's lackeys in broad daylight.

Have you ever visited some still country town after a lapse of years, and wondered, oh, fast-living reader, to find the people you knew in your last visit still alive and thriving, with hair unbleached as yet, although you have lived and suffered whole centuries since then? Surely Providence gives us this sublimely egotistical sense of Time as a set-off against the brevity of our lives! I might make this book a companion in bulk to the Catalogue of the British Museum if I were to tell all that Talbot Bulstrode felt and suffered in the month of January, 1858—if I were to anatomize the doubts, and confessions, and self-contradictions, the mental resolutions, made one moment to be broken the next. I refrain, therefore, and will set down nothing but the fact that, on a certain Sunday, midway in the month, the captain, sitting in the family pew at Bulstrode church, directly facing the monument of Admiral Hartley Bulstrode, who fought and died in the days of Queen Elizabeth, registered a silent oath that, as he was a gentleman and a Christian, he would henceforth abstain from holding any voluntary communication with Aurora Floyd. But for this vow he must have broken down, and yielded to his yearning fear and love, and gone to Felden Woods to throw himself, blind and unquestioning, at the feet of the sick woman.

The tender green of the earliest leaflets was breaking out in bright patches upon the hedge-rows round Felden Woods; the ash-buds were no longer black upon the front of March, and pale violets and primroses made exquisite tracery in the shady nooks beneath the oaks and beeches; all nature was rejoicing in the mild April weather when Aurora Floyd lifted her dark eyes to her father's face with something of their old look and familiar light. The battle had been a long and severe one, but it was wellnigh over now, the physicians said; defeated Death drew back for a while, to wait a better opportunity for making his fatal spring; and the feeble victor was to be carried down stairs to sit in the drawing-room for the first time since the night of December the 25th.

John Mellish, happening to be at Felden that day, was allowed the supreme privilege of carrying the fragile burden in his strong arms from the door of the sick-chamber to the great sofa by the fire in the drawing-room, attended by a procession of happy people bearing shawls and pillows, vinaigrettes and scent-bottles, and other invalid paraphernalia. Every creature at Felden was devoted to this adored convalescent. Archibald Floyd lived only to minister to her; gentle Lucy waited on her night and day, fearful to trust the service to menial hands; Mrs. Powell, like some pale and quiet shadow, lurked amid the bed-curtains, soft of foot and watchful of eye, invaluable in the sick-chamber, as the doctors said. Throughout her illness, Aurora had never mentioned the name of Talbot Bulstrode. Not even when the fever was at its worst, and the brain most distraught, had that familiar name escaped her lips. Other names, strange to Lucy, had been repeated by her again and again: the names of places and horses, and slangy technicalities of the turf, had interlarded the poor girl's brain-sick babble; but, whatever were her feelings with regard to Talbot, no word had revealed their depth or sadness. Yet I do not think that my poor, dark-eyed heroine was utterly feelingless upon this point. When they first spoke of carrying her down stairs, Mrs. Powell and Lucy proposed the little bay-windowed chamber, which was small and snug, and had a southern aspect, as the fittest place for the invalid; but Aurora cried out, shuddering, that she would never enter that hateful chamber again.

As soon as ever she was strong enough to bear the fatigue of the journey, it was considered advisable to remove her from Felden, and Leamington was suggested by the doctors as the best place for the change—a mild climate and a pretty inland retreat, a hushed and quiet town, peculiarly adapted to invalids, being almost deserted by other visitors after the hunting-season.

Shakespeare's birthday had come and gone, and the high festivals at Stratford were over, when Archibald Floyd took his pale daughter to Leamington. A furnished cottage had been engaged for them a mile and a half out of the town; a pretty place, half villa, half farm-house, with walls of white plaster, checkered with beams of black wood, and wellnigh buried in a luxuriant and trimly-kept flower-garden; a pleasant place, forming one of a little cluster of rustic buildings crowded into a gray old church in a nook of the roadway, where two or three green lanes met, and went branching off between overhanging hedges; a most retired spot, yet clamorous with that noise which is of all others cheerful and joyous—the hubbub of farm-yards, the cackle of poultry, the cooing of pigeons, the monotonous lowing of lazy cattle, and the squabbling grunt of quarrelsome pigs. Archibald could not have brought his daughter to a better place. The checkered farm-house seemed a haven of rest to this poor, weary girl of nineteen. It was so pleasant to lie wrapped in shawls, on a chintz-covered sofa, in the open window, listening to the rustic noises in the straw-littered yard upon the other side of the hedge, with her faithful Bow-wow's big fore paws resting on the cushions at her feet. The sounds in the farm-yard were pleasanter to Aurora than the monotonous inflections of Mrs. Powell's voice; but as that lady considered it a part of her duty to read aloud for the invalid's delectation, Miss Floyd was too good-natured to own how tired she was of Marmion and Childe Harold, Evangeline and The Queen of the May, and how she would have preferred, in her present state of mind, to listen to a lively dispute between a brood of ducks round the pond in the farm-yard, or a trifling dissension in the pig-sty, to the sublimest lines ever penned by poet, living or dead. The poor girl had suffered very much, and there was a certain nervous, lazy pleasure in this slow recovery, this gradual return

4

to strength. Her own nature revived in unison with the bright revival of the genial summer weather. As the trees in the garden put forth new strength and beauty, so the glorious vitality of her constitution returned with much of its wonted power. The bitter blows had left their scars behind them, but they had not killed her after all. They had not utterly changed her even, for glimpses of the old Aurora appeared day by day in the pale convalescent; and Archibald Floyd, whose life was at best but a reflected existence, felt his hopes revive as he looked at his daughter. Lucy and her mother had gone back to the villa at Fulham, and to their own family duties; so the Leamington party consisted only of Aurora and her father, and that pale shadow of propriety, the ensign's light-haired widow. But they were not long without a visitor. John Mellish, artfully taking the banker at a disadvantage in some moment of flurry and confusion at Felden Woods, had extorted from him an invitation to Leamington, and a fortnight after their arrival he presented his stalwart form and fair face at the low, wooden gates of the checkered cottage. Aurora laughed (for the first time since her illness) as she saw that faithful adorer come, carpet-bag in hand, through the labyrinth of grass and flower-beds toward the open window at which she and her father sat; and Archibald seeing that first gleam of gayety in the beloved face, could have hugged John Mellish for being the cause of it. He would have embraced a street-tumbler, or the low comedian of a booth at a fair, or a troop of performing dogs and monkeys, or anything upon earth that could win a smile from his sick child. Like the Eastern potentate in the fairy tale, who always offers half his kingdom and his daughter's hand to any one who can cure the princess of her bilious headache, or extract her carious tooth, Archibald would have opened a banker's account in Lombard street, with a fabulous sum to start with, for any one who could give pleasure to this black-eyed girl, now smiling, for the first time in that year, at sight of the big, fair-faced Yorkshireman coming to pay his foolish worship at her shrine.

It was not to be supposed that Mr. Floyd had felt no wonder as to the cause of the rupture of his daughter's engagement to Talbot Bulstrode. The anguish and terror endured by him during her long illness had left no room for any other thought; but since the passing away of the danger he had pondered not a little upon the abrupt rupture between the lovers. He ventured once, in the first week of their stay at Leamington, to speak to her upon the subject, asking why it was she had dismissed the captain. Now if there was one thing more hateful than another to Aurora Floyd, it was a lie. I do not say that she had never told one in the course of her life. There

are some acts of folly which carry falsehood and dissimulation at their heels—as certainly as the shadows which follow us when we walk toward the evening sun; and we very rarely swerve from the severe boundary-line of right without being dragged ever so much farther than we calculated upon across the border. Alas! my heroine is not faultless. She would take her shoes off to give them to the bare-footed poor; she would take the heart from her breast, if she could by so doing heal the wounds she has inflicted upon the loving heart of her father. But a shadow of mad folly has blotted her motherless youth, and she has a terrible harvest to reap from that lightly-sown seed, and a cruel expiation to make for that unforgotten wrong. Yet her natural disposition is all truth and candor; and there are many young ladies, whose lives have been as primly ruled and ordered as the fair pleasure-gardens of a Tyburnian Square, who could tell a falsehood with a great deal better grace than Aurora Floyd. So, when her father asked her why she had dismissed Talbot Bulstrode, she made no answer to that question, but simply told him that the quarrel had been a very painful one, and that she hoped never to hear the captain's name again, although at the same time she assured Mr. Floyd that her lover's conduct had been in nowise unbecoming a gentleman and a man of honor. Archibald implicitly obeyed his daughter in this matter, and, the name of Talbot Bulstrode never being spoken, it seemed as if the young man had dropped out of their lives, or as if he had never had any part in the destiny of Aurora Floyd. Heaven knows what Aurora herself felt and suffered in the quiet of her low-roofed, white-curtained little chamber, with the soft May moonlight stealing in at the casement windows, and creeping in wan radiance about the walls. Heaven only knows the bitterness of the silent battle. Her vitality made her strong to suffer; her vivid imagination intensified every throb of pain. In a dull and torpid soul grief is a slow anguish; but with her it was a fierce and tempestuous emotion, in which past and future seemed rolled together with the present to make a concentrated agony. But, by an all-wise dispensation, the stormy sorrow wears itself out by reason of its very violence, while the dull woe drags its slow length sometimes through weary years, becoming at last ingrafted in the very nature of the patient sufferer, as some diseases become part of our constitutions. Aurora was fortunate in being permitted to fight her battle in silence, and to suffer unquestioned. If the dark hollow rings about her eyes told of sleepless nights, Archibald Floyd forbore to torment her with anxious speeches and trite consolations. The clairvoyance of love told him that it was better to let her alone. So the trouble hanging over the little circle was neither seen nor spoken of. Aurora kept her skeleton in some quiet corner, and no one saw the grim skull, or heard the rattle of the dry bones. Archibald Floyd read his newspapers and wrote his letters; Mrs. Walter Powell tended the convalescent, who reclined during the best part of the day on the sofa in the open window; and John Mellish loitered about the garden and the farm - yard, leaned on the low white gate, smoking his cigar, and talking to the men about the place, and was in and out of the house twenty times in an hour. The banker pondered sometimes in serio - comic perplexity as to what was to be done with this big Yorkshireman, who hung upon him like a good - natured monster of six feet two, conjured into existence by the hospitality of a modern Frankenstein. He had invited him to dinner, and, lo! he appeared to be saddled with him for life. He could not tell the friendly, generous, loud-spoken creature to go away. Besides, Mr. Mellish was, on the whole, very useful, and he did much toward keeping Aurora in apparently good spirits. Yet, on the other hand, was it right to tamper with this great loving heart? Was it just to let the young man linger in the light of those black eyes, and then send him away when the invalid was equal to the effort of giving him his *congé*? Archibald Floyd did not know that John had been rejected by his daughter on a certain morning at Brighton, so he made up his mind to speak frankly, and sound the depths of his visitor's feelings.

Mrs. Powell was making tea at a little table near one of the windows. Aurora had fallen asleep with an open book in her hand, and the banker walked with John Mellish up and down an espaliered alley in the golden sunset.

Archibald freely communicated his perplexities to the Yorkshireman. "I need not tell you, my dear Mellish," he said, "how pleasant it is to me to have you here. I never had a son; but if it had pleased God to give me one, I could have wished him to be just such a frank, noble-hearted fellow as yourself. I'm an old man, and have seen a great deal of trouble—the sort of trouble which strikes deeper home to the heart than any sorrows that begin in Lombard street or on 'Change; but I feel younger in your society, and I find myself clinging to you and leaning on you as a father might upon his son. You may believe, then, that *I* don't wish to get rid of you."

"I do, Mr. Floyd; but do you think that any one else wishes to get rid of me? Do you think I'm a nuisance to Miss Floyd?"

"No, Mellish," answered the banker, energetically. "I am sure that Aurora takes pleasure in your society, and seems to treat you almost as if you were her brother; but—but—I know your feelings, my dear boy, and what I fear is, that you may perhaps never inspire a warmer feeling in her heart."

"Let me stay and take my chance, Mr. Floyd," cried John, throwing his cigar across the espaliers, and coming to a dead stop upon the gravel walk in the warmth of his enthusiasm. "Let me stay and take my chance. It there's any disappointment to be borne, I'll bear it like a man; I'll go back to the Park, and you shall never be bothered with me again. Miss Floyd has rejected me once already; but perhaps I was in too great a hurry. I've grown wiser since then, and I've learned to bide my time. I've one of the finest estates in Yorkshire; I'm not worse looking than the generality of fellows, or worse educated than the generality of fellows. I may n't have straight hair, and a pale face, and look as if I'd walked out of a three-volume novel, like Talbot Bulstrode. I may be a stone or two over the correct weight for winning a young lady's heart; but I'm sound, wind and limb. I never told a lie, or committed a mean action; and I love your daughter with as true and pure a love as ever man felt for woman. May I try my luck once more?"

"You may, John."

"And have I — thank you, sir, for calling me John — have I your good wishes for my success?"

The banker shook Mr. Mellish by the hand as he answered this question.

"You have, my dear John, my best and heartiest wishes."

So there were three battles of the heart being fought in that springtide of fifty-eight. Aurora and Talbot, separated from each other by the length and breadth of half England, yet united by an impalpable chain, were struggling day by day to break its links; while poor John Mellish quietly waited in the background, fighting the sturdy fight of the strong heart, which very rarely fails to win the prize it is set upon, however high or far away that prize may seem to be.

CHAPTER XI.

AT THE CHATEAU D'ARQUES.

John Mellish made himself entirely at home in the little Leamington circle after this interview with Mr. Floyd. No one could have been more tender in his manner, more respectful, untiring, and devoted, than was this rough Yorkshireman to the broken old man. Archibald must have been less than human had he not in somewise returned this devotion, and it is therefore scarcely to be wondered that he became very warmly attached to his daughter's adorer. Had John Mellish been the most designing disciple of Machiavelli, instead of the most transparent and candid of living creatures, I scarcely think he could have adopted a truer means of making for himself a ? m up in the gratitude of Aurora Floyd t . by the affecti he evinced for her father,

And this affection was as genuine as all else in that simple nature. How could he do otherwise than love Aurora's father? He *was* her father. He had a sublime claim upon the devotion of the man who loved her—who loved her as John loved—unreservedly, undoubtingly, childishly; with such blind, unquestioning love as an infant feels for its mother. There may be better women than that mother, perhaps, but who shall make the child believe so?

John Mellish could not argue with himself upon his passion as Talbot Bulstrode had done. He could not separate himself from his love, and reason with the mild madness. How could he divide himself from that which was himself—more than himself—a diviner self? He asked no questions about the past life of the woman he loved. He never sought to know the secret of Talbot's departure from Felden. He saw her, beautiful, fascinating, perfect, and he accepted her as a great and wonderful fact, like the moon and the stars shining down on the rustic flower-beds and espaliered garden-walks in the balmy June nights.

So the tranquil days glided slowly and monotonously past that quiet circle. Aurora bore her silent burden—bore her trouble with a grand courage, peculiar to such rich organizations as her own, and none knew whether the serpent had been rooted from her breast, or had made for himself a permanent home in her heart. The banker's most watchful care could not fathom the womanly mystery; but there were times when Archibald Floyd ventured to hope that his daughter was at peace, and Talbot Bulstrode wellnigh forgotten. In any case, it was wise to keep her away from Felden Woods; so Mr. Floyd proposed a tour through Normandy to his daughter and Mrs. Powell. Aurora consented, with a tender smile and gentle pressure of her father's hand. She divined the old man's motive, and recognized the all-watchful love which sought to carry her from the scene of her trouble. John Mellish, who was not invited to join the party, burst forth into such raptures at the proposal that it would have required considerable hardness of heart to have refused his escort. He knew every inch of Normandy, he said, and promised to be of infinite use to Mr. Floyd and his daughter; which, seeing that his knowledge of Normandy had been acquired in his attendance at the Dieppe steeple-chases, and that his acquaintance with the French language was very limited, seemed rather doubtful. But, for all this, he contrived to keep his word. He went up to town and hired an all-accomplished courier, who conducted the little party from town to village, from church to ruin, and who could always find relays of Normandy horses for the banker's roomy travelling carriage. The little party travelled from place to place until pale gleams of color returned in transient flushes to Au-

rora's cheeks. Grief is terribly selfish. I fear that Miss Floyd never took into consideration the havoc that might be going on in the great, honest heart of John Mellish. I dare say that if she had ever considered the matter, she would have thought that a broad-shouldered Yorkshireman of six feet two could never suffer seriously from such a passion as love. She grew accustomed to his society; accustomed to have his strong arm handy for her to lean upon when she grew tired; accustomed to his carrying her sketch-book, and shawls, and camp-stools; accustomed to be waited upon by him all day, and served faithfully by him at every turn; taking his homage as a thing of course, but making him superlatively and dangerously happy by her tacit acceptance of it.

September was half gone when they bent their way homeward, lingering for a few days at Dieppe, where the bathers were splashing about in semi-theatrical costume, and the Etablissement des Bains was all aflame with colored lanterns and noisy with nightly concerts.

The early autumnal days were glorious in their balmy beauty. The best part of a year had gone by since Talbot Bulstrode had bade Aurora that adieu which, in one sense at least, was to be eternal. They two, Aurora and Talbot, might meet again, it is true. They might meet, ay, and even be cordial and friendly together, and do each other good service in some dim time to come; but the two lovers who had parted in the little bay-windowed room at Felden Woods could *never* meet again. Between *them* there was death and the grave.

Perhaps some such thoughts as these had their place in the breast of Aurora Floyd as she sat with John Mellish at her side, looking down upon the varied landscape from the height upon which the ruined walls of the Chateau d'Arques still rear the proud memorials of a day that is dead. I don't suppose that the banker's daughter troubled herself much about Henry the Fourth, or any other dead and gone celebrity who may have left the impress of his name upon that spot. She felt a tranquil sense of the exquisite purity and softness of the air, the deep blue of the cloudless sky, the spreading woods and grassy plains, the orchards, where the trees were rosy with their plenteous burden, the tiny streamlets, the white villa-like cottages and struggling gardens, outspread in a fair panorama beneath her. Carried out of her sorrow by the sensuous rapture we derive from nature, and for the first time discovering in herself a vague sense of happiness, she began to wonder how it was she had outlived her grief by so many months.

She had never, during those weary months, heard of Talbot Bulstrode. Any change might have come to him without her knowledge. He might have married—might have chosen a prouder and worthier bride to share his lofty name. She might meet him on her return to England, with that happier woman leaning upon his arm. Would some good-natured friend tell the bride how Talbot had loved and wooed the banker's daughter? Aurora found herself pitying this happier woman, who would, after all, win but the second love of that proud heart—the pale reflection of a sun that has set; the feeble glow of expiring embers when the great blaze has died out. They had made her a couch with shawls and carriage-rugs, outspread upon a rustic seat, for she was still far from strong, and she lay in the bright September sunshine, looking down at the fair landscape, and listening to the hum of beetles and the chirp of grasshoppers upon the smooth turf.

Her father had walked to some distance with Mrs. Powell, who explored every crevice and cranny of the ruins with the dutiful perseverance peculiar to commonplace people; but faithful John Mellish never stirred from her side. He was watching her musing face, trying to read its meaning—trying to gather a gleam of hope from some chance expression floating across it. Neither he nor she knew how long he had watched her thus, when, turning to speak to him about the landscape at her feet, she found him on his knees imploring her to have pity upon him, and to love him, or to let him love her, which was much the same.

"I don't expect you to love me, Aurora," he said, passionately; "how should you? What is there in a big, clumsy fellow like me to win your love? I don't ask that. I only ask you to let me love you, to let me worship you, as the people we see kneeling in the churches here worship their saints. You won't drive me away from you, will you, Aurora, because I presume to forget what you said to me that cruel day at Brighton? You would never have suffered me to stay with you so long, and to be so happy, if you had meant to drive me away at the last! You never could have been so cruel!"

Miss Floyd looked at him with a sudden terror in her face. What was this? What had she done? More wrong, more mischief! Was her life to be one of perpetual wrong-doing? Was she to be for ever bringing sorrow upon good people? Was this John Mellish to be another sufferer by her folly?

"Oh, forgive me!" she cried, "forgive me! I never thought—"

"You never thought that every day spent by your side must make the anguish of parting from you more cruelly bitter. Oh, Aurora, women should think of these things! Send me away from you, and what shall I be for the rest of my life?—a broken man, fit for nothing better than the race-course and the betting-rooms; a reckless man, ready to go

to the bad by any road that can take me there—worthless alike to myself and to others. You must have seen such men, Aurora; men whose unblemished youth promised an honorable manhood, but who break up all of a sudden, and go to ruin in a few years of mad dissipation. Nine times out of ten a woman is the cause of that sudden change. I lay my life at your feet, Aurora; I offer you more than my heart—I offer you my destiny. Do with it as you will."

He rose in his agitation, and walked a few paces away from her. The grass-grown battlements sloped away from his feet; outer and inner moat lay below him, at the bottom of a steep declivity. What a convenient place for suicide, if Aurora should refuse to take pity upon him! The reader must allow that he had availed himself of considerable artifice in addressing Miss Floyd. His appeal had taken the form of an accusation rather than a prayer, and he had duly impressed upon this poor girl the responsibility she would incur in refusing him. And this, I take it, is a meanness of which men are often guilty in their dealings with the weaker sex.

Miss Floyd looked up at her lover with a quiet, half-mournful smile.

"Sit down there, Mr. Mellish," she said, pointing to a camp-stool at her side.

John took the indicated seat, very much with the air of a prisoner in a criminal dock about to answer for his life.

"Shall I tell you a secret?" asked Aurora, looking compassionately at his pale face.

"A secret?"

"Yes; the secret of my parting with Talbot Bulstrode. It was not I who dismissed him from Felden; it was he who refused to fulfil his engagement with me."

She spoke slowly, in a low voice, as if it were painful to her to say the words which told of so much humiliation.

"He did!" cried John Mellish, rising, red and furious, from his seat, eager to run to look for Talbot Bulstrode then and there, in order to inflict chastisement upon him.

"He did, John Mellish, and he was justified in doing so," answered Aurora, gravely. "You would have done the same."

"Oh, Aurora, Aurora!"

"You would. You are as good a man as he, and why should your sense of honor be less strong than his? A barrier arose between Talbot Bulstrode and me, and separated us for ever. That barrier was a secret."

She told him of the missing year in her young life; how Talbot had called upon her for an explanation, and how she had refused to give it. John listened to her with a thoughtful face, which broke out into sunshine as she turned to him and said,

"How would you have acted in such a case, Mr. Mellish?"

"How should I have acted, Aurora? I

should have trusted you. But I can give you a better answer to your question, Aurora. I can answer it by a renewal of the prayer I made you five minutes ago. Be my wife."

"In spite of this secret?"

"In spite of a hundred secrets. I could not love you as I do, Aurora, if I did not believe you to be all that is best and purest in woman. I can not believe this one moment, and doubt you the next. I give my life and honor into your hands. I would not confide them to the woman whom I could insult by a doubt."

His handsome Saxon face was radiant with love and trustfulness when he spoke. All his patient devotion, so long unheeded, or accepted as a thing of course, recurred to Aurora's mind. Did he not deserve some reward, some requital, for all this? But there was one who was nearer and dearer to her, dearer than even Talbot Bulstrode had ever been, and that one was the white-haired old man pottering about among the ruins on the other side of the grassy platform.

"Does my father know of this, Mr. Mellish?" she asked.

"He does, Aurora. He has promised to accept me as his son; and Heaven knows I will try to deserve that name. Do not let me distress you, Aurora. The murder is out now. You know that I still love you, still hope. Let time do the rest."

She held out both her hands to him with a tearful smile. He took those little hands in his own broad palms, and, bending down, kissed them reverently.

"You are right," she said; "let time do the rest. You are worthy of the love of a better woman than me, John Mellish; but, with the help of Heaven, I will never give you cause to regret having trusted me."

CHAPTER XII.

STEEVE HARGRAVES, "THE SOFTY."

Early in October Aurora Floyd returned to Felden Woods, once more "engaged." The county families opened their eyes when the report reached them that the banker's daughter was going to be married, not to Talbot Bulstrode, but to Mr. John Mellish, of Mellish Park, near Doncaster. The unmarried ladies—rather hanging on hand about Beckenham and West Wickham—did not approve of all this chopping and changing. They recognized the taint of the Prodder blood in this fickleness. The spangles and the sawdust were breaking out, and Aurora was, as they had always said, her mother's own daughter. She was a very lucky young woman, they remarked, in being able, after jilting one rich man, to pick up another; but,

of course, a young person whose father could give her fifty thousand pounds on her wedding-day might be permitted to play fast and loose with the male sex, while worthier Marianas moped in their moated granges till gray hairs showed themselves in glistening bandeaux, and cruel crow's-feet gathered about the corners of bright eyes. It is well to be merry and wise, and honest and true, and to be off with the old love, etc., but it is better to be Miss Floyd, of the senior branch of Floyd, Floyd, and Floyd, for then you need be none of these things. At least to such effect was the talk about Beckenham when Archibald brought his daughter back to Felden Woods, and a crowd of dress-makers and milliners set to work at the marriage garments as busily as if Miss Floyd had never had any clothes in her life before.

Mrs. Alexander and Lucy came back to Felden to assist in the preparations for the wedding. Lucy had improved very much in appearance since the preceding winter; there was a happier light in her soft blue eyes, and a healthier hue in her cheeks; but she blushed crimson when she first met Aurora, and hung back a little from Miss Floyd's caresses.

The wedding was to take place at the end of November. The bride and bridegroom were to spend the winter in Paris, where Archibald Floyd was to join them, and return to England "in time for the Craven Meeting," as John Mellish said; for I am sorry to say that, having been so happily successful in his love-affair, this young man's thoughts returned into their accustomed channels; and the creature he held dearest on earth, next to Miss Floyd and those belonging to her, was a bay filly called Aurora, and entered for the Oaks and Leger of a future year.

Ought I to apologize for my heroine because she has forgotten Talbot Bulstrode, and that she entertains a grateful affection for this adoring John Mellish? She ought, no doubt, to have died of shame and sorrow after Talbot's cruel desertion: and Heaven knows that only her youth and vitality carried her through a very severe battle with the grim rider of the pale horse; but, having once passed through that dread encounter, she was, however feeble, in a fair way to recover. These passionate griefs, to kill at all, must kill suddenly. The lovers who die for love in our tragedies die in such a vast hurry that there is generally some mistake or misapprehension about the business, and the tragedy might have been a comedy if the hero or heroine had only waited for a quarter of an hour. If Othello had but lingered a little before smothering his wife, Mistress Emilia might have come in and sworn and protested; and Cassio, with the handkerchief about his leg, might have been in time to set the mind of the valiant Moor at rest, and put the Venetian dog to confusion. How happily

Mr and Mrs Romeo Montague might have lived and died, thanks to the dear, good friar, if the foolish bridegroom had not been in such a hurry to swallow the vile stuff from the apothecary's, and, as people are, I hope and believe, a little wiser in real life than they appear to be upon the stage, the worms very rarely get an honest meal off men and women who have died for love. So Aurora walked through the rooms at Felden in which Talbot Bulstrode had so often walked by her side, and, if there was any regret at her heart, it was a quiet sorrow, such as we feel for the dead — a sorrow not unmingled with pity, for she thought that the proud son of Sir John Raleigh Bulstrode might have been a happier man if he had been as generous and trusting as John Mellish. Perhaps the healthiest sign of the state of her health was, that she could speak of Talbot freely, cheerfully, and without a blush. She asked Lucy if she had met Captain Bulstrode that year, and the little hypocrite told her cousin Yes, that he had spoken to them one day in the Park, and that she believed he had gone into Parliament. She *believed*! Why, she knew his maiden speech by heart, though it was on some hopelessly uninteresting bill in which the Cornish mines were in some vague manner involved with the national survey, and she could have repeated it as correctly as her youngest brother could declaim to his "Romans, countrymen, and lovers." Aurora might forget him and basely marry a fair-haired Yorkshireman, but for Lucy Floyd, earth only held this dark knight, with the severe gray eyes and the stiff leg. Poor Lucy, therefore, loved, and was grateful to her brilliant cousin for that fickleness which had brought about such a change in the programme of the gay wedding at Felden Woods. The fair young confidante and bridesmaid could assist in the ceremonial now with a good grace. She no longer walked about like a "corpse alive," but took a hearty womanly interest in the whole affair, and was very much concerned in a discussion as to the merits of pink *versus* blue for the bonnets of the bridesmaids.

The boisterous happiness of John Mellish seemed contagious, and made a genial atmosphere about the great mansion at Felden. Stalwart Andrew Floyd was delighted with his young cousin's choice. No more refusals to join him in the hunting-field, but half the county breakfasting at Felden and the long terrace and garden luminous with "pink."

Not a ripple disturbed the smooth current of that brief courtship. The Yorkshireman contrived to make himself agreeable to everybody belonging to his dark-eyed divinity. He flattered their weaknesses, he gratified their caprices, he studied their wishes, and paid them all such insidious court, that I 'm afraid invidious comparisons were drawn be-tween John and Talbot, to the disadvantage of the proud young officer.

It was impossible for any quarrel to arise between the lovers, for John followed his mistress about like some big slave, who only lived to do her bidding and Aurora accepted his devotion with a sultana-like grace, which became her amazingly. Once more she visited the stables and inspected her father's stud, for the first time since she had left Felden for the Parisian finishing school. Once more she rode across country, wearing a hat which provoked considerable criticism—a hat which was no other than the now universal turban, or pork-pie, but which was new to the world in the autumn of fifty-eight. Her earlier girlhood appeared to return to her once more. It seemed almost as if the two years and a half in which she had left and returned to her home, and had met and parted with Talbot Bulstrode, had been blotted from her life, leaving her spirits fresh and bright as they were before that stormy interview in her father's study in the June of fifty-six.

The county families came to the wedding at Beckenham church, and were fain to confess that Miss Floyd looked wondrously handsome in her virginal crown of orange-buds and flowers, and her voluminous Mechlin veil; she had pleaded hard to be married in a bonnet, but had been overruled by a posse of female cousins. Mr Richard Gunter provided the marriage feast, and sent a man down to Felden to superintend the arrangements, who was more dashing and splendid to look upon than any of the Kentish guests. John Mellish alternately laughed and cried throughout that eventful morning. Heaven knows how many times he shook hands with Archibald Floyd, carrying the banker off into solitary corners, and swearing, with the tears running down his broad cheeks, to be a good husband to the old man's daughter, so that it must have been a relief to the white-haired old Scotchman when Aurora descended the staircase, rustling in violet moiré antique, and surrounded by her bridesmaids, to take leave of this dear father before the prancing steeds carried Mr. and Mrs Mellish to that most prosaic of hymeneal stages, the London Bridge station.

Mrs. Mellish! Yes, she was Mrs Mellish now Talbot Bulstrode read of her marriage in that very column of the newspaper in which he had thought, perhaps, to see her death. How flatly the romance ended! With what a dull cadence the storm died out, and what a commonplace, gray, every-day sky succeeded the terrors of the lightning! Less than a year since, the globe had seemed to him to collapse, and creation to come to a stand-still because of his trouble, and he was now in Parliament legislating for the Cornish miners, and getting stout, his ill-natured friends said; and she — she who ought, in accordance with all dramatic propriety, to have died out of hand long before this, she had married a Yorkshire land-owner, and would, no doubt, take her place in the county, and play My Lady Bountiful in the village, and be chief patroness at the race-balls, and live happily ever afterward. He crumpled the *Times* newspaper, and flung it from him in his rage and mortification. "And I once thought that she loved me," he cried.

And she did love you, Talbot Bulstrode — loved you as she can never love this honest, generous, devoted John Mellish, though she may by and by bestow upon him an affection which is a great deal better worth having. She loved you with the girl's romantic fancy and reverent admiration, and tried humbly to fashion her very nature anew, that she might be worthy of your sublime excellence. She loved you as women only love in their first youth, and as they rarely love the men they ultimately marry. The tree is perhaps all the stronger when these first frail branches are lopped away to give place to strong and spreading arms, beneath which a husband and children may shelter.

But Talbot could not see all this. He saw nothing but that brief announcement in the *Times:* "Aurora, only daughter of Archibald Floyd, Banker, of Felden Woods, Kent, to John Mellish, Esq., of Mellish Park, near Doncaster." He was angry with his some-time love, and more angry with himself for feeling that anger; and he plunged furiously into blue-books, to prepare himself for the coming session; and again he took his gun and went out upon the "barren, barren moorland," as he had done in the first violence of his grief, and wandered down to the dreary sea-shore, where he raved about his "Amy, shallow-hearted," and tried the pitch of his voice against the ides of February should come round, and the bill for the Cornish miners be laid before the speaker.

Toward the close of January, the servants at Mellish Park prepared for the advent of Master John and his bride. It was a work of love in that disorderly household, for it pleased them that master would have some one to keep him at home, and that the county would be entertained, and festivals held in the roomy, rambling mansion. Architects, upholsterers, and decorators had been busy through the short winter days preparing a suite of apartments for Mrs. Mellish; and the western, or, as it was called, the Gothic wing of the house, had been restored and remodelled for Aurora, until the oak-roofed chambers blazed with rose-color and gold, like a mediæval chapel. If John could have expended half his fortune in the purchase of a roc's egg to hang in these apartments, he would have gladly done so. He was so proud of his Cleopatra-like bride, his jewel beyond all parallel amid all gems, that he fancied he could not build a shrine

rich enough for his treasure. So the house in which honest country squires and their sensible motherly wives had lived contentedly for nearly three centuries was almost pulled to pieces before John thought it worthy of the banker's daughter. The trainers, and grooms, and stable-boys shrugged their shoulders superciliously, and spat fragments of straw disdainfully upon the paved stable-yard, as they heard the clatter of the tools of the stone-masons and glaziers busy about the *façade* of the restored apartments. The stable would be *naught* now, they supposed, and Master Mellish would be always tied to his wife's apron-string. It was a relief to them to hear that Mrs. Mellish was fond of riding and hunting, and would, no doubt, take to horse-racing in due time, as the legitimate taste of a lady of position and fortune.

The bells of the village church rang loudly and joyously in the clear winter air as the carriage and four, which had met John and his bride at Doncaster, dashed into the gates of Mellish Park, and up the long avenue to the semi-Gothic, semi-barbaric portico of the great door. Hearty Yorkshire voices rang out in loud cheers of welcome as Aurora stepped from the carriage, and passed under the shadow of the porch and into the old oak hall, which had been hung with evergreens and adorned with floral devices, among which figured the legend, "WELLCOME TO MELLISH!" and other such friendly inscriptions, more conspicuous for their kindly meaning than their strict orthography. The servants were enraptured with their master's choice. She was so brightly handsome that the simple-hearted creatures accepted her beauty as we accept the sunlight, and felt a genial warmth in that radiant loveliness which the most classical perfection could never have inspired. Indeed, a Grecian outline might have been thrown away upon the Yorkshire servants, whose uncultivated tastes were a great deal more disposed to recognize splendor of color than purity of form. They could not choose but admire Aurora's eyes, which they unanimously declared to be "regular shiners;" and the flash of her white teeth, glancing between the full crimson lips; and the bright flush which lighted up her pale olive skin; and the purple lustre of her massive coronal of plaited hair. Her beauty was of that luxuriant and splendid order which has always most effect upon the masses, and the fascination of her manner was almost akin to sorcery in its power over simple people. I lose myself when I try to describe the feminine intoxications, the wonderful fascination exercised by this dark-eyed siren. Surely the secret of her power to charm must have been the wonderful vitality of her nature, by virtue of which she carried life and animal spirits about with her as an atmosphere, till dull people grew merry by reason of her contagious presence, or perhaps the true charm of her manner was that childlike and exquisite unconsciousness of self which made her for ever a new creature—for ever impulsive and sympathetic, acutely sensible of all sorrow in others, though of a nature originally joyous in the extreme

Mrs Walter Powell had been transferred from Felden Woods to Mellish Park, and was comfortably installed in her prim apartments when the bride and bridegroom arrived The Yorkshire housekeeper was to abandon the executive power to the ensign's widow, who was to take all trouble of administration off Aurora's hands

"Heaven help your friends if they ever had to eat a dinner of my ordering, John," Mrs Mellish said, making a free confession of her ignorance, "I am glad, too, that we have no occasion to turn the poor soul out upon the world once more Those long columns of advertisements in the *Times* give me a sick pain at my heart when I think of what a governess must have to encounter. I can not loll back in my carriage and be 'grateful for my advantages,' as Mrs Alexander says, when I remember the sufferings of others I am rather inclined to be discontented with my lot, and to think it a poor thing after all, to be rich and happy in a world where so many must suffer, so I am glad we can give Mrs Powell something to do at Mellish Park "

The ensign's widow rejoiced very much in that she was to be retained in such comfortable quarters, but she did not thank Aurora for the benefits received from the open hands of the banker's daughter She did not thank her, because—she hated her. Why did she hate her? She hated her for the very benefits she received, or rather because she, Aurora, had power to bestow such benefits She hated her as such slow sluggish, narrow-minded creatures always hate the frank and generous, hated her as envy will for ever hate prosperity, as Haman hated Mordecai from the height of his throne, and as the man of Haman nature would hate were he supreme in the universe If Mrs Walter Powell had been a duchess, and Aurora a crossing-sweeper, she would still have envied her: she would have envied her glorious eyes and flashing teeth, her imperial carriage and generous soul This pale, whity-brown haired woman felt herself contemptible in the presence of Aurora, and she resented the bounteous vitality of this nature which made her conscious of the sluggishness of her own She detested Mrs Mellish for the possession of attributes which she felt were richer gifts than all the wealth of the house of Floyd, Floyd, and Floyd, melted into one mountain of ore. But it is not for a dependent to hate, except in a decorous and gentle womanly manner—secretly, in the dim recesses of her soul, while she dresses her face with an unvarying smile—a

smile which she puts on every morning with her clean collar, and takes off at night when she goes to bed

Now as, by an all-wise dispensation of Providence, it is not possible for one person so to hate another without that other having a vague consciousness of the deadly sentiment, Aurora felt that Mrs Powell's attachment to her was of no very profound a nature But the reckless girl did not seek to fathom the depth of any inimical feeling which might lurk in her dependent's breast

"She is not very fond of me, poor soul," she said, "and I dare say I torment and annoy her with my careless follies If I were like that dear, considerate little Lucy, now—" And with a shrug of her shoulders, and an unfinished sentence such as this, Mrs Mellish dismissed the insignificant subject from her mind

You can not expect these grand, courageous creatures to be frightened of quiet people And yet, in the great dramas of life, it is the quiet people who do the mischief Iago was not a noisy person, though, thank Heaven! it is no longer the fashion to represent him an oily sneak, whom even the most foolish of Moors could not have trusted

Aurora was at peace The storms that had so nearly shipwrecked her young life had passed away, leaving her upon a fair and fertile shore. Whatever griefs she had inflicted upon her father's devoted heart had not been mortal, and the old banker seemed a very happy man when he came, in the bright April weather, to see the young couple at Mellish Park Among all the hangers-on of that large establishment there was only one person who did not join in the general voice when Mrs Mellish was spoken of, and that one person, was so very insignificant that his fellow-servants scarcely cared to ascertain his opinion He was a man of about forty, who had been born at Mellish Park, and had pottered about the stables from his boyhood doing odd jobs for the grooms, and being reckoned, although a little "fond" upon common matters, a very acute judge of horse-flesh This man was called Stephen, or more commonly, Steeve Hargraves. He was a squat, broad-shouldered fellow, with a big head, a pale, haggard face—a face whose ghastly pallor seemed almost unnatural—reddish-brown eyes, and bushy, sandy eyebrows, which formed a species of penthouse over those sinister-looking eyes He was the sort of man who is generally called repulsive—a man from whom you recoil with a feeling of instinctive dislike, which is, no doubt, both wicked and unjust, for we have no right to take objection to a man because he has an ugly glitter in his eyes, and shaggy tufts of red hair meeting on the bridge of his nose, and big splay feet which seem made to crush and destroy whatever comes in their way, and this was what Aurora Mellish thought when, a few days after her arrival at the Park, she saw Steeve Hargraves for the first time, coming out of the harness-room with a bridle across his room. She was angry with herself for the involuntary shudder with which she drew back at the sight of this man, who stood at a little distance polishing the brass ornaments upon a set of harness, and furtively regarding Mrs. Mellish as she leaned on her husband's arm, talking to the trainer about the foals at grass in the meadows outside the Park.

Aurora asked who the man was.

"Why, his name is Hargraves, ma'am," answered the trainer; "but we call him Steeve. He 's a little bit touched in the upper story—a little bit 'fond,' as we call it here; but he 's useful about the stables when he pleases, for he 's rather a queer temper, and there 's none of us has ever been able to get the upper hand of him, as master knows."

John Mellish laughed.

"No," he said; "Steeve has pretty much his own way in the stables, I fancy. He was a favorite groom of my father's twenty years ago; but he got a fall in the hunting-field, which did him some injury about the head, and he 's never been quite right since. Of course this, with my poor father's regard for him, gives him a claim upon us, and we put up with his queer ways—don't we, Langley?"

"Well, we do, sir," said the trainer; "though, upon my honor, I 'm sometimes half afraid of him, and think he 'll get up in the middle of the night and murder some of us."

"Not till some of you have won a hatful of money, Langley. Steeve's a little too fond of the brass to murder any of you for nothing. You shall see his face light up presently, Aurora," said John, beckoning to the stable-man. "Come here, Steeve. Mrs. Mellish wishes you to drink her health."

He dropped a sovereign into the man's broad, muscular palm—the hand of a gladiator, with horny flesh and sinews of iron. Steeve's red eyes glistened as his fingers closed upon the money.

"Thank you kindly, my lady," he said, touching his cap.

He spoke in a low, subdued voice, which contrasted so strangely with the physical power manifest in his appearance that Aurora drew back with a start.

Unhappily for this poor "fond" creature, whose person was in itself repulsive, there was something in this inward, semi-whispering voice which gave rise to an instinctive dislike in those who heard him speak for the first time.

He touched his greasy woollen cap once more, and went slowly back to his work.

"How white his face is!" said Aurora. "Has he been ill?"

"No. He has had that pale face ever since his fall. I was too young when it happened to remember much about it, but I have heard my father say that when they brought the poor creature home his face, which had been florid before, was as white as a sheet of writing-paper, and his voice, until that period strong and gruff, was reduced to the half-whisper in which he now speaks. The doctors did all they could for him, and carried him through an awful attack of brain fever, but they could never bring back his voice, nor the color to his cheeks."

"Poor fellow!" said Mrs. Mellish, gently; "he is very much to be pitied."

She was reproaching herself, as she said this, for that feeling of repugnance which she could not overcome. It was a repugnance closely allied to terror; she felt as if she could scarcely be happy at Mellish Park while that man was on the premises. She was half inclined to beg her indulgent husband to pension him off, and send him to the other end of the county; but the next moment she was ashamed of her childish folly, and a few hours afterward had forgotten Steeve Hargraves, the "softy," as he was politely called in the stables.

Reader, when any creature inspires you with this instinctive, unreasoning abhorrence, avoid that creature. He is dangerous. Take warning, as you take warning by the clouds in the sky and the ominous stillness of the atmosphere when there is a storm coming. Nature can not lie; and it is nature which has planted that shuddering terror in your breast; an instinct of self-preservation rather than of cowardly fear, which, at the first sight of some fellow-creature, tells you more plainly than words can speak, "That man is my enemy!"

Had Aurora suffered herself to be guided by this instinct; had she given way to the impulse which she despised as childish, and caused Stephen Hargraves to be dismissed from Mellish Park, what bitter misery, what cruel anguish, might have been spared to herself and others.

The mastiff Bow-wow had accompanied his mistress to her new home; but Bow-wow's best days were done. A month before Aurora's marriage he had been run over by a pony-carriage in one of the roads about Felden, and had been conveyed, bleeding and disabled, to the veterinary surgeon's, to have one of his hind legs put into splints, and to be carried through his sufferings by the highest available skill in the science of dog-doctoring. Aurora drove every day to Croydon to see her sick favorite; and at the worst Bow-wow was always well enough to recognize his beloved mistress, and roll his listless, feverish tongue over her white hands, in token of that unchanging brute affection which can only perish with life. So the mastiff was quite lame as well as half blind when he arrived at Mellish Park with the rest of Aurora's goods and chattels. He was a privileged creature in the roomy mansion, a tiger-skin was spread for him upon the hearth in the drawing-room, and he spent his declining days in luxurious repose, basking in the firelight or sunning himself in the windows, as it pleased his royal fancy; but, feeble as he was, always able to limp after Mrs. Mellish when she walked on the lawn or in the woody shrubberies which skirted the gardens.

One day, when she had returned from her morning's ride with John and her father, who accompanied them sometimes upon a quiet gray cob, and seemed a younger man for the exercise, she lingered on the lawn in her riding-habit after the horses had been taken back to the stables, and Mr. Mellish and his father-in-law had re-entered the house. The mastiff saw her from the drawing-room window, and crawled out to welcome her. Tempted by the exquisite softness of the atmosphere, she strolled, with her riding-habit gathered under her arm and her whip in her hand, looking for primroses under the clumps of trees upon the lawn. She gathered a cluster of wild flowers, and was returning to the house when she remembered some directions respecting a favorite pony that was ill, which she had omitted to give to her groom.

She crossed the stable-yard, followed by Bow-wow, found the groom, gave him her orders, and went back to the gardens. While talking to the man she had recognized the white face of Steeve Hargraves at one of the windows of the harness-room. He came out while she was giving her directions, and carried a set of harness across to a coach-house on the opposite side of the quadrangle. Aurora was on the threshold of the gates opening from the stables into the gardens when she was arrested by a howl of pain from the mastiff Bow-wow. Rapid as lightning in every movement, she turned round in time to see the cause of this cry. Steeve Hargraves had sent the animal reeling away from him with a kick from his iron-bound clog. Cruelty to animals was one of the failings of the "softy." He was not cruel to the Mellish horses, for he had sense enough to know that his daily bread depended upon his attention to them, but Heaven help any outsider that came in his way. Aurora sprang upon him like a beautiful tigress, and, catching the collar of his fustian jacket in her slight hands, rooted him to the spot upon which he stood. The grasp of those slender hands, convulsed by passion, was not to be easily shaken off, and Steeve Hargraves, taken completely off his guard, stared aghast at his assailant. Taller than the stable-man by a foot and a half, she towered above him, her cheeks white with rage, her eyes flashing fury, her hat fallen off, and her black hair tumbling about her shoulders, sublime in her passion.

The man crouched beneath the grasp of the imperious creature.

"Let me go," he gasped, in his inward whisper, which had a hissing sound in his agitation, "let me go, or you'll be sorry; let me go!"

"How dared you!" cried Aurora—"how dared you hurt him? My poor dog! My poor, lame, feeble dog! How dared you do it? You cowardly dastard! you—"

She disengaged her right hand from his collar, and rained a shower of blows upon his clumsy shoulders with her slender whip, a mere toy with emeralds set in its golden head, but stinging like a rod of flexible steel in that little hand.

"How dared you!" she repeated again and again, her cheeks changing from white to scarlet in the effort to hold the man with one hand. Her tangled hair had fallen to her waist by this time, and the whip was broken in half a dozen places.

John Mellish, entering the stable-yard by chance at this very moment, turned white with horror at beholding the beautiful fury.

"Aurora! Aurora!" he cried, snatching the man's collar from her grasp, and hurling him half a dozen paces off. "Aurora, what is it?"

She told him, in broken gasps, the cause of her indignation. He took the splintered whip from her hand, picked up her hat which she had trodden upon in her rage, and led her across the yard toward the back entrance to the house. It was such bitter shame to him to think that this peerless, this adored creature should do anything to bring disgrace or even ridicule upon herself. He would have stripped off his coat and fought with half a dozen coal-heavers, and thought nothing of it, but that she—

"Go in, go in, my darling girl," he said, with sorrowful tenderness, "the servants are peeping and prying about, I dare say. You should not have done this; you should have told me."

"I should have told you!" she cried, impatiently. "How could I stop to tell you when I saw him strike my dog—my poor, lame dog?"

"Go in, darling, go in! There, there, calm yourself, and go in."

He spoke as if he had been trying to soothe an agitated child, for he saw by the convulsive heaving of her breast that the violent emotion would terminate in hysteria, as all womanly fury must, sooner or later. He half led, half carried her up a back staircase to her own room, and left her lying on a sofa in her riding-habit. He thrust the broken whip into his pocket, and then, setting his strong white teeth and clenching his fist, went to look for Stephen Hargraves. As he crossed the hall in his way out, he selected a stout leather-thonged hunting-whip from a stand of formidable implements. Steeve, the softy, was sitting on a horse-block when John re-entered the stable-yard. He was rubbing his shoulders with a very doleful face, while a couple of grinning stable-boys, who had perhaps witnessed his chastisement, watched him from a respectful distance. They had no inclination to go too near him just then, for the softy had a play-ful habit of brandishing a big clasp-knife when he felt himself aggrieved, and the bravest lad in the stables had no wish to die from a stab in the abdomen, with the pleasant conviction that his murderer's heaviest punishment might be a fortnight's imprisonment or an easy fine.

"Now, Mr. Hargraves," said John Mellish, lifting the softy off the horse-block and plant-ing him at a convenient distance for giving full play to the hunting-whip, "it was n't Mrs. Mellish's business to horsewhip you, but it was her duty to let me do it for her; so take that, you coward."

The leathern thong whistled in the air, and curled about Steeve's shoulders; but John felt there was something despicable in the unequal contest. He threw his whip away, and, still holding him by the collar, conducted the softy to the gates of the stable-yard.

"You see that avenue," he said, pointing down a fair glade that stretched before them, "it leads pretty straight out of the park, and I strongly recommend you, Mr. Stephen Hargraves, to get to the end of it as quick as ever you can, and never to show your ugly white face upon an inch of ground belong-ing to me again. D'ye hear?"

"E-es, sir."

"Stay! I suppose there's wages or some-thing due to you." He took a handful of money from his waistcoat-pocket and threw it on the ground, sovereigns and half-crowns rolling hither and thither on the gravel path; then, turning on his heel, he left the softy to pick up the scattered treasure. Steeve Har-graves dropped on his knees, and groped about till he had found the last coin; then, as he slowly counted the money from one hand into the other, his white face relapsed into a grin; John Mellish had given him gold and silver amounting to upward of two years of his ordinary wages.

He walked a few paces down the avenue, and then, looking back, shook his fist at the house he was leaving behind him.

"You 're a fine-spirited madam, Mrs. John Mellish, sure enough," he muttered; "but never you give me a chance of doing you any mischief, or by the Lord, *fond* as I am, I 'll do it! They think the softy 's up to naught, perhaps. Wait a bit."

He took his money from his pocket again, and counted it once more as he walked slowly toward the gates of the park.

It will be seen, therefore, that Aurora had two enemies, one without and one within her pleasant home; one for ever brooding discon-tent and hatred within the holy circle of the domestic hearth, the other plotting ruin and vengeance without the walls of the citadel.

CHAPTER XIII.

THE SPRING MEETING.

The early spring brought Lucy Floyd on a visit to her cousin, a wondering witness of the happiness that reigned at Mellish Park.

Poor Lucy had expected to find Aurora held as something better than the dogs, and a little higher than the horses in that York-shire household, and was considerably sur-prised to find her dark-eyed cousin a despotic and capricious sovereign, reigning with un-disputed sway over every creature, biped or quadruped, upon the estate. She was sur-prised to see the bright glow in her cheeks, the merry sparkle in her eyes — surprised to hear the light tread of her footstep, the gush-ing music of her laugh — surprised, in fact, to discover that, instead of weeping over the dry bones of her dead love for Talbot Bul-strode, Aurora had learned to love her hus-band.

Have I any need to be ashamed of my heroine in that she had forgotten her straight-nosed, gray-eyed Cornish lover, who had set his pride and his pedigree between himself and his affection, and had loved her at best with a reservation, although Heaven only knows how dearly he had loved her? Have I any cause to blush for this poor, impetuous girl if, turning in the sickness of her sorrow-ful heart with a sense of relief and gratitude to the honest shelter of John's love, she had quickly learned to feel for him an affection which repaid him a thousand-fold for his long-suffering devotion? Surely it would have been impossible for any true-hearted woman to withhold some such repayment for such love as that which in every word, and look, and thought, and deed John Mellish be-stowed upon his wife. How could she be for ever his creditor for such a boundless debt? Are hearts like his common among our clay? Is it a small thing to be beloved with this loyal and pure affection? Is it laid so often at the feet of any mortal woman that she should spurn and trample upon the holy offering?

He had loved, and, more, he had trusted her — he had trusted her, when the man who passionately loved her had left her in an agony of doubt and despair. The cause of this lay in the difference between the two men. John Mellish had as high and stern a sense of honor as Talbot Bulstrode; but while the Cornishman's strength of brain lay in the reflective faculties, the Yorkshireman's acute intellect was strongest in its power of percep-tion. Talbot drove himself half mad with imagining what might be: John saw what was, and he saw, or fancied he saw, that the woman he loved was worthy of all love, and he gave his peace and honor freely into her keeping

He had his reward   He had his reward in her frank, womanly affection, and in the delight of seeing that she was happy; no cloud upon her face, no shadow on her life, but ever-beaming joy in her eyes, ever-changing smiles upon her lips   She was happy in the calm security of her home happy in that pleasant strong-hold in which she was so fenced about and guarded by love and devotion   I do not know that she ever felt any romantic or enthusiastic love for this big Yorkshireman, but I do know that from the first hour in which she laid her head upon his broad breast she was true to him — true as a wife should be, true in every thought, true in the merest shadow of a thought   A wide gulf yawned around the altar of her home, separating her from every other man in the universe, and leaving her alone with that one man whom she had accepted as her husband She had accepted him in the truest and purest sense of the word.   She had accepted him from the hand of God as the protector and shelterer of her life, and, morning and night, upon her knees she thanked the gracious Creator who had made this man for her helpmeet

But, after duly setting down all this, I have to confess that poor John Mellish was cruelly hen-pecked   Such big, blustering fellows are created to be the much-enduring subjects of petticoat government, and they carry the rosy garlands until then dying hour with a sublime consciousness that those floral chains are not very easy to be broken   Your little man is self-assertive, and for ever on his guard against womanly domination   All tyrannical husbands on record have been little men, from Mr Daniel Quilp upward, but who could ever convince a fellow of six feet two in his stockings that he was afraid of his wife?   He submits to the petty tyrant with a quiet smile of resignation   What does it matter?   She is so little, so fragile   he could break that tiny wrist with one twist of his big thumb and finger; and, in the meantime, till affairs get desperate, and such measures become necessary, it is as well to let her have her own way

John Mellish did not even debate the point He loved her, and he laid himself down to be trampled upon by her gracious feet   Whatever she did or said was charming, bewitching, and wonderful to him   If she ridiculed or laughed at him, her laughter was the sweetest harmony in creation, and it pleased him to think that his absurdities could give birth to such music.   If she lectured him, she arose to the sublimity of a priestess, and he listened to her and worshipped her as the most noble of living creatures   And, with all this, his innate manliness of character preserved him from any taint of that quality our argot has christened spooneyism   It was only those who knew him well and watched him closely who could fathom the full depths of his tender weakness   The noblest sentiments approach most nearly to the universal, and this love of John's was in a manner universal   It was the love of husband, father, mother, brother, melted into one comprehensive affection   He had a mother's weak pride in Aurora, a mother's foolish vanity in the wonderful creature, the wild ass he had won from her nest to be his wife

If Mrs Mellish was complimented while John stood by, he simpered like a school-girl who blushes at a handsome man's first flatteries   I'm afraid he bored his male acquaintance about "my wife;" her marvellous leap over the bullfinch   the plan she drew for the new stables, "which the architect said was a better plan than he could have drawn himself, sir, by gad" (a clever man, that Doncaster architect), the surprising manner she had discovered the fault of the chestnut colt's off fore leg; the pencil sketch she had made of her dog Bow-wow ("Sir Edwin Landseer might have been proud of such spirit and dash, sir") — all these things did the country gentlemen hear, until, perhaps, they grew a shade weary of John's talk of "my wife" But they were never weary of Aurora herself   She took her place at once among them, and they bowed down to her and worshipped her, envying John Mellish the ownership of such a high-bred filly, as I fear they were but likely, unconsciously, to designate my black-eyed heroine.

The domain over which Aurora found herself empress was no inconsiderable one   John Mellish had inherited an estate which brought him an income of something between £16,000 and £17,000 a year.   Far-away farms, upon wide Yorkshire wolds and fenny Lincolnshire flats, owned him master, and the intricate secrets of his possessions were scarcely known to himself — known perhaps, to none but his land-steward and solicitor, a grave gentleman who lived in Doncaster, and drove about once a fortnight down to Mellish Park, much to the horror of his light-hearted master   to whom "business' was a terrible bugbear   Not that I would have the reader for a moment imagine John Mellish an empty-headed blockhead with no comprehension save for his own daily pleasures   He was not a reading man, nor a business man, nor a politician, nor a student of the natural sciences.

There was an observatory in the park, but John had fitted it up as a smoking-room, the revolving openings in the roof being very convenient for letting out the effluvia of his guests' cheroots and Havanas, Mr Mellish caring for the stars very much after the fashion of that Assyrian monarch who was content to see them shine, and thank their Maker for their beauty. He was not a spiritualist, and, unless one of the tables at Mellish could have given him "a tip" for the "Sellinger" or Great Ebor, he would have cared very little if every inch of walnut and rose-wood in his house had grown oracular. But, for all this, he was no fool; he had that brightly clear intellect which very often accompanies perfect honesty of purpose, and which is the very intellect of all others most successful in the discomfiture of all knavery. He was not a creature to despise, for his very weaknesses were manly. Perhaps Aurora felt this, and that it was something to rule over such a man. Sometimes, in an outburst of loving gratitude, she would nestle her handsome head upon his breast — tall as she was, she was only tall enough to take shelter under his wing — and tell him that he was the dearest and the best of men, and that, although she might love him to her dying day, she could never, never, never love him half as much as he deserved. After which, half ashamed of herself for the sentimental declaration, she would alternately ridicule, lecture, and tyrannize over him for the rest of the day.

Lucy beheld this state of things with silent bewilderment. Could the woman who had once been loved by Talbot Bulstrode sink to this — the happy wife of a fair-haired Yorkshireman, with her fondest wishes concentred in her namesake, the bay filly, which was to run in a weight-for-age race at the York Spring, and was entered for the ensuing Derby; interested in a tan-gallop, a new stable; talking of mysterious but evidently all-important creatures, called by such names as Scott, and Fobert, and Challoner; and, to all appearance, utterly forgetful of the fact that there existed upon the earth a divinity with fathomless gray eyes, known as the heir of Bulstrode? Poor Lucy was like to have been driven wellnigh demented by the talk about this bay filly Aurora as the spring meeting drew near. She was taken to see it every morning by Aurora and John, who, in their anxiety for the improvement of their favorite, looked at the animal upon each visit as if they expected some wonderful physical transformation to have occurred in the stillness of the night. The loose box in which the filly was lodged was watched night and day by an amateur detective force of stable-boys and hangers-on; and John Mellish once went so far as to dip a tumbler into the pail of water provided for the bay filly Aurora, to ascertain, of his own experience, that the crystal fluid was innocuous; for he grew nervous as the eventful day drew nigh, and was afraid of lurking danger to the filly from dark-minded touts who might have heard of her in London. I fear the touts troubled their heads very little about this graceful two-year old,

though she had the blood of Old Melbourne and West Australian in her veins, to say nothing of other aristocracy upon the maternal side.

The suspicious gentlemen hanging about York and Doncaster in those early April days were a great deal too much occupied with Lord Glasgow's lot, and John Scott's lot, and Lord Zetland's, and Mr. Merry's lot, and other lots of equal distinction, to have much time to prowl about Mellish Park, or peer into that meadow which the young man had caused to be surrounded by an eight-foot fence for the privacy of the Derby winner *in futuro*.

Lucy declared the filly to be the loveliest of creatures, and safe to win any number of cups and plates that might be offered for equine competition; but she was always glad, when the daily visit was over, to find herself safely out of reach of those high-bred hind legs, which seemed to possess a faculty for being in all four corners of the loose box at one and the same moment.

The first day of the meeting came, and found half the Mellish household established at York; John and his family at a hotel near the betting-rooms; and the trainer, his satellites, and the filly, at a little inn close to the Knavesmire.

Archibald Floyd did his best to be interested in the event which was so interesting to his children; but he freely confessed to his grand-niece Lucy that he heartily wished the meeting over, and the merits of the bay filly decided. She had stood her trial nobly, John said; not winning with a rush, it is true; in point of fact, being in a manner beaten; but evincing a power to stay, which promised better for the future than any two-year-old velocity. When the saddling-bell rang, Aurora, her father, and Lucy were stationed in the balcony, a crowd of friends about them; Mrs. Mellish, with a pencil in her hand, putting down all manner of impossible bets in her excitement, and making such a book as might have been preserved as a curiosity in sporting annals. John was pushing in and out of the ring below, tumbling over small bookmen in his agitation, dashing from the ring to the weighing-house, and hanging about the small, pale-faced boy who was to ride the filly as anxiously as if the jockey had been a prime minister, and John a family man with half a dozen sons in need of government appointments. I tremble to think how many bonuses, in the way of five-pound notes, John promised the pale-faced lad on condition that the stakes (some small matter amounting to about £60) were pulled off — pulled off where, I wonder — by the bay filly Aurora. If the youth had not been of that preternatural order of being who seem born of an emotionless character to wear silk for the good of their fellow-men, his brain must certainly have been dazed by the variety of conflicting directions which John Mellish gave him within the critical last quarter of an hour; but, having received his orders early that morning from the trainer, accompanied with a warning not to suffer himself to be *tewed* (Yorkshire *patois* for worried) by anything Mr. Mellish might say, the sallow-complexioned lad walked about in the calm serenity of innocence — there are honest jockeys in the world, thank Heaven! and took his seat in the saddle with as even a pulse as if he had been about to ride in an omnibus.

There were some people upon the stand that morning who thought the face of Aurora Mellish as pleasant a sight as the smooth green sward of the Knavesmire, or the best horse-flesh in the county of York. All forgetful of herself in her excitement, with her natural vivacity multiplied by the animation of the scene before her, she was more than usually lovely; and Archibald Floyd looked at her with a fond emotion, so intermingled with gratitude to Heaven for the happiness of his daughter's destiny as to be almost akin to pain. She was happy — she was thoroughly happy at last — the child of his dead Eliza, this sacred charge left to him by the woman he had loved; she was happy, and she was safe; he could go to his grave resignedly tomorrow, if it pleased God, knowing this. Strange thoughts, perhaps, for a crowded race-course; but our most solemn fancies do not come always in solemn places. Nay, it is often in the midst of crowds and confusion that our souls wing their loftiest flights, and the saddest memories return to us. You see a man sitting at some theatrical entertainment with a grave, abstracted face, over which no change of those around him has any influence. He may be thinking of his dead wife, dead ten years ago; he may be acting over well-remembered scenes of joy and sorrow; he may be recalling cruel words, never to be atoned for upon earth — angry looks, gone to be registered against him in the skies, while his children are laughing at the clown on the stage below him. He may be moodily meditating inevitable bankruptcy or coming ruin, holding imaginary meetings with his creditors, and contemplating prussic acid upon the refusal of his certificate, while his eldest daughter is crying with Pauline Deschapelles. So Archibald Floyd, while the numbers were going up, and the jockeys being weighed, and the bookmen clamoring below him, leaned over the broad ledge of the stone balcony, and, looking far away across the grassy amphitheatre, thought of his dead wife who had bequeathed to him this precious daughter.

The bay filly Aurora was beaten ignominiously. Mrs. Mellish turned white with despair, as she saw the amber jacket, black belt, and blue cap crawling in at the heels of the ruck, the jockey looking pale defiance at the by-standers; as who should say that the filly had never been meant to win, and that the defeat of to-day was but an artfully-concocted ruse whereby fortunes were to be made in the future? John Mellish, something used to such disappointments, crept away to hide his discomfiture outside the ring; but Aurora dropped her card and pencil, and, stamping her foot upon the stone flooring of the balcony, told Lucy and the banker that it was a shame, and that the boy must have sold the race, as it was impossible that the filly could have been fairly beaten. As she turned to say this, her cheeks flushed with passion, and her eyes flashing bright indignation on any one who might stand in the way to receive the angry electric light, she became aware of a pale face and a pair of gray eyes earnestly regarding her from the threshold of an open window two or three paces off, and in another moment both she and her father had recognized Talbot Bulstrode.

The young man saw that he was recognized, and approached them, hat in hand — very, very pale, as Lucy always remembered — and, with a voice that trembled as he spoke, wished the banker and the two ladies "Good-day."

And it was thus that they met, these two who had "parted in silence and tears," more than "half broken-hearted," to sever, as they thought, for eternity; it was thus, upon this commonplace, prosaic, half-guinea grand stand — that Destiny brought them once more face to face.

A year ago, and how often in the spring twilight Aurora Floyd had pictured her possible meeting with Talbot Bulstrode! He would come upon her suddenly, perhaps, in the still moonlight, and she would swoon away and die at his feet of the unendurable emotion; or they would meet in some crowded assembly, she dancing, laughing with hollow, simulated mirth, and the shock of one glance of those eyes would slay her in her painted glory of jewels and grandeur. How often, ah! how often she had acted the scene and felt the anguish! only a year ago, less than a year ago, ay! even so lately as on that balmy September day when she had laid on the rustic couch at the Chateau d'Arques, looking down at the fair Normandy landscape, with faithful John at watch by her side, the tame goats browsing upon the grassy platform behind her, and preternaturally ancient French children teasing the mild, long-suffering animals; and to-day she met him with her thoughts so full of the horse that had just been beaten that she scarcely knew what she said to her sometime lover. Aurora Floyd was dead and buried, and Aurora Mellish, looking critically at Talbot Bulstrode, wondered how any one could have ever gone near to the gates of death for the love of him.

It was Talbot who grew pale at this un-

looked-for encounter; it was Talbot whose
voice was shaken in the utterance of those
few every-day syllables which common courtesy demanded of him. The captain had not
so easily learned to forget. He was older
than Aurora, and he had reached the age of
two-and-thirty without having ever loved
woman, only to be more desperately attacked
by the fatal disease when his time came. He
suffered acutely at that sudden meeting.—
Wounded in his pride by her serene indifference, dazzled afresh by her beauty, mad with
jealous fury at the thought that he had lost
her, Captain Bulstrode's feelings were of no
very enviable nature; and, if Aurora had
ever wished to avenge that cruel scene at
Felden Woods, her hour of vengeance had
most certainly come. But she was too generous a creature to have harbored such a
thought. She had submitted in all humility
to Talbot's decree; she had accepted his decision, and had believed in its justice; and,
seeing his agitation to-day, she was sorry for
him. She pitied him with a tender, matronly
compassion, such as she, in the safe harbor of
a happy home, might be privileged to feel for
this poor wanderer still at sea on life's troubled ocean. Love, and the memory of love,
must indeed have died before we can feel like
this. The terrible passion must have died
that slow and certain death from the grave
of which no haunting ghost ever returns to
torment the survivors. It was, and it is not.
Aurora might have been shipwrecked and
cast on a desert island with Talbot Bulstrode,
and might have lived ten years in his company without ever feeling for ten seconds as
she had felt for him once. With these impetuous and impressionable people, who live
quickly, a year is sometimes as twenty years;
so Aurora looked back at Talbot Bulstrode
across a gulf which stretched for weary miles
between them, and wondered if they had
really ever stood side by side, allied by hope
and love, in the days that were gone.

While Aurora was thinking of these things,
as well as a little of the bay filly, and while
Talbot, half choked by a thousand confused
emotions, tried to appear preternaturally at
his ease, John Mellish, having refreshed his
spirits with bottled beer, came suddenly upon
the party, and slapped the captain on the
back.

He was not jealous, this happy John. Secure in his wife's love and truth, he was ready
to face a regiment of her old admirers; indeed, he rather delighted in the idea of
avenging Aurora upon this cowardly lover.
Talbot glanced involuntarily at the members
of the York constabulary on the course below, wondering how they would act if he
were to fling John Mellish over the stone
balcony, and do a murder then and there. He
was thinking this while John was nearly
wringing off his hand in cordial salutation,
and asking what the deuce had brought him
to the York Spring.

Talbot explained rather lamely that, being
knocked up by his Parliamentary work, he
had come down to spend a few days with an
old brother-officer, Captain Hunter, who had
a place between York and Leeds.

Mr. Mellish declared that nothing could be
more lucky than this. He knew Hunter
well; the two men must join them at dinner
that day! and Talbot must give them a week
at the Park after he left the captain's place.

Talbot murmured some vague protestation
of the impossibility of this, to which John
paid no attention whatever, hustling his some-
time rival away from the ladies in his eagerness to get back to the ring, where he had to
complete his book for the next race.

So Captain Bulstrode was gone once more,
and throughout the brief interview no one
had cared to notice Lucy Floyd, who had
been pale and red by turns half a dozen times
within the last ten minutes.

John and Talbot returned after the start,
with Captain Hunter, who was brought on to
the stand to be presented to Aurora, and who
immediately entered into a very animated
discussion upon the day's racing. How Captain Bulstrode abhorred this idle babble of
horse-flesh, this perpetual jargon, alike in
every mouth, from Aurora's rosy Cupid's bow
to the tobacco-tainted lips of the bookmen in
the ring! Thank Heaven, this was not his
wife, who knew all the slang of the course,
and, with lorgnette in hand, was craning her
swan-like throat to catch sight of a wind in the
Knavesmire and the horse that had a lead of
half a mile.

Why had he ever consented to come into
this accursed horse-racing county? Why
had he deserted the Cornish miners even for
a week? Better to be wearing out his brains
over Dryasdust pamphlets and Parliamentary
minutes than to be here, desolate among this
shallow-minded, clamorous multitude, who
have nothing to do but to throw up caps and
cry huzza for any winner of any race. Talbot, as a by-stander, could not but remark
this, and draw from this something of a philo-
sophical lesson on life. He saw that there
was always the same clamor and the same rejoicing in the crowd, whether the winning
jockey wore blue and black belt, yellow and
black cap, white with scarlet spots, or any
other variety of color, even to dismal sable;
and he could but wonder how this was. Did
the unlucky speculators run away and hide
themselves while the uplifted voices were rejoicing? When the welkin was rent with
the name of Kettledrum, where were the
men who had backed Dundee unflinchingly
up to the dropping of the flag and the ringing of the bell? When Thormanby came in
with a rush, where were the wretched creatures whose fortunes hung on Umpire or

Wizard? They were voiceless, these poor unlucky ones, crawling away with sick white faces, to gather in groups and explain to each other, with stable jargon intermingled with oaths, how it ought not to have been, and never could have been, but for some unlooked-for and preposterous combination of events never before witnessed upon any mortal course. How little is ever seen of the losers in any of the great races run upon this earth? For years and years the name of Louis Napoleon is an empty sound, signifying nothing; when, lo! a few master-strokes of policy and *finesse*, a little juggling with those pieces of pasteboard out of which are built the shaky card-palaces men call empires, and creation rings with the same name; the outsider emerges from the ruck, and the purple jacket, spotted with golden bees, is foremost in the mighty race.

Talbot Bulstrode leaned with folded arms upon the stone balustrade, looking down at the busy life below him, and thinking of these things. Pardon him for his indulgence in dreary platitudes and wornout sentimentalities. He was a desolate, purposeless man; entered for no race himself; scratched for the matrimonial stakes; embittered by disappointment; soured by doubt and suspicion. He had spent the dull winter months upon the Continent, having no mind to go down to Bulstrode to encounter his mother's sympathy and his cousin Constance Trevyllian's chatter. He was unjust enough to nourish a secret dislike to that young lady for the good service she had done him by revealing Aurora's flight.

Are we ever really grateful to the people who tell us of the iniquity of those we love? Are we ever really just to the kindly creatures who give us friendly warning of our danger? No, never. We hate them; always involuntarily reverting to them as the first cause of our anguish; always repeating to ourselves that, had they been silent, that anguish need never have been; always ready to burst forth in one wild rage with the mad cry that "it is better to be much abused than but to know 't a little." When the friendly Ancient drops his poisoned hints into poor Othello's ear, it is not Mrs. Desdemona, but Iago himself, whom the noble Moor first has a mind to strangle. If poor, innocent Constance Trevyllian had been born the veriest cur in the county of Cornwall, she would have had a better chance of winning Talbot's regard than she had now.

Why had he come into Yorkshire? I left that question unanswered just now, for I am ashamed to tell the reasons which actuated this unhappy man. He came, in a paroxysm of curiosity, to learn what kind of life Aurora led with her husband, John Mellish. He had suffered horrible distractions of mind upon this subject, one moment imagining her the most despicable of coquettes, ready to marry any man who had a fair estate and a good position to offer her, and by and by depicting her as some white-robed Iphigenia, led a passive victim to the sacrificial shrine. So, when happening to meet this good-natured brother-officer at the United Service Club, he had consented to run down to Captain Hunter's country place for a brief respite from Parliamentary minutes and red tape, the artful hypocrite had never owned to himself that he was burning to hear tidings of his false and fickle love, and that it was some lingering fumes of the old intoxication that carried him down to Yorkshire. But now — now that he met her — met her, the heartless, abominable creature, radiant and happy—mere simulated happiness and feverish mock radiance, no doubt, but too well put on to be quite pleasing to him — now he knew her. He knew her at last, the wicked enchantress, the soulless siren. He knew that she had never loved him; that she was, of course, powerless to love; good for nothing but to wreathe her white arms and flash the dark splendor of her eyes for weak man's destruction; fit for nothing but to float in her beauty above the waves that concealed the bleached bones of her victims. Poor John Mellish! Talbot reproached himself for his hardness of heart in nourishing one spiteful feeling toward a man who was so deeply to be pitied.

When the race was done Captain Bulstrode turned and beheld the black-eyed sorceress in the midst of a group gathered about a grave patriarch, with gray hair, and the look of one accustomed to command.

This grave patriarch was John Pastern.

I write his name with respect, even as it was reverentially whispered there, till, travelling from lip to lip, every one present knew that a great man was among them. A very quiet, unassuming veteran, sitting with his womankind about him — his wife and daughter, as I think — self-possessed and grave, while men were busy with his name in the crowd below, and while tens of thousands were staked in trusting dependence on his acumen. What golden syllables might have fallen from those oracular lips had the veteran been so pleased! What hundreds would have been freely bidden for a word, a look, a nod, a wink, a mere significant pursing-up of the lips from that great man! What is the fable of the young lady who discoursed pearls and diamonds to a truth such as this! Pearls and diamonds must be of a large size which would be worth the secrets of those Richmond stables, the secrets which Mr. Pastern might tell if he chose. Perhaps it is the knowledge of this which gives him a calm, almost clerical gravity of manner. People come to him, and fawn upon him, and tell him that such and such a horse from his stable has won, or looks safe to win; and he nods pleasantly, thanking them for the kind information, while perhaps his thoughts are far away on Epsom Downs or Newmarket Flats, winning future Derbys and two thousands with colts that are as yet un-foaled.

John Mellish is on intimate terms with the great man, to whom he presents Aurora, and of whom he asks advice upon a matter that has been troubling him for some time. His trainer's health is failing him, and he wants assistance in the stables — a younger man, honest and clever. Does Mr. Pastern know such a one ?

The veteran tells him, after due consideration, that he does know of a young man — honest, he believes, as times go — who was once employed in the Richmond stables, and who had written to him only a few days before, asking for his influence in getting him a situation. "But the lad's name has slipped my memory," added Mr. Pastern; "he was but a lad when he was with me; but, bless my soul, that 's ten years ago! I 'll look up his letter when I go home, and write to you about him. I know he 's clever, and I believe he 's honest; and I shall be only too happy," concluded the old gentleman, gallantly, "to do anything to oblige Mrs. Mellish."

CHAPTER XIV.

"LOVE TOOK UP THE GLASS OF TIME AND TURNED IT IN HIS GLOWING HANDS."

Talbot Bulstrode yielded at last to John's repeated invitations, and consented to pass a couple of days at Mellish Park.

He despised and hated himself for the absurd concession. In what a pitiful farce had the tragedy ended! A visitor in the house of his rival—a calm spectator of Aurora's every-day, commonplace happiness. For the space of two days he had consented to occupy this most preposterous position. Two days only; then back to the Cornish miners, and the desolate bachelor's lodgings in Queen's Square, Westminster; back to his tent in life's great Sahara. He could not, for the very soul of him, resist the temptation of beholding the inner life of that Yorkshire mansion. He wanted to know for certain — what was it to him, I wonder — whether she was really happy, and had utterly forgotten him. They all returned to the Park together — Aurora, John, Archibald Floyd, Lucy, Talbot Bulstrode, and Captain Hunter. The last-named officer was a jovial gentleman, with a hook nose and auburn whiskers; a gentleman whose intellectual attainments were of no very oppressive order, but a hearty, pleasant guest in an honest country mansion, where there is cheer and welcome for all.

Talbot could but inwardly confess that Au-rora became her new position. How every-body loved her! What an atmosphere of happiness she created about her wherever she went! How joyously the dogs barked and leaped at sight of her, straining their chains in the desperate effort to approach her! How fearlessly the thorough-bred mares and foals ran to the paddock-gates to bid her welcome, bending down their velvet nostrils to nestle upon her shoulder, or respond to the touch of her caressing hand! Seeing all this, how could Talbot refrain from remembering that the same sunlight might have shone upon that dreary castle far away by the surging Western Sea? She might have been his, this beautiful creature; but at what price? At the price of honor; at the price of every principle of his mind, which had set up for himself a holy and perfect standard — a pure and spotless ideal for the wife of his choice. Forbid it, manhood! He might have weakly yielded; he might have been happy, with the blind happiness of a lotus-eater, but not the reasonable bliss of a Christian. Thank Heaven for the strength which had been given him to escape from the silken net! Thank Heaven for the power which had been granted to him to fight the battle!

Standing by Aurora's side in one of the wide windows at Mellish Park, looking far out over the belted lawn to the glades in which the deer lay basking drowsily in the April sunlight, he could not repress the thought uppermost in his mind.

"I am — very glad — to see you so happy, Mrs. Mellish."

She looked at him with frank, truthful eyes, in whose brightness there was not one latent shadow.

"Yes," she said, "I am very, very happy. My husband is very good to me. He loves — and trusts me."

She could not resist that one little stab — the only vengeance she ever took upon him, but a stroke that pierced him to the heart.

"Aurora! Aurora! Aurora!" he cried.

That half-stifled cry revealed the secret of wounds that were not yet healed. Mrs. Mellish turned pale at the traitorous sound. This man must be cured. The happy wife, secure in her own strong-hold of love and confidence, could not bear to see this poor fellow still adrift.

She by no means despaired of his cure, for experience had taught her that although love's passionate fever takes several forms there are very few of them incurable. Had she not passed safely through the ordeal herself, without one scar to bear witness of the old wounds ?

She left Captain Bulstrode staring moodily out of the window, and went away to plan the saving of this poor shipwrecked soul.

She ran, in the first place, to tell Mr. John Mellish of her discovery, as it was her custom to carry to him every scrap of intelligence, great and small.

"My dearest old Jack," she said — it was another of her customs to address him by every species of exaggeratedly endearing appellation; it may be that she did this for the quieting of her own conscience, being well aware that she tyrannized over him — "my darling boy, I have made a discovery."

"About the filly?"

"About Talbot Bulstrode."

John's blue eyes twinkled maliciously. He was half prepared for what was coming.

"What is it, Lolly?"

Lolly was a corruption of Aurora, devised by John Mellish.

"Why, I 'm really afraid, my precious darling, that he has n't quite got over—"

"My taking you away from him!" roared John. "I thought as much. Poor devil—poor Talbot! I could see that he would have liked to fight me on the stand at York. Upon my word, I pity him!" and, in token of his compassion, Mr. Mellish burst into that old joyous, boisterous, but musical laugh, which Talbot might almost have heard at the other end of the house.

This was a favorite delusion of John's. He firmly believed that he had won Aurora's affection in fair competition with Captain Bulstrode, pleasantly ignoring that the captain had resigned all pretensions to Miss Floyd's hand nine or ten months before his own offer had been accepted.

The genial, sanguine creature, had a habit of deceiving himself in this manner. He saw all things in the universe just as he wished to see them—all men and women good and honest; life one long, pleasant voyage, in a well-fitted ship, with only first-class passengers on board. He was one of those men who are likely to cut their throats or take prussic acid upon the day they first encounter the black visage of Care.

"And what are we to do with this poor fellow, Lolly?"

"Marry him!" exclaimed Mrs. Mellish.

"Both of us?" said John, simply.

"My dearest pet, what an obtuse old darling you are! No; marry him to Lucy Floyd, my first cousin once removed, and keep the Bulstrode estate in the family."

"Marry him to Lucy!"

"Yes; why not? She has studied enough, and learned history, and geography, and astronomy, and botany, and geology, and conchology, and entomology enough; and she has covered I don't know how many China jars with impossible birds and flowers; and she has illuminated missals, and read High-Church novels; so the next best thing she can do is to marry Talbot Bulstrode."

John had his own reasons for agreeing with Aurora in this matter. He remembered that secret of poor Lucy's which he had discovered more than a year before at Felden Woods—the secret which had been revealed to him by some mysterious sympathetic power belonging to hopeless love. So Mr. Mellish declared his hearty concurrence in Aurora's scheme, and the two amateur match-makers set to work to devise a complicated man-trap, in the which Talbot was to be entangled; never for a moment imagining that, while they were racking their brains in the endeavor to bring this piece of machinery to perfection, the intended victim was quietly strolling across the sunlit lawn toward the very fate they desired for him.

Yes, Talbot Bulstrode lounged with languid step to meet his destiny in a wood upon the borders of the Park —a part of the Park, indeed, inasmuch as it was within the boundary fence of John's domain. The wood-anemones trembled in the spring breezes deep in those shadowy arcades; pale primroses showed their mild faces amid their sheltering leaves; and in shady nooks, beneath low spreading boughs of elm and beech, oak and ash, the violets hid their purple beauty from the vulgar eye. A lovely spot, soothing by its harmonious influence; a very forest sanctuary, without whose dim arcades man cast his burden down, to enter in a child. Captain Bulstrode had felt in no very pleasant humor as he walked across the lawn, but some softening influence stole upon him on the threshold of that sylvan shelter which made him feel a better man. He began to question himself as to how he was playing his part in the great drama of life.

"Good Heavens!" he thought, "what a shameful coward, what a negative wretch I have become by this one grief of my manhood! An indifferent son, a careless brother, a useless, purposeless creature, content to dawdle away my life in feeble pottering with political economy. Shall I ever be in earnest again? Is this dreary doubt of every living creature to go with me to my grave? Less than two years ago my heart sickened at the thought that I had lived to two-and-thirty years of age and had never been loved. Since then—since then — since then I have lived through life's brief fever; I have fought manhood's worst and sharpest battle, and find myself—where? Exactly where I was before—still companionless upon the dreary journey, only a little nearer to the end."

He walked slowly onward into the woodland aisle, other aisles branching away from him right and left into deep glades and darkening shadow. A month or so later, and the mossy ground beneath his feet would be one purple carpet of hyacinths, the very air thick with a fatal scented vapor from the perfumed bulbs.

"I asked too much," said Talbot, in that voiceless argument we are perpetually carrying on with ourselves; "I asked too much—I yielded to the spell of the siren, and was angry because I missed the white wings of the angel. I was bewitched by the fascinations of a beautiful woman, when I should have sought for a noble-minded wife."

He went deeper and deeper into the wood, going to his fate, as another man was to do before the coming summer was over; but to what a different fate! The long arcades of beech and elm had reminded him from the first of the solemn aisles of a cathedral. The saint was only needed. And, coming suddenly to a spot where a new arcade branched off abruptly on his right hand, he saw, in one of the sylvan niches, as fair a saint as had ever been modelled by the hand of artist and believer—the same golden-haired angel he had seen in the long drawing-room at Felden Woods—Lucy Floyd, with the pale aureola about her head, her large straw hat in her lap, filled with anemones and violets, and the third volume of a novel in her hand.

How much in life often hangs, or seems to us to hang, upon what is called by playwrights "a situation!" But for this sudden encounter, but for coming thus upon this pretty picture, Talbot Bulstrode might have dropped into his grave ignorant to the last of Lucy's love for him. But, given a sunshiny April morning (April's fairest bloom, remember, when the capricious nymph is mending her manners, aware that her lovelier sister May is at hand, and anxious to make a good impression before she drops her farewell courtesy, and weeps her last brief shower of farewell tears)—given a balmy spring morning, solitude, a wood, wild flowers, golden hair, and blue eyes, and is the problem difficult to solve?

Talbot Bulstrode, leaning against the broad trunk of a beech, looked down at the fair face, which crimsoned under his eyes, and the first glimmering hint of Lucy's secret began to dawn upon him. At that moment he had no thought of profiting by the discovery, no thought of what he was afterward led on to say. His mind was filled with the storm of emotion that had burst from him in that wild cry to Aurora. Rage and jealousy, regret, despair, envy, love, and hate—all the conflicting feelings that had struggled like so many demons in his soul at sight of Aurora's happiness, were still striving for mastery in his breast, and the first words he spoke revealed the thoughts that were uppermost.

"Your cousin is very happy in her new life, Miss Floyd?" he said.

Lucy looked up at him with surprise. It was the first time he had spoken to her of Aurora.

"Yes," she answered quietly, "I think she is happy."

Captain Bulstrode whisked the end of his cane across a group of anemones, and decapitated the tremulous blossoms. He was thinking, rather savagely, what a shame it was that this glorious Aurora could be happy with big, broad-shouldered, jovial-tempered John Mellish. He could not understand the strange anomaly; he could not discover the clew to the secret; he could not comprehend that the devoted love of this sturdy Yorkshireman was in itself strong enough to conquer all difficulties, to outweigh all differences.

Little by little he and Lucy began to talk of Aurora, until Miss Floyd told her companion all about that dreary time at Felden Woods during which the life of the heiress was wellnigh despaired of. So she had loved him truly, then, after all; she had loved and had suffered, and had lived down her trouble, and had forgotten him and was happy. The story was all told in that one sentence. He looked blankly back at the irrecoverable past, and was angry with the pride of the Bulstrodes, which had stood between himself and his happiness.

He told sympathizing Lucy something of his sorrow; told her that misapprehension—mistaken pride—had parted him from Aurora. She tried, in her gentle, innocent fashion, to comfort the strong man in his weakness, and in trying revealed—ah! how simply and transparently—the old secret, which had so long been hidden from him.

Heaven help the man whose heart is caught at the rebound by a fair-haired divinity, with dove-like eyes, and a low, tremulous voice, softly attuned to his grief. Talbot Bulstrode saw that he was beloved, and in very gratitude made a dismal offer of the ashes of that fire which had burnt so fiercely at Aurora's shrine. Do not despise this poor Lucy if she accepted her cousin's forgotten lover with humble thankfulness, nay, with a tumult of wild delight, and with joyful fear and trembling. She loved him so well, and had loved him so long. Forgive and pity her, for she was one of those pure and innocent creatures whose whole being resolves itself into affection; to whom passion, anger, and pride are unknown; who live only to love, and who love until death. Talbot Bulstrode told Lucy Floyd that he had loved Aurora with the whole strength of his soul, but that now the battle was over, he, the stricken warrior, needed a consoler for his declining days; would she, could she, give her hand to one who would strive to the uttermost to fulfil a husband's duty, and to make her happy? Happy! She would have been happy if he had asked her to be his slave—happy if she could have been a scullery-maid at Bulstrode Castle, so that she might have seen the dark face she loved once or twice a day through the obscure panes of some kitchen-window.

But she was the most undemonstrative of women, and, except by her blushes, and her drooping eyelids, and the teardrop trembling upon the soft auburn lashes, she made no reply to the captain's appeal, until at last, taking her hand in his, he won from her a low consenting murmur, which meant Yes.

Good Heavens! how hard it is upon such women as these that they feel so much and yet display so little feeling. The dark-eyed, impetuous creatures, who speak out fearlessly, and tell you that they love or hate you, flinging their arms around your neck or throwing the carving-knife at you, as the case may be, get full value for all their emotion; but these gentle creatures love, and make no sign. They sit, like Patience on a monument, smiling at grief, and no one reads the mournful meaning of that sad smile. Concealment, like the worm i' the bud, feeds on their damask cheeks, and compassionate relatives tell them that they are bilious, and recommend Cockle's pills, or some other homely remedy, for their pallid complexions. They are always at a disadvantage. Their inner life may be a tragedy, all blood and tears, while their outward existence is some dull domestic drama of every-day life. The only outward sign Lucy Floyd gave of the condition of her heart was that one tremulous, half-whispered affirmative, and yet what a tempest of emotion was going forward within! The muslin folds of her dress rose and fell with the surging billows, but for the very life of her she could have uttered no better response to Talbot's pleading.

It was only by and by, after she and Captain Bulstrode had wandered slowly back to the house, that her emotion betrayed itself. Aurora met her cousin in the corridor out of which their rooms opened, and, drawing Lucy into her own dressing-room, asked the truant where she had been.

"Where have you been, you runaway girl? John and I have wanted you half a dozen times."

Miss Lucy Floyd explained that she had been in the wood with the last new novel—a High-Church novel, in which the heroine rejected the clerical hero because he did not perform the service according to the Rubric. Now, Miss Lucy Floyd made this confession with so much confusion and so many blushes that it would have appeared as if there were some lurking criminality in the fact of spending an April morning in a wood; and, being farther examined as to why she had staid so long, and whether she had been alone all the time, poor Lucy fell into a pitiful state of embarrassment, saying that she had been alone, that is to say, part of the time, or at least most of the time, but that Captain Bulstrode——"

But, in trying to pronounce his name—this beloved, this sacred name—Lucy Floyd's utterance failed her; she fairly broke down, and burst into tears.

Aurora laid her cousin's face upon her breast, and looked down with a womanly, matronly glance into those tearful blue eyes.

"Lucy, my darling," she said, "is it really and truly as I think—as I wish—Talbot loves you?"

"He has asked me to marry him," Lucy whispered.

"And you—you have consented—you love him?"

Lucy Floyd only answered by a new burst of tears.

"Why, my darling, how this surprises me! How long has it been so, Lucy? How long have you loved him?'

"From the hour I first saw him," murmured Lucy; "from the day he first came to Felden. Oh, Aurora! I know how foolish and weak it was; I hate myself for the folly; but he is so good, so noble, so—"

"My silly darling; and because he is good and noble, and asked you to be his wife, you shed as many tears as if you had been asked to go to his funeral. My loving, tender Lucy, you loved him all the time then; and you were so gentle and good to me—to me, who was selfish enough never to guess! My dearest, you are a hundred times better suited to him than ever I was, and you will be as happy—as happy as I am with that ridiculous old John."

Aurora's eyes filled with tears as she spoke. She was truly and sincerely glad that Talbot was in a fair way to find consolation, still more glad that her sentimental cousin was to be made happy.

Talbot Bulstrode lingered on a few days at Mellish Park—happy, ah! too happy days for Lucy Floyd—and then departed, after receiving the congratulations of John and Aurora.

He was to go straight to Alexander Floyd's villa at Fulham, and plead his cause with Lucy's father. There was little fear of his meeting other than a favorable reception, for Talbot Bulstrode, of Bulstrode Castle, was a very great match for a daughter of the junior branch of Floyd, Floyd, and Floyd, a young lady whose expectations were considerably qualified by half a dozen brothers and sisters.

So Captain Bulstrode went back to London as the betrothed lover of Lucy Floyd—went back with a subdued gladness in his heart all unlike the stormy joys of the past. He was happy in the choice he had made, calmly and dispassionately. He had loved Aurora for her beauty and her fascination; he was going to marry Lucy because he had seen much of her, had observed her closely, and believed her to be all that a woman should be. Perhaps, if stern truth must be told, Lucy's chief charm in the captain's eyes lay in that reverence for himself which she so naively betrayed. He accepted her worship with a quiet, unconscious serenity, and thought her the most sensible of women.

Mrs. Alexander was utterly bewildered when Aurora's sometime lover pleaded for his daughter's hand. She was too busy a woman to watch her flock to be the most ....

suspected the state of Lucy's heart. She was glad, therefore, to find that her daughter did justice to her excellent education, and had too much good sense to refuse so advantageous an offer as that of Captain Bulstrode; and she joined with her husband in perfect approval of Talbot's suit. So, there being no let or hinderance, and as the lovers had long known and esteemed each other, it was decided, at the captain's request, that the wedding should take place early in June, and that the honeymoon should be spent at Bulstrode Castle. At the end of May Mr. and Mrs. Mellish went to Felden on purpose to attend Lucy's wedding, which took place with great style at Fulham, Archibald Floyd presenting his grand-niece with a check for five thousand pounds after the return from church.

Once during that marriage ceremony Talbot Bulstrode was nigh rubbing his eyes, thinking that the pageant must be a dream. A dream surely; for here was a pale, fair-haired girl by his side, while the woman he had chosen two years before stood amid a group behind him, and looked on at the ceremony a pleased spectator. But when he felt the little gloved hand trembling upon his arm as the bride and bridegroom left the altar he remembered that it was no dream, and that life held new and solemn duties for him from that hour.

Now, my two heroines being married, the reader versed in the physiology of novel-writing may conclude that my story is done, that the green curtain is ready to fall upon the last act of the play, and that I have nothing more to do than to entreat indulgence for the shortcomings of the performance and the performers. Yet, after all, does the business of the real life-drama always end upon the altar-steps? Must the play needs be over when the hero and heroine have signed their names in the register? Does man cease to be, to do, and to suffer when he gets married? And is it necessary that the novelist, after devoting three volumes to the description of a courtship of six weeks' duration, should reserve for himself only half a page in which to tell us the events of two-thirds of a lifetime? Aurora is married, and settled, and happy; sheltered, as one would imagine, from all dangers, safe under the wing of her stalwart adorer; but it does not therefore follow that the story of her life is done. She has escaped shipwreck for a while, and has safely landed on a pleasant shore; but the storm may still lower darkly upon the horizon, while the hoarse thunder grumbles threateningly in the distance.

CHAPTER XV.

MR. PASTERN'S LETTER.

Mr. John Mellish reserved to himself one room upon the ground-floor of his house, a cheerful, airy apartment, with French windows opening upon the lawn — windows that were sheltered from the sun by a veranda, overhung with jessamine and roses. It was altogether a pleasant room for the summer season, the floor being covered with an India matting instead of a carpet, and many of the chairs being made of light basket-work. Over the chimney-piece hung a portrait of John's father, and opposite to this work of art there was the likeness of the deceased gentleman's favorite hunter, surmounted by a pair of brightly-polished spurs, the glistening rowels of which had often pierced the sides of that faithful steed. In this chamber Mr. Mellish kept his whips, canes, foils, single-sticks, boxing-gloves, spurs, guns, pistols, powder and shot flasks, fishing-tackle, boots and tops, and many happy mornings were spent by the master of Mellish Park in the pleasing occupation of polishing, repairing, inspecting, and otherwise setting in order these possessions. He had as many pairs of hunting-boots as would have supplied half Leicestershire, with tops to match. He had whips enough for half the Melton Hunt. Surrounded by these treasures, as it were in a temple sacred to the deities of the race-course and the hunting-field, Mr. John Mellish used to hold solemn audiences with his trainer and his head groom upon the business of the stable.

It was Aurora's custom to peep into this chamber perpetually, very much to the delight and distraction of her adoring husband, who found the black eyes of his divinity a terrible hinderance to business, except, indeed, when he could induce Mrs. Mellish to join in the discussion upon hand, and lend the assistance of her powerful intellect to the little conclave. I believe that John thought she could have handicapped the horses for the Chester Cup as well as Mr. Topham himself. She was such a brilliant creature that every little smattering of knowledge she possessed appeared to such good account as to make her seem an adept in any subject of which she spoke, and the simple Yorkshireman believed in her as the wisest, as well as the noblest and fairest of women.

Mr. and Mrs. Mellish returned to Yorkshire immediately after Lucy's wedding. Poor John was uneasy about his stables: for his trainer was a victim to chronic rheumatism, and Mr. Pastern had not as yet made any communication respecting the young man of whom he had spoken on the stand at York.

"I shall keep Langley," John said to Aurora, speaking of his old trainer; "for he's an honest fellow, and his judgment will always be of use to me. He and his wife can still occupy the rooms over the stables, and the new man, whoever he may be, can live in the lodge on the north side of the Park. Nobody ever goes in at that gate, so the lodge-keeper's post is a sinecure, and the cottage has been shut up for the last year or two. I wish John Pastern would write."

"And I wish whatever you wish, my dearest life," Aurora said, dutifully, to her happy slave.

Very little had been seen of Steeve Hargraves, the softy, since the day upon which John Mellish had turned him neck and crop out of his service. One of the grooms had seen him in a little village close to the Park, and Stephen had informed the man that he was getting his living by doing odd jobs for the doctor of the parish, and looking after that gentleman's horse and gig; but the softy had seemed inclined to be sulky, and had said very little about himself or his sentiments. He made very particular inquiries, though, about Mrs. Mellish, and asked so many questions as to what Aurora did and said, where she went, whom she saw, and how she agreed with her husband, that at last the groom, although only a simple country lad, refused to answer any more interrogatories about his mistress.

Steeve Hargraves rubbed his coarse, sinewy hands, and chuckled as he spoke of Aurora.

"She 's a rare proud one— a regular high-spirited lady," he said, in that whispering voice that always sounded strange. "She laid in on me with that riding-whip of hers; but I bear no malice— I bear no malice. She 's a beautiful creature, and I wish Mr. Mellish joy of his bargain."

The groom scarcely knew how to take this, not being fully aware whether it was intended as a compliment or an impertinence. So he nodded to the softy and strode off, leaving him still rubbing his hands and whispering about Aurora Mellish, who had long ago forgotten her encounter with Mr. Stephen Hargraves.

How was it likely that she should remember him or take heed of him? How was it likely that she should take alarm because the pale-faced widow, Mrs. Walter Powell, sat by her hearth and hated her? Strong in her youth and beauty, rich in her happiness, sheltered and defended by her husband's love, how should she think of danger? How should she dread misfortune? She thanked God every day that the troubles of her youth were past, and that her path in life led henceforth through smooth and pleasant places, where no perils could come.

Lucy was at Bulstrode Castle, winning upon the affections of her husband's mother, who patronized her daughter-in-law with lofty kindness, and took the blushing, timorous creature under her sheltering wing. Lady Bulstrode was very well satisfied with her son's choice. He might have done better, certainly, as to position and fortune, the lady hinted to Talbot; and, in her maternal anxiety, she would have preferred his marrying any one rather than the cousin of that Miss Floyd, who ran away from school and caused such a scandal at the Parisian seminary. But Lady Bulstrode's heart warmed to Lucy, who was so gentle and humble, and who always spoke of Talbot as if he had been a being far "too bright and good," etc., much to the gratification of her ladyship's maternal vanity.

"She has a very proper affection for you, Talbot," Lady Bulstrode said, "and, for so young a creature, promises to make an excellent wife; far better suited to you, I 'm sure, than her cousin could ever have been."

Talbot turned fiercely upon his mother, very much to the lady's surprise.

"Why will you be for ever bringing Aurora's name into the question, mother?" he cried. "Why can not you let her memory rest? You parted us for ever—you and Constance—and is not that enough? She is married, and she and her husband are a very happy couple. A man might have a worse wife than Mrs. Mellish, I can tell you; and John seems to appreciate her value in his rough way."

"You need not be so violent, Talbot," Lady Bulstrode said with offended dignity. "I am very glad to hear that Miss Floyd has altered since her school-days, and I hope that she may continue to be a good wife," she added, with an emphasis which expressed that she had no very great hopes of the continuance of Mr. Mellish's happiness.

"My poor mother is offended with me," Talbot thought, as Lady Bulstrode swept out of the room. "I know I am an abominable bear, and that nobody will ever truly love me so long as I live. My poor little Lucy loves me after her fashion— loves me in fear and trembling, as if she and I belonged to different orders of beings—very much as the flying woman must have loved my countryman, Peter Wilkins, I think. But, after all, perhaps my mother is right, and my gentle little wife is better suited to me than Aurora would have been."

So we dismiss Talbot Bulstrode for a while, moderately happy, and yet not quite satisfied. What mortal ever was quite satisfied in this world? It is a part of our earthly nature always to find something wanting, always to have a vague, dull, ignorant yearning which can not be appeased. Sometimes, indeed, we are happy; but in our wildest happiness we are still unsatisfied, for it seems then sin if the cup of joy were too full, and we grow cold with terror at the thought that, even because of its fulness, it may possibly be dashed to the ground. What a mistake this life would be, what a wild, feverish dream, what an unfinished and imperfect story, if it were not a prelude to something better! Taken by itself, it is all trouble and confusion; but, taking the future as the key-note of the present, how wondrously harmonious the whole becomes! How little does it signify that our hearts are not complete, our wishes not fulfilled, if the completion and the fulfilment are to come hereafter!

Little more than a week after Lucy's wedding Aurora ordered her horse immediately after breakfast, upon a sunny summer morning, and, accompanied by the old groom who had ridden behind John's father, went out on an excursion among the villages round Mellish Park, as it was her habit to do once or twice a week.

The poor in the neighborhood of the Yorkshire mansion had good reason to bless the coming of the banker's daughter. Aurora loved nothing better than to ride from cottage to cottage, chatting with the simple villagers, and finding out their wants. She never found the worthy creatures very remiss in stating their necessities, and the housekeeper at Mellish Park had enough to do in distributing Aurora's bounties among the cottagers who came to the servants' hall with pencil orders from Mrs. Mellish. Mrs. Walter Powell sometimes ventured to take Aurora to task on the folly and sinfulness of what she called indiscriminate almsgiving; but Mrs. Mellish would pour such a flood of eloquence upon her antagonist that the ensign's widow was always glad to retire from the unequal contest. Nobody had ever been able to argue with Archibald Floyd's daughter. Impulsive and impetuous, she had always taken her own course, whether for weal or woe, and nobody had been strong enough to hinder her.

Returning on this lovely June morning from one of these charitable expeditions, Mrs. Mellish dismounted from her horse at a little turnstile leading into the wood, and ordered the groom to take the animal home.

"I have a fancy for walking through the wood, Joseph," she said, "it's such a lovely morning. Take care of Mazeppa; and if you see Mr. Mellish, tell him that I shall be home directly."

The man touched his hat, and rode off, leading Aurora's horse.

Mrs. Mellish gathered up the folds of her habit and strolled slowly into the wood under whose shadow Talbot Bulstrode and Lucy had wandered on that eventful April day which sealed the young lady's fate.

Now, Aurora had chosen to ramble homeward through this wood because, being thoroughly happy, the warm gladness of the summer weather filled her with a sense of delight which she was loath to curtail. The drowsy hum of the insects, the rich coloring of the woods, the scent of wild flowers, the ripple of water, all blended into one delicious whole, and made the earth lovely.

There is something satisfactory, too, in the sense of possession; and Aurora felt, as she looked down the long avenues, and away through distant loop-holes in the wood to the wide expanse of park and lawn, and the picturesque irregular pile of building beyond, half Gothic, half Elizabethan, and so lost in a rich tangle of ivy and bright foliage as to be beautiful at every point—she felt, I say, that all the fair picture was her own, or her husband's, which was the same thing. She had never for one moment regretted her marriage with John Mellish. She had never, as I have said already, been inconstant to him by one thought.

In one part of the wood the ground rose considerably, so that the house, which lay low, was distinctly visible whenever there was a break in the trees. The rising ground was considered the prettiest spot in the wood, and here a summer-house had been erected—a fragile wooden building, which had fallen into decay of late years, but which was still a pleasant resting-place upon a summer's day, being furnished with a wooden table and a broad bench, and sheltered from the sun and wind by the lower branches of a magnificent beech. A few paces away from this summer-house there was a pool of water, the surface of which was so covered with lilies and tangled weeds as to have beguiled a short-sighted traveller into forgetfulness of the danger beneath. Aurora's way led her past this spot, and she started with a momentary sensation of terror on seeing a man lying asleep by the side of the pool. She quickly recovered herself, remembering that John allowed the public to use the footpath through the wood; but she started again when the man, who must have been a bad sleeper, to be aroused by her light footstep, lifted his head and displayed the white face of the softy.

He rose slowly from the ground upon seeing Mrs. Mellish, and crawled away, looking at her as he went, but not making any acknowledgment of her presence.

Aurora could not repress a brief terrified shudder; it seemed as if her footfall had startled some viperish creature, some loathsome member of the reptile race, and scared it from its lurking-place.

Steeve Hargraves disappeared among the trees as Mrs. Mellish walked on, her head proudly erect, but her cheek a shade paler than before this unexpected encounter with the softy.

Her joyous gladness in the bright summer's day had forsaken her as suddenly as she had met Stephen Hargraves; that bright smile, which was even brighter than the morning sunshine, faded out, and left her face unnaturally grave.

"Good Heavens!" she exclaimed, "how foolish I am! I am actually afraid of that man—afraid of that pitiful coward who could hurt my feeble old dog. As if such a creature as that could do one any mischief!"

Of course this was very wisely argued, as no coward ever by any chance worked any mischief upon this earth, since the Saxon prince was stabbed in the back while drinking at his kinswoman's gate, or since brave King John and his creature plotted together what they should do with the little boy Arthur.

Aurora walked slowly across the lawn toward that end of the house at which the apartment sacred to Mr. Mellish was situated. She entered softly at the open window, and laid her hand upon John's shoulder as he sat at a table covered with a litter of account-books, racing-lists, and disorderly papers.

He started at the touch of the familiar hand.

"My darling, I'm so glad you've come in. How long you've been!"

She looked at her little jewelled watch. Poor John had loaded her with trinkets and gewgaws. His chief grief was that she was a wealthy heiress, and that he could give her nothing but the adoration of his simple, honest heart.

"Only half-past one, you silly old John," she said. "What made you think me late?"

"Because I wanted to consult you about something, and to tell you something. Such good news!"

"About what?"

"About the trainer."

She shrugged her shoulders, and pursed up her red lips with a bewitching little gesture of indifference.

"Is that all?" she said.

"Yes; but a'n't you glad we've got the man at last—the very man to suit us, I think? Where's John Pastern's letter?"

Mr. Mellish searched among the litter of papers upon the table, while Aurora, leaning against the frame-work of the open window, watched him, and laughed at his embarrassment.

She had recovered her spirits, and looked the very picture of careless gladness as she leaned in one of those graceful and unstudied attitudes peculiar to her, supported by the frame-work of the window, and with the trailing jessamine waving round her in the soft summer breeze. She lifted her ungloved hand and gathered the roses above her head as she talked to her husband.

"You most disorderly and unmethodic of men," she said, laughing, "I would n't mind betting you won't find it."

I'm afraid that Mr. Mellish muttered an oath as he tossed about the heterogeneous mass of papers in his search for the missing document.

"I had it five minutes before you came in Aurora," he said, "and now there's no sign of it—oh, here it is!"

Mr. Mellish unfolded the letter, and, smoothing it out upon the table before him, cleared his throat preparatory to reading the epistle. Aurora still leaned against the window-frame, half in and half out of the room, singing a snatch of a popular song, and trying to gather an obstinate half-blown rose which grew provokingly out of reach.

"You're attending, Aurora?"

"Yes, dearest and best."

"But do come in. You can't hear a word there."

Mrs. Mellish shrugged her shoulders, as who should say, "I submit to the command of a tyrant," and advanced a couple of paces from the window; then, looking at John with an enchantingly insolent toss of her head, she folded her hands behind her, and told him she would "be good." She was a careless, impetuous creature, dreadfully forgetful of what Mrs. Walter Powell called her "responsibilities;" every mortal thing by turns, and never any one thing for two minutes together; happy, generous, affectionate; taking life as a glorious summer's holiday, and thanking God for the bounty which made it so pleasant to her.

Mr. John Pastern began his letter with an apology for having so long deferred writing. He had lost the address of the person he had wished to recommend, and had waited until the man wrote to him.

"I think he will suit you very well," the letter went on to say, "as he is well up in his business, having had plenty of experience as groom, jockey, and trainer. He is only thirty years of age, but met with an accident some time since, which lamed him for life. He was half killed in a steeple-chase in Prussia, and was for upward of a year in a hospital at Berlin. His name is James Conyers, and he can have a character from—"

The letter dropped out of John Mellish's hand as he looked up at his wife. It was not a scream which she had uttered. It was a gasping cry, more terrible to hear than the shrillest scream that ever came from the throat of woman in all the long history of womanly distress.

"Aurora! Aurora!"

He looked at her, and his own face changed and whitened at the sight of hers. So terrible a transformation had come over her during the reading of that letter that the shock could scarcely have been greater had he looked up and seen another person in her place.

"It's wrong! it's wrong!" she cried, hoarsely; "you've read the wrong name. It can't be that!"

"What name?"

"What name?" she echoed fiercely, her face flaming up with a wild fury—"that name! I tell you it can't be. Give me the letter."

He obeyed her mechanically, picking up the paper and handing it to her, but never removing his eyes from her face.

She snatched it from him; looked at it for a few moments with her eyes dilated and her lips apart; then, reeling back two or three paces, her knees bent under her, and she fell heavily to the ground.

CHAPTER XVI.

MR. JAMES CONYERS.

The first week in July brought James Conyers, the new trainer, to Mellish Park. John had made no particular inquiries as to the man's character of any of his former employers, as a word from Mr. Pastern was all-sufficient.

Mr. Mellish had endeavored to discover the cause of Aurora's agitation at the reading of Mr. Pastern's letter. She had fallen like a dead creature at his feet; she had been hysterical throughout the remainder of the day, and delirious in the ensuing night, but she had not uttered one word calculated to throw any light upon the secret of her strange manifestation of emotion.

Her husband sat by her bedside upon the day after that on which she had fallen into the death-like swoon, watching her with a grave, anxious face, and earnest eyes that never wandered from her own.

He was suffering very much the same agony that Talbot Bulstrode had endured at Felden on the receipt of his mother's letter. The dark wall was slowly rising and separating him from the woman he loved. He was now to discover the tortures known only to the husband whose wife is parted from him by that which has more power to sever than any width of land or wild extent of ocean — *a secret*.

He watched the pale face lying on the pillow; the large, black, haggard eyes, wide open, and looking blankly out at the faraway purple tree-tops in the horizon; but there was no clew to the mystery in any line of that beloved countenance; there was little more than an expression of weariness, as if the soul, looking out of that white face, was so utterly enfeebled as to have lost all power to feel anything but a vague yearning for rest.

The wide casement windows were open, but the day was hot and oppressive — oppressively still and sunny; the landscape sweltering under a yellow haze, as if the very atmosphere had been opaque with melted gold. Even the roses in the garden seemed to feel the influence of the blazing summer sky, dropping their heavy heads like human sufferers from headache. The mastiff Bow-wow, lying under an acacia upon the lawn,

was as peevish as any captious elderly gentleman, and snapped spitefully at a frivolous butterfly that wheeled, and spun, and threw summersaults about the dog's head. Beautiful as was this summer's day, it was one on which people are apt to lose their tempers, and quarrel with each other by reason of the heat; every man feeling a secret conviction that his neighbor is in some way to blame for the sultriness of the atmosphere, and that it would be cooler if he were out of the way. It was one of those days on which invalids are especially fractious, and hospital nurses murmur at their vocation; a day on which third-class passengers travelling long distances by excursion-trains are savagely clamorous for beer at every station, and hate each other for the narrowness and hardness of the carriage-seats, and for the inadequate means of ventilation provided by the Railway Company; a day on which stern business men revolt against the ceaseless grinding of the wheel, and, suddenly reckless of consequences, rush wildly to the Crown and Sceptre, to cool their overheated systems with water souchy and still hock; an abnormal day, upon which the machinery of every-day life gets out of order, and runs riot throughout twelve suffocating hours.

John Mellish, sitting patiently by his wife's side, thought very little of the summer weather. I doubt if he knew whether the month was January or June. For him earth only held one creature, and she was ill and in distress from which he was powerless to save her — distress the very nature of which he was ignorant.

His voice trembled when he spoke to her.

"My darling, you have been very ill," he said.

She looked at him with a smile so unlike her own that it was more painful to him to see than the loudest agony of tears, and stretched out her hand. He took the burning hand in his, and held it while he talked to her.

"Yes, dearest, you have been ill; but Morton says the attack was merely hysterical, and that you will be yourself again to-morrow, so there's no occasion for anxiety on that score. What grieves me, darling, is to see that there is something on your mind — something which has been the real cause of your illness."

She turned her face upon the pillow, and tried to snatch her hand from his in her impatience, but he held it tightly in both his own.

"Does my speaking of yesterday distress you, Aurora?" he asked, gravely.

"Distress me? Oh, no."

"Then tell me, darling, why the mention of that man, the trainer's name, had such a terrible effect upon you."

"The doctor told you that the attack was

hysterical," she said, coldly; "I suppose I was
hysterical and nervous yesterday."

"But the name, Aurora, the name. This
James Conyers, who is he?" He felt the
hand he held tighten convulsively upon his
own as he mentioned the trainer's name.

"Who is this man? Tell me, Aurora. For
God's sake, tell me the truth."

She turned her face toward him once more
as he said this.

"If you only want the truth from me, John,
you must ask me nothing. Remember what I
said to you at the Chateau d'Arques. It was
a secret that parted me from Talbot Bulstrode. You trusted me then, John — you
must trust me to the end; or, if you can not
trust me"— she stopped suddenly, and the
tears welled slowly up to her large, mournful
eyes as she looked at her husband.

"What, dearest?"

"We must part — as Talbot and I parted."

"Part!" he cried; "my love, my love! Do
you think there is anything upon this earth
strong enough to part us, except death? Do
you think that any combination of circumstances, however strange, however inexplicable, would ever cause me to doubt your honor,
or to tremble for my own? Could I be here
if I doubted you? could I sit by your side,
asking you these questions, if I feared the
issue? Nothing shall shake my confidence —
nothing can. But have pity on me; think
how bitter a grief it is to sit here with your
hand in mine, and to know that there is a
secret between us. Aurora, tell me — this
man, this Conyers — what is he, and who
is he?"

"You know that as well as I do. A groom
once; afterward a jockey; and now a trainer."

"But you know him?"

"I have seen him."

"When?"

"Some years ago, when he was in my father's service."

John Mellish breathed more freely for a
moment. The man had been a groom at Felden Woods, that was all. This accounted for
the fact of Aurora's recognizing his name, but
not for her agitation. He was no nearer the
clew to the mystery than before.

"James Conyers was in your father's service,' he said, thoughtfully; "but why should
the mention of his name yesterday have
caused you such emotion?"

"I can not tell you."

"It is another secret, then, Aurora," he
said, reproachfully; "or has this man anything to do with the old secret of which you
told me at the Chateau d'Arques?"

She did not answer him.

"Ah! I see — I understand, Aurora," he
added, after a pause. "This man was a servant at Felden Woods; a spy, perhaps; and
he discovered the secret, and traded upon it,
as servants often have done before. This

caused your agitation at hearing his name.
You were afraid that he would come here and
annoy you, making use of this secret to extort
money, and keeping you in perpetual terror
of him. I think I can understand it all. I
am right, am I not?"

She looked at him with something of the
expression of a hunted animal that finds itself
at bay.

"Yes, John."

"This man — this groom — knows something of — of the secret?"

"He does."

John Mellish turned away his head, and
buried his face in his hands. What cruel anguish! what bitter degradation! This man,
a groom, a servant, was in the confidence of
his wife, and had such power to harass and
alarm her that the very mention of his name
was enough to cast her to the earth, as if
stricken by sudden death. What, in the
name of Heaven, could this secret be, which
was in the keeping of a servant, and yet could
not be told to him? He bit his lip till his
strong teeth met upon the quivering flesh, in
the silent agony of that thought. What could
it be? He had sworn, only a minute before,
to trust in her blindly to the end; and yet —
and yet — His massive frame shook from
head to heel in that noiseless struggle; doubt
and despair rose like twin demons in his soul;
but he wrestled with them, and overcame
them; and, turning with a white face to his
wife, said quietly:

"I will press these painful questions no
farther, Aurora. I will write to Pastern, and
tell him that the man will not suit us; and —"

He was rising to leave her bedside, when
she laid her hand upon his arm.

"Don't write to Mr. Pastern, John," she
said; "the man will suit you very well, I dare
say. I had rather he came."

"You wish him to come here?"

"Yes."

"But he will annoy you; he will try to extort money from you."

"He would do that in any case, since he is
alive. I thought that he was dead."

"Then you really wish him to come here?"

"I do."

John Mellish left his wife's room inexpressibly relieved. The secret could not be so
very terrible after all, since she was willing
that the man who knew it should come to
Mellish Park, where there was at least a remote chance of his revealing it to her husband. Perhaps, after all, this mystery involved others rather than herself—her father's
commercial integrity — her mother? He had
heard very little of her mother's history;
perhaps she— Pshaw! why weary himself
with speculative surmises? he had promised
to trust her, and the hour had come in which
he was called upon to keep his promise. He
wrote to Mr. Pastern, accepting his recom-

mendation of James Conyers, and waited rather impatiently to see what kind of man the trainer was.

He received a letter from Conyers, very well written and worded, to the effect that he would arrive at Mellish Park upon the third of July.

Aurora had recovered from her brief hysterical attack when this letter arrived; but, as she was still weak and out of spirits, her medical man recommended change of air; so Mr. and Mrs. Mellish drove off to Harrowgate upon the 28th of June, leaving Mrs. Powell behind them at the Park.

The ensign's widow had been scrupulously kept out of Aurora's room during her short illness, being held at bay by John, who coolly shut the door in the lady's sympathetic face, telling her that he'd wait upon his wife himself, and that when he wanted female assistance he would ring for Mrs. Mellish's maid.

Now, Mrs. Walter Powell, being afflicted with that ravenous curiosity common to people who live in other people's houses, felt herself deeply injured by this line of conduct. There were mysteries and secrets afloat, and she was not to be allowed to discover them; there was a skeleton in the house, and she was not to anatomize the bony horror. She scented trouble and sorrow as carnivorous animals scent their prey, and yet she, who hated Aurora, was not to be allowed to riot at the unnatural feast.

Why is it that the dependents in a household are so feverishly inquisitive about the doings and sayings, the manners and customs, the joys and sorrows of those who employ them? Is it that, having abnegated for themselves all active share in life, they take an unhealthy interest in those who are in the thick of the strife? Is it because, being cut off, in a great measure, by the nature of their employments from family ties and family pleasures, they feel a malicious delight in all family trials and vexations, and the ever-recurring breezes which disturb the domestic atmosphere? Remember this, husbands and wives, fathers and sons, mothers and daughters, brothers and sisters, when you quarrel. *Your servants enjoy the fun.* Surely that recollection ought to be enough to keep you for ever peaceful and friendly. Your servants listen at your doors, and repeat your spiteful speeches in the kitchen, and watch you while they wait at table, and understand every sarcasm, every innuendo, every look, as well as those at whom the cruel glances and the stinging words are aimed. They understand your sulky silence, your studied and overacted politeness. The most polished form your hate and anger can take is as transparent to those household spies as if you threw knives at each other, or pelted your enemy with the side-dishes and vegetables, after the fashion of disputants in a pantomime. Nothing that is done in the

parlor is lost upon these quiet, well-behaved watchers from the kitchen. They laugh at you; nay, worse, they pity you. They discuss your affairs, and make out your income, and settle what you can afford to do and what you can't afford to do; they prearrange the disposal of your wife's fortune, and look prophetically forward to the day when you will avail yourself of the advantages of the new Bankruptcy Act. They know why you live on bad terms with your eldest daughter, and why your favorite son was turned out of doors; and they take a morbid interest in every dismal secret of your life. You don't allow them followers; you look blacker than thunder if you see Mary's sister or John's poor old mother sitting meekly in your hall; you are surprised if the postman brings them letters, and attribute the fact to the pernicious system of over-educating the masses; you shut them from their homes and their kindred, their lovers and their friends; you deny them books, you grudge them a peep at your newspaper, and then you lift up your eyes and wonder at them because they are inquisitive, and because the staple of their talk is scandal and gossip.

Mrs. Walter Powell, having been treated by most of her employers as a species of upper servant, had acquired all the instincts of a servant, and she determined to leave no means untried in order to discover the cause of Aurora's illness, which the doctor had darkly hinted to her had more to do with the mind than the body. John Mellish had ordered a carpenter to repair the lodge at the north gate for the accommodation of James Conyers, and John's old trainer, Langley, was to receive his colleague and introduce him to the stables.

The new trainer made his appearance at the lodge-gates in the glowing July sunset; he was accompanied by no less a person than Steeve Hargraves, the softy, who had been lurking about the station upon the look-out for a job, and who had been engaged by Mr. Conyers to carry his portmanteau.

To the surprise of the trainer, Stephen Hargraves set down his burden at the Park gates.

"You'll have to find some one else to carry it th' rest 't' ro-ad," he said, touching his greasy cap, and extending his broad palm to receive the expected payment.

Mr. James Conyers was rather a dashing fellow, with no small amount of that quality which is generally termed "swagger," so he turned sharply round upon the softy and asked him what the devil he meant.

"I mean that I may n't go inside yon gates," muttered Stephen Hargraves; "I mean that I've been turned out of yon place that I've lived in, man and boy, for forty years—turned out like a dog, neck and crop."

Mr. Conyers threw away the stump of his cigar, and stared superciliously at the softy.

"What does the man mean?" he asked of the woman who had opened the gates.

"Why, poor fellow, he's a bit fond, sir, and him and Mrs. Mellish didn't get on very well; she has a rare spirit, and I *have* heard that she horsewhipped him for beating her favorite dog. Anyways, master turned him out of his service."

"Because my lady had horsewhipped him. Servants'-hall justice all the world over," said the trainer, laughing, and lighting a second cigar from a metal fusee-box in his waistcoat-pocket.

"Yes, that's justice, a'n't it?" the softy said, eagerly. "You would n't like to be turned out of a place as you 'd lived in forty year, would you? But Mrs. Mellish has a rare spirit, bless her pretty face!"

The blessing enunciated by Mr. Stephen Hargraves had such a very ominous sound that the new trainer, who was evidently a shrewd, observant fellow, took his cigar from his mouth on purpose to stare at him. The white face, lighted up by a pair of red eyes with a dim glimmer in them, was by no means the most agreeable of countenances; but Mr. Conyers looked at the man for some moments, holding him by the collar of his coat in order to do so with more deliberation; then, pushing the softy away with an affably contemptuous gesture, he said, laughing:

"You 're a character, my friend, it strikes me, and not too safe a character either. I 'm dashed if I should like to offend you. There 's a shilling for your trouble, my man," he added, tossing the money into Steeve's extended palm with careless dexterity.

"I suppose I can leave my portmanteau here till to-morrow, ma'am?" he said, turning to the woman at the lodge. "I 'd carry it down to the house myself, if I was n't lame."

He was such a handsome fellow, and had such an easy, careless manner, that the simple Yorkshirewoman was quite subdued by his fascinations.

"Leave it here, sir, and welcome," she said, courtesying, "and my master shall take it to the house for you as soon as he comes in. Begging your pardon, sir, but I suppose you 're the new gentleman that 's expected in the stables?"

"Precisely."

"Then I was to tell you, sir, that they 've fitted up the north lodge for you; but you was to please go straight to the house, and the housekeeper was to make you comfortable and give you a bed for to-night."

Mr. Conyers nodded, thanked her, wished her good-night, and limped slowly away, through the shadows of the evening, and under the shelter of the overarching trees. He stepped aside from the broad carriage-drive on to the dewy turf that bordered it, choosing the softest, mossiest places, with a sybarite's instinct. Look at him as he takes his slow way under those glorious branches, in the holy stillness of the summer sunset, his face sometimes lighted by the low, lessening rays, sometimes dark with the shadows from the leaves above his head. He is wonderfully handsome—wonderfully and perfectly handsome—the very perfection of physical beauty; faultless in proportion, as if each line in his face and form had been measured by the sculptor's rule, and carved by the sculptor's chisel. He is a man about whose beauty there can be no dispute, whose perfection servant-maids and duchesses must alike confess, albeit they are not bound to admire; yet it is rather a sensual type of beauty, this splendor of form and color, unallied to any special charm of expression. Look at him now, as he stops to rest, leaning against the trunk of a tree, and smoking his big cigar with easy enjoyment. He is thinking. His dark blue eyes, deeper in color by reason of the thick black lashes which fringe them, are half closed, and have a dreamy, semi-sentimental expression, which might lead you to suppose the man was musing upon the beauty of the summer sunset. He is thinking of his losses on the Chester Cup, the wages he is to get from John Mellish, and the perquisites likely to appertain to the situation. You give him credit for thoughts to match with his dark, violet-hued eyes, and the exquisite modelling of his mouth and chin; you give him a mind as æsthetically perfect as his face and figure, and you recoil on discovering what a vulgar every-day sword may lurk under that beautiful scabbard. Mr. James Conyers is, perhaps, no worse than other men of his station, but he is decidedly no better. He is only very much handsomer; and you have no right to be angry with him because his opinions and sentiments are exactly what they would have been if he had had red hair and a pug nose. With what wonderful wisdom has George Eliot told us that people are not any better because they have long eyelashes! Yet it must be that there is something anomalous in this outward beauty and inward ugliness; for, in spite of all experience, we revolt against it, and are incredulous to the last, believing that the palace which is outwardly so splendid can scarcely be ill furnished within. Heaven help the woman who sells her heart for a handsome face, and awakes, when the bargain has been struck, to discover the foolishness of such an exchange.

It took Mr. Conyers a long while to walk from the lodge to the house. I do not know how, technically, to describe his lameness. He had fallen, with his horse, in the Prussian steeple-chase, which had so nearly cost him his life, and his left leg had been terribly injured. The bones had been set by wonderful German surgeons, who put the shattered leg together as if it had been a Chinese puzzle, but who, with all their skill, could not prevent the contraction of the sinews, which had left the jockey lamed for life, and no longer fit to ride in any race whatever. He was of the middle height, and weighed something over eleven stone, and had never ridden except in Continental steeple-chases.

Mr. James Conyers paused a few paces from the house, and gravely contemplated the irregular pile of buildings before him.

"A snug crib," he muttered; "plenty of tin hereabouts, I should think, from the look of the place."

Being ignorant of the geography of the neighborhood, and being, moreover, by no means afflicted by an excess of modesty, Mr. Conyers went straight to the principal door, and rang the bell sacred to visitors and the family.

He was admitted by a grave old man-servant, who, after deliberately inspecting his brown shooting-coat, colored shirt-front, and felt hat, asked him, with considerable asperity, what he was pleased to want.

Mr. Conyers explained that he was the new trainer, and that he wished to see the house-keeper; but he had hardly finished doing so when a door in an angle of the hall was softly opened, and Mrs. Walter Powell peeped out of the snug little apartment sacred to her hours of privacy.

"Perhaps the young man will be so good as to step in here," addressing herself apparently to space, but indirectly to James Conyers.

The young man took off his hat, uncovering a mass of luxuriant brown curls, and limped across the hall in obedience to Mrs. Powell's invitation.

"I dare say I shall be able to give you any information you require."

James Conyers smiled, wondering whether the bilious-looking party, as he mentally designated Mrs. Powell, could give him any information about the York summer meeting; but he bowed politely, and said he merely wanted to know where he was to hang out— he stopped and apologized — where he was to sleep that night, and whether there were any letters for him. But Mrs. Powell was by no means inclined to let him off so cheaply. She set to work to pump him, and labored so assiduously that she soon exhausted that very small amount of intelligence which he was disposed to afford her, being perfectly aware of the process to which he was subjected, and more than equal to the lady in dexterity. The ensign's widow, therefore, ascertained little more than that Mr. Conyers was a perfect stranger to John Mellish and his wife, neither of whom he had ever seen.

Having failed to gain much by this interview, Mrs. Powell was anxious to bring it to a speedy termination.

"Perhaps you would like a glass of wine after your walk?" she said; "I 'll ring for some, and I can inquire at the same time about your letters. I dare say you are anxious to hear from the relatives you have left at home."

Mr. Conyers smiled for the second time. He had neither had a home nor any relatives to speak of since the most infantine period of his existence, but had been thrown upon the world a sharp-witted adventurer at seven or eight years old. The "relatives" for whose communication he was looking out so eagerly were members of the humbler class of book-men with whom he did business.

The servant despatched by Mrs. Powell returned with a decanter of sherry and about half a dozen letters for Mr. Conyers.

"You 'd better bring the lamp, William," said Mrs. Powell, as the man left the room, "for I 'm sure you 'll never be able to read your letters by this light," she added politely to Mr. Conyers.

The fact was, that Mrs. Powell, afflicted by that diseased curiosity of which I have spoken, wanted to know what kind of correspondents these were whose letters the trainer was so anxious to receive, and sent for the lamp in order that she might get the full benefit of any scraps of information to be got at by rapid glances and dexterously stolen peeps.

The servant brought a brilliant camphene lamp, and Mr. Conyers, not at all abashed by Mrs. Powell's condescension, drew his chair close to the table, and, after tossing off a glass of sherry, settled himself to the perusal of his letters.

The ensign's widow, with some needle-work in her hand, sat directly opposite to him at the small round table, with nothing but the pedestal of the lamp between them.

James Conyers took up the first letter, examined the superscription and seal, tore open the envelope, read the brief communication upon half a sheet of note-paper, and thrust it into his waistcoat-pocket. Mrs. Powell, using her eyes to the utmost, saw nothing but a few lines in a scratchy, plebeian handwriting, and a signature which, seen at a disadvantage upside down, did n't look unlike "Johnson." The second envelope contained only a tissue-paper betting-list; the third held a dirty scrap of paper with a few words scrawled in pencil; but at sight of the uppermost envelope of the remaining three Mr. James Conyers started as if he had been shot. Mrs. Powell looked from the face of the trainer to the superscription of the letter, and was scarcely less surprised than Mr. Conyers. The superscription was in the handwriting of Aurora Mellish.

It was a peculiar hand — a hand about which there could be no mistake; not an elegant Italian hand, sloping, slender, and feminine, but large and bold, with ponderous up-strokes and down-strokes, easy to recognize at a greater distance than that which

eparated Mrs. Powell from the trainer.
There was no room for any doubt. Mrs.
Iellish had written to her husband's servant,
nd the man was evidently familiar with
er hand, yet surprised at receiving her
etter.

He tore open the envelope, and read the
ontents eagerly twice over, frowning darkly
s he read.

Mrs. Powell suddenly remembered that she
ad left part of her needle-work upon a
hiffonnier behind the young man's chair, and
ose quietly to fetch it. He was so much
ngrossed by the letter in his hand that he
ras not aware of the pale face which peered
or one brief moment over his shoulder, as the
aded, hungry eyes stole a glance at the
riting on the page.

The letter was written on the first side of a
heet of note-paper, with only a few words
arried over to the second page. It was this
econd page which Mrs. Powell saw. The
ords written at the top of the leaf were
hese: "Above all, *express no surprise*.—A."

There was no ordinary conclusion to the
etter; no other signature than this big
apital A.

CHAPTER XVII.

THE TRAINER'S MESSENGER.

Mr. James Conyers made himself very
much at home at Mellish Park. Poor Lang-
ey, the invalid trainer, who was a Yorkshireman, felt himself almost bewildered by the
easy insolence of the town-bred trainer. He
ooked so much too handsome and dashing for
is office that the grooms and stable-boys
owed down to him, and paid court to him as
hey had never done to simple Langley, who
ad been very often obliged to enforce his
ommands with a horsewhip or a serviceable
eather strap. James Conyers' handsome face
ras a capital with which that gentleman
new very well how to trade, and he took
he full amount of interest that was to be got
or it without compunction. I am sorry to be
bliged to confess that this man, who had sat
n the artists' studios and the life academies
or Apollo and Antinous, was selfish to the
ackbone; and, so long as he was well fed,
nd clothed, and housed, and provided for,
ared very little whence the food and cloth-
ng came, or who kept the house that shel-
ered him, or filled the purse which he jingled
n his trousers-pocket. Heaven forbid that I
hould be called upon for his biography. I
nly know that he sprang from the mire of
he streets, like some male Aphrodite rising
rom the mud; that he was a black[?] g[?]n the
utter at four years of age, and a w[?] [?]'1
he matter of marbles and hardbake be[?]
is fifth birthday. Even then he was [?]

reaping the advantage of a handsome face;
for tender-hearted matrons, who would have
been deaf to the cries of a snub-nosed urchin,
petted and compassionated the pretty boy.

In his earliest childhood he learned therefore to trade upon his beauty, and to get the
most that he could for that merchandise; and
he grew up utterly unprincipled, and carried
his handsome face out into the world to help
him on to fortune. He was extravagant, lazy,
luxurious, and selfish; but he had that easy,
indifferent grace of manner which passes
with shallow observers for good-nature. He
would not have gone three paces out of his
way to serve his best friend; but he smiled
and showed his handsome white teeth with
equal liberality to all his acquaintance, and
took credit for being a frank, generous-
hearted fellow on the strength of that smile.
He was skilled in the uses of that gilt gin-
gerbread of generosity which so often passes
current for sterling gold. He was dexterous
in the handling of those cogged dice which
have all the rattle of the honest ivories. A
slap on the back, a hearty shake of the hand,
often went as far from him as the loan of
a sovereign from another man; and Jim Conyers was firmly believed in by the doubtful
gentlemen with whom he associated as a good-
natured fellow who was nobody's enemy but
his own. He had that superficial Cockney
cleverness which is generally called knowledge of the world — knowledge of the worst
side of the world—and utter ignorance of all
that is noble upon earth, it might perhaps be
more justly called; he had matriculated in
the streets of London, and graduated on the
race-course; he had never read any higher
literature than the Sunday papers and the
Racing Calendar, but he contrived to make a
very little learning go a long way, and was
generally spoken of by his employers as a
superior young man, considerably above his
station.

Mr. Conyers expressed himself very well
contented with the rustic lodge which had
been chosen for his dwelling-house. He con-
descendingly looked on while the stable-lads
carried the furniture selected for him by the
housekeeper from the spare servants' rooms
from the house to the lodge, and assisted in
the arrangement of the tiny rustic chambers,
limping about in his shirt-sleeves, and showing himself wonderfully handy with a hammer and a pocket full of nails. He sat upon
a table and drank beer with such charming
affability that the stable-lads were as grateful to him as if he had treated them to that
beverage. Indeed, seeing the frank cordiality
with which James Conyers smote the lads
upon the back, and prayed them to be active
w[?] [?] an, it w[?] [?] [?] diffi[c]ult to re-
[?] t all w[?] [?] the giver of the
[?] and that it w[?] Mr John Mellish who
[?] h[?] to [?]y [?] [?] w[?] ill. What,

among all the virtues which adorn this earth, can be more charming than the generosity of upper servants! With what hearty hospitality they pass the bottle! how liberally they throw the seven-shilling gunpowder into the teapot! how unsparingly they spread the twenty-penny fresh butter on the toast! and what a glorious welcome they give to the droppers-in of the servants' hall! It is scarcely wonderful that the recipients of their bounty forget that it is the master of the household who will be called upon for the expenses of the banquet, and who will look ruefully at the total of the quarter's housekeeping.

It was not to be supposed that so dashing a fellow as Mr. James Conyers could, in the lodging-house-keeper's *patois*, "do for" himself. He required a humble drudge to black his boots, make his bed, boil his kettle, cook his dinner, and keep the two little chambers at the lodge in decent order. Casting about in a reflective mood for a fitting person for this office, his recreant fancy hit upon Steeve Hargraves, the softy. He was sitting upon the sill of an open window in the little parlor of the lodge, smoking a cigar and drinking out of a can of beer, when this idea came into his head. He was so tickled by the notion that he took his cigar from his mouth in order to laugh at his ease.

"The man 's a character," he said, still laughing, "and I 'll have him to wait upon me. He 's been forbid the place, has he? turned out neck and crop because my Lady Highropes horsewhipped him. Never mind that; I 'll give him leave to come back, if it 's only for the fun of the thing." ·

He limped out upon the high-road half an hour after this, and went into the village to find Steeve Hargraves. He had little difficulty in doing this, as everybody knew the softy, and a chorus of boys volunteered to fetch him from the house of the doctor, in whose service he did odd jobs, and brought him to Mr. Conyers five minutes afterward, looking very hot and dirty, but as pale of complexion as usual.

Stephen Hargraves agreed very readily to abandon his present occupation, and to wait upon the trainer, in consideration of five shillings a week and his board and lodging; but his countenance fell when he discovered that Mr. Conyers was in the service of John Mellish, and lived on the outskirts of the Park.

"You 're afraid of setting foot upon his estate, are you?" said the trainer, laughing. "Never mind, Steeve, *I* give you leave to come, and I should like to see the man or woman in that house who 'll interfere with any whim of mine. *I* give you leave. You understand."

The softy touched his cap, and tried to look as if he understood; but it was very evident

that he did not understand, and it was some time before Mr. Conyers could persuade him that his life would be safe within the gates of Mellish Park; but he was ultimately induced to trust himself at the north lodge, and promised to present himself there in the course of the evening.

Now, Mr. James Conyers had exerted himself as much in order to overcome the cowardly objections of this rustic clown as he could have done if Steeve Hargraves had been the most accomplished body-servant in the three ridings. Perhaps there was some deeper motive than any regard for the man himself in this special preference for the softy; some lurking malice, some petty spite, the key to which was hidden in his own breast. If, while standing smoking in the village street, *chaffing* the softy for the edification of the lookers-on, and taking so much trouble to secure such an ignorant and brutish esquire—if one shadow of the future, so very near at hand, could have fallen across his path, surely he would have instinctively recoiled from the striking of that ill-omened bargain.

But James Conyers had no superstition; indeed, he was so pleasantly free from that weakness as to be a disbeliever in all things in heaven and on earth, except himself and his own merits; so he hired the softy, for the fun of the thing, as he called it, and walked slowly back to the Park gates to watch for the return of Mr. and Mrs. Mellish, who were expected that afternoon.

The woman at the lodge brought him out a chair, and begged him to rest himself under the portico. He thanked her with a pleasant smile, and sat down among the roses and honeysuckles, and lighted another cigar.

"You 'll find the north lodge dull, I 'm thinking, sir," the woman said, from the open window, where she had rescated herself with her needle-work.

"Well, it is n't very lively, ma'am, certainly," answered Mr. Conyers, "but it serves my purpose well enough. The place is lonely enough for a man to be murdered there and nobody be any the wiser; but, as I have nothing to lose, it will answer well enough for me."

He might, perhaps, have said a good deal more about the place, but at this moment the sound of wheels upon the high-road announced the return of the travellers, and two or three minutes afterward the carriage dashed through the gate, and past Mr. James Conyers.

Whatever power this man might have over Aurora, whatever knowledge of a compromising secret he might have obtained and traded upon, the fearlessness of her nature showed itself now as always, and she never flinched at the sight of him. If he had placed himself in her way on purpose to watch the effect of his presence, he must have been disappointed; for, except that a cold shadow of disdain passed over her face as the carriage drove by him, he might have imagined himself unseen. She looked pale and careworn, and her eyes seemed to have grown larger since her illness; but she held her head as erect as ever, and had still the air of imperial grandeur which constituted one of her chief charms.

"So that is Mr. Mellish," said Conyers, as the carriage disappeared. "He seems very fond of his wife."

"Yes, sure; and he is, too. Fond of her! Why, they say there is n't another such couple in all Yorkshire. And she 's fond of him, too, bless her handsome face! But who would n't be fond of Master John ?"

Mr. Conyers shrugged his shoulders; these patriarchal habits and domestic virtues had no particular charm for him.

"She had plenty of money, had n't she ?" he asked, by way of bringing the conversation into a more rational channel.

"Plenty of money! I should think so. They say her pa gave her fifty thousand pounds down on her wedding-day; not that our master wants money; he 's got enough, and to spare."

"Ah! to be sure," answered Mr. Conyers; "that 's always the way of it. The banker gave her fifty thousand, did he? If Miss Floyd had married a poor devil, now, I don't suppose her father would have given her fifty sixpences."

"Well, no; if she 'd gone against his wishes, I don't suppose he would. He was here in the spring—a nice, white-haired old gentleman, but failing fast."

"Failing fast. And Mrs. Mellish will come into a quarter of a million, at his death, I suppose. Good afternoon, ma'am. It 's a queer world." Mr. Conyers took up his stick, and limped away under the trees, repeating this ejaculation as he went. It was a habit with this gentleman to attribute the good fortune of other people to some eccentricity in the machinery of life, by which he, the only really deserving person in the world, had been deprived of his natural rights. He went through the wood into a meadow where some of the horses under his charge were at grass, and spent upward of an hour lounging about the hedge-rows, sitting on gates, smoking his pipe, and staring at the animals, which seemed about the hardest work he had to do in his capacity of trainer. "It is n't a very hard life, when all 's said and done," he thought, as he looked at a group of mares and foals, who, in their eccentric diversions, were performing a species of Sir Roger de Coverly up and down the meadow. "It is n't a very hard life; for as long as a fellow swears hard and fast at the lads, and gets rid of plenty of oats, he 's right enough. These country gentlemen always judge a man's merits by the

quantity of corn they have to pay for. Feed their horses as fat as pigs, and never enter 'em except among such a set of screws as an active pig could beat, and they 'll swear by you. They 'd think more of having a horse win the Margate plate, or the Hampstead Heath sweepstakes, than if he ran a good fourth in the Derby. Bless their innocent hearts! I should think fellows with plenty of money and no brains must have been invented for the good of fellows with plenty of brains and no money; and that 's how we contrive to keep our equilibrium in the universal see-saw."

Mr. James Conyers, puffing lazy clouds of transparent blue smoke from his lips, and pondering thus, looked as sentimental as if he had been ruminating upon the last three pages of the *Bride of Abydos*, or the death of Paul Dombey. He had that romantic style of beauty peculiar to dark blue eyes and long black lashes, and he could not wonder what he should have for dinner without a dreamy pensiveness in the purple shadows of those deep blue orbs. He had found the sentimentality of his beauty almost of greater use to him than the beauty itself. It was this sentimentality which always put him at an advantage with his employers. He looked like an exiled prince doing menial service in bitterness of spirit and a turned-down collar. He looked like Lara returned to his own domains to train the horses of a usurper. He looked, in short, like anything but what he was — a selfish, good-for-nothing, lazy scoundrel, who was well up in the useful art of doing the minimum of work, and getting the maximum of wages.

He strolled slowly back to his rustic habitation, where he found the softy waiting for him; the kettle boiling upon a handful of bright fire, and some tea-things laid out upon the little round table. Mr. Conyers looked rather contemptuously at the humble preparations.

"I 've mashed the tea for 'ee," said the softy; "I thought you 'd like a coop."

The trainer shrugged his shoulders.

"I can't say I am particularly attached to the cat-lap," he said, laughing; "I 've had rather too much of it when I 've been in training — half-and-half, warm tea, and cold-drawn castor-oil. I 'll send you into Doncaster for some spirits to-morrow, my man — or to-night, perhaps," he added, reflectively, resting his elbow upon the table and his chin in the hollow of his hand.

He sat for some time in this thoughtful attitude, his retainer, Steeve Hargraves, watching him intently all the while, with that half wondering, half admiring stare with which a very ugly creature — a creature so ugly as to know w c is ugly — looks at a very handsome one.

At the close of his reverie, Mr. Conyers

took out a clumsy silver watch, and sat for a few minutes staring vacantly at the dial.

"Close upon six," he muttered at last. "What time do they dine at the house, Steeve ?"

"Seven o'clock," answered the softy.

"Seven o'clock. Then you 'd have time to run there with a message, or a letter, and catch 'em just as they 're going in to dinner."

The softy stared aghast at his new master.

"A message or a letter," he repeated, "for Mr. Mellish ? "

"No; for Mrs. Mellish."

"But I dare n't," exclaimed Stephen Hargraves; "I dare n't go nigh the house, least of all to speak to her. I don't forget the day she horsewhipped me. I 've never seen her since, and I don't want to see her. You think I am a coward, don't 'ee ?" he said, stopping suddenly, and looking at the trainer, whose handsome lips were curved into a contemptuous smile. "You think I 'm a coward, don't 'ee, now ?" he repeated.

"Well. I do n't think you are over valiant," answered Mr. Conyers, "to be afraid of a woman, though she was the veriest devil that ever played fast and loose with a man."

"Shall I tell you what it is I 'm afraid of ?" said Steeve Hargraves, hissing the words through his closed teeth in that unpleasant whisper peculiar to him. "It 's n't Mrs. Mellish. It 's myself. It 's *this*"—he grasped something in the loose pocket of his trowsers as he spoke—"it 's *this*. I 'm afraid to trust myself anigh her, for fear I should spring upon her, and cut her throat from ear to ear. I 've seen her in my dreams sometimes, with her beautiful white throat laid open, and streaming oceans of blood; but, for all that, she 's always had the broken whip in her hand, and she 's always laughed at me. I 've had many a dream about her, but I 've never seen her dead or quiet, and I 've never seen her without the whip."

The contemptuous smile died away from the trainer's lips as Steeve Hargraves made this revelation of his sentiments, and gave place to a darkly thoughtful expression, which overshadowed the whole of his face.

"I 've no such wonderful love for Mrs. Mellish myself," he said; "but she might live to be as old as Methuselah for aught I care, if she 'd"—he muttered something between his teeth, and walked up the little staircase to his bedroom, whistling a popular tune as he went.

He came down again with a dirty-looking leather desk in his hand, which he flung carelessly on to the table. It was stuffed with crumpled, untidy-looking letters and papers, from among which he had considerable difficulty in selecting a tolerably clean sheet of note-paper.

"You 'll take a letter to Mrs. Mellish, my friend," he said to Stephen, stooping over the table and writing as he spoke, "and you 'll please to deliver it safely into her own hands. The windows will all be open this sultry weather, and you can watch till you see her in the drawing-room; and when you do, contrive to beckon her out, and give her this."

He had folded the sheet of paper by this time, and had sealed it carefully in an adhesive envelope.

"There 's no need of any address," he said, as he handed the letter to Steeve Hargraves; "you know who it 's for, and you won't give it to anybody else. There, get along with you. She 'll say nothing to *you*, man, when she sees who the letter comes from."

The softy looked darkly at his new employer; but Mr. James Conyers rather piqued himself upon a quality which he called determination, but which his traducers designated obstinacy, and he made up his mind that no one but Steeve Hargraves should carry the letter.

"Come," he said, "no nonsense, Mr. Stephen. Remember this: if I choose to employ you, and if I choose to send you on any errand whatsoever, there 's no one in that house will dare to question my right to do it. Get along with you."

He pointed as he spoke, with the stem of his pipe, to the Gothic roofs and ivied chimneys of the old house gleaming among a mass of foliage. "Get along with you, Mr. Stephen, and bring me an answer to that letter," he added, lighting his pipe, and seating himself in his favorite attitude upon the window-sill—an attitude which, like everything about him, was a half careless, half defiant protest of his superiority to his position. "You need n't wait for a written answer. Yes or no will be quite enough, you may tell Mrs. Mellish."

The softy whispered something half inaudible between his teeth; but he took the letter, and, pulling his shabby rabbit-skin cap over his eyes, walked slowly off in the direction to which Mr. Conyers had pointed, with a half-contemptuous action, a few moments before.

"A queer fish," muttered the trainer, lazily watching the awkward figure of his attendant; "a queer fish; but it 's rather hard if I can't manage *him*. I 've twisted his betters round my little finger before to-day."

Mr. Conyers forgot that there are some natures which, although inferior in everything else, are strong by reason of their stubbornness, and not to be twisted out of their natural crookedness by any trick of management or skilfulness of handling.

The evening was sunless, but sultry; there was a lowering darkness in the leaden sky, and an unnatural stillness in the atmosphere that prophesied the coming of a storm. The elements were taking breath for the struggle, and lying silently in wait against the wreak-ing of their fury. It would come by and by, the signal for the outburst, in a long, crackling peal of thunder, that would shake the distant hills and flutter every leaf in the wood.

The trainer looked with an indifferent eye at the ominous aspect of the heavens. "I must go down to the stables, and send some of the boys to get the horses under shelter," he said; "there 'll be a storm before long." He took his stick and limped out of the cottage, still smoking; indeed, there were very few hours in the day, and not many during the night, in which Mr. Conyers was unprovided with his pipe or cigar.

Steeve Hargraves walked very slowly along the narrow pathway which led across the Park to the flower-garden and lawn before the house. This north side of the Park was wilder and less well-kept than the rest; but the thick undergrowth swarmed with game, and the young hares flew backward and forward across the pathway, startled by the softy's shambling tread, while every now and then the partridges rose in pairs from the tangled grass, and skimmed away under the low roof of foliage.

"If I was to meet Mr. Mellish's keeper here, he 'd look at me black enough, I dare say," muttered the softy, "though I a'n't after the game. Looking at a pheasant 's high treason in his mind, curse him."

He put his hands low down in his pockets, as if scarcely able to resist the temptation to wring the neck of a splendid cock-pheasant that was strutting through the high grass, with a proud serenity of manner that implied a knowledge of the game-laws. The trees on the north side of the Park formed a species of leafy wall which screened the lawn, so that, coming from this northern side, the softy emerged at once from the shelter into the smooth grass bordering this lawn, which was separated from the Park by an invisible fence.

As Steeve Hargraves, still sheltered from observation by the trees, approached this place, he saw that his errand was shortened, for Mrs. Mellish was leaning upon a low iron gate, with the dog Bow-wow, the dog that he had beaten, at her side.

He had left the narrow pathway and struck in among the undergrowth, in order to make a shorter cut to the flower-garden, and as he came from under the shelter of the low branches which made a leafy cave about him, he left a long track of parted grass behind him, like the track of the footstep of a tiger, or the trail of a slow, ponderous serpent creeping toward its prey.

Aurora looked up at the sound of the shambling footsteps, and, for the second time since she had beaten him, she encountered the gaze of the softy. She was very pale, almost as pale as her white dress, which was unenli-

vened by any scrap of color, and which hung about her in loose folds that gave a statuesque grace to her figure. She was dressed with such evident carelessness that every fold of muslin seemed to tell how far away her thoughts had been when that hasty toilet was made. Her black brows contracted as she looked at the softy.

"I thought Mr. Mellish had dismissed you," she said, "and that you had been forbidden to come here."

"Yes, ma'am, Muster Mellish did turn me out of the house I 'd lived in, man and boy, nigh upon forty year, but I 've got a new place now, and my new master sent me to you with a letter."

Watching the effect of his words, the softy saw a leaden change come over the pale face of his listener.

"What new master?" she asked.

Steeve Hargraves lifted his hand and pointed across his shoulder. She watched the slow motion of that clumsy hand, and her eyes seemed to grow larger as she saw the direction to which it pointed.

"Your new master is the trainer, James Conyers, the man who lives at the north lodge?" she said.

"Yes, ma'am."

"What does he want with you?" she asked.

"I keep his place in order for him, ma'am, and run errands for him; and I 've brought a letter."

"A letter? Ah! yes, give it me."

The softy handed her the envelope. She took it slowly, without removing her eyes from his face, but watching him with a fixed and earnest look that seemed as if it would have fathomed something beneath the dull red eyes which met hers — a look that betrayed some doubtful terror hidden in her own breast, and a vague desire to penetrate the secrets of his.

She did not look at the letter, but held it half crushed in the hand hanging by her side.

"You can go," she said.

"I was to wait for an answer."

The black brows contracted again, and this time a bright gleam of fury kindled in the great black eyes.

"There is no answer," she said, thrusting the letter into the bosom of her dress, and turning to leave the gate; "there is no answer, and there shall be none till I choose. Tell your master that."

"It was n't to be a written answer," persisted the softy; "it was to be yes or no; that's all; but I was to be sure and wait for it."

The half-witted creature saw some feeling of hate and fury in her face beyond her contemptuous hatred of himself, and took a savage pleasure in tormenting her. She struck her foot impatiently upon the grass, and, plucking the letter from her breast, tore open the envelope, and read the few lines it contained. Few as they were, she stood for nearly five minutes with the open letter in her hand, separated from the softy by the iron fence, and lost in thought. The silence was only broken during this pause by an occasional growl from the mastiff, who lifted his heavy lip and showed his feeble teeth for the edification of his old enemy.

She tore the letter into a hundred morsels, and flung it from her before she spoke. "Yes," she said at last; "tell your master that."

Steeve Hargraves touched his cap, and went back through the grassy trail he had left, to carry this message to the trainer.

"She hates me bad enough," he muttered, as he stopped once to look back at the quiet white figure on the lawn, "but she hates him worse."

CHAPTER XVIII.

OUT IN THE RAIN.

The second dinner-bell rang five minutes after the softy had left Aurora, and Mr. John Mellish came out upon the lawn to look for his wife. He came whistling across the grass, and whisking the roses with his pocket-handkerchief in very gayety of heart. He had quite forgotten the anguish of that miserable morning after the receipt of Mr. Pastern's letter. He had forgotten all but that his Aurora was the loveliest and dearest of women, and that he trusted her with the boundless faith of his big, honest heart. "Why should I doubt such a noble, impetuous creature?" he thought; "does n't every feeling and every sentiment write itself upon her lovely, expressive face in characters the veriest fool could read? If I please her, what bright smiles light up in her black eyes! If I vex her—as I do, poor awkward idiot that I am, a hundred times a day—how the two black arches contract over her pretty impertinent nose, while the red lips pout defiance and disdain! Shall I doubt her because she keeps one secret from me, and freely tells me I must for ever remain ignorant of it, when an artful woman would try to set my mind at rest with some shallow fiction invented to deceive me? Heaven bless her! no doubt of her shall ever darken my life again, come what may."

It was easy for Mr. Mellish to make this mental vow, believing fully that the storm was past, and that lasting fair weather had set in.

"Lolly, darling," he said, winding his great arm round his wife's waist, "I thought I had lost you."

She looked up at him with a sad smile.

"Would it grieve you much, John," she said, in a low voice, "if you were really to lose me?"

He started as if he had been struck, and looked anxiously at her pale face.

"Would it grieve me, Lolly!" he repeated; "not for long; for the people who came to your funeral would come to mine. But, my darling, my darling, what can have made you ask this question? Are you ill, dearest? You have been looking pale and tired for the last few days, and I have thought nothing of it. What a careless wretch I am!"

"No, no, John," she said, "I don't mean that. I know you would grieve dear, if I were to die. But suppose something were to happen which would separate us for ever—something which would compel me to leave this place never to return to it—what then?"

"What then, Lolly?" answered her husband, gravely. "I would rather see your coffin laid in the empty niche beside my mother's in the vault yonder"—he pointed in the direction of the parish church, which was close to the gates of the Park—"than I would part with you thus. I would rather know you to be dead and happy than I would endure any doubt about your fate. Oh, my darling, why do you speak of these things? I could n't part with you—I could n't. I would rather take you in my arms and plunge with you into the pond in the wood; I would rather send a bullet into your heart, and see you lying murdered at my feet."

"John, John, my dearest and truest," she said, her face lighting up with a new brightness, like the sudden breaking of the sun through a leaden cloud, "not another word, dear; we will never part. Why should we? There is very little upon this wide earth that money can not buy, and it shall help to buy our happiness. We will never part, darling, never."

She broke into a joyous laugh as she watched his anxious, half-wondering face.

"Why, you foolish John, how frightened you look!" she said. "Have n't you discovered yet that I like to torment you now and then with such questions as these, just to see your big blue eyes open to their widest extent? Come, dear; Mrs. Powell' will look white thunder at us when we go in, and make some meek conventional reply to our apologies for this delay, to the effect that she does n't care in the least how long she waits for dinner, and that, on the whole, she would rather never have any dinner at all. Is n't it strange, John, how that woman hates me?"

"Hates you, dear, when you 're so kind to her!"

"But she hates me for being kind to her, John. If I were to give her my diamond necklace, she 'd hate me for having it to give. She hates us because we 're rich, and young, and handsome," said Aurora, laughing, "and the very opposite of her namby-pamby, pale-faced self."

It was strange that from this moment Aurora seemed to regain her natural gayety of spirits, and to be what she had been before the receipt of Mr. Pastern's letter. Whatever dark cloud had hovered over her head since the day upon which that simple epistle had caused such a terrible effect, that threatening shadow seemed to have been suddenly removed. Mrs. Walter Powell was not slow to perceive this change. The eyes of love, clear-sighted though they may be, are dull indeed beside the eyes of hate. *Those* are never deceived. Aurora had wandered out of the drawing-room, listless and dispirited, to stroll wearily upon the lawn — Mrs. Powell, seated in one of the windows, had watched her every movement, and had seen her in the distance speaking to some one (she had been unable to distinguish the softy from her post of observation) — and this same Aurora returned to the house almost another creature. There was a look of determination about the beautiful mouth (which female critics called too wide), a look not usual to the rosy lips, and a resolute brightness in the eyes, which had some significance surely. Mrs. Powell thought, if she could only have found the key to that hidden meaning. Ever since Aurora's brief illness the poor woman had been groping for this key — groping in mazy darknesses which baffled her utmost powers of penetration. Who and what was this groom, that Aurora should write to him, as she most decidedly had written? Why was he to express no surprise, and what cause could there be for his expressing any surprise in the simple economy of Mellish Park? The mazy darknesses were more impenetrable than the blackest night, and Mrs. Powell wellnigh gave up all hope of ever finding any clew to the mystery. And now, behold, a new complication had arisen in Aurora's altered spirits. John Mellish was delighted with this alteration. He talked and laughed until the glasses near him vibrated with his noisy mirth. He drank so much sparkling Moselle that his butler Jarvis (who had grown gray in the service of the old squire, and had poured out Master John's first glass of Champagne) refused at last to furnish him with any more of that beverage, offering him in its stead some very expensive Hock, the name of which was in fourteen unpronounceable syllables, and which John tried to like, but did n't.

"We 'll fill the house with visitors for the shooting-season, Lolly, darling," said Mr. Mellish. "If they come on the first of September, they 'll all be comfortably settled for the Leger. The dear old dad will come of course, and trot about on his white pony like the best of men and bankers in Christendom. Captain and Mrs. Bulstrode will come too; and we shall see how our little Lucy looks, and whether solemn Talbot bears her in the silence of the matrimonial chamber. Then there 's Hunter, and a host of fellows; and

you must write me a list of any nice people you 'd like to ask down here, and we 'll have a glorious autumn — won't we, Lolly ?"

"I hope so, dear," said Mrs. Mellish, after a little pause, and a repetition of John's eager question. She had not been listening very attentively to John's plans for the future, and she startled him rather by asking him a question very wide from the subject upon which he had been speaking.

"How long do the fastest vessels take going to Australia, John ?" she asked, quietly.

Mr. Mellish stopped with his glass in his hand to stare at his wife as she asked this question.

"How long do the fastest vessels take to go to Australia ?" he repeated. "Good gracious me, Lolly, how should I know ? Three weeks or a month — no, I mean three months; but, in mercy's name, Aurora, why do you want to know ?"

"The average length of the voyage is, I believe, about three months; but some fast-sailing packets do it in seventy, or even in sixty-eight days," interposed Mrs. Powell, looking sharply at Aurora's abstracted face from under cover of her white eyelashes.

"But why, in goodness name, do you want to know, Lolly ?" repeated John Mellish. "You don't want to go to Australia, and you don't know anybody who 's going to Australia ?"

"Perhaps Mrs. Mellish is interested in the Female Emigration movement," suggested Mrs. Powell: "it is a most delightful work."

Aurora replied neither to the direct nor the indirect question. The cloth had been removed (for no modern customs had ever disturbed the conservative economy of Mellish Park), and Mrs. Mellish sat, with a cluster of pale cherries in her hand, looking at the reflection of her own face in the depths of the shining mahogany.

"Lolly !" exclaimed John Mellish, after watching his wife for some minutes, "you are as grave as a judge. What can you be thinking of ?"

She looked up at him with a bright smile, and rose to leave the dining-room.

"I 'll tell you one of these days, John," she said. "Are you coming with us, or are you going out upon the lawn to smoke ?"

"If you 'll come with me, dear," he answered, returning her smile with a frank glance of unchangeable affection, which always beamed in his eyes when they rested on his wife. "I 'll go out and smoke a cigar if you 'll come with me, Lolly."

"You foolish old Yorkshireman," said Mrs. Mellish, laughing, "I verily believe you 'd like me to smoke one of your choice Manillas, by way of keeping you company."

"No, darling. I 'd never wish to see you do anything that did n't square — that was n't compatible," interposed Mr. Mellish gravely, "with the manners of the noblest lady, and the duties of the truest wife in England. If I love to see you ride across country with a red feather in your hat, it is because I think that the good old sport of English gentlemen was meant to be shared by their wives rather than by people whom I would not like to name, and because there is a fair chance that the sight of your Spanish hat and scarlet plume at the meet may go some way toward keeping Miss Wilhelmina de Lancy (who was born plain Scroggins, and christened Sarah) out of the field. I think our British wives and mothers might have the battle in their own hands, and win the victory for themselves and their daughters, if they were a little braver in standing to their ground—if they were not quite so tenderly indulgent to the sins of eligible young noblemen, and, in their estimate of a man's qualifications for the marriage state, were not so entirely guided by the figures in his banker's book. It's a sad world, Lolly, but John Mellish, of Mellish Park, was never meant to set it right."

Mr. Mellish stood on the threshold of a glass door which opened to a flight of steps leading to the lawn as he delivered himself of this homily, the gravity of which was quite at variance with the usual tenor of his discourse. He had a cigar in his hand, and was going to light it, when Aurora stopped him.

"John, dear," she said, "my most unbusiness-like of darlings, have you forgotten that poor Langley is so anxious to see you, that he may give up your old accounts before the new trainer takes the stable business into his hands? He was here half an hour before dinner, and begged that you would see him to-night."

Mr. Mellish shrugged his shoulders.

"Langley 's as honest a fellow as ever breathed," he said. "I don't want to look into his accounts. I know what the stable costs me yearly on an average, and that 's enough."

"But for his satisfaction, dear."

"Well, well, Lolly, to-morrow morning, then."

"No, dear, I want you to ride out with me to-morrow."

"To-morrow evening."

"'You meet the captains at the Citadel,'" said Aurora, laughing; "that is to say, you dine at Holmbush with Colonel Pevensey. Come, darling, I insist on your being business-like for once in a way; come to your *sanctum sanctorum*, and we 'll send for Langley, and look into the accounts."

The pretty tyrant linked her arm in his, and led him to the other end of the house, and into the very room in which she had swooned away at the hearing of Mr. Pastern's letter. She looked thoughtfully out at the dull evening sky as she closed the windows. The storm had not yet come, but the ominous clouds still brooded low over the earth, and the sultry atmosphere was heavy and airless. Mrs. Mellish made a wonderful show of her business habits, and appeared to be very much interested in the mass of corn-chandlers', veterinary surgeons', saddlers', and harness-makers' accounts with which the old trainer respectfully bewildered his master. But about ten minutes after John had settled himself to his weary labor Aurora threw down the pencil with which she had been working a calculation (by a process of so wildly original a nature as to utterly revolutionize Cocker, and annihilate the hackneyed notion that twice two are four), and floated lightly out of the room, with some vague promise of coming back presently, leaving Mr. Mellish to arithmetic and despair.

Mrs. Walter Powell was seated in the drawing-room reading when Aurora entered the apartment with a large black lace shawl wrapped about her head and shoulders. Mrs. Mellish had evidently expected to find the room empty, for she started and drew back at the sight of the pale-faced widow, who was seated in a distant window, making the most of the last faint rays of summer twilight. Aurora paused for a moment a few paces within the door, and then walked deliberately across the room toward the farthest window from that at which Mrs. Powell was seated.

"Are you going out in the garden this dull evening, Mrs. Mellish?" asked the ensign's widow.

Aurora stopped half way between the window and the door to answer her.

"Yes," she said coldly.

"Allow me to advise you not to go far. We are going to have a storm."

"I don't think so."

"What, my dear Mrs. Mellish, not with that thunder-cloud yonder?"

"I will take my chance of being caught in it, then. The weather has been threatening all the afternoon. The house is insupportable to-night."

"But you will not surely go far?"

Mrs. Mellish did not appear to overhear this remonstrance. She hurried through the open window, and out upon the lawn, striking northward toward that little iron gate across which she had talked to the softy.

The arch of the leaden sky seemed to contract above the tree-tops in the Park, shutting in the earth as if with a roof of hot iron, after the fashion of those cunningly contrived metal torture-chambers which we read of; but the rain had not yet come.

"What can take her into the garden on such an evening as this?" thought Mrs. Powell, as she watched the white dress receding in the dusky twilight. "It will be dark in ten minutes, and she is not usually so fond of going out alone."

The ensign's widow laid down the book in

which she had appeared so deeply interested, and went to her own room, where she selected a comfortable gray cloak from a heap of primly-folded garments in her capacious wardrobe. She muffled herself in this cloak, hurried down stairs with a soft but rapid step, and went out into the garden through a little lobby near John Mellish's room. The blinds in the little *sanctum* were not drawn down, and Mrs. Powell could see the master of the house bending over his paper under the light of a reading-lamp, with the rheumatic trainer sitting by his side. It was by this time quite dark, but Aurora's white dress was faintly visible upon the other side of the lawn.

Mrs. Mellish was standing beside the little iron gate when the ensign's widow emerged from the house. The white dress was motionless for some time, and the pale watcher, lurking under the shade of a long veranda, began to think that her trouble was wasted, and that perhaps, after all, Aurora had no special purpose in this evening ramble.

Mrs. Walter Powell felt cruelly disappointed. Always on the watch for some clew to the secret whose existence she had discovered, she had fondly hoped that even this unseasonable ramble might be some link in the mysterious chain she was so anxious to fit together. But it appeared that she was mistaken. The unseasonable ramble was very likely nothing more than one of Aurora's caprices — a womanly foolishness signifying nothing.

No! The white dress was no longer motionless, and in the unnatural stillness of the hot night Mrs. Powell heard the distant, scrooping noise of a hinge revolving slowly, as if guided by a cautious hand. Mrs. Mellish had opened the iron gate, and had passed to the other side of the invisible barrier which separated the gardens from the Park. In another moment she had disappeared under the shadow of the trees which made a belt about the lawn.

Mrs. Powell paused, almost terrified by her unlooked-for discovery.

What, in the name of all that was darkly mysterious, could Mrs. Mellish have to do between nine and ten o'clock on the north side of the Park — the wildly-kept, deserted north side, in which, from year's end to year's end, no one but the keepers ever walked.

The blood rushed hotly up to Mrs. Powell's pale face as she suddenly remembered that the disused, dilapidated lodge upon this north side had been given to the new trainer as a residence. Remembering this was nothing, but remembering this in connection with that mysterious letter signed "A" was enough to send a thrill of savage, horrible joy through the dull veins of the dependent. What should she do? Follow Mrs. Mellish, and discover where she was going? How far would this be a safe thing to attempt?

She turned back and looked once more through the windows of John's room. He was still bending over the papers, still in an apparently hopeless confusion of mind. There seemed little chance of his business being finished very quickly. The starless night and her dark dress alike sheltered the spy from observation.

"If I were close behind her, she would never see me," she thought.

She struck across the lawn to the iron gate, and passed into the Park. The brambles and the tangled undergrowth caught at her dress as she paused for a moment looking about her in the summer night.

There was no trace of Aurora's white figure among the leafy alleys stretching in wild disorder before her.

"I 'll not attempt to find the path she took," thought Mrs. Powell; "I know where to find her."

She groped her way into the narrow footpath leading to the lodge. She was not sufficiently familiar with the place to take the short cut which the softy had made for himself through the grass that afternoon, and she was some time walking from the iron gate to the lodge.

The front windows of this rustic lodge faced the road and the disused north gates; the back of the building looked toward the path down which Mrs. Powell went, and the two small windows in this back wall were both dark.

The ensign's widow crept softly round to the front, looked about her cautiously, and listened. There was no sound but the occasional rustle of a leaf, tremulous even in the still atmosphere, as if by some internal prescience of the coming storm. With a slow, careful footstep, she stole toward the little rustic window, and looked into the room within.

She had not been mistaken when she had said that she knew where to find Aurora.

Mrs. Mellish was standing with her back to the window. Exactly opposite to her sat James Conyers, the trainer, in an easy attitude, and with his pipe in his mouth. The little table was between them, and the one candle which lighted the room was drawn close to Mr. Conyers' elbow, and had evidently been used by him for the lighting of his pipe. Aurora was speaking. The eager listener could hear her voice, but not her words; and she could see by the trainer's face that he was listening intently. He was listening intently; but a dark frown contracted his handsome eyebrows, and it was very evident that he was not too well satisfied with the bent of the conversation.

He looked up when Aurora ceased speaking, shrugged his shoulders, and took his pipe out of his mouth. Mrs. Powell, with her pale face close against the window-pane, watched him intently.

He pointed with a careless gesture to an empty chair near Aurora, but she shook her head contemptuously, and suddenly turned toward the window; so suddenly that Mrs. Powell had scarcely time to recoil into the darkness before Aurora had unfastened the iron latch and flung the narrow casement open.

"I can not endure this intolerable heat," she exclaimed, impatiently; "I have said all I have to say, and need only wait for your answer."

"You don't give me much time for consideration," he said, with an insolent coolness which was in strange contrast to the restless vehemence of her manner. "What sort of answer do you want?"

"Yes or no."

"Nothing more?"

"No, nothing more. You know my conditions; they are all written here," she added, putting her hand upon an open paper which lay upon the table; "they are all written clearly enough for a child to understand. Will you accept them? Yes or no?"

"That depends upon circumstances," he answered, filling his pipe, and looking admiringly at the nail of his little finger as he pressed the tobacco into the bowl.

"Upon what circumstances?"

"Upon the inducement which you offer, my dear Mrs. Mellish."

"You mean the price?"

"That 's a low expression," he said, laughing; "but I suppose we both mean the same thing. The inducement must be a strong one which will make me do all that"—he pointed to the written paper — "and it must take the form of solid cash. How much is it to be?"

"That is for you to say. Remember what I have told you. Decline to-night, and I telegraph to my father to-morrow morning, telling him to alter his will."

"Suppose the old gentleman should be carried off in the interim, and leave that pleasant sheet of parchment standing as it is. I hear that he 's old and feeble; it might be worth while calculating the odds upon such an event. I 've risked my money on a worst chance before to-night."

She turned upon him with so dark a frown as he said this that the insolently heartless words died upon his lips, and left him looking at her gravely.

"Egad," he said, "you 're as great a devil as ever you were. I doubt if that is n't a good offer after all. Give me ten thousand down, and I 'll take it."

"Ten thousand pounds!"

"I ought to have said twenty, but I 've always stood in my own light."

Mrs. Powell, crouching down beneath the open casement, had heard every word of this brief dialogue; but at this juncture, half-forgetful of all danger in her eagerness to listen, she raised her head until it was nearly on a level with the window-sill. As she did so, she recoiled with a sudden thrill of terror. She felt a puff of hot breath upon her cheek, and the garments of a man rustling against her own.

She was not the only listener.

The second spy was Stephen Hargraves, the softy.

"Hush!" he whispered, grasping Mrs. Powell by the wrist, and pinning her in her crouching attitude by the muscular force of his horny hand; "it 's only me, Steeve the Softy, you know; the stable-helper that *she*" (he hissed out the personal pronoun with such a furious impetus that it seemed to whistle sharply through the stillness) — "the fondy that she horsewhipped. I know you, and I know you 're here to listen. He sent me into Doncaster to fetch this " (he pointed to a bottle under his arm); "he thought it would take me four or five hours to go and get back; but I ran all the way, for I knew there was summat oop."

He wiped his streaming face with the ends of his coarse neckerchief as he finished speaking. His breath came in panting gasps, and Mrs. Powell could hear the laborious beating of his heart in the stillness.

"I won't tell o' you," he said, "and you won't tell o' me. I 've got the stripes upon my shoulder where she cut me with the whip to this day; I look at 'm sometimes, and they help to keep me in mind. She 's a fine madam, a'n't she, and a great lady too? Ay, sure she is; but she comes to meet her husband's servant on the sly, after dark, for all that. Maybe the day is n't far off when *she 'll* be turned away from these gates, and warned off this ground, and the merciful Lord send that I live to see it. Hush!"

With her wrist still pinioned in his strong grasp, he motioned her to be silent, and bent his pale face forward, every feature rigid in the listening expectancy of his hungry gaze.

"Listen," he whispered; "listen! Every fresh word damns her deeper than the last."

The trainer was the first to speak after this pause in the dialogue within the cottage. He had quietly smoked out his pipe, and had emptied the ashes of his tobacco upon the table before he took up the thread of the conversation at the point at which he had dropped it.

"Ten thousand pounds," he said; "that is the offer, and I think it ought to be taken freely. Ten thousand down, in Bank of England notes (fives and tens; higher figures might be awkward), or sterling coin of the realm. You understand; ten thousand down. That 's *my* alternative; or I leave this place to-morrow morning, with all belonging to me."

"By which course you would get nothing," said Mrs. John Mellish, quietly.

"Should n't I? What does the chap in the play get for his trouble when the blackamoor smothers his wife? I should get nothing—but my revenge upon a tiger-cat whose claws have left a mark upon me that I shall carry to my grave." He lifted his hair with careless gesture of his hand, and pointed to a scar upon his forehead — a white mark, barely visible in the dim light of the tallow-candle. "I 'm a good-natured, easy-going fellow, Mrs John Mellish, but I don't forget. Is it to be the ten thousand pounds, or war to the knife?"

Mrs Powell waited eagerly for Aurora's answer; but before it came a round, heavy rain-drop pattered upon the light hair of the ensign's widow. The hood of her cloak had fallen back, leaving her head uncovered. This one large drop was the warning of the coming storm. The signal peal of thunder rumbled slowly and hoarsely in the distance, and a pale flash of lightning trembled upon the white faces of the two listeners.

"Let me go," whispered Mrs Powell, "let me go, I must get back to the house before the rain begins."

The softly slowly relaxed his iron grip upon her wrist. He had held it unconsciously in his utter abstraction to all things except the two speakers in the cottage.

Mrs Powell rose from her knees, and crept noiselessly away from the lodge. She remembered the vital necessity of getting back to the house before Aurora, and of avoiding the shower. Her wet garments would betray her, she did not succeed in escaping the coming storm. She was of spare, wizen figure, encumbered with no superfluous flesh, and she ran rapidly along the narrow sheltered pathway leading to the iron gate through which she had followed Aurora.

The heavy rain-drops fell at long intervals upon the leaves. A second and a third peal of thunder rattled along the earth like the terrible roar of some hungry animal creeping nearer and nearer to its prey. Blue flashes of faint lightning lit up the tangled intricacies of the wood, but the fullest fury of the storm had not yet burst forth.

The rain-drops came at shorter intervals as Mrs Powell passed out of the wood, through the little iron gate, faster still as she hurried across the lawn, faster yet as she reached the lobby-door, which she had left ajar an hour before, and sat down panting upon a little bench within, to recover her breath before she went any farther. She was still sitting on this bench, when the fourth peal of thunder shook the low roof above her head, and the rain dropped from the starless sky with such rushing impetus that it seemed as if a huge trap-door had been opened in the heavens, and celestial ocean let down to flood the earth.

"I think my lady will be nicely caught," muttered Mrs Walter Powell.

She threw her cloak aside upon the lobby-bench, and went through a passage leading to the hall. One of the servants was shutting the hall-door.

"Have you shut the drawing-room windows, Wilson?" she asked.

"No, ma'am; I am afraid Mrs Mellish is out in the rain. Jarvis is getting ready to go and look for her, with a lantern and the gig-umbrella."

"Then Jarvis can stop where he is; Mrs Mellish came in half an hour ago. You may shut all the windows, and close the house for the night."

"Yes, ma'am."

"By the by, what o'clock is it, Wilson? My watch is slow."

"A quarter past ten, ma'am, by the dining-room clock."

The man locked the hall-door, and put up an immense iron bar which worked with some rather complicated machinery, and had a bell hanging at one end of it, for the frustration of all burglarious and designing ruffians.

From the hall the man went to the drawing-room, where he carefully fastened the long range of windows; from the drawing-room to the lobby, and from the lobby to the dining-room, where he locked the half-glass door opening into the garden. This being done, all communication between the house and the garden was securely cut off.

"He shall know of her goings on, at any rate," thought Mrs Powell, as she dogged the footsteps of the servant to see that he did his work. The Mellish household did not take very kindly to this deputy mistress, and when the footman went back to the servants' hall, he informed his colleagues that sura was pryin' and pokin' about sharper than hever, and watchin' of a feller like a hold 'ouse-cat. Mr Wilson was a Cockney, and had been newly imported into the establishment.

When the ensign's widow had seen the last bolt driven home to its socket, and the last key turned in its lock, she went back to the drawing-room and seated herself at the lamp-lit table, with some delicate morsel of old-maidish fancy-work, which seemed to be the converse of Penelope's embroidery, as it appeared to advance at night and retrograde by day. She had hastily smoothed her hair and rearranged her dress, and she looked as uncomfortably neat as when she came down to breakfast in the fresh primness of her matutinal toilette.

She had been sitting at her work for about ten minutes when John Mellish entered the room, emerging weary but triumphant from his struggle with the simple rules of multiplication and subtraction. Mr Mellish had evidently suffered severely in the contest. His thick brown hair was tumbled into a rough mass that stood nearly upright upon his head, his cravat was untied, and his shirt collar was thrown open for the relief of his capacious throat; and these and many other marks of the struggle he bore upon him when he entered the drawing-room.

"I 've broken loose from school at last, Mrs. Powell," he said, flinging his big frame upon one of the sofas, to the imminent peril of the German spring cushions; "I 've broken away before the flag dropped, for Langley would have liked to keep me there till midnight. He followed me to the door of this room with fourteen bushels of oats that was down in the corn-chandler's account and was not down in the book he keeps to check the corn-chandler. Why the deuce don't he put it down in his book and make it right, then, I ask, instead of bothering me? What 's the good of his keeping an account to check the corn-chandler if he don't make his account the same as the corn-chandler's? But it 's all over," he added, with a great sigh of relief, "it 's all over; and all I can say is, I hope the new trainer is n't honest."

"Do you know much of the new trainer, Mr. Mellish?" asked Mrs. Powell, blandly, rather as if she wished to amuse her employer by the exertion of her conversational powers than for the gratification of any mundane curiosity.

"Deuced little," answered John indifferently. "I have n't even seen the fellow yet; but John Pastern recommended him, and he 's sure to be all right; besides, Aurora knows the man; he was in her father's service once."

"Oh, indeed!" said Mrs. Powell, giving the two insignificant words a significant little jerk; "oh, indeed! Mrs. Mellish knows him, does she? Then of course he 's a trustworthy person. He 's a remarkably handsome young man."

"Remarkably handsome, is he?" said Mr. Mellish, with a careless laugh. "Then I suppose all the maids will be falling in love with him, and neglecting their work to look out of the windows that open on to the stable-yard, hey? That 's the sort of thing when a man has a handsome groom, a'n't it? Susan and Sarah, and all the rest of 'em, take to cleaning the windows, and wearing new ribbons in their caps?"

"I don't know anything about that, Mr. Mellish," answered the ensign's widow, simpering over her work as if the question they were discussing was so very far away that it was impossible for her to be serious about it; "but my experience has thrown me into a very large number of families." (She said this with perfect truth, as she had occupied so many situations that her enemies had come to declare she was unable to remain in any one household above a twelvemonth, by reason of her employer's discovery of her real nature.) "I have occupied positions of trust and confidence," continued Mrs. Powell, "and

I regret to say that I have seen much domestic misery arise from the employment of handsome servants, whose appearance and manners are superior to their station. Mr. Conyers is not at all the sort of person I should like to see in a household in which I had the charge of young ladies."

A sick, half-shuddering faintness crept through John's herculean frame as Mrs. Powell expressed herself thus; so vague a feeling that he scarcely knew whether it was mental or physical, any better than he knew what it was that he disliked in this speech of the ensign's widow. The feeling was as transient as it was vague. John's honest blue eyes looked wonderingly round the room.

"Where 's Aurora?" he said; "gone to bed?"

"I believe Mrs. Mellish has retired to rest," Mrs. Powell answered.

"Then I shall go too. The place is as dull as a dungeon without her," said Mr. Mellish, with agreeable candor. "Perhaps you 'll be good enough to make me a glass of brandy and water before I go, Mrs. Powell, for I 've got the cold shivers after those accounts."

He rose to ring the bell; but, before he had gone three paces from the sofa, an impatient knocking at the closed outer shutters of one of the windows arrested his footsteps.

"Who, in mercy's name, is that?" he exclaimed, staring at the direction from which the noise came, but not attempting to respond to the summons.

Mrs. Powell looked up to listen, with a face expressive of nothing but innocent wonder.

The knocking was repeated more loudly and impatiently than before.

"It must be one of the servants," muttered John; "but why does n't he go round to the back of the house? I can't keep the poor devil out upon such a night as this, though," he added, good-naturedly, unfastening the window as he spoke. The sashes opened inward, the Venetian shutters outward. He pushed these shutters open, and looked out into the darkness and the rain.

Aurora, shivering in her drenched garments, stood a few paces from him, with the rain beating down straight and heavily upon her head.

Even in that obscurity her husband recognized her.

"My darling," he cried, "is it you? You out at such a time, and on such a night! Come in, for mercy's sake; you must be drenched to the skin."

She came into the room: the wet hanging in her muslin dress streamed out upon the carpet on which she trod, and the folds of her lace shawl clung tightly about her figure.

"Why did you let them shut the windows?" she said, turning to Mrs. Powell, who had risen, and was looking the picture of lady-like neasiness and sympathy. "You know that I was in the garden."

"Yes, but I thought you had returned, my dear Mrs. Mellish," said the ensign's widow, busying herself with Aurora's wet shawl, which she attempted to remove, but which Mrs. Mellish plucked impatiently away from her. "I saw you go out, certainly, and I saw you leave the lawn in the direction of the north lodge, but I thought you had returned some time since."

The color faded out of John Mellish's face. "The north lodge!" he said. "Have you been to the north lodge?"

"I have been in the *direction of the north lodge*," Aurora answered, with a sneering emphasis upon the words. "Your information is perfectly correct, Mrs. Powell, though I did not know you had done me the honor of watching my actions."

Mr. Mellish did not appear to hear this. He looked from his wife to his wife's companion with a half-bewildered expression—an expression of newly-awakened doubt, of dim, struggling perplexity, which was very painful to see.

"The north lodge!" he repeated; "what were you doing at the north lodge, Aurora?"

"Do you wish me to stand here in my wet clothes while I tell you?" asked Mrs. Mellish, her great black eyes blazing up with indignant pride. "If you want an explanation for Mrs. Powell's satisfaction, I can give it here; only for your own, it will do as well up stairs."

She swept toward the door, trailing her wet shawl after her, but not less queenly, even in her dripping garments (Semiramide and Cleopatra may have been out in wet weather); but at the door she paused and looked back at him.

"I shall want you to take me to London to-morrow, Mr. Mellish," she said. Then, with one haughty toss of her beautiful head, and one bright flash of her glorious eyes, which seemed to say, "Slave, obey and tremble!" she disappeared, leaving Mr. Mellish to follow her, meekly, wonderingly, fearfully, with terrible doubts and anxieties creeping, like venomous living creatures, stealthily into his heart.

CHAPTER XIX.

MONEY MATTERS.

Archibald Floyd was very lonely at Felden Woods without his daughter. He took no pleasure in the long drawing-room, or the billiard-room and library, or the pleasant galleries, in which there were all manner of easy corners, with abutting bay-windows, damask-cushioned oaken benches, china vases as high as tables, all enlivened by the alternately sternly masculine and simperingly feminine faces of those ancestors whose painted representations the banker had bought in Wardour-street. (Indeed, I fear those Scottish warriors, those bewigged worthies of the Northern Circuit, those taper-waisted ladies with pointed stomachers, tucked-up petticoats, pannier hoops, and blue-ribbon bedizened crooks, had been painted to order, and that there were such items in the account of the Wardour-street rococo merchant as, "To one knight banneret, killed at Bosworth, £25 5s.") The old banker, I say, grew sadly weary of his gorgeous mansion, which was of little avail to him without Aurora.

People are not so very much happier for living in handsome houses, though it is generally considered such a delightful thing to occupy a mansion which would be large enough for a hospital, and take your simple meal at the end of a table long enough to accommodate a board of railway directors. Archibald Floyd could not sit beside both the fireplaces in his long drawing-room, and he felt strangely lonely looking from the easy-chair on the hearth-rug, through a vista of velvet-pile and satin-damask, walnut-wood, buhl, malachite, china, parian, crystal, and ormolu, at that solitary second hearth-rug and those empty easy-chairs. He shivered in his dreary grandeur. His five-and-forty by thirty feet of velvet-pile might have been a patch of yellow sand in the great Sahara for any pleasure he derived from its occupation. The billiard-room, perhaps, was worse; for the cues and balls were every one made precious by Aurora's touch; and there was a great fine drawn seam upon the green cloth, which marked the spot where Miss Floyd had ripped it open what time she made her first juvenile essay at billiards.

The banker locked the doors of both these splendid apartments, and gave the keys to his housekeeper.

"Keep the rooms in order, Mrs. Richardson," he said, "and keep them thoroughly aired; but I shall only use them when Mr. and Mrs. Mellish come to me."

And, having shut up these haunted chambers, Mr. Floyd retired to that snug little study in which he kept his few relics of the sorrowful past.

It may be said that the Scottish banker was a very stupid old man, and that he might have invited the county families to his gorgeous mansion; that he might have summoned his nephews and their wives, with all grand-nephews and nieces appertaining, and might thus have made the place merry with the sound of fresh young voices, and the long corridors noisy with the patter of restless little feet. He might have lured literary and artistic celebrities to his lonely hearth-rug, and paraded the lions of the London season upon his velvet-pile. He might have entered the political arena, and have had himself nominated for Beckenham, Croydon, or West Wickham. He might have done almost anything; for he had very nearly as much money as Aladdin, and could have carried dishes of uncut diamonds to the father of any princess whom he might take it into his head to marry. He might have done almost anything, this ridiculous old banker; yet he did nothing but sit brooding over his lonely hearth—for he was old and feeble, and he sat by the fire even in the bright summer weather—thinking of the daughter who was far away.

He thanked God for her happy home, for her devoted husband, for her secure and honorable position; and he would have given the last drop of his blood to obtain for her these advantages; but he was, after all, only mortal, and he would rather have had her by his side.

Why did he not surround himself with society, as brisk Mrs. Alexander urged, when she found him looking pale and care-worn?

Why? Because society was not Aurora. Because all the brightest *bon-mots* of all the literary celebrities who have ever walked this earth seemed dull to him when compared with his daughter's idlest babble. Literary lions! Political notabilities! Out upon them! When Sir Edward Bulwer Lytton and Mr. Charles Dickens should call in Mr. Makepeace Thackeray and Mr. Wilkie Collins to assist them in writing a work, in fifteen volumes or so, about Aurora, the banker would be ready to offer them a handsome sum for the copyright. Until then, he cared very little for the best book in Mr. Mudie's collection. When the members of the Legislature should bring their political knowledge to bear upon Aurora, Mr. Archibald Floyd would be happy to listen to them. In the interim, he would have yawned in Lord Palmerston's face, or turned his back upon Earl Russell.

The banker had been a kind uncle, a good master, a warm friend, and a generous patron; but he had never loved any creature except his wife Eliza and the daughter she had left to his care. Life is not long enough to hold many such attachments as these; and the people who love very intensely are apt to concentrate the full force of their affection upon one object. For twenty years this black-eyed girl had been the idol before which the old man had knelt; and now that the divinity is taken away from him, he falls prostrate and desolate before the empty shrine. Heaven knows how bitterly this beloved child had made him suffer, how deeply she had plunged the reckless dagger to the very core of his loving heart, and how freely, gladly, tearfully, and hopefully he had forgiven her. But she had never atoned for the past. It is poor consolation which Lady Macbeth gives to her remorseful husband when she tells him that "what's done can not be undone;" but it is

painfully and terribly true. Aurora could not restore the year which she had taken out of her father's life, and which his anguish and despair had multiplied by ten. She could not restore the equal balance of the mind which had once experienced a shock so dreadful as to shatter its serenity, as we shatter the mechanism of a watch when we let it fall violently to the ground. The watchmaker patches up the damage, and gives us a new wheel here, and a spring there, and sets the hands going again, but they never go so smoothly as when the watch was fresh from the hands of the maker, and they are apt to stop suddenly with no shadow of warning. Aurora could not atone. Whatever the nature of that girlish error which made the mystery of her life, it was not to be undone. She could more easily have baled the ocean dry with a soup-ladle—and I dare say she would gladly have gone to work to spoon out the salt water if by so doing she could have undone that by-gone mischief. But she could not; she could not! Her tears, her penitence, her affection, her respect, her devotion could do much, but they could not do this.

The old banker invited Talbot Bulstrode and his young wife to make themselves at home at Felden, and drive down to the Woods as freely as if the place had been some country mansion of their own. They came sometimes, and Talbot entertained his great-uncle-in-law with the troubles of the Cornish miners, while Lucy sat listening to her husband's talk with unmitigated reverence and delight. Archibald Floyd made his guests very welcome upon these occasions, and gave orders that the oldest and costliest wines in the cellar should be brought out for the captain's entertainment; but sometimes, in the very middle of Talbot's discourse upon political economy, the old man would sigh wearily, and look with a dimly-yearning gaze far away over the tree-tops in a northward direction, toward that distant Yorkshire household in which his daughter was the queen.

Perhaps Mr. Floyd had never quite forgiven Talbot Bulstrode for the breaking off of the match between him and Aurora. The banker had, certainly, of the two suitors, preferred John Mellish; but he would have considered it only correct if Captain Bulstrode had retired from the world upon the occasion of Aurora's marriage, and broken his heart in foreign exile, rather than advertising his indifference by a union with poor little Lucy. Archibald looked wonderingly at his fair-haired niece as she sat before him in the deep bay-window, with the sunshine upon her amber tresses and the crisp folds of her peach-colored silk dress, looking for all the world like one of the painted heroines so dear to the pre-Raphaelite brotherhood, and marvelled how it was that Talbot could have ome to admire her. She was very pretty, ertainly, with pink cheeks, a white nose, and ose-colored nostrils, and a species of beauty hich consists in very careful finishing-off nd picking-out of the features; but oh, how me, how cold, how weak, beside that gyptian goddess, that Assyrian queen with ae flashing eyes and the serpentine coils of urple-black hair!

Talbot Bulstrode was very calm, very quiet, ut apparently sufficiently happy. I use that ord "sufficiently" advisedly. It is a dan- erous thing to be too happy. Your high- ressure happiness, your sixty-miles-an-hour njoyment, is apt to burst up and come to hard end. Better the quietest parliamen- ary train, which starts very early in the iorning, and carries its passengers safe into he terminus when the shades of night come own, than that rabid, rushing express, which oes the journey in a quarter of the time, nt occasionally topples over a bank, or rides ickaback upon a luggage-train in its fiery npetuosity.

Talbot Bulstrode was substantially happier ith Lucy than he ever could have been with .urora. His fair young wife's undemonstra- ve worship of him soothed and flattered him. ler gentle obedience, her entire concurrence i his every thought and whim, set his pride t rest. She was not eccentric, she was not npetuous. If he left her alone all day in the iug little house in Half-Moon street which e had furnished before his marriage, he had o fear of her calling for her horse and ampering away into Rotten Row, with not) much as a groom to attend upon her. She as not strong-minded. She could be happy ithout the society of Newfoundlands and kye terriers. She did not prefer Landseer's og-pictures above all other examples of mod- rn art. She might have walked down Regent :reet a hundred times without being once :mpted to loiter upon the curb-stone and argain with suspicious-looking merchants for "noice leetle dawg." She was altogether entle and womanly, and Talbot had no fear) trust her to her own sweet will, and no need) impress upon her the necessity of lending er feeble little hands to the mighty task of sus- aining the dignity of the Raleigh Bulstrodes. She would cling to him sometimes half ovingly, half timidly, and, looking up with a retty, deprecating smile into his coldly hand- ome face, ask him, falteringly, if he was ally, REALLY happy.

"Yes, my darling girl," the Cornish captain ould answer, being very well accustomed to ae question, "decidedly, very happy."

His calm business-like tone would rather isappoint poor Lucy, and she would vaguely 'ish that her husband had been a little more ke the heroes in the High-Church novels, nd a little less devoted to Adam Smith, Me- 'ulloch, and the Cornish mines.

"But you don't love me as you loved Au- rora, Talbot?" (There were profane people who corrupted the captain's Christian name into "Tal;" but Mrs. Bulstrode was not more likely to avail herself of that disrespectful abbreviation than she was to address her gra- cious sovereign as "Vic.") "But you don't love me as you loved Aurora, Talbot, dear?" the pleasing voice would urge, so tenderly anxious to be contradicted.

"Not as I loved Aurora, perhaps, darling."

"Not as much?"

"As much and better, my pet; with a more enduring and a wiser love."

If this was a little bit of a fib when the captain first said it, is he to be utterly con- demned for the falsehood? How could he resist the loving blue eyes so ready to fill with tears if he had answered coldly; the softly pensive voice, tremulous with emotion; the earnest face; the caressing hand laid so lightly upon his coat-collar? He must have been more than mortal had he given any but loving answers to those loving questions. The day soon came when his answers were no longer tinged with so much as the shadow of falsehood. His little wife crept stealthily, almost imperceptibly into his heart; and if he remembered the fever-dream of the past, it was only to rejoice in the tranquil security of the present.

Talbot Bulstrode and his wife were staying at Felden Woods for a few days during the burning July weather, and sat down to dinner with Mr. Floyd upon the day succeeding the night of the storm. They were disturbed in the very midst of that dinner by the unex- pected arrival of Mr. and Mrs. Mellish, who rattled up to the door in a hired vehicle, just as the second course was being placed upon the table.

Archibald Floyd recognized the first mur- mur of his daughter's voice, and ran out into the hall to welcome her.

She showed no eagerness to throw herself into her father's arms, but stood looking at John Mellish with a weary, absent expression, while the stalwart Yorkshireman allowed himself to be gradually disencumbered of a chaotic load of travelling-bags, sun-umbrellas, shawls, mag- azines, newspapers, and overcoats.

"My darling, my darling!" exclaimed the banker, "what a happy surprise, what an un- expected pleasure!"

She did not answer him, but, with her arms about his neck, looked mournfully into his face.

"She would come," said Mr. John Mellish, addressing himself generally; "she would come. The doose knows why! But she said she must come, and what could I do but bring her? If she asked me to take her to the moon, what could I do but take her? But she would n't bring any luggage to speak of, because we 're going back to-morrow."

"Going back to-morrow!" repeated Mr. Floyd; "impossible."

"Bless your heart!" cried John, "what 's impossible to Lolly? If she wanted to go to the moon, she 'd go, don't I tell you? She 'd have a special engine, or a special balloon, or a special something or other, and she 'd go. When we were in Paris she wanted to see the big fountains play, and she told me to write to the emperor and ask him to have them set going for her. She did, by Jove!"

Lucy Bulstrode came forward to bid her cousin welcome; but I fear that a sharp, jealous pang thrilled through that innocent heart at the thought that those fatal black eyes were again brought to bear upon Talbot's life.

Mrs. Mellish put her arms about her cousin as tenderly as if she had been embracing a child.

"You here, dearest Lucy!" she said. "I am so very glad."

"He loves me," whispered little Mrs. Bulstrode, "and I never, never can tell you how good he is."

"Of course not, my darling," answered Aurora, drawing her cousin aside while Mr. Mellish shook hands with his father-in-law and Talbot Bulstrode. "He is the most glorious of princes, the most perfect of saints, is he not? and you worship him all day; you sing silent hymns in his praise, and perform high mass in his honor, and go about telling his virtues upon an imaginary rosary. Ah! Lucy, how many kinds of love there are; and who shall say which is the best or highest? I see plain, blundering John Mellish yonder with unprejudiced eyes; I know his every fault, I laugh at his every awkwardness. Yes, I laugh now, for he is dropping those things faster than the servants can pick them up."

She stopped to point to poor John's chaotic burden.

"I see all this as plainly as I see the deficiencies of the servant who stands behind my chair; and yet I love him with all my heart and soul, and I would not have one fault corrected, or one virtue exaggerated, for fear it should make him different to what he is."

Lucy Bulstrode gave a little half-resigned sigh.

"What a blessing that my poor cousin is happy," she thought; "and yet how can she be otherwise than miserable with that absurd John Mellish?"

What Lucy meant perhaps was this. How could Aurora be otherwise than wretched in the companionship of a gentleman who had neither a straight nose nor dark hair. Some women never outlive that school-girl infatuation for straight noses and dark hair. Some girls would have rejected Napoleon the Great because he was n't "tall," or would have turned up their noses at the author of *Childe*

Harold if they had happened to see him in a stand-up collar. If Lord Byron had never turned down his collars, would his poetry have been as popular as it was. If Mr. Alfred Tennyson were to cut his hair, would that operation modify our opinion of *The Queen of the May?* Where does that marvellous power of association begin and end? Perhaps there may have been a reason for Aurora's contentment with her commonplace, prosaic husband. Perhaps she had learned at a very early period of her life that there are qualities even more valuable than exquisitely modelled features or clustering locks. Perhaps, having begun to be foolish very early, she had outstripped her contemporaries in the race, and had early learned to be wise.

Archibald Floyd led his daughter and her husband into the dining-room, and the dinner-party sat down again with the two unexpected guests, and the second course was served, and the lukewarm salmon brought in again for Mr. and Mrs. Mellish.

Aurora sat in her old place on her father's right hand. In the old girlish days Miss Floyd had never occupied the bottom of the table, but had loved best to sit close to that foolishly doting parent, pouring out his wine for him in defiance of the servants, and doing other loving offices which were deliciously inconvenient to the old man.

To-day Aurora seemed especially affectionate. That fondly clinging manner had all its ancient charm to the banker. He put down his glass with a tremulous hand to gaze at his darling child, and was dazzled with her beauty, and drunken with the happiness of having her near him.

"But, my darling," he said, by and by, "what do you mean by talking about going back to Yorkshire to-morrow?"

"Nothing, papa, except that I *must* go," answered Mrs. Mellish, determinedly.

"But why come, dear, if you could only stop one night?"

"Because I wanted to see you, dearest father, and to talk to you about—about money matters."

"That 's it," exclaimed John Mellish, with his mouth half full of salmon and lobster-sauce. "That 's it! Money matters! That 's all I can get out of her. She goes out late last night, and roams about the garden, and comes in wet through and through, and says she must come to London about money matters. What should she want with money matters? If she wants money, she can have as much as she wants. She shall write the figures, and I 'll sign the check; or she shall have a dozen blank checks to fill in just as she pleases. What is there upon this earth that I 'd refuse her? If she dipped a little too deep, and put more money than she could afford upon the bay filly, why does n't she come to me, instead of bothering you about oney matters? You know I said so in the ain, Aurora, ever so many times. Why ither your poor papa about it?"

The poor papa looked wonderingly from his ughter to his daughter's husband. What d it all mean? Trouble, vexation, weariss of spirit, humiliation, disgrace?

Ah! Heaven help that enfeebled mind hose strength has been shattered by one eat shock. Archibald Floyd dreaded the ken of a coming storm in every chance oud on the summer's sky.

"Perhaps I may prefer to spend my *own* oney, Mr. John Mellish," answered Aurora, and pay any foolish bets I have chosen to ake out of my *own* purse, without being ider an obligation to any one."

Mr. Mellish returned to his salmon in since.

"There is no occasion for a great mystery, apa," resumed Aurora; "I want some money r a particular purpose, and I have come to msult with you about my affairs. There is thing very extraordinary in that, I suppse?"

Mrs. John Mellish tossed her head, and ng this sentence at the assembly as if it ad been a challenge. Her manner was so fiant that even Talbot and Lucy felt called pon to respond with a gentle dissenting murur.

"No, no, of course not; nothing more natul," muttered the captain; but he was think-g all the time, "Thank God I married the her one."

After dinner the little party strolled out of e drawing-room windows on to the lawn, nd away toward that iron bridge upon which urora had stood, with her dog by her side, ss than two years ago, on the occasion of albot Bulstrode's second visit to Felden Woods. Lingering upon that bridge on this anquil summer's evening, what could the aptain do but think of that September day, arely two years agone? Barely two years! ot two years! And how much had been one, and thought, and suffered since! How ontemptible was the narrow space of time! et what terrible eternities of anguish, what enturies of heart-break, had been compressed to that pitiful sum of days and weeks! When the fraudulent partner in some house f business puts the money which is not his wn upon a Derby favorite, and goes home at ight a loser, it is strangely difficult for that retched defaulter to believe that it is not welve hours since he travelled the road to psom confident of success, and calculating ow he should invest his winnings. Talbot lulstrode was very silent, thinking of the fluence which this family of Felden Woods ad had upon his destiny. His little Lucy saw hat silence and thoughtfulness, and, stealing oftly to her husband, linked her arm in his. he had a right to do it now—yes, to pass her

little soft white hand under his coat sleeve, and even look up, almost boldly, in his face.

"Do you remember when you first came to Felden, and we stood upon this very bridge?" she asked; for she too had been thinking of that far-away time in the bright September of '57. "Do you remember, Talbot, dear?"

She had drawn him away from the banker and his children in order to ask this all-important question.

"Yes, perfectly, darling. As well as I remember your graceful figure seated at the piano in the long drawing-room, with the sunshine on your hair."

"You remember that! you remember *me!*" exclaimed Lucy, rapturously.

"Very well, indeed."

"But I thought—that is, I know—that you were in love with Aurora then."

"I think not."

"You only think not."

"How can I tell!" cried Talbot. "I freely confess that my first recollection connected with this place is of a gorgeous black-eyed creature, with scarlet in her hair; and I can no more disassociate her image from Felden Woods than I can, with my bare right hand, pluck up the trees which give the place its name. But if you entertain one distrustful thought of that pale shadow of the past, you do yourself and me a grievous wrong. I made a mistake, Lucy; but, thank Heaven, I saw it in time."

It is to be observed that Captain Bulstrode was always peculiarly demonstrative in his gratitude to Providence for his escape from the bonds which were to have united him to Aurora. He also made a great point of the benign compassion in which he held John Mellish. But, in despite of this, he was apt to be rather captious and quarrelsomely disposed toward the Yorkshireman; and I doubt if John's little stupidities and weaknesses were, on the whole, very displeasing to him. There are some wounds which never heal. The jagged flesh may reunite; cooling medicines may subdue the inflammation; even the scar left by the dagger-thrust may wear away, until it disappears in that gradual transformation which every atom of us is supposed by physiologists to undergo; but the wound *has been*, and to the last hour of our lives there are unfavorable winds which can make us wince with the old pain.

Aurora treated her cousin's husband with the calm cordiality which she might have felt for a brother. She bore no grudge against him for the old desertion, for she was happy with her husband—happy with the man who loved and believed in her, surviving every trial of his simple faith. Mrs. Mellish and Lucy wandered among the flower-beds by the waterside, leaving the gentlemen on the bridge.

"So you are very, very happy, my Lucy?" said Aurora.

"Oh, yes, yes, dear. How could I be otherwise. Talbot is so good to me. I know, of course, that he loved you first, and that he does n't love me quite—in the same way, you know—perhaps, in fact—not as much." Lucy Bulstrode was never tired of harping on this unfortunate minor string. "But I am very happy. You must come and see us, Aurora, dear. Our house is so pretty!".

Mrs. Bulstrode hereupon entered into a detailed description of the furniture and decorations in Half-Moon street, which is perhaps scarcely worthy of record. Aurora listened rather absently to the long catalogue of upholstery, and yawned several times before her cousin had finished.

"It's a very pretty house, I dare say, Lucy," she said at last, "and John and I will be very glad to come and see you some day. I wonder, Lucy, if I were to come in any trouble or disgrace to your door, whether you would turn me away ?"

"Trouble! disgrace!" repeated Lucy, looking frightened.

"You would n't turn me away, Lucy, would you? No; I know you better than that. You 'd let me in secretly, and hide me away in one of the servants' bedrooms, and bring me food by stealth, for fear the captain should discover the forbidden guest beneath his roof. You 'd serve two masters, Lucy, in fear and trembling."

Before Mrs. Bulstrode could make any answer to this extraordinary speech, the approach of the gentlemen interrupted the feminine conference.

It was scarcely a lively evening, this July sunset at Felden Woods. Archibald Floyd's gladness in his daughter's presence was something damped by the peculiarity of her visit; John Mellish had some shadowy remnants of the previous night's disquietude hanging about him; Talbot Bulstrode was thoughtful and moody; and poor little Lucy was tortured by vague fears of her brilliant cousin's influence. I don't suppose that any member of that "attenuated" assembly felt very much regret when the great clock in the stable-yard struck eleven, and the jingling bedroom candlesticks were brought into the room.

Talbot and his wife were the first to say good-night. Aurora lingered at her father's side, and John Mellish looked doubtfully at his dashing white sergeant, waiting to receive the word of command.

"You may go, John," she said; "I want to speak to papa."

"But I can wait, Lolly."

"On no account," answered Mrs. Mellish, sharply. "I am going into papa's study to have a quiet confabulation with him. What end would be gained by your waiting? You 've been yawning in our faces all the evening. You 're tired to death, I know, John; so go at once, my precious pet, and leave papa and

me to discuss our money matters." She pouted her rosy lips, and stood upon tiptoe, while the big Yorkshireman kissed her.

"How you do henpeck me, Lolly!" he said, rather sheepishly. "Good - night, sir. God bless you! Take care of my darling."

He shook hands with Mr. Floyd, parting from him with that half-affectionate, half-reverent manner which he always displayed to Aurora's father. Mrs. Mellish stood for some moments silent and motionless, looking after her husband, while her father, watching her looks, tried to read their meaning.

How quiet are the tragedies of real life! That dreadful scene between the Moor and his Ancient takes place in the open street of Cyprus. According to modern usage, I can not fancy Othello and Iago debating about poor Desdemona's honesty in St. Paul's churchyard, or even in the market-place of a country town; but perhaps the Cyprus street was a dull one, a cul-de-sac, it may be, or at least a deserted thoroughfare, something like that in which Monsieur Melnotte falls upon the shoulder of General Damas and sobs out his lamentations. But our modern tragedies seem to occur in-doors, and in places where we should least look for scenes of horror. Even while I write this the London flaneurs are staring all agape at a shop-window in a crowded street as if every pitiful feather, every poor shred of ribbon in that milliner's window had a mystical association with the terrors of a room up stairs. But to the ignorant passers - by how commonplace the spot must seem; how remote in its every-day associations from the terrors of life's tragedy!

Any chance traveller driving from Beckenham to West Wickham would have looked, perhaps enviously, at the Felden mansion, and sighed to be lord of that fair expanse of park and garden; yet I doubt if in the county of Kent there was any creature more disturbed in mind than Archibald Floyd, the banker. Those few moments during which Aurora stood in thoughtful silence were as so many hours to his anxious mind. At last she spoke.

"Will you come to the study, papa?" she said; "this room is so big, and so dimly lighted, I always fancy there are listeners in the corners."

She did not wait for an answer, but led the way to a room on the other side of the hall —the room in which she and her father had been so long closeted together upon the night before her departure for Paris. The crayon portrait of Eliza Floyd looked down upon Archibald and his daughter. The face wore so bright and genial a smile that it was difficult to believe it was the face of the dead.

The banker was the first to speak.

"My darling girl," he said, "what is it you want of me ?"

"Money, papa. Two thousand pounds."

She checked his gesture of surprise, and resumed before he could interrupt her:

"The money you settled upon me on my marriage with John Mellish is invested in our own bank, I know. I know, too, that I can draw upon my account when and how I please; but I thought that if I wrote a check for two thousand pounds the unusual amount might attract attention, and it might possibly fall into your hands. Had this occurred, you would perhaps have been alarmed, at any rate astonished. I thought it best, therefore, to come to you myself and ask you for the money, especially as I must have it in notes."

Archibald Floyd grew very pale. He had been standing while Aurora spoke, but as she finished he dropped into a chair near his little office-table, and, resting his elbow upon an open desk, leaned his head on his hand.

"What do you want the money for, my dear?" he asked, gravely.

"Never mind what, papa. It is my own money, is it not, and I may spend it as I please?"

"Certainly, my dear, certainly," he answered, with some slight hesitation. "You shall spend whatever you please. I am rich enough to indulge any whim of yours, however foolish, however extravagant. But your marriage settlement was rather intended for the benefit of your children—than—than for—anything of this kind, and I scarcely know if you are justified in touching it without your husband's permission, especially as your pin-money is really large enough to enable you to gratify any reasonable wish."

The old man pushed his gray hair away from his forehead with a weary action and a tremulous hand. Heaven knows that even in that desperate moment Aurora took notice of the feeble hand and the whitening hair.

"Give me the money, then, papa," she said. "Give it me from your own purse. You are rich enough to do that."

"Rich enough! Yes, if it were twenty times the sum," answered the banker, slowly. Then, with a sudden burst of passion, he exclaimed, "Oh, Aurora, Aurora, why do you treat me so badly? Have I been so cruel a father that you can't confide in me. Aurora, why do you want this money?"

She clasped her hands tightly together, and stood looking at him for a few moments irresolutely.

"I can not tell you," she said, with grave determination. "If I were to tell you—what—what I think of doing, you might thwart me in my purpose. Father! father!" she cried, with a sudden change in her voice and manner, "I am hemmed in on every side by difficulty and danger, and there is only one way of escape—except death. Unless I take that one way, I must die. I am very young—too young and happy, perhaps, to die willingly. Give me the means of escape."

"You mean this sum of money?"

"Yes."

"You have been pestered by some connection—some old associate of—his?"

"No."

"What then?"

"I can not tell you."

They were silent for some moments. Archibald Floyd looked imploringly at his child, but she did not answer that earnest gaze. She stood before him with a proudly downcast look; the eyelids drooping over the dark eyes, not in shame, not in humiliation, only in the stern determination to avoid being subdued by the sight of her father's distress.

"Aurora," he said at last, "why not take the wisest and the safest step? Why not tell John Mellish the truth? The danger would disappear; the difficulty would be overcome. If you are persecuted by this low rabble, who so fit as he to act for you? Tell him, Aurora—tell him all!"

"No, no, no!"

She lifted her hands, and clasped them upon her pale face.

"No, no; not for all this wide world!" she cried.

"Aurora," said Archibald Floyd, with a gathering sternness upon his face, which overspread the old man's benevolent countenance like some dark cloud, "Aurora—God forgive me for saying such words to my own child—but I must insist upon your telling me that this is no new infatuation, no new madness, which leads you to—" He was unable to finish his sentence.

Mrs. Mellish dropped her hands from before her face, and looked at him with her eyes flashing fire, and her cheeks in a crimson blaze.

"Father," she cried, "how dare you ask me such a question? New infatuation! New madness! Have I suffered so little, do you think, from the folly of my youth? Have I paid so small a price for the mistake of my girlhood that you should have cause to say these words to me to-night? Do I come of so bad a race," she said, pointing indignantly to her mother's portrait, "that you should think so vilely of me? Do I—"

Her tragical appeal was rising to its climax, when she dropped suddenly at her father's feet, and burst into a tempest of sobs.

"Papa, papa, pity me," she cried, "pity me!"

He raised her in his arms, and drew her to him, and comforted her, as he had comforted her for the loss of a Scotch terrier-pup twelve years before, when she was small enough to sit on his knee, and nestle her head in his waistcoat.

"Pity you, my dear!" he said. "What is there I would not do for you to save you one moment's sorrow? If my worthless life could help you; if—"

7

"You will give me the money, papa?" she asked, looking up at him half coaxingly through her tears.

"Yes, my darling, to-morrow morning."

"In bank-notes?"

"In any manner you please. But, Aurora, why see these people? Why listen to their disgraceful demands? Why not tell the truth?"

"Ah! why, indeed!" she said, thoughtfully. "Ask me no questions, dear papa, but let me have the money to-morrow, and I promise you that this shall be the very last you hear of my old troubles."

She made this promise with such perfect confidence that her father was inspired with a faint ray of hope.

"Come, darling papa," she said, "your room is near mine; let us go up stairs together."

She entwined her arms in his, and led him up the broad staircase, only parting from him at the door of his room.

Mr. Floyd summoned his daughter into the study early the next morning, while Talbot Bulstrode was opening his letters, and Lucy strolling up and down the terrace with John Mellish.

"I have telegraphed for the money, my darling," the banker said. "One of the clerks will be here with it by the time we have finished breakfast."

Mr. Floyd was right. A card inscribed with the name of a Mr. George Martin was brought to him during breakfast.

"Mr. Martin will be good enough to wait in my study," he said.

Aurora and her father found the clerk seated at the open window, looking admiringly through festoons of foliage, which clustered round the frame of the lattice, into the richly-cultivated garden. Felden Woods was a sacred spot in the eyes of the junior clerks in Lombard street, and a drive to Beckenham in a Hansom cab on a fine summer's morning, to say nothing of such chance refreshment as pound-cake and old Madeira, or cold fowl and Scotch ale, was considered no small treat.

Mr. George Martin, who was laboring under the temporary affliction of being only nineteen years of age, rose in a confused flutter of respect and surprise, and blushed very violently at sight of Mrs. Mellish.

Aurora responded to his reverential salute with such a pleasant nod as she might have bestowed upon the younger dogs in the stable-yard, and seated herself opposite to him at the little table by the window. It was such an excruciatingly narrow table that Aurora's muslin dress rustled against the drab trowsers of the junior clerk as Mrs. Mellish sat down.

The young man unlocked a little morocco pouch which he wore suspended from a strap across his shoulder, and produced a roll of crisp notes; so crisp, so white and new, that, in their unsullied freshness, they looked more like notes on the Bank of Elegance than the circulating medium of this busy, money-making nation.

"I have brought the cash for which you telegraphed, sir," said the clerk.

"Very good, Mr. Martin," answered the banker. "Here is my check ready written for you. The notes are—"

"Twenty fifties, twenty-five twenties, fifty tens," the clerk said, glibly.

Mr. Floyd took the little bundle of tissue-paper, and counted the notes with the professional rapidity which he still retained.

"Quite correct," he said, ringing the bell, which was speedily answered by a simpering footman. "Give this gentleman some lunch. You will find the Madeira very good," he added, kindly, turning to the blushing junior; "it's a wine that is dying out, and by the time you're my age, Mr. Martin, you won't be able to get such a glass as I can offer you to-day. Good-morning."

Mr. George Martin clutched his hat nervously from the empty chair on which he had placed it, knocked down a heap of papers with his elbow, bowed, blushed, and stumbled out of the room, under convoy of the simpering footman, who nourished a profound contempt for the young men from the h'office.

"Now, my darling," said Mr. Floyd, "here is the money. Though, mind, I protest against—"

"No, no, papa, not a word," she interrupted; "I thought that was all settled last night."

He sighed, with the same weary sigh as on the night before, and, seating himself at his desk, dipped a pen into the ink.

"What are you going to do, papa?"

"I'm only going to take the numbers of the notes."

"There is no occasion."

"There is always occasion to be business-like," said the old man, firmly, as he checked the numbers of the notes one by one upon a sheet of paper with rapid precision.

Aurora paced up and down the room impatiently while this operation was going forward.

"How difficult it has been to me to get this money!" she exclaimed. "If I had been the wife and daughter of two of the poorest men in Christendom, I could scarcely have had more trouble about this two thousand pounds. And now you keep me here while you number the notes, not one of which is likely to be exchanged in this country."

"I learned to be business-like when I was very young, Aurora," answered Mr. Floyd, "and I have never been able to forget my old habits."

He completed his task in defiance of his

daughter's impatience, and handed her the packet of notes when he had done.

"I will keep the list of numbers, my dear," he said. "If I were to give it to you, you would most likely lose it."

He folded the sheet of paper, and put it in a drawer of his desk.

"Twenty years hence, Aurora," he said, "should I live so long, I should be able to produce this paper, if it were wanted."

"Which it never will be, you dear methodical papa," answered Aurora. "My troubles are ended now. Yes," she added, in a graver tone, "I pray God that my troubles may be ended now."

She encircled her arms about her father's neck, and kissed him tenderly.

"I must leave you, dearest, to-day," she said; "you must not ask me why—you must ask me nothing. You must only love and trust me—as my poor John trusts me—faithfully, hopefully, through everything."

CHAPTER XX.

CAPTAIN PRODDER.

While the Doncaster express was carrying Mr. and Mrs. Mellish northward, another express journeyed from Liverpool to London with its load of passengers.

Among these passengers there was a certain broad-shouldered and rather bull-necked individual, who attracted considerable attention during the journey, and was an object of some interest to his fellow-travellers and the railway officials at the two or three stations where the train stopped.

He was a man of about fifty years of age, but his years were worn very lightly, and only recorded by some wandering streaks and patches of gray among his thick blue-black stubble of hair. His complexion, naturally dark, had become of such a bronzed and coppery tint by perpetual exposure to meridian suns, tropical hot winds, the fiery breath of the simoon, and the many other inconveniences attendant upon an out-door life, as to cause him to be frequently mistaken for the inhabitant of some one of those countries in which the complexion of the natives fluctuates between burnt sienna, Indian red, and Vandyke brown. But it was rarely long before he took an opportunity to rectify this mistake, and to express that hearty contempt and aversion for all *furriners* which is natural to the unspoiled and unsophisticated Briton.

Upon this particular occasion he had not been half an hour in the society of his fellow-passengers before he had informed them that he was a native of Liverpool, and the captain of a merchant vessel, trading, in a manner of speaking, he said, everywhere; that he had run away from his father and his home at a

very early period of his life, and had shifted for himself in different parts of the globe ever since; that his Christian name was Samuel, and his surname Prodder, and that his father had been, like himself, a captain in the merchant service. He chewed so much tobacco, and drank so much fiery Jamaica rum from a pocket-pistol in the intervals of his conversation, that the first-class compartment in which he sat was odorous with the compound perfume. But he was such a hearty, loud-spoken fellow, and there was such a pleasant twinkle in his black eyes, that the passengers (with the exception of one crusty old lady) treated him with great good-humor, and listened very patiently to his talk.

"Chewin' a'n't smokin', you know, is it?" he said, with a great guffaw, as he cut himself a terrible block of Cavendish; "and railway companies a'n't got any laws against that. They can put a fellow's pipe out, but he can chew his quid in their faces; though I won't say which is wust for their carpets, neither."

I am sorry to be compelled to confess that this brown-visaged merchant-captain, who said *wust* and chewed Cavendish tobacco, was uncle to Mrs. John Mellish, of Mellish Park; and that the motive for this very journey was neither more nor less than his desire to become acquainted with his niece.

He imparted this fact—as well as much other information relating to himself, his tastes, habits, adventures, opinions, and sentiments—to his travelling companions in the course of the journey.

"Do you know for why I'm going to London by this identical train?" he asked generally, as the passengers settled themselves into their places after taking refreshment at Rugby.

The gentlemen looked over their newspapers at the talkative sailor, and a young lady looked up from her book, but nobody volunteered to speculate an opinion upon the mainspring of Mr. Prodder's actions.

"I'll tell you for why," resumed the merchant-captain, addressing the assembly as if in answer to their eager questioning. "I'm going to see my niece, which I have never seen before. When I ran away from father's ship, the *Ventur'some*, nigh upon forty years ago, and went aboard the craft of a captain by the name of Mobley, which was a good master to me for many a day, I had a little sister as I had left behind at Liverpool, which was dearer to me than my life." He paused to refresh himself with rather a demonstrative sip from the pocket-pistol. "But if *you*," he continued generally, "if *you* had a father that 'd fetch you a clout of the head as soon as look at you, *you*'d run away, perhaps, and so did I. I took the opportunity to be missin' one night as father was settin' sail from Yarmouth Harbor; and, not settin' that wonderful store by me which some folks do by their only sons, he shipped his anchor without stoppin' to ask many questions, and left me hidin' in one of the little alleys which cut the town of Yarmouth through and across like they cut the cakes they make there. There was many in Yarmouth that knew me, and there wasn't one that didn't say, 'Sarve him right,' when they heard how I'd given father the slip, and the next day Cap'en Mobley gave me a berth as cabin-boy about the *Mariar Anne*."

Mr. Prodder again paused to partake of refreshment from his portable spirit store, and this time politely handed the pocket-pistol to the company.

"Now, perhaps you'll not believe me," he resumed, after his friendly offer had been refused, and the wicker-covered vessel replaced in his capacious pocket — "you won't perhaps believe me when I tell you, as I tell you candid, that up to last Saturday week I never could find the time nor the opportunity to go back to Liverpool, and ask after the little sister that I'd left no higher than the kitchen-table, and that had cried fit to break her poor little heart when I went away. But whether you believe it or whether you don't, it's as true as gospel," cried the sailor, thumping his ponderous fist upon the padded elbow of the compartment in which he sat; "it's as true as gospel. I've coasted America, North and South. I've carried West-Indian goods to the East Indies, and East-Indian goods to the West Indies. I've traded in Norwegian goods between Norway and Hull. I've carried Sheffield goods from Hull to South America. I've traded between all manner of countries and all manner of docks; but somehow or other I've never had the time to spare to go on shore at Liverpool, and find out the narrow little street in which I left my sister Eliza, no higher than the table, more than forty years ago, until last Saturday was a week. Last Saturday was a week I touched at Liverpool with a cargo of furs and poll-parrots—what you may call fancy goods; and I said to my mate, I said, 'I'll tell you what I'll do, Jack: I'll go ashore and see my little sister Eliza.'"

He paused once more, and a softening change came over the brightness of his black eyes. This time he did not apply himself to the pocket-pistol. This time he brushed the back of his brown hand across his eye-lashes, and brought it away with a drop or two of moisture glittering upon the bronzed skin. Even his voice was changed when he continued, and had mellowed to a richer and more mournful depth, until it very much resembled the melodious utterance which twenty-one years before had assisted to render Miss Eliza Percival the popular tragedian of the Preston and Bradford circuit.

"God forgive me," continued the sailor, in that altered voice: "but throughout my voyages I'd never thought of my sister Eliza but in two ways—sometimes one, sometimes t' other. One way of thinking of her, and expecting to see her, was as the little sister that I'd left, not altered by so much as one lock of her hair being changed from the identical curl into which it was twisted the morning she cried and clung about me on board the *Ventur'some*, having come aboard to wish father and me good-by. Perhaps I oftenest thought of her in this way. Anyhow, it was in this way, and no other, that I always saw her in my dreams. The other way of thinking of her, and expectin' to see her, was as a handsome, full-grown, buxom married woman, with a troop of saucy children hanging on to her apron-string, and every one of 'em askin' what Uncle Samuel had brought 'em from foreign parts. Of course this fancy was the most rational of the two; but the other fancy, of the little child with the long, black, curly hair, would come to me very often, especially at night, when all was quiet aboard, and when I took the wheel in a spell while the helmsman turned in. Lord bless you, ladies and gentlemen, many a time of a starlight night, when we've been in them latitudes where the stars are brighter than common, I've seen the floating mists upon the water take the very shape of that light figure of a little girl in a white pinafore, and come skipping toward me across the waves. I don't mean that I've seen a ghost, you know, but I mean that I could have seen one if I'd had the mind, and that I've seen as much of a one as folks ever do see upon this earth—the ghosts of their own memories and their own sorrows, mixed up with the mists of the sea or the shadows of the trees wavin' back'ard and for'ard in the moonlight, or a white curtain agen a window, or something of that sort. Well, I was such a precious old fool with these fancies and fantigs"—Mr. Samuel Prodder seemed rather to pride himself upon the latter word, as something out of the common—"that when I went ashore at Liverpool last Saturday was a week, I couldn't keep my eyes off the little girls in white pinafores as passed me by in the streets, thinkin' to see my Eliza skippin' along, with her black curls flyin' in the wind, and a bit of chalk, to play hop-scotch with, in her hand; so I was obliged to say to myself, quite serious, 'Now, Samuel Prodder, the little girl you're a lookin' for must be fifty years of age, if she's a day, and it's more than likely that she's left off playin' hop-scotch and wearin' white pinafores by this time.' If I hadn't kept repeatin' this, internally like, all the way I went, I should have stopped half the little girls in Liverpool to ask 'em if their name was Eliza, and if they'd ever had a brother as ran away and was lost. I had only one thought of how to set about findin' her, and that was to walk straight to the back street in which I remembered leavin' her forty years before. I'd no thought that those forty years could make any more change than to change her from a girl to a woman, and it seemed almost strange to me that they could make as much change as that. There was one thing I never thought of; and if my heart beat loud and quick when I knocked at the little front door of the very identical house in which we'd lodged, it was with nothing but hope and joy. The forty years that had sent railways spinning all over England had n't made much difference in the old house; it was forty years dirtier, perhaps, and forty years shabbier, and it stood in the very heart of the town instead of on the edge of the open country; but, exceptin' that, it was pretty much the same, and I expected to see the same landlady come to open the door, with the same dirty artificial flowers in her cap, and the same old slippers down at heel scrapin' after her along the bit of oil-cloth. It gave me a kind of a turn when I did n't see this identical landlady, though she'd have been turned a hundred years old if she'd been alive; and I might have prepared myself for the disappointment if I'd thought of that, but I had n't; and when the door was opened by a young woman with sandy hair, brushed backward as if she'd been a Chinese, and no eyebrows to speak of, I did feel disappointed. The young woman had a baby in her arms—a black-eyed baby, with its eyes opened so wide that it seemed as if it had been very much surprised with the look of things on first comin' into the world, and had n't quite recovered itself yet; so I thought to myself, as soon as I clapped eyes on the little one, why, as sure as a gun, that 's my sister Eliza's baby, and my sister Eliza 's married, and lives here still. But the young woman had never heard the name of Prodder, and did n't think there was anybody in the neighborhood as ever had. I felt my heart, which had been beatin' louder and quicker every minute, stop all of a sudden when she said this, and seem to drop down like a dead weight; but I thanked her for her civil answers to my questions, and went on to the next house to inquire there. I might have saved myself the trouble, for I made the same inquiries at every house on each side of the street, going straight from door to door, till the people thought I was a sea-farin' tax-gatherer; but nobody had ever heard the name of Prodder, and the oldest inhabitant in the street had n't lived there ten years. I was quite disheartened when I left the neighborhood, which had once been so familiar, and which seemed so strange, and small, and mean, and shabby now. I'd had so little thought of failing to find Eliza in the very house in which I'd left her, that I'd made no plans beyond. So I was brought to a dead stop; and I went back to the tavern where I'd left

my carpet-bag, and I had a chop brought me for my dinner, and I sat with my knife and fork before me thinkin' what I was to do next. When Eliza and I had parted, forty years before, I remembered father leaving her in charge of a sister of my mother's (my poor mother had been dead a year), and I thought to myself, the only chance there is left for me now is to find Aunt Sarah."

By the time Mr. Prodder arrived at this stage of his narrative his listeners had dropped off gradually, the gentlemen returning to their newspapers, and the young lady to her book, until the merchant-captain found himself reduced to communicate his adventures to one good-natured looking young fellow, who seemed interested in the brown-faced sailor, and encouraged him every now and then with an assenting nod or a friendly "Ay, ay, to be sure."

"The only chance I can see, ses I," continued Mr. Prodder, "is to find Aunt Sarah. I found Aunt Sarah. She'd been keepin' a shop in the general line when I went away forty years ago, and she was keepin' the same shop in the general line when I came back last Saturday week; and there was the same fly-blown handbills of ships that was to sail immediate, and that had sailed two years ago, accordin' to the date upon the bills; and the same wooden sugar-loaves wrapped up in white paper; and the same lattice-work gate, with a bell that rang as loud as if it was meant to give the alarm to all Liverpool as well as to my Aunt Sarah in the parlor behind the shop. The poor old soul was standing behind the counter, serving two ounces of tea to a customer when I went in. Forty years had made so much change in her that I should n't have known her if I had n't known the shop. She wore black curls upon her forehead, and a brooch like a brass butterfly in the middle of the curls, where the parting ought to have been; and she wore a beard; and the curls were false, but the beard was n't; and her voice was very deep, and rather manly, and she seemed to me to have grown manly altogether in the forty years that I'd been away. She tied up the two ounces of tea, and then asked me what I pleased to want. I told her that I was little Sam, and that I wanted my sister Eliza."

The merchant-captain paused and looked out of the window for upward of five minutes before he resumed his story. When he did resume it, he spoke in a very low voice, and in short, detached sentences, as if he could n't trust himself with long ones, for fear he should break down in the middle of them.

"Eliza had been dead one-and-twenty years. Aunt Sarah told me all about it. She'd tried the artificial flower-makin', and she had n't liked it. And she turned play-actress. And when she was nine-and-twenty she'd married—she'd married a gentleman that had no end of money, and she 'd gone to live at a fine place somewhere in Kent. I 've got the name of it wrote down in my memorandum-book. But she 'd been a good and generous friend to Aunt Sarah; and Aunt Sarah was to have gone to Kent to see her, and to stop all the summer with her. But while aunt was getting ready to go for that very visit, my sister Eliza died, leaving a daughter behind her, which is the niece that I 'm going to see. I sat down upon the three-legged wooden stool against the counter, and hid my face in my hands; and I thought of the little girl that I 'd seen playin' at hop-scotch forty years before, until I thought my heart would burst; but I did n't shed a tear. Aunt Sarah took a big brooch out of her collar, and showed me a ring of black hair behind a bit of glass, with a gold frame round it. 'Mr Floyd had this brooch made a purpose for me,' she said; 'he has always been a liberal gentleman to me, and he comes down to Liverpool once in two or three years, and takes tea with me in yon back parlor; and I 've no call to keep a shop, for he allows me a handsome income; but I should die of the mopes if it was n't for the business.' There was Eliza's name and the date of her death engraved upon the back of the brooch. I tried to remember where I 'd been, and what I 'd been doing that year. But I could n't, sir. All the life that I looked back upon seemed muddled and mixed up, like a dream; and I could only think of the little sister I 'd said good-by to aboard the *Ventur'some* forty years before. I got round by little and little, and I was able half an hour afterward to listen to Aunt Sarah's talk. She was nigh upon seventy, poor old soul, and she 'd always been a good one to talk. She asked me if it was n't a great thing for the family that Eliza had made such a match; and if I was n't proud to think that my niece was a young heiress, that spoke all manner of languages, and rode in her own carriage; and if that ought n't to be a consolation to me? But I told her that I 'd rather have found my sister married to the poorest man in Liverpool, and alive and well, to bid me welcome back to my native town. Aunt Sarah said if those were my religious opinions, she did n't know what to say to me. And she showed me a picture of Eliza's tomb in Beckenham church-yard, that had been painted expressly for her by Mr. Floyd's orders. Floyd was the name of Eliza's husband. And then she showed me a picture of Miss Floyd, the heiress, at the age of ten, which was the image of Eliza, all but the pinafore; and it 's that very Miss Floyd that I 'm going to see."

"And I dare say," said the kind listener, "that Miss Floyd will be very much pleased to see her sailor uncle."

"Well, sir, I think she will," answered the captain. "I don't say it from any pride I

take in myself, Lord knows; for I know I 'm a rough and ready sort of a chap, that 'ud be no great ornament in a young lady's drawing-room: but if Eliza's daughter 's anything like Eliza, I know what she 'll say and what she 'll do as well as if I see her saying it and doing it. She 'll clap her pretty little hands together, and she 'll clasp her arms round my neck, and she 'll say, 'Lor, uncle, I am *so* glad to see you.' And when I tell her that I was her mother's only brother, and that me and her mother was very fond of one another, she 'll burst out a cryin', and she 'll hide her pretty face upon my shoulder, and she 'll sob as if her dear little heart was going to break for love of the mother that she never saw. That 's what she 'll do," said Captain Prodder, "and I don't think the truest born lady that ever was could do any better."

The good-natured traveller heard a good deal more from the captain of his plans for going to Beckenham to claim his niece's affections, in spite of all the fathers in the world.

"Mr. Floyd 's a good man, I dare say, sir," he said: "but he 's kept his daughter apart from her aunt Sarah, and it 's but likely he 'll try to keep her from me. But if he does, he 'll find he 's got a toughish customer to deal with in Captain Samuel Prodder."

The merchant-captain reached Beckenham as the evening shadows were deepening among the Felden oaks and beeches, and the long rays of red sunshine fading slowly out in the low sky. He drove up to the old red-brick mansion in a hired fly, and presented himself at the hall-door just as Mr. Floyd was leaving the dining-room to finish the evening in his lonely study.

The banker paused to glance with some slight surprise at the loosely-clad, weather-beaten looking figure of the sailor, and mechanically put his hand among the gold and silver in his pocket. He thought the seafaring man had come to present some petition for himself and his comrades. A life-boat was wanted somewhere on the Kentish coast, perhaps, and this good-tempered looking, bronze-colored man had come to collect funds for the charitable work.

He was thinking this, when, in reply to the town-bred footman's question, the sailor uttered the name of Prodder; and in the one moment of its utterance his thoughts flew back over one-and-twenty years, and he was in love with a beautiful actress, who owned blushingly to that plebeian cognomen. The banker's voice was faint and husky as he turned to the captain and bade him welcome to Felden Woods.

"Step this way, Mr. Prodder," he said, pointing to the open door of the study. "I am very glad to see you. I—I—have often heard of you. You are my dead wife's runaway brother."

Even amid his sorrowful recollection of

that brief happiness of the past, some natural alloy of pride had its part, and he closed the study-door carefully before he said this,

"God bless you, sir," he said, holding out his hand to the sailor. "I see I am right. Your eyes are like Eliza's. You and yours will always be welcome beneath my roof. Yes, Samuel Prodder — you see I know your Christian name — and when I die you will find that you have not been forgotten."

The captain thanked his brother-in-law heartily, and told him that he neither asked nor wished for anything except permission to see his niece, Aurora Floyd.

As he made this request, he looked toward the door of the little room, evidently expecting that the heiress might enter at any moment. He looked terribly disappointed when the banker told him that Aurora was married, and lived near Doncaster; but that, if he had happened to come ten hours earlier, he would have found her at Felden Woods.

Ah! who has not heard those common words? Who has not been told that, if they had come sooner, or gone earlier, or hurried their pace, or slackened it, or done something that they have not done, the whole course of life would have been otherwise? Who has not looked back regretfully at the past, which, differently fashioned, would have made the present other than it is? We think it hard that we can not take the fabric of our life to pieces, as a mantua-maker unpicks her work, and make up the stuff another way. How much waste we might save in the cloth, how much better a shape we might make the garment, if we only had the right to use our scissors and needle again, and refashion the past by the experience of the present.

"To think, now, that I should have been comin' yesterday!" exclaimed the captain, "but put off my journey because it was a Friday! If I'd only knowed!"

Of course, Captain Prodder, if you had only known what it was not given you to know, you would, no doubt, have acted more prudently; and so would many other people. If Mr. William Palmer had known that detection was to dog the footsteps of crime, and the gallows to follow at the heels of detection, he would most likely have hesitated long before he mixed the strychnine pills for the friend whom, with cordial voice, he was entreating to be of good cheer. If the speculators upon this year's Derby had known that Caractacus was to be the winner, they would scarcely have hazarded their money upon Buckstone and the Marquis. We spend the best part of our lives in making mistakes, and the poor remainder in reflecting how very easily we might have avoided them.

Mr. Floyd explained, rather lamely perhaps, how it was that the Liverpool spinster had never been informed of her grand-niece's marriage with Mr. John Mellish; and the

merchant-captain announced his intention of starting for Doncaster early the next morning.

"Don't think that I want to intrude upon your daughter, sir," he said, as if perfectly acquainted with the banker's nervous dread of such a visit. "I know her station 's high above me, though she 's my own sister's only child; and I make no doubt that those about her would be ready enough to turn up their noses at a poor old salt that has been tossed and tumbled about in every variety of weather for this forty year. I only want to see her once in a way, and to hear her say, perhaps, 'Lor, uncle, what a rum old chap you are!' There!" exclaimed Samuel Prodder, suddenly, "I think, if I could only once hear her call me uncle, I could go back to sea and die happy, though I never came ashore again."

CHAPTER XXI.

"HE ONLY SAID I AM A-WEARY."

Mr. James Conyers found the long summer's day hang rather heavily upon his hands at Mellish Park, in the society of the rheumatic ex-trainer, the stable-boys, and Steeve Hargraves, the softy, and with no literary resources except the last Saturday's *Bell's Life*, and sundry flimsy sheets of shiny, slippery tissue-paper, forwarded him by post from King Charles' Croft, in the busy town of Leeds.

He might have found plenty of work to do in the stables, perhaps, if he had had a mind to do it; but after the night of the storm there was a perceptible change in his manner, and the showy pretense of being very busy, which he had made on his first arrival at the Park, was now exchanged for a listless and undisguised dawdling and an unconcerned indifference, which caused the old trainer to shake his gray head, and mutter to his hangers-on that the new chap warn't up to mooch, and was evidently too grand for his business.

Mr. James cared very little for the opinion of these simple Yorkshiremen; and he yawned in their faces, and stifled them with his cigar-smoke, with a dashing indifference that harmonized well with the gorgeous tints of his complexion and the lustrous splendor of his lazy eyes. He had taken the trouble to make himself very agreeable on the day succeeding his arrival, and had distributed his hearty slaps on the shoulder and friendly digs in the ribs right and left, until he had slapped and dug himself into considerable popularity among the friendly rustics, who were ready to be bewitched by his handsome face and flashy manner. But after his interview with Mr. Mellish in the cottage by the north gates, he seemed to abandon all desire to please, and to grow suddenly restless and discontented — so restless and so discontented that he felt inclined even to quarrel with the unhappy softy, and led his red-haired retainer a sufficiently uncomfortable life with his whims and vagaries.

Stephen Hargraves bore this change in his new master's manner with wonderful patience. Rather too patiently, perhaps; with that slow, dogged, uncomplaining patience of those who keep something in reserve as a set-off against present forbearance, and who invite rather than avoid injury, rejoicing in anything which swells the great account, to be squared in future storm and fury. The softy was a man who could hoard his hatred and vengeance, hiding the bad passions away in the dark corners of his poor shattered mind, and bringing them out in the dead of the night to " kiss and talk to," as the Moor's wife kissed and conversed with the strawberry-embroidered cambric. There must surely have been very little "society" at Cyprus, or Mrs. Othello could scarcely have been reduced to such insipid company.

However it might be, Steeve bore Mr. Conyers' careless insolence so very meekly that the trainer laughed at his attendant for a poor-spirited hound, whom a pair of flashing black eyes and a lady's toy riding-whip could frighten out of the poor remnant of wit left in his muddled brain. He said something to this effect when Steeve displeased him once, in the course of the long, temper-trying summer's day, and the softy turned away with something very like a chuckle of savage pleasure in acknowledgment of the compliment. He was more obsequious than ever after it, and was humbly thankful for the ends of cigars which the trainer liberally bestowed upon him, and went into Doncaster for more spirits and more cigars in the course of the day, and fetched and carried as submissively as that craven-spirited hound to which his employer had politely compared him.

Mr. Conyers did not even make a pretence of going to look at the horses on this blazing 5th of July, but lolled on the window-sill, with his lame leg upon a chair, and his back against the frame-work of the little easement, smoking, drinking, and reading his price-lists all through the sunny day. The cold brandy and water which he poured, without half an hour's intermission, down his handsome throat, seemed to have far less influence upon him than the same amount of liquid would have had upon a horse. It would have put the horse out of condition, perhaps, but it had no effect whatever upon the trainer.

Mrs. Powell, walking for the benefit of her health, in the north shrubberies, and incurring imminent danger of a sun-stroke for the same praiseworthy reason, contrived to pass the lodge, and to see Mr. Conyers lounging, dark and splendid, on the window-sill, exhibiting a kitcat of his handsome person framed in the clustering foliage which hung about the cottage walls. She was rather embarrassed by the presence of the softy, who was sweeping the door-step, and who gave her a glance of recognition as she passed — a glance which might perhaps have said, " We know his secrets, you and I, handsome and insolent as he is; we know the paltry price at which he can be bought and sold. But we keep our counsel — we keep our counsel till time ripens the bitter fruit upon the tree, though our fingers itch to pluck it while it is still green."

Mrs. Powell stopped to give the trainer good-day, expressing as much surprise at seeing him at the north lodge as if she had been given to understand that he was travelling to Kamtchatka: but Mr. Conyers cut her civilities short with a yawn, and told her, with easy familiarity, that she would be conferring a favor upon him by sending him that morning's *Times* as soon as the daily papers arrived at the Park. The ensign's widow was too much under the influence of the graceful impertinence of his manner to resist it as she might have done, and returned to the house, bewildered and wondering, to comply with his request. So through the oppressive heat of the summer's day the trainer smoked, drank, and took his ease, while his dependent and follower watched him with a puzzled face, revolving vaguely and confusedly in his dull, muddled brain the events of the previous night.

But Mr. James Conyers grew weary at last even of his own ease; and that inherent restlessness which caused Rasselas to tire of his happy valley, and sicken for the free breezes on the hill-tops and the clamor of the distant cities, arose in the bosom of the trainer, and grew so strong that he began to chafe at the rural quiet of the north lodge, and to shuffle his poor lame leg wearily from one position to another in sheer discontent of mind, which, by one of those many subtle links between spirit and matter that tell us we are mortal, communicated itself to his body, and gave him that chronic disorder which is popularly called " the fidgets " — an unquiet fever, generated amid the fibres of the brain, and finding its way by that physiological telegraph, the spinal marrow, to the remotest station on the human railway.

Mr. James suffered from this common complaint to such a degree that, as the solemn strokes of the church clock vibrated in sonorous music above the tree-tops of Mellish Park in the sunny evening atmosphere, he threw down his pipe with an impatient shrug of the shoulders, and called to the softy to bring him his hat and walking-stick.

" Seven o'clock," he muttered; " only seven o'clock. I think there must have been twenty-four hours in this blessed summer's day."

He stood looking from the little easement window with a discontented frown contracting his handsome eyebrows, and a peevish expression distorting his full, classically-moulded lips as he said this. He glanced through the little casement, made smaller by its clustering frame of roses and clematis, jessamine and myrtle, and looking like the port-hole of a ship that sailed upon a sea of summer verdure. He glanced through the circular opening left by that scented frame-work of leaves and blossoms into the long glades, where the low sunlight was flickering upon waving fringes of 'ern. He followed with his listless glance the wandering intricacies of the underwood, until they led his weary eyes away to distant patches of blue water, slowly changing to opal and rose-color in the declining light. He saw all these things with a lazy apathy, which had no power to recognize their beauty, or to inspire one latent thrill of gratitude to Him who had made them. He had better have been blind; surely he had better have been blind.

He turned his back upon the evening sunshine, and looked at the white face of Steeve Hargraves, the softy, with every whit as much pleasure as he had felt in looking at Nature in her loveliest aspect.

"A long day," he said: "an infernally tedious, wearisome day. Thank God, it 's over."

Strange that, as he uttered this impious thanksgiving, no subtle influence of the future crept through his veins to chill the slackening pulses of his heart, and freeze the idle words upon his lips. If he had known what was so soon to come: if he had known, as he thanked God for the death of one beautiful summer's day, never to be born again, with its twelve hours of opportunity for good or evil, surely he would have grovelled on the earth, stricken with a sudden terror, and wept aloud for the shameful history of the life which lay behind him.

He had never shed tears but once since his childhood, and then those tears were scalding drops of baffled rage and vengeful fury at the utter defeat of the greatest scheme of his life.

"I shall go into Doncaster to-night, Hargraves," he said to the softy, who stood deferentially awaiting his master's pleasure, and watching him, as he had watched him all day, furtively but incessantly: "I shall spend the evening in Doncaster, and—and—see if I can pick up a few wrinkles about the September meeting; not that there 's anything worth entering among this set of screws, Lord knows," he added, with undisguised contempt for poor John's beloved stable. "Is there a dog-cart, or a trap of any kind, I can drive over in?" he asked of the softy.

Mr. Hargraves said that there was a Newport Pagnell, which was sacred to Mr. John Mellish, and a gig that was at the disposal of any of the upper servants when they had occasion to go into Doncaster, as well as a cov-

ered van, which some of the lads drove into the town every day for the groceries and other matters required at the house.

"Very good," said Mr. Conyers; "you may run down to the stables, and tell one of the boys to put the fastest pony of the lot into the Newport Pagnell, and to bring it up here, and to look sharp."

"But nobody but Muster Mellish rides in the Newport Pagnell," suggested the softy, with an accent of alarm.

"What of that, you cowardly hound?" cried the trainer, contemptuously. "I 'm going to drive it to-night, don't you hear? D—n his Yorkshire insolence! Am I to be put down by him? It 's his handsome wife that he takes such pride in, is it? Lord help him! Whose money bought the dog-cart, I wonder? Aurora Floyd's, perhaps. And I 'm not to ride in it, I suppose, because it 's my lord's pleasure to drive his black-eyed lady in the sacred vehicle. Look you here, you brainless idiot, and understand me, if you can," cried Mr. James Conyers, in a sudden rage, which crimsoned his handsome face, and lit up his lazy eyes with a new fire—"look you here, Stephen Hargraves; if it was n't that I 'm tied hand and foot, and have been plotted against and thwarted by a woman's cunning at every turn, I could smoke my pipe in yonder house, or in a better house this day."

He pointed with his finger to the pinnacled roof, and the reddened windows glittering in the evening sun, visible far away among the trees.

"Mr. John Mellish!" he said. "If his wife was n't such a she-devil as to be too many guns for the cleverest man in Christendom, I 'd soon make him sing small. Fetch the Newport Pagnell," he cried, suddenly, with an abrupt change of tone; "fetch it, and be quick. I 'm not safe to myself when I talk of this. I 'm not safe when I think how near I was to half a million of money," he muttered under his breath.

He limped out into the open air, fanning himself with the wide brim of his felt hat, and wiping the perspiration from his forehead.

"Be quick," he cried, impatiently, to his deliberate attendant, who had listened eagerly to every word of his master's passionate talk, and who now stood watching him even more intently than before; "be quick, man, can't you? I don't pay you five shillings a week to stare at me. Fetch the trap. I 've worked myself into a fever, and nothing but a rattling drive will set me right again."

The softy shuffled off as rapidly as it was within the range of his ability to walk. He had never been seen to run in his life, but had a slow, sidelong gait, which had some faint resemblance to that of the lower reptiles, but very little in common with the motions of his fellow-men.

Mr. James Conyers limped up and down the little grassy lawn in front of the north lodge. The excitement which had crimsoned his face gradually subsided as he vented his disquietude in occasional impatient exclamations. "Two thousand pound," he muttered; "a pitiful, paltry two thousand. Not a twelvemonth's interest on the money I ought to have had—the money I should have had, if—"

He stopped abruptly, and growled something like an oath between his set teeth as he struck his stick with angry violence into the soft grass. It is especially hard when we are reviling our bad fortune, and quarrelling with our fate, to find at last, on wandering backward to the source of our ill luck, that the primary cause of all has been our own evil-doing. It was this that made Mr. Conyers stop abruptly in his reflections upon his misfortunes, and break off with a smothered oath, and listen impatiently for the wheels of the Newport Pagnell.

The softy appeared presently, leading the horse by the bridle. He had not presumed to seat himself in the sacred vehicle, and he stared wonderingly at James Conyers as the trainer tumbled about the chocolate-cloth cushions, arranging them afresh for his own ease and comfort. Neither the bright varnish of the dark brown panels, nor the crimson crest, nor the glittering steel ornaments on the neat harness, nor any of the exquisitely finished appointments of the light vehicle, provoked one word of criticism from Mr. Conyers. He mounted as easily as his lame leg would allow him, and, taking the reins from the softy, lighted his cigar, preparatory to starting.

"You need n't sit up for me to-night," he said, as he drove into the dusty high-road; "I shall be late."

Mr. Hargraves shut the iron gates with a loud clanking noise upon his new master.

"But I shall, though," he muttered, looking askant through the bars at the fast-disappearing Newport Pagnell, which was now little more than a black spot in a white cloud of dust; "but I shall sit up, though. You 'll come home drunk, I lay." (Yorkshire is so preeminently a horse-racing and betting county, that even simple country folk who have never wagered a sixpence in the quiet course of their lives say "I lay" where a Londoner would say "I dare say.") "You 'll come home drunk, I lay; folks generally do from Doncaster; and I shall hear some more of your wild talk. Yes, yes," he said, in a slow, reflecting tone, "it 's very wild talk, and I can't make top nor tail of it yet—not yet; but it seems to me somehow as if I knew what it all meant, only I can't put it together—I can't put it together. There 's something missin', and the want of that something hinders me putting it together."

He rubbed his stubble of coarse red hair with his two strong, awkward hands, as if he would fain have rubbed some wanting intelligence into his head.

"Two thousand pound," he said, walking slowly back to the cottage—"two thousand pound. It 's a power of money. Why it 's two thousand pound that the winner gets by the great race at Newmarket, and there 's all the gentlefolks ready to give their ears for it. There 's great lords fighting and struggling against each other for it; so it 's no wonder a poor fond chap like me thinks summat about it."

He sat down upon the step of the lodge-door to smoke the cigar-ends which his benefactor had thrown him in the course of the day; but he still ruminated upon this subject, and he still stopped sometimes, between the extinction of one cheroot stump and the illuminating of another, to mutter, "Two thousand pound. Twenty hundred pound. Forty times fifty pound," with an unctuous chuckle after the enunciation of each figure, as if it was some privilege even to be able to talk of such vast sums of money. So might some doting lover, in the absence of his idol, murmur the beloved name to the summer breeze.

The last crimson lights upon the patches of blue water died out beneath the gathering darkness; but the softy sat, still smoking, and still ruminating, till the stars were high in the purple vault above his head. A little after ten o'clock he heard the rattling of wheels and the tramp of horses' hoofs upon the high-road, and, going to the gate, he looked out through the iron bars. As the vehicle dashed by the north gates, he saw that it was one of the Mellish-Park carriages which had been sent to the station to meet John and his wife.

"A short visit to Loon'on," he muttered. "I lay she 's been to fetch the brass."

The greedy eyes of the half-witted groom peered through the iron bars at the passing carriage, as if he would have fain looked through its opaque panels in search of that which he had denominated "the brass." He had a vague idea that two thousand pounds would be a great bulk of money, and that Aurora would carry it in a chest or a bundle that might be perceptible through the carriage-window.

"I 'll lay she 's been to fetch t' brass," he repeated, as he crept back to the lodge-door.

He resumed his seat upon the door-step, his cigar-ends, and his reverie, rubbing his head very often, sometimes with one hand, sometimes with both, but always as if he were trying to rub some wanting sense or power of perception into his wretched brains. Sometimes he gave a short restless sigh, as if he had been trying all this time to guess some difficult enigma, and was on the point of giving it up.

It was long after midnight when Mr. James

Conyers returned, very much the worse for brandy and water and dust. He tumbled over the softy, still sitting on the step of the open door, and then cursed Mr. Hargraves for being in the way.

"B't s'ne'y'h'v ch's'n t' s't 'p," said the trainer, speaking a language entirely composed of consonants, "y' m'y dr'v' tr'p b'ck t' st'bl's."

By which rather obscure speech he gave the softy to understand that he was to take the dog-cart back to Mr. Mellish's stable-yard.

Steeve Hargraves did his drunken master's bidding, and, leading the horse homeward through the quiet night, found a cross boy with a lantern in his hand waiting at the gate of the stable-yard, and by no means disposed for conversation, except, indeed, to the extent of the one remark that he, the cross boy, hoped the new trainer was n't going to be up to this game every night, and hoped the mare, which had been bred for a racer, had n't been ill used.

All John Mellish's horses seemed to have been bred for racers, and to have dropped gradually from prospective winners of the Derby, Oaks, Chester Cup, Great Ebor, Yorkshire Stakes, Leger, and Doncaster Cup, to say nothing of minor victories in the way of Northumberland Plates, Liverpool Autumn Cups, and Curragh Handicaps, through every variety of failure and defeat, into the everyday ignominy of harness. Even the van which carried groceries was drawn by a slim-legged, narrow-chested, high-shouldered animal, called the "Yorkshire Childers," and bought, in its sunny colthood, at a great price by poor John.

Mr. Convers was snoring aloud in his little bedroom when Steeve Hargraves returned to the lodge. The softy stared wonderingly at the handsome face brutalized by drink, and the classical head flung back upon the crumpled pillow in one of those wretched positions which intoxication always chooses for its repose. Steeve Hargraves rubbed his head harder even than before as he looked at the perfect profile, the red, half-parted lips, the dark fringe of lashes on the faintly crimson-tinted cheeks.

"Perhaps I might have been good for summat if I 'd been like you," he said, with a half-savage melancholy. "I should n't have been shamed of myself then. I should n't have crept into dark corners to hide myself, and think why I was n't like other people, and what a bitter, cruel shame it was that I was n't like 'em. You 've no call to hide yourself from other folks; nobody tells you to get out of the way for an ugly hound, as you told me this morning, hang you. The world 's smooth enough for you."

So may Caliban have looked at Prospero, with envy and hate in his heart, before going to his obnoxious tasks of dish-washing and trencher-scraping.

He shook his fist at the unconscious sleeper as he finished speaking, and then stooped to pick up the trainer's dusty clothes, which were scattered upon the floor.

"I suppose I 'm to brush these before I go to bed," he muttered, "that my lord may have 'em ready when he wakes in th' morning."

He took the clothes on his arm and the light in his hand, and went down to the lower room, where he found a brush, and set to work sturdily, enveloping himself in a cloud of dust, like some ugly Arabian *génie* who was going to transform himself into a handsome prince.

He stopped suddenly in his brushing by and by, and crumpled the waistcoat in his hand.

"There 's some paper," he exclaimed. "A paper sewed up between stuff and linin'."

He omitted the definite article before each of the substantives, as is a common habit with his countrymen when at all excited.

"A bit o' paper," he repeated, "between stuff and linin'. I 'll rip t' waistcoat open and see what 't is."

He took his clasp-knife from his pocket, carefully unripped a part of one of the seams in the waistcoat, and extracted a piece of paper folded double — a decent-sized square of rather thick paper, partly printed, partly written.

He leaned over the light with his elbows on the table, and read the contents of this paper, slowly and laboriously, following every word with his thick forefinger, sometimes stopping a long time upon one syllable, sometimes trying back half a line or so, but always plodding patiently with his ugly forefinger.

When he came to the last word, he burst suddenly into a loud chuckle, as if he had just succeeded in guessing that difficult enigma which had puzzled him all the evening.

"I know it all now," he said. "I can put it all together now, his words, and hers, and the money. I can put it all together, and make out the meaning of it. She 's going to give him the two thousand pound to go away from here and say nothing about this."

He refolded the paper, replaced it carefully in its hiding-place between the stuff and lining of the waistcoat, then searched in his capacious pocket for a fat leathern book, in which, among all sorts of odds and ends, there were some needles and a tangled skein of black thread. Then, stooping over the light, he slowly sewed up the seam which he had ripped open, dexterously and neatly enough, in spite of the clumsiness of his big fingers.

CHAPTER XXII.

STILL CONSTANT.

Mr. James Convers took his breakfast in his own apartment upon the morning of his visit to Doncaster, and Stephen Hargraves waited upon him, carrying him a basin of muddy coffee, and enduring his ill humor with the long-suffering which seemed peculiar to this hump-backed, low-voiced stable-helper.

The trainer rejected the coffee, and called for a pipe, and lay smoking half the summer morning, with the scent of the roses and honeysuckle floating into his close chamber, and the July sunshine glorifying the sham roses and blue lilies that twisted themselves in floricultural monstrosity about the cheap paper on the walls.

The softy cleaned his master's boots, set them in the sunshine to air, washed the break-fast things, swept the door-step, and then seated himself upon it to ruminate, with his elbows on his knees and his hands twisted in his coarse red hair. The silence of the summer atmosphere was only broken by the drowsy hum of the insects in the wood, and the occasional dropping of some early-blighted leaf.

Mr. Conyers' temper had been in no manner improved by his night's dissipation in the town of Doncaster. Heaven knows what entertainment he had found in those lonely streets, the grass-grown market-place and tenantless stalls, or that dreary and hermetically-sealed building, which looks like a prison on three sides and a chapel on the fourth, and which, during the September meeting, bursts suddenly into life and light with huge posters flaring against its gaunt walls, and a bright blue-ink announcement of Mr. and Mrs. Charles Mathews, or Mr. and Mrs. Charles Kean, for five nights only. Normal amusement in the town of Doncaster between those two oases in the year's dreary circle, the spring and autumn meetings, there is none; but of abnormal and special entertainment there may be much, only known to such men as Mr. James Conyers, to whom the most sinuous alley is a pleasant road, so long as it leads, directly or indirectly, to the betting-man's god—Money.

However this might be, Mr. Conyers bore upon him all the symptoms of having, as the popular phrase has it, made a night of it. His eyes were dim and glassy; his tongue hot and furred, and uncomfortably large for his parched mouth; his hand so shaky that the operation which he performed with a razor before his looking-glass was a toss-up between suicide and shaving. His heavy head seemed to have been transformed into a leaden box full of buzzing noises; and after getting half through his toilet, he gave it up for a bad job, and threw himself upon the bed he had just left, a victim to that biliary derangement which inevitably follows an injudicious admixture of alcoholic and malt liquors.

"A tumbler of Hockheimer," he muttered, "or even the third-rate Chablis they give one at a *table d'hôte*, would freshen me up a little; but there 's nothing to be had in this abominable place except brandy and water."

He called to the softy, and ordered him to mix a tumbler of the last-named beverage cold and weak.

Mr. Conyers drained the cool and lucid draught, and flung himself back upon the pillow with a sigh of relief. He knew that he would be thirsty again in five or ten minutes, and that the respite was a brief one; but still it was a respite.

"Have they come home?" he asked.

"Who?"

"Mr. and Mrs. Mellish, you idiot!" answered the trainer, fiercely. "Who else should bother my head about? Did they come home last night while I was away?"

The softy told his master that he had seen one of the carriages drive past the north gate at a little after ten o'clock upon the preceding night, and that he supposed it contained Mr. and Mrs. Mellish.

"Then you 'd better go up to the house and make sure," said Mr. Conyers; "I want to know."

"Go up to th' house?"

"Yes, coward! yes, sneak! Do you suppose that Mrs. Mellish will eat you?"

"I don't suppose naught o' t' sort," answered the softy, sulkily, "but I 'd rather not go."

"But I tell you I want to know," said Mr. Conyers; "I want to know if Mrs. Mellish at home, and what she 's up to, and whether there are any visitors at the house, and all about her. Do you understand?"

"Yes; it 's easy enough to understand, but it 's rare and difficult to do," replied Steeve Hargraves. "How am I to find out? What 's to tell me?"

"How do I know?" cried the trainer, impatiently; for Stephen Hargrave's slow, dogged stupidity was throwing the dashing James Conyers into a fever of vexation. "How do I know? Don't you see that I 'm too ill to stir from this bed? I 'd go myself if I wasn't. And can't you go and do what I tell you without standing arguing there until you drive me mad?"

Steeve Hargraves muttered some sulky apology, and shuffled out of the room. Mr. Conyers' handsome eyes followed him with a dark frown. It is not a pleasant state of health which succeeds a drunken debauch, and the trainer was angry with himself for the weakness which had taken him to Doncaster upon the preceding evening, and thereby inclined to vent his anger upon other people.

There is a great deal of vicarious penance done in this world. Lady's-maids are apt to suffer for the follies of their mistresses, and Lady Clara Vere de Vere's French abigail extremely likely to have to atone for young Laurence's death by patient endurance of my lady's ill temper, and much unpicking and remaking of bodices, which would have fitted her ladyship well enough in any other state of mind than the remorseful misery which is el-

ndered of an evil conscience. The ugly
sh across young Laurence's throat, to say
thing of the cruel slanders circulated after
e inquest, may make life almost unendur-
le to the poor, meek nursery-governess who
neates Lady Clara's younger sisters; and
e younger sisters themselves, and mamma
d papa, and my lady's youthful confidantes,
d even her haughtiest adorers, all have
eir share in the expiation of her ladyship's
ckedness. For she will not—or she can not
meekly own that she has been guilty, and
ut herself away from the world, to make
r own atonement, and work her own re-
mption. So she thrusts the burden of her
s upon other people's shoulders, and travels
e first stage to captious and disappointed
l-maidism.

The commercial gentlemen who make awk-
rd mistakes in the city, the devotees of the
rf whose misfortunes keep them away from
r. Tattersall's premises on a settling-day,
n make innocent women and children carry
e weight of their sins, and suffer the penal-
s of their foolishness. Papa still smokes
Cabanas at fourpence half-penny apiece,
his mild Turkish at nine shillings a pound,
d still dines at the "Crown and Sceptre"
the drowsy summer weather, when the
es are asleep in the flowers at Morden Col-
ge, and the fragrant hay newly stacked in
e meadows beyond Blackheath. But mam-
a must wear her faded silk, or have it dyed,
the case may be; and the children must
rego the promised happiness, the wild de-
ht of sunny rambles on a shingly beach,
rdered by yellow sands that stretch away
hug an ever-changeful and yet ever-con-
nt ocean in their tawny arms. And not
ly mamma and the little ones, but other
thers and other little ones, must help in the
avy sum of penance for the defaulter's in-
ities. The baker may have calculated
on receiving that long-standing account,
d may have planned a new gown for his
fe, and a summer treat for his little ones, to
paid for by the expected money; and the
nest tradesman, soured by the disappoint-
nt of having to disappoint those he loves, is
ely to be cross to them in the bargain, and
en to grudge her Sunday out to the house-
ld drudge who waits at his little table. The
uence of the strong man's evil deed slowly
rcolates through insidious channels of which
never knows or dreams. The deed of folly
of guilt does its fatal work when the sinner
o committed it has forgotten his wicked-
ss. Who shall say where or when the
ults of one man's evil-doing shall cease?
e seed of sin engenders no common root,
ooting straight upward through the earth,
d bearing a given crop. It is the germ of a
il running weed, whose straggling suckers
ivel underground, beyond the ken of mortal
e, beyond the power of mortal calculation.

If Louis XV had been a conscientious man,
terror and murder, misery and confusion,
might never have reigned upon the darkened
face of beautiful France. If Eve had rejected the fatal fruit, we might all have been in
Eden to-day.

Mr. James Conyers, then, after the manner
of mankind, vented his spleen upon the only
person who came in his way, and was glad to
be able to despatch the softy upon an unpleasant errand, and make his attendant as uncomfortable as he was himself.

"My head rocks as if I was on board a
steam-packet," he muttered, as he lay alone
in his little bedroom, "and my hand shakes
so that I can't hold my pipe steady while I
fill it. I 'm in a nice state to have to talk to
her. As if it was n't as much as I can do at
the best of times to be a match for her."

He flung aside his pipe half filled, and
turned his head wearily upon the pillow.
The hot sun and the buzz of the insects tormented him. There was a big blue-bottle fly
blundering and wheeling about among the
folds of the dimity bed-curtains—a fly which
seemed the very genius of delirium tremens;
but the trainer was too ill to do more than
swear at his purple-winged tormentor.

He was awakened from a half doze by the
treble voice of a small stable-boy in the room
below. He called out angrily for the lad to
come up and state his business. His business
was a message from Mr. John Mellish, who
wished to see the trainer immediately.

"Mr. Mellish," muttered James Conyers to
himself. "Tell your master I 'm too ill to
stir, but that I 'll wait upon him in the evening," he said to the boy. "You can see I 'm
ill, if you 've got any eyes, and you can say
that you found me in bed."

The lad departed with these instructions,
and Mr. Conyers returned to his own thoughts,
which appeared to be by no means agreeable
to him.

To drink spirituous liquors and play all-
fours in the sanded tap-room of a sporting
public is no doubt a very delicious occupation,
and would be altogether Elysian and unob-
jectionable if one could always be drinking
spirits and playing all-fours. But as the finest
picture ever painted by Raphael or Rubens is
but a dead blank of canvas upon the reverse,
so there is generally a disagreeable *other* side
to all the pleasures of earth, and a certain re-
action after card-playing and brandy-drink-
ing which is more than equivalent in misery
to the pleasures which have preceded it.
Mr. Conyers, tossing his hot head from side
to side upon a pillow which seemed even hot-
ter, took a very different view of life to that
which he had expounded to his boon companions only the night before in the tap-room of
the "Lion and Lamb," Doncaster.

"I should liked to have stopped over the
Leger," he muttered, "for I meant to make a

hatful of money out of the Conjurer; for if what they say at Richmond is anything like truth, he's safe to win. But there's no going against my lady when her mind's made up. It's take it or leave it — yes or no — and be quick about it."

Mr. Conyers garnished his speech with two or three expletives common enough among the men with whom he had lived, but not to be recorded here, and, closing his eyes, fell into a doze — a half-waking, half-sleeping torpidity, in which he felt as if his head had become a ton-weight of iron, and was dragging him backward through the pillow into a bottomless abyss.

While the trainer lay in this comfortless semi-slumber, Stephen Hargraves walked slowly and sulkily through the wood on his way to the invisible fence, from which point he meant to reconnoitre the premises.

The irregular *façade* of the old house fronted him across the smooth breadth of lawn, dotted and broken by parti-colored flowerbeds; by rustic clumps of gnarled oak supporting mighty clusters of vivid scarlet geraniums, all aflame in the sunshine; by trellised arches laden with trailing roses of every varying shade, from palest blush to deepest crimson; by groups of evergreens, whose every leaf was rich in beauty and luxuriance, whose every tangled garland would have made a worthy chaplet for a king.

The softy, in the semi-darknesses of his soul, had some glimmer of that light which was altogether wanting in Mr. James Conyers. He felt that these things were beautiful. The broken lines of the ivy-covered house-front, Gothic here, Elizabethan there, were in some manner pleasant to him. The scattered rose-leaves on the lawn; the flickering shadows of the evergreens upon the grass; the song of a skylark too lazy to soar, and content to warble among the bushes; the rippling sound of a tiny water-fall far away in the wood, made a language of which he only understood a few straggling syllables here and there, but which was not altogether a meaningless jargon to him, as it was to the trainer, to whose mind Holborn Hill would have conveyed as much of the sublime as the untrodden pathways of the Jungfrau. The softy dimly perceived that Mellish Park was beautiful, and he felt a fiercer hatred against the person whose influence had ejected him from his old home.

The house fronted the south, and the Venetian shutters were all closed upon this hot summer's day. Stephen Hargraves looked for his old enemy Bow-wow, who was likely enough to be lying on the broad stone steps before the hall-door; but there was no sign of the dog's presence anywhere about. The hall-door was closed, and the Venetian shutters, under the rose and clematis shadowed veranda which sheltered John Mellish's room,

were also closed. The softy walked round by the fence which encircled the lawn to another iron gate which opened close to John's room and which was so completely overshadowed by a clump of beeches as to form a safe point of observation. This gate had been left ajar by Mr. Mellish himself, most likely, for that gentleman had a happy knack of forgetting to shut the doors and gates which he opened and the softy, taking courage from the stillness around and about the house, ventured into the garden, and crept stealthily toward the closed shutters before the windows of Mr. Mellish's apartment, with much of the manner which might distinguish some wretched mongrel cur who trusts himself within earshot of a mastiff's kennel.

The mastiff was out of the way on this occasion, for one of the shutters was ajar; and when Stephen Hargraves peeped cautiously into the room, he was relieved to find it empty. John's elbow-chair was pushed a little way from the table, which was laden with open pistol-cases and breech-loading revolvers. These, with two or three silk handkerchiefs, a piece of chamois leather, and a bottle of oil, bore witness that Mr. Mellish had been beguiling the morning by the pleasing occupation of inspecting and cleaning the fire-arms which formed the chief ornaments of his study.

It was his habit to begin this operation with great preparation, and altogether upon a gigantic scale; to reject all assistance with scorn; to put himself in a violent perspiration at the end of half an hour, and to send one of the servants to finish the business, and restore the room to its old order.

The softy looked with a covetous eye at the noble array of guns and pistols. He had that innate love of these things which seems to be implanted in every breast, whatever its owner's state or station. He had hoarded his money once to buy himself a gun; but when he had saved the five-and-thirty shillings demanded by a certain pawnbroker of Doncaster for an old-fashioned musket, which was almost as heavy as a small cannon, his courage failed him, and he could not bring himself to part with the precious coins, whose very touch could send a thrill of rapture through the slow current of his blood. No, he could not surrender such a sum of money to the Doncaster pawnbroker even for the possession of his heart's desire; and as the stern money-lender refused to take payment in weekly instalments of sixpences, Stephen was fain to go without the gun, and to hope that some day or other Mr. John Mellish would reward his services by the gift of some disused fowling-piece by Forsythe or Manton. But there was no hope of such happiness now. A new dynasty reigned at Mellish, and a black-eyed queen, who hated him, had forbidden him to sully her domain with the traces of his shambling foot. He felt that he was in momentary peril upon the threshold of that sacred chamber, which, during his long service at Mellish Park, he had always regarded as a very temple of the beautiful; but the sight of fire-arms upon the table had a magnetic attraction for him, and he drew the Venetian shutters a little way farther ajar, and slid himself in through the open window. Then, flushed and trembling with excitement, he dropped into John's chair, and began to handle the precious implements of warfare upon pheasants and partridges, and to turn them about in his big, clumsy hands.

Delicious as the guns were, and delightful though it was to draw one of the revolvers up to his shoulder, and take aim at an imaginary pheasant, the pistols were even still more attractive, for with them he could not refrain from taking imaginary aim at his enemies; sometimes at James Conyers, who had snubbed and abused him, and had made the bread of dependence bitter to him; very often at Aurora; once or twice at poor John Mellish; but always with a darkness upon his pallid face which would have promised little mercy had the pistol been loaded and the enemy near at hand.

There was one pistol, a small one, and an odd one apparently, for he could not find its fellow, which took a peculiar hold upon his fancy. It was as pretty as a lady's toy, and small enough to be carried in a lady's pocket; but the hammer snapped upon the nipple, when the softy pulled the trigger, with a sound that evidently meant mischief.

"To think that such a little thing as this could kill a big man like you," muttered Mr. Hargraves, with a jerk of his head in the direction of the north lodge.

He had this pistol still in his hand when the door was suddenly opened, and Aurora Mellish stood upon the threshold.

She spoke as she opened the door, almost before she was in the room.

"John, dear," she said, "Mrs. Powell wants to know whether Colonel Maddison dines here to-day with the Lofthouses."

She drew back with a shudder that shook her from head to foot as her eyes met the softy's hated face instead of John's familiar glance.

In spite of the fatigue and agitation which she had endured within the last few days, she was not looking ill. Her eyes were unnaturally bright, and a feverish color burned in her cheeks. Her manner, always impetuous, was restless and impatient to-day, as if her nature had been charged with a terrible amount of electricity, till she were likely at any moment to explode in some tempest of anger or woe.

"You here!" she exclaimed.

The softy, in his embarrassment, was at a loss for an excuse for his presence. He pulled

his shabby hare-skin cap off, and twisted it round and round in his great hands, but he made no other recognition of his late master's wife.

"Who sent you to this room?" asked Mrs. Mellish; "I thought you had been forbidden this place — the house at least," she added, her face crimsoning indignantly as she spoke, "although Mr. Conyers may choose to bring you to the north lodge. Who sent you here?"

"Him," answered Mr. Hargraves, doggedly, with another jerk of his head toward the trainer's abode.

"James Conyers?"

"Yes."

"What does he want here, then?"

"He told me to come down t' th' house, and see if you and the master'd come back."

"Then you can go and tell him that we have come back," she said contemptuously, "and that if he'd waited a little longer, he would have had no occasion to send his spies after me."

The softy crept toward the window, feeling that his dismissal was contained in these words, and looking rather suspiciously at the array of driving and hunting whips over the mantle-piece. Mrs. Mellish might have a fancy for laying one of these about his shoulders if he happened to offend her.

"Stop!" she said, impetuously, as he laid his hand upon the shutter to push it open; "since you are here, you can take a message, or a scrap of writing," she said, contemptuously, as if she could not bring herself to call any communication between herself and Mr. Conyers a note or letter. "Yes; you can take a few lines to your master. Stop there while I write."

She waved her hand with a gesture which expressed plainly, "Come no nearer; you are too obnoxious to be endured except at a distance," and seated herself at John's writing-table.

She scratched two lines with a quill pen upon a slip of paper, which she folded while the ink was still wet. She looked for an envelope among her husband's littered paraphernalia of account-books, bills, receipts, and price-lists, and, finding one after some little trouble, put the folded paper into it, fastened the gummed flaps with her lips, and handed the missive to Mr. Hargraves, who had watched her with hungry eyes, eager to fathom this new stage in the mystery.

Was the two thousand pounds in that envelope? he thought. No, surely such a sum of money must be a huge pile of gold and silver — a mountain of glittering coin. He had seen checks sometimes, and bank-notes, in the hands of Langley, the trainer, and he had wondered how it was that money could be represented by those pitiful bits of paper.

"I'd rayther have 't i' goold," he thought:

"if 't was mine, I'd have it all i' goold and silver."

He was very glad when he found himself safely clear of the whips and Mrs. John Mellish, and, as soon as he reached the shelter of the thick foliage upon the northern side of the Park, he set to work to examine the packet which had been intrusted to him.

Mrs. Mellish had liberally moistened the adhesive flap of the envelope, as people are apt to do when they are in a hurry; the consequence of which carelessness was that the gum was still so wet that Stephen Hargraves found no difficulty in opening the envelope without tearing it. He looked cautiously about him, convinced himself that he was unobserved, and then drew out the slip of paper. It contained very little to reward him for his trouble—only these few words, scrawled in Aurora's most careless hand:

"Be on the southern side of the wood, near the turnstile, between half-past eight and nine."

The softy grinned as he slowly made himself master of this communication.

"It 's oncommon hard writin', t' make out th' shapes o' th' letters," he said, as he finished his task. "Why can't gentlefolks wroit like Ned Tiller oop at th' Red Lion — printin' loike. It 's easier to read, and a deal prettier to look at."

He refastened the envelope, pressing it down with his dirty thumb to make it adhere once more, and not much improving its appearance thereby.

"He 's one of your rare careless chaps," he muttered, as he surveyed the letter; "he won't stop t' examine if it 's been opened before. What 's insoide were hardly worth th' trouble of openin' it; but perhaps it 's as well to know it too."

Immediately after Stephen Hargraves had disappeared through the open window, Aurora turned to leave the room by the door, intending to go in search of her husband.

She was arrested on the threshold by Mrs. Powell, who was standing at the door, with the submissive and deferential patience of paid companionship depicted in her insipid face.

"Does Colonel Maddison dine here, my dear Mrs. Mellish?" she asked meekly, yet with a pensive earnestness which suggested that her life, or, at any rate, her peace of mind, depended upon the answer. "I am so anxious to know, for of course it will make a difference with the fish — and perhaps we ought to have some mulligatawny, or, at any rate, a dish of curry among the entrées, for these elderly East-Indian officers are so—"

"I don't know," answered Aurora, curtly. "Were you standing at the door long before I came out, Mrs. Powell?"

"Oh, no," answered the ensign's widow, "not long. Did you not hear me knock?"

Mrs. Powell would not have allowed herself to be betrayed into anything so vulgar as an abbreviation by the torments of the rack, and would have neatly rounded her periods while the awful wheel was stretching every muscle of her agonized frame, and the executioner waiting to give the *coup de grace*.

"Did you not hear me knock?" she asked.

"No," said Aurora, "you did n't knock! Did you?"

Mrs. Mellish made an alarming pause between the two sentences.

"Oh, yes, too-wice," answered Mrs. Powell, with as much emphasis as was consistent with gentility upon the elongated word; "I knocked too-wice; but you seemed so very much preoccupied that—"

"I did n't hear you," interrupted Aurora; "you should knock rather louder when you *want* people to hear, Mrs. Powell. I—I came here to look for John, and I shall stop to put away his guns. Careless fellow — he always leaves them lying about."

"Shall I assist you, dear Mrs. Mellish?"

"Oh, no, thank you."

"But pray allow me—guns are *so* interesting. Indeed, there is very little either in art or nature which, properly considered, is not—"

"You had better find Mr. Mellish, and ascertain if the colonel *does* dine here, I think, Mrs. Powell," interrupted Aurora, shutting the lids of the pistol-cases, and replacing them upon their accustomed shelves.

"Oh, if you wish to be alone, certainly," said the ensign's widow, looking furtively at Aurora's face bending over the breech-loading revolvers, and then walking genteelly and noiselessly out of the room.

"Who was she talking to?" thought Mrs. Powell. "I could hear her voice, but not the other person's. I suppose it was Mr. Mellish; and yet he is not generally so quiet."

She stopped to look out of a window in the corridor, and found the solution of her doubts in the shambling figure of the softy making his way northward, creeping stealthily under shadow of the plantation that bordered the lawn. Mrs. Powell's faculties were all cultivated to a state of unpleasant perfection, and she was able, actually as well as figuratively, to see a great deal farther than most people.

John Mellish was not to be found in the house, and, on making inquiries of some of the servants, Mrs. Powell learned that he had strolled up to the north lodge to see the trainer, who was confined to his bed.

"Indeed!" said the ensign's widow; "then I think, as we really ought to know about the colonel and the mulligatawny, I will walk to the north lodge myself and see Mr. Mellish."

She took a sun-umbrella from the stand in the hall, and crossed the lawn northward at a smart pace, in spite of the heat of the July noontide. "If I can get there before Hargraves," she thought; "I may be able to find out why he came to the house."

The ensign's widow did reach the lodge before Stephen Hargraves, who stopped, as we know, under shelter of the foliage in the loneliest pathway of the wood to decipher Aurora's scrawl. She found John Mellish seated with the trainer, in the little parlor of the lodge, discussing the stable arrangement; the master talking with considerable animation, the servant listening with a listless *nonchalance* which had a certain air of depreciation, not to say contempt, for poor John's racing-stud. Mr. Conyers had risen from his bed at the sound of his employer's voice in the little room below, and had put on a dusty shooting-coat and a pair of shabby slippers, in order to come down and hear what Mr. Mellish had to say.

"I 'm sorry to hear you 're ill, Conyers," John said, heartily, with a freshness in his strong voice which seemed to carry health and strength in its every tone; "as you were n't well enough to look in at the house, I thought I 'd come over here and talk to you about business. I want to know whether we ought to take Monte Cristo out of his York engagement, and if you think it would be wise to let Northern Dutchman take his chance for the Great Ebor. Hey ?"

Mr. Mellish's query resounded through the small room, and made the languid trainer shudder. Mr. Conyers had all the peevish susceptibility to discomfort or inconvenience which go to make a man above his station. Is it a merit to be above one's station, I wonder, that people make such a boast of their unfitness for honest employments, and sturdy but progressive labor? The flowers, in the fables, that want to be trees, always get the worst of it, I remember. Perhaps that is because they can do nothing but complain. There is no objection to their growing into trees, if they can, I suppose, but a great objection to their being noisy and disagreeable because they can't. With the son of the simple Corsican advocate, who made himself Emperor of France, the world had every sympathy, but with poor Louis Philippe, who ran away from a throne at the first shock that disturbed its equilibrium, I fear, very little. Is it quite right to be angry with the world because it worships success; for is not success, in some manner, the stamp of divinity ? Self-assertion may deceive the ignorant for a time, but, when the noise dies away, we cut open the drum, and find that it was emptiness that made the music. Mr. Conyers contented himself with declaring that he walked on a road which was unworthy of his footsteps, but as he never contrived to get an inch farther upon the great highway of life, there is some reason to suppose that he had his opinion entirely to himself. Mr. Mellish and his trainer were still discussing stable matters when Mrs. Powell reached the north lodge. She stopped for a few minutes in the rustic doorway, waiting for a pause in the conversation. She was too well-bred to interrupt Mr. Mellish in his talk, and there was a chance that she might hear something by lingering. No contrast could be stronger than that presented by the two men. John, broad-shouldered and stalwart; his short, crisp chestnut hair brushed away from his square forehead; his bright, open blue eyes beaming honest sunshine upon all they looked at; his loose gray clothes neat and well made; his shirt in the first freshness of the morning's toilet; everything about him made beautiful by the easy grace which is the peculiar property of the man who has been born a gentleman, and which neither all the cheap finery which Mr. Moses can sell, nor all the expensive absurdities which Mr. Tittlebat Titmouse can buy, will ever bestow upon the *parvenu* or the vulgarian; the trainer, handsomer than his master by as much as Antinous in Grecian marble is handsomer than the substantially-shod and loose-coated young squires in Mr. Millais's designs; as handsome as it is possible for this human clay to be, with every feature moulded to the highest type of positive beauty, and yet every inch of him a boor; his shirt soiled and crumpled, his hair rough and uncombed; his unshaven chin dark with the blue bristles of his budding beard, and smeared with the traces of last night's liquor; his dingy hands supporting his dingy chin, and his elbows bursting half out of the frayed sleeves of his shabby shooting-jacket, leaning on the table in an attitude of indifferent insolence; his countenance expressive of nothing but dissatisfaction with his own lot, and contempt for the opinions of other people. All the homilies that could be preached upon the time-worn theme of beauty and its worthlessness could never argue so strongly as this mute evidence presented by Mr. Conyers himself in his slouching posture and his unkempt hair. Is beauty, then, so little, one asks, on looking at the trainer and his employer? Is it better to be clean, and well-dressed, and gentlemanly, than to have a classical profile and a thrice-worn shirt?

Finding very little to interest her in John's stable-talk, Mrs. Powell made her presence known, and once more asked the all-important question about Colonel Maddison.

"Yes," John answered, "the old boy is sure to come. Let 's have plenty of chutnee, and boiled rice, and preserved ginger, and all the rest of the unpleasant things that Indian officers live upon. Have you seen Lolly ?"

Mr. Mellish put on his hat, gave a last instruction to the trainer, and left the cottage.

"Have you seen Lolly ?" he asked again.

"Ye-es," replied Mrs. Powell; "I have only lately left Mrs. Mellish in your room;

8

she had been speaking to that half-witted person — Hargraves I think he is called."

"Speaking to *him?*" cried John; "speaking to him in my room? Why, the fellow is forbidden to cross the threshold of the house, and Mrs. Mellish abominates the sight of him. Don't you remember the day he flogged her dog, you know, and Lolly horse — had hysterics?" added Mr. Mellish, choking himself with one word and substituting another.

"Oh, yes, I remember that little — ahem — unfortunate occurrence perfectly," replied Mrs. Powell, in a tone which, in spite of its amiability, implied that Aurora's escapade was not a thing to be easily forgotten.

"Then it 's not likely, you know, that Lolly would talk to the man. You must be mistaken, Mrs. Powell."

The ensign's widow simpered, and lifted her eyebrows, gently shaking her head with a gesture that seemed to say, "Did you ever find *me* mistaken?"

"No, no, my dear Mr. Mellish," she said, with a half-playful air of conviction, "there was no mistake on my part. Mrs. Mellish was talking to the half-witted person; but you know the person is a sort of servant to Mr. Conyers, and Mrs. Mellish may have had a message for Mr. Conyers."

"A message for *him!*" roared John, stopping suddenly, and planting his stick upon the ground in a movement of unconcealed passion; "what messages should she have for *him?* Why should she want people fetching and carrying between her and him?"

Mrs. Powell's pale eyes lit up with a faint yellow flame in their greenish pupils as John broke out thus. "It is coming—it is coming —it is coming!" her envious heart cried, and she felt that a faint flush of triumph was gathering in her sickly cheeks.

But in another moment John Mellish recovered his self-command. He was angry with himself for that transient passion. "Am I going to doubt her again?" he thought. "Do I know so little of the nobility of her generous soul that I am ready to listen to every whisper, and terrify myself with every look?"

They had walked about a hundred yards away from the lodge by this time. John turned irresolutely, as if half inclined to go back.

"A message for Conyers," he said to Mrs. Powell; "ay, ay, to be sure. It 's likely enough she might want to send him a message, for she 's cleverer at all the stable business than I am. It was she who told me not to enter Cherry-stone for the Chester Cup, and, egad! I was obstinate, and I was licked—as I deserved to be, for not listening to my dear girl."

Mrs. Powell would fain have boxed John's ear, had she been tall enough to reach that organ. Infatuated fool! would he never open

his dull eyes and see the ruin that was preparing for him?

"You *are* a good husband, Mr. Mellish," she said, with gentle melancholy. "Your wife *ought* to be happy!" she added, with a sigh which plainly hinted that Mrs. Mellish was miserable.

"A good husband!" cried John; "not half good enough for her. What can I do to prove that I love her? What can I do? Nothing, except to let her have her own way; and what a little that seems! Why, if she wanted to set that house on fire, for the pleasure of making a bonfire," he added, pointing to the rambling mansion in which his blue eyes had first seen the light, "I 'd let her do it, and look on with her at the blaze."

"Are you going back to the lodge?" Mrs. Powell asked quietly, not taking any notice of this outbreak of marital enthusiasm.

They had retraced their steps, and were within a few paces of the little garden before the north lodge.

"Going back?" said John; "no—yes."

Between his utterance of the negative and the affirmative he had looked up and seen Stephen Hargraves entering the little garden-gate. The softy had come by the short cut through the wood. John Mellish quickened his pace, and followed Steeve Hargraves across the little garden to the threshold of the door. At the threshold he paused. The rustic porch was thickly screened by the spreading branches of the roses and honeysuckle, and John was unseen by those within. He did not himself deliberately listen; he only waited for a few moments, wondering what to do next. In those few moments of indecision he heard the trainer speak to his attendant:

"Did you see her?" he asked.

"Ay, sure, I see her."

"And she gave you a message?"

"No, she gave me this here."

"A letter!" cried the trainer's eager voice; "give it me."

John Mellish heard the tearing of the envelope and the crackling of the crisp paper, and knew that his wife had been writing to his servant. He clenched his strong right hand until the nails dug into the muscular palm; then turning to Mrs. Powell, who stood close behind him, simpering meekly, as she would have simpered at an earthquake, or a revolution, or any other national calamity not peculiarly affecting herself, he said quietly:

"Whatever directions Mrs. Mellish has given are sure to be right; I won't interfere with them." He walked away from the north lodge as he spoke, looking straight before him, homeward, as if the unchanging load-star of his honest heart were beckoning to him across the dreary Slough of Despond, and bidding him take comfort.

"Mrs. Powell," he said, turning rather

sharply upon the ensign's widow, "I should be very sorry to say anything likely to offend you, in your character of—of a guest beneath my roof; but I shall take it as a favor to myself if you will be so good as to remember that I require no information respecting my wife's movements from you, or from any one. Whatever Mrs. Mellish does, she does with my full consent, my perfect approbation. Cæsar's wife must not be suspected, and, by Jove, ma'am—you'll pardon the expression—John Mellish's wife must not be watched."

"Watched! information!" exclaimed Mrs. Powell, lifting her pale eyebrows to the extreme limits allowed by nature. "My dear Mr. Mellish, when I really only casually remarked, in reply to a question of your own, that I believed Mrs. Mellish had—"

"Oh yes," answered John, "I understand. There are several ways by which you can go to Doncaster from this house. You can go across the fields, or round by Harper's Common, an out-of-the-way, roundabout route, but you get there all the same, you know, ma'am. I generally prefer the high-road. It may n't be the shortest way, perhaps, but it's certainly the straightest."

The corners of Mrs. Powell's thin lower lip dropped perhaps the eighth of an inch as John made these observations, but she very quickly recovered her habitual genteel simper, and told Mr. Mellish that he really had such a droll way of expressing himself as to make his meaning scarcely so clear as could be wished.

But John had said all that he wanted to say, and walked steadily onward, looking always toward that quarter in which the polestar might be supposed to shine, guiding him back to his home.

That home so soon to be desolate! with such ruin brooding above it as in his darkest doubts, his wildest fears, he had never shadowed forth.

CHAPTER XXIII.

ON THE THRESHOLD OF DARKER MISERIES.

John went straight to his own apartment to look for his wife; but he found the guns put back in their usual places, and the room empty. Aurora's maid, a smartly-dressed girl, came tripping out of the servants' hall, where the rattling of knives and forks announced that a very substantial dinner was being done substantial justice to, to answer John's eager inquiries. She told him that Mrs. Mellish had complained of a headache, and had gone to her room to lie down. John went up stairs, and crept cautiously along the carpeted corridor, fearful of every footfall which might break the repose of his wife. The door of her dressing-room was ajar; he pushed it softly open, and went in. Aurora was lying

upon the sofa, wrapped in a loose white dressing-gown, her masses of ebon hair uncoiled and falling about her shoulders in serpentine tresses that looked like shining blue-black snakes released from poor Medusa's head to make their escape amid the folds of her garments. Heaven knows what a stranger sleep may have been for many a night to Mrs. Mellish's pillow, but she had fallen into a heavy slumber on this hot summer's day. Her cheeks were flushed with a feverish crimson, and one small hand lay under her head, twisted in the tangled masses of her glorious hair.

John bent over her with a tender smile.

"Poor girl," he thought; "Thank God that she can sleep, in spite of the miserable secrets which have come between us. Talbot Bulstrode left her because he could not bear the agony that I am suffering now. What cause had he to doubt her? What cause compared to that which I have had a fortnight ago—the other night—this morning? And yet—and yet I trust her, and will trust her, please God, to the very end."

He seated himself in a low easy-chair close beside the sofa upon which his sleeping wife lay, and, resting his head upon his arm, watched her, thought of her, perhaps prayed for her, and after a little while fell asleep, snoring in bass harmony with Aurora's regular breathing. He slept and snored, this horrible man, in the hour of his trouble, and behaved himself altogether in a manner most unbecoming in a hero. But then he is not a hero. He is stout and strongly built, with a fine broad chest, and unromantically robust health.— There is more chance of his dying of apoplexy than of fading gracefully in a decline, or breaking a blood-vessel in a moment of intense emotion. He sleeps calmly, with the warm July air floating in upon him from the open window, and comforting him with its balmy breath, and he fully enjoys that rest of body and mind. Yet even in his tranquil slumber there is a vague something, some lingering shadow of the bitter memories which sleep has put away from him, that fills his breast with a dull pain, an oppressive heaviness, which can not be shaken off. He slept until half a dozen different clocks in the rambling old house had come to one conclusion, and declared it to be five in the afternoon; and he awoke with a start, to find his wife watching him, Heaven knows how intently, with her black eyes filled with solemn thought, and a strange earnestness in her face.

"My poor John," she said, bending her beautiful head and resting her burning forehead upon his hand, "how tired you must have been to sleep so soundly in the middle of the day! I have been awake for nearly an hour, watching you."

"Watching me. Lolly—why?"

"And thinking how good you are to me. Oh, John, John, what can I ever do—what can I ever do to atone to you for all—"

"Be happy, Aurora," he said, huskily, "be happy, and—and send that man away."

"I will, John; he shall go soon. dear — to-night!"

"What! then that letter was to dismiss him?" asked Mr. Mellish.

"You know that I wrote to him?"

"Yes, darling, it was to dismiss him — say that it was so, Aurora. Pay him what money you like to keep the secret that he discovered, but send him away, Lolly, send him away. The sight of him is hateful to me. Dismiss him, Aurora, or I must do so myself."

He rose in his passionate excitement, but Aurora laid her hand softly upon his arm.

"Leave all to me," she said, quietly. "Believe me that I will act for the best. For the best, at least, if you could n't bear to lose me; and you could n't bear that, could you, John?"

"Lose you! My God, Aurora, why do you say such things to me? I *would n't* lose you. Do you hear, Lolly? I *would n't*. I 'd follow you to the farthest end of the universe; and Heaven take pity upon those that came between us."

His set teeth, the fierce light in his eyes, and the iron rigidity of his mouth gave an emphasis to his words which my pen could never give if I used every epithet in the English language.

Aurora rose from her sofa, and, twisting her hair into a thickly-rolled mass at the back of her head, seated herself near the window, and pushed back the Venetian shutter.

"These people dine here to-day, John?" she asked, listlessly.

"The Lofthouses and Colonel Maddison? Yes, darling; and it 's ever so much past five. Shall I ring for your afternoon cup of tea?"

"Yes, dear, and take some with me, if you will."

I 'm afraid that in his inmost heart Mr. Mellish did not cherish any very great affection for the decoctions of bohea and gunpowder with which his wife dosed him; but he would have dined upon cod-liver oil had she served the banquet, and he strung his nerves to their extreme tension at her supreme pleasure, and affected to highly relish the post-meridian dishes of tea which his wife poured out for him in the sacred seclusion of her dressing-room.

Mrs. Powell heard the comfortable sound of the chinking of the thin egg-shell china and the rattling of the spoons as she passed the half-open door on her way to her own apartment, and was mutely furious as she thought that love and harmony reigned within the chamber where the husband and wife sat at tea.

Aurora went down to the drawing-room an hour after this, gorgeous in maize-colored silk and voluminous flouncings of black lace, with her hair plaited in a diadem upon her head, and fastened with three diamond stars which John had bought for her in the Rue de la Paix, and which were cunningly fixed upon wire springs, which caused them to vibrate with every chance movement of her beautiful head. You will say, perhaps, that she was arrayed too gaudily for the reception of an old Indian officer and a country clergyman and his wife; but if she loved handsome dresses better than simpler attire, it was from no taste for display, but rather from an innate love of splendor and expenditure, which was a part of her expansive nature. She had always been taught to think of herself as Miss Floyd, the banker's daughter, and she had been taught also to spend money as a duty which she owed to society.

Mrs. Lofthouse was a pretty little woman, with a pale face and hazel eyes. She was the youngest daughter of Colonel Maddison, and was, "by birth, you know, my dear, far superior to poor Mrs. Mellish, who, in spite of her wealth, is only, etc., etc., etc.," as Margaret Lofthouse remarked to her female acquaintance. She could not very easily forget that her father was the younger brother of a baronet, and had distinguished himself in some terrific manner by blood-thirsty demolition of Sikhs far away in the untractable East, and she thought it rather hard that Aurora should possess such cruel advantages through some pettifogging commercial genius on the part of her Glasgow ancestors.

But, as it was impossible for honest people to know Aurora without loving her, Mrs. Lofthouse heartily forgave her her fifty thousand pounds, and declared her to be the dearest darling in the wide world; while Mrs. Mellish freely returned her friendliness, and caressed the little woman as she had caressed Lucy Bulstrode, with a superb yet affectionate condescension, such as Cleopatra may have had for her handmaidens.

The dinner went off pleasantly enough. Colonel Maddison attacked the side-dishes specially provided for him, and praised the Mellish-Park cook. Mr. Lofthouse explained to Aurora the plan of a new school-house which Mrs. Mellish was going to build for her husband's parish. She listened patiently to the rather wearisome details, in which a bake-house, and a wash-house, and a Tudor chimney seemed the leading features. She had heard so much of this before; for there was scarcely a church, or a hospital, or a model lodging-house, or a refuge for any misery or destitution whatever that had been lately elevated to adorn this earth for which the banker's daughter had not helped to pay. But her heart was wide enough for them all, and she was always glad to hear of the bake-house, and wash-house, and the Tudor chimney all over again. If she was a little less interested upon this occasion than usual, Mr. Lofthouse did not observe her inattention, for in the simple earnestness of his own mind he thought it scarcely possible that the school-house topic could fail to be interesting. Nothing is so difficult as to make people understand that you don't care for what they themselves especially affect. John Mellish could not believe that the entries for the Great Ebor were not interesting to Mr. Lofthouse, and the country clergyman was fully convinced that the details of his philanthropic schemes for the regeneration of his parish could not be otherwise than delightful to his host. But the master of Mellish Park was very silent, and sat with his glass in his hand, looking across the dinner-table and Mrs. Lofthouse's head at the sunlit tree-tops between the lawn and the north lodge. Aurora, from her end of the table, saw that gloomy glance, and a resolute shadow darkened her face, expressive of the strengthening of some rooted purpose deep hidden in her heart. She sat so long at dessert, with her eyes fixed upon an apricot in her plate, and the shadow upon her face deepening every moment, that poor Mrs. Lofthouse was in utter despair of getting the significant look which was to release her from the bondage of hearing her father's stories of tiger-shooting and pig-sticking for the two or three hundredth time. Perhaps she never would have got that feminine signal had not Mrs. Powell, with a little significant "hem," made some observation about the sinking sun.

The ensign's widow was one of those people who declare that there is a perceptible difference in the length of the days upon the twenty-third or twenty-fourth of June, and who go on announcing the same fact until the long winter evenings come with the twenty-first of December, and it is time for them to declare the converse of their late proposition. It was some remark of this kind that aroused Mrs. Mellish from her reverie, and caused her to start up suddenly, quite forgetful of the conventional simpering beck to her guest.

"Past eight!" she said; "no, it 's surely not so late?"

"Yes it is, Lolly," John Mellish answered, looking at his watch, "a quarter past."

"Indeed! I beg your pardon, Mrs. Lofthouse; shall we go into the drawing-room?"

"Yes, dear, do," said the clergyman's wife, "and let 's have a nice chat. Papa will drink too much claret if he tells the pig-sticking stories," she added, in a confidential whisper. "Ask your dear, kind husband not to let him have too much claret, because he 's sure to suffer with his liver to-morrow, and say that Lofthouse ought to have restrained him. He always says that it 's poor Riginald's fault for not restraining him."

John looked anxiously after his wife as he stood with the door in his hand, while the three ladies crossed the hall. He bit his lip

as he noticed Mrs. Powell's unpleasantly precise figure close at Aurora's shoulder.

"I think I spoke pretty plainly, though, this morning," he thought, as he closed the door and returned to his friends.

A quarter past eight; twenty minutes past; five-and-twenty minutes past. Mrs. Lofthouse was rather a brilliant pianist, and was never happier than when interpreting Thalberg and Benedict upon her friends' Collard and Collards. There were old-fashioned people round Doncaster who believed in Collard and Collard, and were thankful for the melody to be got out of a good, honest grand, in a solid rosewood case, unadorned with carved glorification or ormolu fretwork. At seven-and-twenty minutes past eight Mrs. Lofthouse was seated at Aurora's piano, in the first agonies of a prelude in six flats; a prelude which demanded such extraordinary uses of the left hand across the right, and the right over the left, and such exercise of the thumbs in all sorts of positions——in which, according to all orthodox theories of the pre-Thalberg-ite school, no pianist's thumbs should ever be used—that Mrs. Mellish felt that her friend's attention was not very likely to wander from the keys.

Within the long, low-roofed drawing-room at Mellish there was a snug little apartment, hung with innocent rosebud-sprinkled chintzes, and furnished with maple-wood chairs and tables. Mrs. Lofthouse had not been seated at the piano more than five minutes when Aurora strolled from the drawing-room to this inner chamber, leaving her guest with no audience but Mrs. Powell. She lingered for a moment on the threshold to look back at the ensign's widow, who sat near the piano in an attitude of rapt attention.

"She is watching me," thought Aurora, "though her pink eyelids are drooping over her eyes, and she seems to be looking at the border of her pocket-handkerchief. She sees me with her chin or her nose, perhaps. How do I know? She is all eyes! Bah! am I going to be afraid of her, when I was never afraid of him? What should I fear except——" her head changed from its defiant attitude to a drooping posture, and a sad smile curved her crimson lips—"except to make you unhappy, my dear, my husband. Yes," with a sudden lifting of her head, and reassumption of its proud defiance, "my own true husband; the husband who has kept his marriage vow as unpolluted as when first it issued from his lips!"

I am writing what she thought, remember, not what she said; for she was not in the habit of thinking aloud, nor did I ever know anybody who was.

Aurora took up a shawl that she had flung upon the sofa, and threw it lightly over her head, veiling herself with a cloud of black lace, through which the ru... shivering diamonds shone out like stars in a midnight sky. She looked like Hecate, as she stood on the threshold of the French window, lingering for a moment, with a deep-laid purpose in her heart, and a resolute light in her eyes. The clock in the steeple of the village church struck the three-quarters after eight while she lingered for those few moments. As the last chime died away in the summer air, she looked up darkly at the evening sky, and walked with a rapid footstep out upon the lawn toward the southern end of the wood that bordered the Park.

CHAPTER XXIV.

CAPTAIN PRODDER CARRIES BAD NEWS TO HIS NIECE'S HOUSE.

While Aurora stood upon the threshold of the open window, a man was lingering upon the broad stone steps before the door of the entrance hall, remonstrating with one of John Mellish's servants, who held supercilious parley with the intruder, and kept him at arm's length with the contemptuous indifference of a well-bred servant.

The stranger was Captain Samuel Prodder, who had arrived at Doncaster late in the afternoon, had dined at the "Reindeer," and had come over to Mellish Park in a gig driven by a hanger-on of that establishment. The gig and the hanger-on were both in waiting at the bottom of the steps; and if there had been anything wanting to turn the balance of the footman's contempt for Captain Prodder's blue coat, loose shirt-collar, and silver watch-chain, the gig from the "Reindeer" would have done it.

"Yes, Mrs. Mellish is at home," the gentleman in plush replied, after surveying the sea-captain with a leisurely and critical air, which was rather provoking to poor Samuel, "but she 's engaged."

"But perhaps she 'll put off her engagements for a bit when she hears who it is as wants to see her," answered the captain, diving into his capacious pocket. "She 'll tell a different story, I dare say, when you take her that bit of pasteboard."

He handed the man a card, or rather let me say a stiff square of thick pasteboard, inscribed with his name, so disguised by the flourishing caprices of the engraver as to be not very easily deciphered by unaccustomed eyes. The card bore Captain Prodder's address as well as his name, and informed his acquaintances that he was part owner of the *Nancy Jane*, and that all consignments of goods were to be made to him at, etc., etc.

The footman took the document between his thumb and finger, and examined it as minutely as if it had been some relic of the Middle Ages. A new light dawned upon him

as he deciphered the information about the *Nancy Jane*, and he looked at the captain for the first time with some approach to human interest in his countenance.

"Is it cigars you want to dispose hoff," he asked, "or bandannas? If it 's cigars, you might come round to our 'all, and show us the harticle."

"Cigars!" roared Samuel Prodder. "Do you take me for a smuggler, you ——?" Here followed one of those hearty seafaring epithets with which polite Mr. Chucks was apt to finish his speeches. "I 'm your missus's own uncle; leastways I—I knew her mother when she was a little gal," he added, in considerable confusion; for he remembered how far away his sea-captainship thrust him from Mrs. Mellish and her well-born husband; "so just take her my card, and look sharp about it, will you?"

"We 've a dinner-party," the footman said, coldly, "and I don't know if the ladies have returned to the drawing-room; but if you 're anyways related to missus—I 'll go and see."

The man strolled leisurely away, leaving poor Samuel biting his nails in mute vexation at having let slip that ugly fact of her relationship.

"That swab in the same cut coat as Lord Nelson wore aboard the *Victory*, will look down upon her now he knows she 's niece to a old sea-captain that carries dry goods on commission, and can't keep his tongue between his teeth," he thought.

The footman came back while Samuel Prodder was upbraiding himself for his folly, and informed him that Mrs. Mellish was not to be found in the house.

"Who 's that playin' upon the pianer, then?" asked Mr. Prodder, with skeptical bluntness.

"Oh, that 's the clugyman's wife," answered the man, contemptuously, "a ciddywong guvness, I should think, for she plays too well for a real lady. Missus don't play—leastways only pawlkers, and that sort of think. Good-night."

He closed the two half-glass doors upon Captain Prodder without farther ceremony, and shut Samuel out of his niece's house.

"To think that I played hop-scotch and swopped marbles for hardbake with this gal's mother," thought the captain, "and that her servant turns up his nose at me, and shuts the door in my face!"

It was in sorrow rather than in anger that the disappointed sailor thought this. He had scarcely hoped for anything better. It was only natural that those about his niece should flout at and contemptuously entreat him. Let him get to *her* — let him come only for a moment face to face with Eliza's child, and he did not fear the issue.

"I 'll walk through the Park," he said to the man who had driven him from Doncaster;

"it 's a nice evenin', and there 's pleasant walks under the trees to win'ard. You can drive back into the high-road, and wait for me agen that 'ere turnstile I took notice of as we come along."

The driver nodded, smacked his whip, and drove his elderly gray pony toward the Park gates. Captain Samuel Prodder went slowly and deliberately enough — the way that it was appointed for him to go. The Park was a strange territory to him; but, while driving past the outer boundaries, he had looked admiringly at chance openings in the wood, revealing grassy amphitheatres enriched by spreading oaks, whose branches made a shadowy tracery upon the sunlit turf. He had looked with a seaman's wonder at the inland beauties of the quiet domain, and had pondered whether it might not be a pleasant thing for an old sailor to end his days amid such monotonous woodland tranquillity, far away from the sound of wreck and tempest, and the mighty voices of the dreadful deep; and, in his disappointment at not seeing Aurora, it was some consolation to the captain to walk across the dewy grass in the evening shadows in the direction where, with a sailor's unerring topographical instinct, he knew the turnstile must be situated.

Perhaps he had some hope of meeting his niece in the pathway across the Park. The man had told him that she was out. She could not be far away, as there was a dinner-party at the house, and she was scarcely likely to leave her guests. She was wandering about the Park most likely with some of them.

The shadows of the trees grew darker upon the grass as Captain Prodder drew nearer to the wood; but it was that sweet summer time in which there is scarcely one positively dark hour among the twenty-four; and though the village clock chimed the half-hour after nine as the sailor entered the wood, he was able to distinguish the outlines of two figures advancing toward him from the other end of the long arcade, that led in a slanting direction to the turnstile.

The figures were those of a man and woman — the woman wearing some light-colored dress, which shimmered in the dusk; the man leaning on a stick, and obviously very lame.

"Is it my niece and one of her visitors?" thought the captain; "maybe it is. I 'll lay by to port of 'em, and let 'em pass me."

Samuel Prodder stepped aside under the shadow of the trees to the left of the grassy avenue through which the two figures were approaching, and waited patiently until they drew near enough for him to distinguish the woman's face. The woman was Mrs. Mellish, and she was walking on the left of the man, and was therefore nearest to the captain. Her head was turned away from her companion, as if in utter scorn and de-

fiance of him, although she was talking to him at that moment. Her face, proud, pale, and disdainful, was visible to the seaman in the chill, shadowy light of the newly-risen moon. A low line of crimson behind the black trunks of a distant group of trees marked where the sun had left its last track in a vivid streak that looked like blood.

Captain Prodder gazed in loving wonder at the beautiful face turned toward him. He saw the dark eyes, with their sombre depth, dark in anger and scorn, and the luminous shimmer of the jewels that shone through the black veil upon her haughty head. He saw her, and his heart grew chill at the sight of her pale beauty in the mysterious moonlight.

"It might be my sister's ghost," he thought, "coming upon me in this quiet place; it 's a'most difficult to believe as it 's flesh and blood."

He would have advanced, perhaps, and addressed his niece, had he not been held back by the words which she was speaking as she passed him—words that jarred painfully upon his heart, telling, as they did, of anger and bitterness, discord and misery.

"Yes, hate you," she said, in a clear voice, which seemed to vibrate sharply in the dusk — "hate you, hate you, hate you!" She repeated the hard phrase, as if there were some pleasure and delight in uttering it, which in her ungovernable anger she could not deny herself. "What other words do you expect from me?" she cried with a low, mocking laugh, which had a tone of deeper misery and more utter hopelessness than any outbreak of womanly weeping. "Would you have me love you, or respect you, or tolerate you?" Her voice rose with each rapid question, merging into an hysterical sob, but never melting into tears. "Would you have me tell you anything else than what I tell you to-night? I hate and abhor you. I look upon you as the primary cause of every sorrow I have ever known, of every tear I have ever shed, of every humiliation I have ever endured — every sleepless night, every weary day, every despairing hour I have ever passed. More than this — yes, a thousand, thousand times more — I look upon you as the first cause of my father's wretchedness. Yes, even before my own mad folly in believing in you, and thinking you — what? — Claude Melnotte, perhaps! A curse upon the man who wrote the play, and the player who acted in it, if it helped to make me what I was when I met you! I say again, I hate you; your presence poisons my home, your abhorred shadow haunts my sleep — no, not my sleep, for how should I ever sleep knowing that you are near?"

Mr. Conyers, being apparently weary of walking, leaned against the trunk of a tree to listen to the end of this outbreak, looking insolent defiance at the speaker. But Aurora's passion had reached that point in which all consciousness of external things passes away in the complete egoism of anger and hate. She did not see his superciliously indifferent look; her dilated eyes stared straight before her into the dark recess from which Captain Prodder watched his sister's only child. Her restless hands rent the fragile border of her shawl in the strong agony of her passion. Have you ever seen this kind of woman in a passion? Impulsive, nervous, sensitive, sanguine; with such a one passion is a madness — brief, thank Heaven! and expending itself in sharply cruel words, and convulsive rendings of laces and ribbons, or coroners' juries might have to sit even oftener than they do. It is fortunate for mankind that speaking daggers is often quite as great a satisfaction to us as using them, and that we can threaten very cruel things without meaning to carry them out. Like the little children who say, "Won't I just tell your mother?" and the terrible editors who write, "Won't I give you a castigation in the Market-Deeping *Spirit of the Times*, or the Walton-on-the-Naze *Athenæum?*"

"If you are going to give us much more of this sort of thing," said Mr. Conyers, with aggravating stolidity, "perhaps you won't object to my lighting a cigar?"

Aurora took no notice of his quiet insolence; but Captain Prodder, involuntarily clenching his fist, bounded a step forward in his retreat, and shook the leaves of the underwood about his legs.

"What 's that?" exclaimed the trainer.

"My dog, perhaps," answered Aurora; "he 's about here with me."

"Curse the purblind cur," muttered Mr. Conyers, with an unlighted cigar in his mouth. He struck a lucifer match against the bark of a tree, and the vivid sulphurous light shone full upon his handsome face.

"A rascal," thought Captain Prodder; "a good-looking, heartless scoundrel. What 's this between my niece and him? He is n't her husband, surely, for he don't look like a gentleman. But if he a'n't her husband, who is he?"

The sailor scratched his head in his bewilderment. His senses had been almost stupefied by Aurora's passionate talk, and he had only a confused feeling that there was trouble and wretchedness of some kind or other around and about his niece.

"If I thought he 'd done anything to injure her," he muttered, "I 'd pound him into such a jelly that his friends would never know his handsome face again as long as there was life in his carcass."

Mr. Conyers threw away the burning match, and puffed at his newly-lighted cigar. He did not trouble himself to take it from his lips as he addressed Aurora, but spoke between his teeth, and smoked in the pauses of his discourse.

"Perhaps, if you 've — calmed yourself down — a bit," he said, "you 'll be so good as — to come to business. What do you want me to do?"

"You know as well as I do," answered Aurora.

"You want me to leave this place?"

"Yes, for ever."

"And to take what you give me — and be satisfied?"

"Yes."

"What if I refuse?"

She turned sharply upon him as he asked this question, and looked at him for a few moments in silence.

"What if I refuse?" he repeated, still smoking.

"Look to yourself!" she cried, between her set teeth; "that 's all. Look to yourself!"

"What! you 'd kill me, I suppose?"

"No," answered Aurora; "but I 'd tell all, and get the release which I ought to have sought for two years ago."

"Oh! ah! to be sure," said Mr. Conyers; "a pleasant thing for Mr. Mellish, and our poor papa, and a nice bit of gossip for the newspapers. But suppose, I remarked just now, we drop to the test, and see if you 've pluck enough to do it, my lady."

She stamped her foot upon the turf, and tore the lace in her hands, throwing the fragments away from her; but she did not answer him.

"You 'd like to stab me, or shoot me, or strangle me, as I stand here, would n't you, now?" asked the trainer, mockingly.

"Yes," cried Aurora, "I would!" She flung her head back with a gesture of disdain as she spoke.

"Why do I waste my time in talking to you?" she said. "My worst words can inflict no wound upon such a nature as yours. My scorn is no more painful to you than it would be to any of the loathsome creatures that creep about the margin of yonder pool."

The trainer took his cigar from his mouth, and struck the ashes away with his little finger.

"No," he said, with a contemptuous laugh, "I 'm not very thin-skinned, and I 'm pretty well used to this sort of thing into the bargain. But suppose, as I remarked just now, we drop this style of conversation, and come to business. We don't seem to be getting on very fast this way."

At this juncture, Captain Prodder, who, in his extreme desire to strangle his niece's companion, had advanced very close upon the two speakers, knocked off his hat against the lower branches of the tree which sheltered him.

There was no mistake this time about the rustling of the leaves. The trainer started, and limped toward Captain Prodder's hiding-place.

"There 's some one listening to us," he said. "I 'm sure of it this time — that fellow Hargraves, perhaps. I fancy he 's a sneak."

Mr. Conyers supported himself against the very tree behind which the sailor stood, and beat among the undergrowth with his stick, but did not succeed in encountering the legs of the listener.

"If that soft-headed fool *is* playing the spy upon me," cried the trainer, savagely, "he 'd better not let me catch him, for I 'll make him remember it if I do."

"Don't I tell you that my dog followed me here ?" exclaimed Aurora, contemptuously.

A low rustling of the grass on the other side of the avenue, and at some distance from the seaman's place of concealment, was heard as Mrs. Mellish spoke.

"*That* 's your dog, if you like," said the trainer; "the other was a man. Come on a little way farther, and let 's make a finish of this business; it 's past ten o'clock."

Mr. Conyers was right. The church clock had struck ten five minutes before, but the solemn chimes had fallen unheeded upon Aurora's ear, lost amid the angry voices raging in her breast. She started as she looked around her at the summer darkness in the woods, and the flaming yellow moon, which brooded low upon the earth, and shed no light upon the mysterious pathways and the water-pools in the wood.

The trainer limped away, Aurora walking by his side, yet holding herself as far aloof from him as the grassy pathway would allow. They were out of hearing, and almost out of sight, before the sea-captain could emerge from a state of utter stupefaction so far as to be able to look at the business in its right bearings.

"I ought to ha' knocked him down," he muttered at last; "whether he 's her husband or whether he is n't. I ought to have knocked him down, and I would have done it too," added the captain, resolutely, "if it had n't been that my niece seemed to have a good fiery spirit of her own, and to be able to fire a jolly good broadside in the way of hard words. I 'll find my skull-thatcher if I can," said Captain Prodder, groping for his hat among the brambles and the long grass, "and then I 'll just run up to the turnstile and tell my mate to lay at anchor a bit longer with the horse and shay. He 'll be wonderin' what I 'm up to: but I won't go back just yet; I 'll keep in the way of my niece and that swab with the game leg."

The captain found his hat, and walked down to the turnstile, where he found the young man from the "Reindeer" fast asleep, with the reins loose in his hands, and his head upon his knees. The horse, with his head in an empty nose-bag, seemed as fast asleep as the driver.

The young man woke at the sound of the turnstile creaking upon its axis, and the step of the sailor in the road.

"I a'n't goin' to get aboard just yet," said Captain Prodder; "I 'll take another turn in the wood, as the evenin' 's so pleasant. I come to tell you I would n't keep you much longer, for I thought you 'd think I was dead."

"I did a'most," answered the charioteer, candidly. "My word, a'n't you been a time!"

"I met Mr. and Mrs. Mellish in the wood," said the captain, "and I stopped to have a look at 'em. She 's a bit of a spitfire, a'n't she ?" asked Samuel, with affected carelessness.

The young man from the "Reindeer" shook his head dubiously.

"I doant know about that," he said; "she 's a rare favorite hereabouts, with poor folks and gentry too. They do say as she horsewhipped a poor fond chap as they 'd got in the stables for ill-usin' her dog; and sarve him right too," added the young man, decisively. "Them softies is allus vicious."

Captain Prodder pondered rather doubtfully upon this piece of information. He was not particularly elated by the image of his sister's child laying a horsewhip upon the shoulders of her half-witted servant. This trifling incident did n't exactly harmonize with his idea of the beautiful heiress, playing upon all manner of instruments, and speaking half a dozen languages.

"Yes," repeated the driver, "they *do* say as she gave t' fondy a good whopping; and damme if I don't admire her for it."

"Ay, ay," answered Captain Prodder, thoughtfully. "Mr. Mellish walks lame, don't he ?" he asked, after a pause.

"Lame !" cried the driver; "Lord bless your heart, not a bit of it. John Mellish is as fine a young man as you 'll meet in this Riding — ay, and finer, too. I ought to know. I 've seen him walk into our house often enough in the race week."

The captain's heart sank strangely at this information. The man with whom he had heard his niece quarrelling was not her husband, then. The squabble had seemed natural enough to the uninitiated sailor while he looked at it in a matrimonial light, but, seen from another aspect, it struck sudden terror to his sturdy heart, and blanched the ruddy hues in his brown face. "Who was he, then ?" he thought; "who was it as my niece was talkin' to—after dark—alone—a mile off her own home, eh ?"

Before he could seek for a solution to the muttered question which agitated and alarmed him, the report of a pistol rang sharply through the wood, and found an echo under a distant hill.

The horse pricked up his ears and jibbed a few paces; the driver gave a low whistle.

"I thought so," he said. "Poachers! This side of the wood 's chock full of game; and, though Squire Mellish is allus threatenin' to prosecute 'em, folks know pretty well as he 'll never do it."

The broad-shouldered, strong-limbed sailor leaned against the turnstile, trembling in every limb.

What was that which his niece had said a quarter of an hour before, when the man had asked her whether she would like to shoot him?

"Leave your horse," he said, in a gasping voice; "tie him to the stile, and come with me. If—if—it 's poachers, we 'll—we 'll catch 'em."

The young man looped the reins across the turnstile. He had no very great terror of any inclination for flight latent in the gray horse from the "Reindeer." The two men ran into the wood, the captain running in the direction in which his sharp ears told him the shot had been fired.

The moon was slowly rising in the tranquil heavens, but there was very little light yet in the wood.

The captain stopped near a rustic summer-house falling into decay, and half buried amid the tangled foliage that clustered about the mouldering thatch and the dilapidated wood-work.

"It was hereabout the shot was fired," muttered the captain; "about a hundred yards due nor'ard of the stile. I could take my oath as it were n't far from this spot I 'm standin' on."

He looked about him in the dim light. He could see no one; but an army might have hidden among the trees that encircled the open patch of turf on which the summer-house had been built. He listened with his hat off, and his big hand pressed tightly on his heart, as if to still its tumultuous beating; he listened as eagerly as he had often listened, far out on a glassy sea, for the first faint breath of a rising wind; but he could hear nothing except the occasional croaking of the frogs in the pond near the summer-house.

"I could have sworn it was about here the shot was fired," he repeated. "God grant as it was poachers, after all; but it 's given me a turn that 's made me feel like some Cockney lubber aboard a steamer betwixt Bristol and Cork. Lord, what a blessed old fool I am!" muttered the captain, after walking slowly round the summer-house to convince himself that there was no one hidden in it. "One 'ud think I 'd never heerd the sound of a ha'p'orth of powder before to-night."

He put on his hat, and walked a few paces forward, still looking about him cautiously, and still listening, but much easier in his mind than when first he had re-entered the wood. He stooped suddenly, arrested by a sound which has of itself, without any reference to its power of association, a mysterious and chilling influence upon the human heart. This sound was the howling of a dog—the prolonged, monotonous howling of a dog. A cold sweat broke out upon the sailor's forehead. That sound, always one of terror to his superstitious nature, was doubly terrible to-night.

"It means death," he muttered, with a groan. "No dog ever howled like that except for death."

He turned back and looked about him. The moonlight glimmered faintly upon the broad patch of stagnant water near the summer-house, and upon its brink the captain saw two figures, black against the summer atmosphere—a prostrate figure, lying close to the edge of the water, and a large dog, with his head uplifted to the sky, howling piteously.

It was the bounden duty of poor John Mellish, in his capacity of host, to sit at the head of his table, pass the claret-jug, and listen to Colonel Maddison's stories of the pig-sticking and the tiger-hunting as long as the Indian officer chose to talk for the amusement of his friend and his son-in-law. It was perhaps lucky that patient Mr. Lofthouse was well up in all the stories, and knew exactly which departments of each narrative were to be laughed at, and which were to be listened to with silent and awe-stricken attention; for John Mellish made a very bad audience upon this occasion. He pushed the filberts toward the colonel at the very moment when "the tigress was crouching for a spring, upon the rising ground exactly above us, sir, and when, by Jove, Charley Maddison felt himself at pretty close quarters with the enemy, sir, and never thought to stretch his legs under this mahogany, or any other man's, sir;" and he spoiled the officer's best joke by asking him for the claret in the middle of it.

The tigers and the pigs were confusion and weariness of spirit to Mr. Mellish. He was yearning for the moment when, with any show of decency, he might make for the drawing-room, and find out what Aurora was doing in the still summer twilight. When the door was opened and fresh wine brought in, he heard the rattling of the keys under Mrs. Lofthouse's manipulation, and rejoiced to think that his wife was seated quietly, perhaps, listening to those sonatas in C flat which the rector's wife delighted to interpret.

The lamps were brought in before Colonel Maddison's stories were finished; and when John's butler came to ask if the gentlemen would like coffee, the worthy Indian officer said "Yes, by all means, and a cheroot with it. No smoking in the drawing-room, eh, Mellish? Petticoat government and window-curtains, I dare say. Clara does n't like my smoke at the Rectory, and poor Lofthouse writes his sermons in the summer-house; for he can't write without a weed, you know, and a volume of Tillotson, or some of those fellows, to prig from, eh, George?" said the facetious gentleman, digging his son-in-law in the ribs with his fat old fingers, and knocking over two or three wine-glasses in his ponderous jocosity. How dreary it all seemed to John Mellish to-night! He wondered how people felt who had no social mystery brooding upon their hearth; no domestic skeleton cowering in their homely cupboard. He looked at the rector's placid face with a pang of envy. There was no secret kept from *him*. There was no perpetual struggle rending *his* heart; no dreadful doubts and fears that would not be quite lulled to rest; no vague terror, incessant and unreasoning; no mute argument for ever going forward, with plaintiff's counsel and defendant's counsel continually pleading the same cause, and arriving at the same result. Heaven take pity upon those who have to suffer such silent misery, such secret despair! We look at our neighbors' smiling faces, and say, in bitterness of spirit, that A is a lucky fellow, and that B can't be as much in debt as his friends say he is; that C and his pretty wife are the happiest couple we know; and to-morrow B is in the *Gazette*, and C is weeping over a dishonored home, and a group of motherless children, who wonder what mamma has done that papa should be so sorry. The battles are very quiet, but they are for ever being fought. We keep the fox bidden under our cloak, but the teeth of the animal are none the less sharp, nor the pain less terrible to bear: a little more terrible, perhaps, for being endured silently. John Mellish gave a long sigh of relief when the Indian officer finished his third cheroot, and pronounced himself ready to join the ladies. The lamps in the drawing-room were lighted, and the curtains drawn before the open windows, when the three gentlemen entered. Mrs. Lofthouse was asleep upon one of the sofas, with a Book of Beauty lying open at her feet, and Mrs. Powell, pale and sleepless—sleepless as trouble and sorrow, as jealousy and hate, as anything that is ravenous and unappeasable—sat at her embroidery, working laborious monstrosities upon delicate cambric muslin.

The colonel dropped heavily into a luxurious easy-chair, and quietly abandoned himself to repose. Mr. Lofthouse awoke his wife, and consulted her about the propriety of ordering the carriage. John Mellish looked eagerly round the room. To him it was empty. The rector and his wife, the Indian officer and the ensign's widow, were only so many "phosphorescent spectralities," "phantasm captains;" in short, they were not Aurora.

"Where's Lolly?" he asked looking from Mrs. Lofthouse to Mrs. Powell, "where's my wife?"

"I really do not know," answered Mrs. Powell, with icy deliberation. "I have not been watching Mrs. Mellish."

The poisoned darts glanced away from John's preoccupied breast. There was no room in his wounded heart for such a petty sting as this.

"Where's my wife?" he cried, passionately; "you *must* know where she is. She's not here. Is she up stairs? Is she out of doors?"

"To the best of my belief," replied the ensign's widow, with more than usual precision, "Mrs. Mellish is in some part of the grounds; she has been out of doors ever since we left the dining-room."

The French clock upon the mantle-piece chimed the three-quarters after ten as she finished speaking, as if to give emphasis to her words, and to remind Mr. Mellish how long his wife had been absent. He bit his lip fiercely, and strode toward one of the windows. He was going to look for his wife; but he stopped as he flung aside the window-curtain, arrested by Mrs. Powell's uplifted hand.

"Hark!" she said, "there is something the matter, I fear. Did you hear that violent ringing at the hall-door?"

Mr. Mellish let fall the curtain, and re-entered the room.

"It's Aurora, no doubt," he said; "they've shut her out again, I suppose. I beg, Mrs. Powell, that you will prevent this in future. Really, ma'am, it is hard that my wife should be shut out of her own house."

He might have said much more, but he stopped, pale and breathless, at the sound of a hubbub in the hall, and rushed to the room-door. He opened it and looked out, with Mrs. Powell and Mr. and Mrs. Lofthouse crowding behind him and looking over his shoulder.

Half a dozen servants were clustered round a roughly-dressed, seafaring-looking man, who, with his hat off and his disordered hair falling about his white face, was telling in broken sentences, scarcely intelligible for the speaker's agitation, that a murder had been done in the wood.

CHAPTER XXV.

THE DEED THAT HAD BEEN DONE IN THE WOOD.

The bareheaded seafaring man who stood in the centre of the hall was Captain Samuel Prodder. The scared faces of the servants gathered round him told more plainly than his words, which came hoarsely from his parched white lips, the nature of the tidings that he brought.

John Mellish strode across the hall with an awful calmness on his white face, and, parting the hustled group of servants with his strong arms as a mighty wind rends asunder the storm-beaten waters, he placed himself face to face with Captain Prodder.

"Who are you?" he asked, sternly; "and what has brought you here?"

The Indian officer had been aroused by the clamor, and had emerged, red and bristling with self-importance, to take his part in the business in hand.

There are some pies in the making of which everybody yearns to have a finger. It is a great privilege, after some social convulsion has taken place, to be able to say, "I was there at the time the scene occurred, sir;" or, "I was standing as close to him when the blow was struck, ma'am, as I am to you at this moment." People are apt to take pride out of strange things. An elderly gentleman at Doncaster, showing me his comfortably furnished apartments, informed me, with evident satisfaction, that Mr. William Palmer had lodged in those very rooms.

Colonel Maddison pushed aside his daughter and her husband, and struggled out into the hall.

"Come, my man," he said, echoing John's interrogatory, "let us hear what has brought you here at such a remarkably unseasonable hour."

The sailor gave no direct answer to the question. He pointed with his thumb across his shoulder toward that dismal spot in the lonely wood, which was as present to his mental vision now as it had been to his bodily eyes a quarter of an hour before.

"A man!" he gasped; "a man—lyin' close agen' the water's edge—shot through the heart."

"Dead?" asked some one, in an awful tone. The voices and the questions came from whom they would in the awe-stricken terror of those first moments of overwhelming horror and surprise. No one knew who spoke except the speakers; perhaps even they were scarcely aware that they had spoken.

"Dead?" asked one of those eager listeners.

"Stone dead."

"A man—shot dead in the wood!" cried John Mellish; "what man?"

"I beg your pardon, sir," said the grave old butler, laying his hand gently upon his master's shoulder, "I think, from what this person says, that the man who has been shot is—the new trainer, Mr.—Mr.—"

"Conyers!" exclaimed John. "Conyers! who—who should shoot him?" The question was asked in a hoarse whisper. It was impossible for the speaker's face to grow whiter than it had been from the moment in which he had opened the drawing-room-door, and looked out into the hall; but some terrible change not to be translated into words came over it at the mention of the trainer's name.

He stood motionless and silent, pushing his hair from his forehead, and staring wildly about him.

The grave butler laid his warning hand for a second time upon his master's shoulder.

"Sir, Mr. Mellish," he said, eager to arouse the young man from the dull, stupid quiet into which he had fallen, "excuse me, sir, but if my mistress should come in suddenly, and hear of this, she might be upset, perhaps. Would n't it be better to—"

"Yes! yes!" cried John Mellish, lifting his head suddenly, as if aroused into immediate action by the mere suggestion of his wife's name—"yes! Clear out of the hall, every one of you," he said, addressing the eager group of pale-faced servants. "And you, sir," he added, to Captain Prodder, "come with me."

He walked toward the dining-room-door. The sailor followed him, still bareheaded, still with a semi-bewildered expression in his dusky face.

"It a'n't the first time I've seen a man shot," he thought, "but it's the first time I've felt like this."

Before Mr. Mellish could reach the dining-room, before the servants could disperse and return to their proper quarters, one of the half-glass doors, which had been left ajar, was pushed open by the light touch of a woman's hand, and Aurora Mellish entered the hall.

"Ah, ha!" thought the ensign's widow, who looked on at the scene snugly sheltered by Mr. and Mrs. Lofthouse, "my lady is caught a second time in her evening rambles. What will he say to her goings on to-night, I wonder?"

Aurora's manner presented a singular contrast to the terror and agitation of the assembly in the hall. A vivid crimson flush glowed in her cheeks and lit up her shining eyes. She carried her head high, in that queenly defiance which was her peculiar grace. She walked with a light step; she moved with easy, careless gestures. It seemed as if some burden which she had long carried had been suddenly removed from her. But at sight of the crowd in the hall she drew back with a look of alarm.

"What has happened, John?" she cried; "what is wrong?"

He lifted his hand with a warning gesture—a gesture that plainly said, Whatever trouble or sorrow there may be, let her be spared the knowledge of it—let her be sheltered from the pain.

"Yes, my darling," he answered, quietly, taking her hand and leading her into the drawing-room, "there is something wrong. An accident has happened—in the wood yonder; but it concerns no one whom you care for. Go, dear; I will tell you all by and by. Mrs. Lofthouse, you will take care of my wife. Lofthouse, come with me. Allow me to shut the door, Mrs. Powell, if you please," he added to the ensign's widow, who did not seem inclined to leave her post upon the threshold of the drawing-room. "Any curiosity which you may have about the business shall be satisfied in due time. For the present, you will oblige me by remaining with my wife and Mrs. Lofthouse."

He paused, with his hand upon the drawing-room-door, and looked at Aurora.

She was standing with her shawl upon her arm, watching her husband; and she advanced eagerly to him as she met his glance.

"John," she exclaimed, "for mercy's sake, tell me the truth! *What* is this accident?"

He was silent for a moment, gazing at her eager face — that face, whose exquisite mobility expressed every thought; then, looking at her with a strange solemnity, he said gravely, "You were in the wood just now, Aurora?"

"I was," she answered; "I have only just left the grounds. A man passed me, running violently, about a quarter of an hour ago. I thought he was a poacher. Was it to him the accident happened?"

"No. There was a shot fired in the wood some time since. Did you hear it?"

"I did," replied Mrs. Mellish, looking at him with sudden terror and surprise. "I knew there were often poachers about near the road, and I was not alarmed by it. Was there anything wrong in that shot? Was any one hurt?"

Her eyes were fixed upon his face, dilated with that look of wondering terror.

"Yes; a—a man was hurt."

Aurora looked at him in silence—looked at him with a stony face, whose only expression was an utter bewilderment. Every other feeling seemed blotted away in that one sense of wonder.

John Mellish led her to a chair near Mrs. Lofthouse, who had been seated, with Mrs. Powell, at the other end of the room, close to the piano, and too far from the door to overhear the conversation which had just taken place between John and his wife. People do not talk very loudly in moments of intense agitation. They are liable to be deprived of some portion of their vocal power in the fearful crisis of terror and despair. A numbness seizes the organ of speech; a partial paralysis disables the ready tongue; the trembling lips refuse to do their duty. The soft pedal of the human instrument is down, and the tones are feeble and muffled, wandering into weak minor shrillness, or sinking to husky basses, beyond the ordinary compass of the speaker's voice. The stentorian accents in which Claude Melnotte bids adieu to Mademoiselle Deschappelle mingle very effectively with the brazen clamor of the Marseillaise Hymn; the sonorous tones in which Mistress Julia appeals to her Hunchback

guardian are pretty sure to bring down the approving thunder of the eighteen-penny gallery; but I doubt if the noisy energy of stage-grief is true to nature, however wise in art. I'm afraid that an actor who would play Claude Melnotte with a pre-Raphaelite fidelity to nature would be an insufferable bore, and utterly inaudible beyond the third row in the pit. The artist must draw his own line between nature and art, and map out the extent of his own territory. If he finds that cream-colored marble is more artistically beautiful than a rigid presentment of actual flesh and blood, let him stain his marble of that delicate hue until the end of time. If he can represent five acts of agony and despair without once turning his back to his audience or sitting down, let him do it. If he is conscientiously true to his *art*, let him choose for himself how true he shall be to nature.

John Mellish took his wife's hand in his own, and grasped it with a convulsive pressure that almost crushed the delicate fingers.

"Stay here, my dear, till I come back to you," he said. "Now, Lofthouse."

Mr. Lofthouse followed his friend into the hall, where Colonel Maddison had been making the best use of his time by questioning the merchant-captain.

"Come, gentlemen," said John, leading the way to the dining-room; "come, colonel, and you too, Lofthouse; and you, sir," he added, to the sailor, "step this way."

The *debris* of the dessert still covered the table, but the men did not advance far into the room. John stood aside as the others went in, and, entering the last, closed the door behind him, and stood with his back against it.

"Now," he said, turning sharply upon Samuel Prodder, "what is this business?"

"I'm afraid it's soocicide—or—or murder," answered the sailor, gravely. "I've told this good gentleman all about it."

This good gentleman was Colonel Maddison, who seemed delighted to plunge into the conversation.

"Yes, my dear Mellish," he said, eagerly, "our friend, who describes himself as a sailor, and who had come down to see Mrs. Mellish, whose mother he knew when he was a boy, has told me all about this shocking affair. Of course the body must be removed immediately, and the sooner your servants go out with lanterns for that purpose the better. Decision, my dear Mellish, decision and prompt action are indispensable in these sad catastrophes."

"The body removed!" repeated John Mellish; "the man is dead, then?"

"Quite dead," answered the sailor; "he was dead when I found him, though it wasn't above seven minutes after the shot was fired. I left a man with him—a young man as drove me from Doncaster—and a dog—some big dog that watched beside him, howling awful, and would n't leave him."

"Did you—see—the man's face?"

"Yes."

"You are a stranger here," said John Mellish; "it is useless, therefore, to ask you if you know who the man is."

"No, sir," answered the sailor, "I did n't know him; but the young man from the Reindeer—"

"He recognized him?"

"Yes; he said he 'd seen the man in Doncaster only the night before; and that he was your—trainer, I think he called him."

"Yes, yes."

"A lame chap."

"Come, gentlemen," said John, turning to his friends, "what are we to do?"

"Send the servants into the wood," replied Colonel Maddison, "and have the body carried—"

"Not here," cried John Mellish, interrupting him, "not here; it would kill my wife."

"Where did the man live?" asked the colonel.

"In the north lodge. A cottage against the northern gates, which are never used now."

"Then let the body be taken there," answered the Indian soldier; "let one of your people run for the parish constable; and you 'd better send for the nearest surgeon immediately, though, from what our friend here says, a hundred of 'em could n't do any good. It 's an awful business. Some poaching fray, I suppose."

"Yes, yes," answered John, quickly, "no doubt."

"Was the man disliked in the neighborhood?" asked Colonel Maddison; "had he made himself in any manner obnoxious?"

"I should scarcely think it likely. He had only been with me about a week."

The servants, who had dispersed at John's command, had not gone very far. They had lingered in corridors and lobbies, ready at a moment's notice to rush out into the hall again, and act their minor parts in the tragedy. They preferred doing anything to returning quietly to their own quarters.

They came out eagerly at Mr. Mellish's summons. He gave his orders briefly, selecting two of the men, and sending the others about their business.

"Bring a couple of lanterns," he said; "and follow us across the Park toward the pond in the wood."

Colonel Maddison, Mr. Lofthouse, Captain Prodder, and John Mellish left the house together. The moon, still slowly rising in the broad, cloudless heavens, silvered the quiet lawn, and shimmered upon the tree-tops in the distance. The three gentlemen walked at a rapid pace, led by Samuel Prodder, who kept

a little way in advance, and followed by a couple of grooms, who carried darkened stable-lanterns.

As they entered the wood, they stopped involuntarily, arrested by that solemn sound which had first drawn the sailor's attention to the dreadful deed that had been done—the howling of the dog. It sounded in the distance like a low, feeble wail—a long, monotonous death-cry.

They followed that dismal indication of the spot to which they were to go. They made their way through the shadowy avenue, and emerged upon the silvery patch of turf and fern where the rotting summer-house stood in its solitary decay. The two figures—the prostrate figure on the brink of the water, and the figure of the dog with uplifted head—still remained exactly as the sailor had left them three-quarters of an hour before. The young man from the Reindeer stood aloof from these two figures, and advanced to meet the new-comers as they drew near.

Colonel Maddison took a lantern from one of the men, and ran forward to the water's edge. The dog rose as he approached, and walked slowly round the prostrate form, sniffling at it, and whining piteously. John Mellish called the animal away.

"This man was in a sitting posture when he was shot," said Colonel Maddison, decisively. "He was sitting upon this bench here."

He pointed to a dilapidated rustic seat close to the margin of the stagnant water.

"He was sitting upon this bench," repeated the colonel, "for he 's fallen close against it, as you see. Unless I 'm very much mistaken, he was shot from behind."

"You don't think he shot himself, then?" asked John Mellish.

"Shot himself!" cried the colonel; "not a bit of it. But we 'll soon settle that. If he shot himself, the pistol must be close against him. Here, bring a loose plank from that summer-house, and lay the body upon it," added the Indian officer, speaking to the servants.

Captain Prodder and the two grooms selected the broadest plank they could find. It was moss-grown and rotten, and straggling wreaths of wild clematis were entwined about it; but it served the purpose for which it was wanted. They laid it upon the grass, and lifted the body of James Conyers on to it, with his handsome face—ghastly and horrible in the fixed agony of sudden death — turned upward to the moonlit sky. It was wonderful how mechanically and quietly they went to work, promptly and silently obeying the colonel's orders.

John Mellish and Mr. Lofthouse searched the slippery grass upon the bank, and groped among the fringe of fern, without result. There was no weapon to be found anywhere within a considerable radius of the body.

While they were searching in every direction for this missing link in the mystery of the man's death, the parish constable arrived with the servant who had been sent to summon him.

He had very little to say for himself, except that he supposed it was poachers as had done it; and that he also supposed all particklars would come out at the inquest. He was a simple rural functionary, accustomed to petty dealings with refractory tramps, contumacious poachers, and impounded cattle, and was scarcely master of the situation in any great emergency.

Mr. Prodder and the servants lifted the plank upon which the body lay, and struck into the long avenue leading northward, walking a little ahead of the three gentlemen and the constable. The young man from the Reindeer returned to look after his horse, and to drive round to the north lodge, where he was to meet Mr. Prodder. All had been done so quietly that the knowledge of the catastrophe had not passed beyond the domains of Mellish Park. In the holy summer-evening stillness James Conyers was carried back to the chamber from whose narrow window he had looked out upon the beautiful world, weary of its beauty, only a few hours before.

The purposeless life was suddenly closed. The careless wanderer's journey had come to an unthought-of end. What a melancholy record, what a meaningless and unfinished page? Nature, blindly bountiful to the children whom she has yet to know, had bestowed her richest gifts upon this man. She had created a splendid image, and had chosen a soul at random, ignorantly enshrining it in her most perfectly-fashioned clay. Of all who read the story of this man's death in the following Sunday's newspapers, there was not one who shed a tear for him; there was not one who could say, "That man once stepped out of his way to do me a kindness; and may the Lord have mercy upon his soul!"

Shall I be sentimental, then, because he is dead, and regret that he was not spared a little longer, and allowed a day of grace in which he might repent? Had he lived for ever, I do not think he would have lived long enough to become that which it was not in his nature to be. May God, in His infinite compassion, have pity upon the souls which He has Himself created, and where He has withheld the light, may he excuse the darkness! The phrenologists who examined the head of William Palmer declared that he was so utterly deficient in moral perception, so entirely devoid of conscientious restraint, that he could not help being what he was. Heaven keep us from too much credence in that horrible fatalism! Is a man's destiny here and hereafter to depend upon bulbous projections scarcely perceptible to uneducated fingers, and good and evil propensities which can be measured by the compass or weighed in the scale?

The dismal *cortège* slowly made its way under the silver moonlight, the trembling leaves making a murmuring music in the faint summer air, the pale glowworm sshining here and there amid the tangled verdure. The bearers of the dead walked with a slow but steady tramp in advance of the rest. All walked in silence. What should they say? In the presence of death's awful mystery life made a pause. There was a brief interval in the hard business of existence — a hushed and solemn break in the working of life's machinery.

"There 'll be an inquest," thought Mr. Prodder, "and I shall have to give evidence. I wonder what questions they 'll ask me?"

He did not think this once, but perpetually, dwelling with a half-stupid persistence upon the thought of that inquisition which must most infallibly be made, and those questions that might be asked. The honest sailor's simple mind was cast astray in the utter bewilderment of this night's mysterious horror. The story of life was changed. He had come to play his humble part in some sweet domestic drama of love and confidence, and he found himself involved in a tragedy — a horrible mystery of hatred, secrecy, and murder — a dreadful maze, from whose obscurity he saw no hope of issue.

A beacon-light glimmered in the lower window of the cottage by the north gates — a feeble ray, that glittered like a gem from out a bower of honeysuckle and clematis. The little garden-gate was closed, but it only fastened with a latch.

The bearers of the body paused before entering the garden, and the constable stepped aside to speak to Mr. Mellish.

"Is there anybody lives in the cottage?" he asked.

"Yes," answered John; "the trainer employed an old hanger-on of my own — a half-witted fellow, called Hargraves."

"It 's him as burns the light in there most likely, then," said the constable. "I 'll go in and speak to him first. Do you wait here till I come out again," he added, turning to the men who carried the body.

The lodge-door was on the latch. The constable opened it softly and went in. A rush-light was burning upon the table, the candle-stick placed in a basin of water. A bottle half filled with brandy, and a tumbler, stood near the light; but the room was empty. The constable took his shoes off, and crept up the little staircase. The upper floor of the lodge consisted of two rooms—one, sufficiently large and comfortable, looking toward the stable-gates; the other, smaller and darker, looked out upon a patch of kitchen-garden and on the fence which separated Mr. Mellish's estate from the high-road. The larger chamber was empty; but the door of the smaller was ajar; and the constable, pausing to listen at that half-open door, heard the regular breathing of a heavy sleeper.

He knocked sharply upon the panel.

"Who 's there?" asked the person within, starting up from a truckle bedstead. "Is 't thou, Muster Conyers?"

"No," answered the constable. "It 's me, William Dork, of Little Meslingham. Come down stairs; I want to speak to you."

"Is there aught wrong?"

"Yes."

"Poachers?"

"That 's as may be," answered Mr. Dork. "Come down stairs, will you?"

Mr. Hargraves muttered something to the effect that he would make his appearance as soon as he could find sundry portions of his rather fragmentary toilet. The constable looked into the room, and watched the softy groping for his garments in the moonlight. Three minutes afterward Stephen Hargraves slowly shambled down the angular wooden stairs, which wound, in a corkscrew fashion affected by the builders of small dwellings, from the upper to the lower floor.

"Now," said Mr. Dork, planting the softy opposite to him, with the feeble rays of the rush-light upon his sickly face, "now then, I want you to answer me a question. At what time did your master leave the house?"

"At half-past seven o'clock," answered the softy, in his whispering voice; "she was strokin' the half-hour as he went out."

He pointed to a small Dutch clock in a corner of the room. His countrymen always speak of a clock as "she."

"Oh, he went out at half-past seven o'clock, did he?" said the constable; "and you have n't seen him since, I suppose?"

"No. He told me he should be late, and I was n't to sit oop for him. He swore at me last night for sitting oop for him. But is there aught wrong?" asked the softy.

Mr. Dork did not condescend to reply to this question. He walked straight to the door, opened it, and beckoned to those who stood without in the summer moonlight, patiently waiting for his summons. "You may bring him in," he said.

They carried their ghastly burden into the pleasant rustic chamber — the chamber in which Mr. James Conyers had sat smoking and drinking a few hours before. Mr. Morton, the surgeon from Meslingham, the village nearest to the Park gates, arrived as the body was being carried in, and ordered a temporary couch of mattresses to be spread upon a couple of tables placed together, in the lower room, for the reception of the trainer s corpse.

John Mellish, Samuel Prodder, and Mr. Lofthouse remained outside of the cottage. Colonel Maddison, the servants, the constable, and the doctor were all clustered round the corpse.

"He has been dead about an hour and a quarter," said the doctor, after a brief inspection of the body. "He has been shot in the back; the bullet has not penetrated the heart, for in that case there would have been no hemorrhage. He has respired after receiving the shot; but death must have been almost instantaneous."

Before making his examination, the surgeon had assisted Mr. Dork, the constable, to draw off the coat and waistcoat of the deceased. The bosom of the waistcoat was saturated with the blood that had flowed from the parted lips of the dead man.

It was Mr. Dork's business to examine these garments, in the hope of finding some shred of evidence which might become a clew to the secret of the trainer's death. He turned out the pockets of the shooting-coat and of the waistcoat; one of these pockets contained a handful of half-pence, a couple of shillings, a fourpenny piece, and a rusty watch-key; another held a little parcel of tobacco wrapped in an old betting-list, and a broken meerschaum pipe, black and greasy with the essential oil of by-gone shag, and bird's eye. In one of the waistcoat-pockets Mr. Dork found the dead man's silver watch, with a blood-stained ribbon and a 'worthless gilt seal. Among all these things there was nothing calculated to throw any light upon the mystery. Colonel Maddison shrugged his shoulders as the constable emptied the paltry contents of the trainer's pockets on to a little dresser at one end of the room.

"There 's nothing here that makes the business any clearer," he said; "but, to my mind, it 's plain enough. The man was new here, and he brought new ways with him from his last situation. The poachers and vagabonds have been used to have it all their own way about Mellish Park, and they did n't like this poor fellow's interference. He wanted to play the tyrant, I dare say, and made himself obnoxious to some of the worst of the lot; and he 's caught it hot, poor chap, that's all I 've got to say."

Colonel Maddison, with the recollection of a refractory Punjaub strong upon him, had no very great reverence for the mysterious spark that lights the human temple. If a man made himself obnoxious to other men, other men were very likely to kill him. This was the soldier's simple theory; and, having delivered himself of his opinion respecting the trainer's death, he emerged from the cottage, and was ready to go home with John Mellish, and drink another bottle of that celebrated tawny port which had been laid in by his host's father twenty years before.

The constable stood close against a candle, that had been hastily lighted and thrust unceremoniously into a disused blacking-bottle, with the waistcoat still in his hands. He was turning the blood-stained garment inside out;

for, while emptying the pockets, he had felt a thick substance that seemed like a folded paper, but the whereabouts of which he had not been able to discover. He uttered a suppressed exclamation of surprise presently, for he found the solution of this difficulty. The paper was sewn between the inner lining and the outer material of the waistcoat. He discovered this by examining the seam, a part of which was sewn with coarse stitches, and a thread of a different color to the rest. He ripped open this part of the seam, and drew out the paper, which was so much bloodstained as to be undecipherable to Mr Dork's rather obtuse vision. "I 'll say naught about it, and keep it to show to th' coroner," he thought; "I 'll lay he 'll make something out of it." The constable folded the document, and secured it in a leathern pocket-book, a bulky receptacle, the very aspect of which was wont to strike terror to rustic defaulters. 'I 'll show it to the coroner," he thought, "and if aught particklar comes out, I may get something for my trouble."

The village surgeon, having done his duty, prepared to leave the crowded little room, where the gaping servants still lingered, as if loath to tear themselves away from the ghastly figure of the dead man, over which Mr. Morton had spread a patchwork coverlet, taken from the bed in the chamber above. The softy had looked on quietly enough at the dismal scene, watching the faces of the small assembly, and glancing furtively from one to another beneath the shadow of his bushy red eyebrows. His haggard face, always of a sickly white, seemed to-night no more colorless than usual. His slow, whispering tones were not more suppressed than they always were. If he had a hangdog manner and a furtive glance, the manner and the glance were both common to him. No one looked at him, no one heeded him. After the first question as to the hour at which the trainer left the lodge had been asked and answered, no one spoke to him. If he got in anybody's way, he was pushed aside; if he said anything, nobody listened to him. The dead man was the sole monarch of that dismal scene. It was to him they looked with awe-stricken glances, it was of him they spoke in subdued whispers. All their questions, their suggestions, their conjectures, were about him, and him alone. There is this to be observed in the physiology of every murder — that before the coroner's inquest the sole object of public curiosity is the murdered man; while immediately after that judicial investigation the tide of feeling turns, the dead man is buried and forgotten, and the suspected murderer becomes the hero of men's morbid imaginations.

John Mellish looked in at the door of the cottage to ask a few questions.

"Have you found anything, Dork?" he asked.

"Nothing particklar, sir."

"Nothing that throws any light upon this business?"

"No, sir."

"You are going home, then, I suppose?"

"Yes, sir, I must be going back now, if you 'll leave some one here to watch —"

"Yes, yes," said John, "one of the servants shall stay."

"Very well, then, sir, I 'll just take the names of the witnesses that 'll be examined at the inquest, and I 'll go over and see the coroner early to-morrow morning."

' The witnesses — ah! to be sure. Who will you want?"

Mr Dork hesitated for a moment, rubbing the bristles upon his chin.

"Well, there 's this man here, Hargraves, I think you called him," he said presently, "we shall want him, for it seems he was the last that saw the deceased alive, leastways as I can hear on yet, then we shall want the gentleman as found the body, and the young man as was with him when he heard the shot: the gentleman as found the body is the most particklar of all, and I 'll speak to him at once."

John Mellish turned round, fully expecting to see Mr Prodder at his elbow, where he had been some time before. John had a perfect recollection of seeing the loosely-clad seafaring figure standing behind him in the moonlight, but, in the terrible confusion of his mind, he could not remember exactly when it was that he had last seen the sailor: it might have been only five minutes before — it might have been a quarter of an hour. John's ideas of time were annihilated by the horror of the catastrophe which had marked this night with the red brand of murder. It seemed to him as if he had been standing for hours in the little cottage garden, with Reginald Lofthouse by his side, listening to the low hum of the voices in the crowded room, and waiting to see the end of the dreary business.

Mr Dork looked about him in the moonlight, entirely bewildered by the disappearance of Samuel Prodder.

"Why, where on earth has he gone ?" exclaimed the constable. "We must have him before the coroner. What 'll Mr Hayward say to me for letting him slip through my fingers ?"

"The man was here a quarter of an hour ago, so he can't be very far off," suggested Mr. Lofthouse. "Does anybody know who he is ?"

No, nobody knew anything about him. He had appeared as mysteriously as if he had risen from the earth, to bring terror and confusion upon it with the evil tidings which he bore. Stay! some one suddenly remembered that he had been accompanied by Bill Jarvis, the young man from the Reindeer, and that he had ordered the young man to drive his

9

trap to the north gates, and wait for him there.

The constable ran to the gates upon receiving this information; but there was no vestige of the horse and gig, or of the young man. Samuel Prodder had evidently taken advantage of the confusion, and had driven off in the gig under cover of the general bewilderment.

"I 'll tell you what I 'll do, sir," said William Dork, addressing Mr. Mellish; "if you 'll lend me a horse and trap, I 'll drive into Doncaster, and see if this man 's to be found at the Reindeer. We *must* have him for a witness."

John Mellish assented to this arrangement. He left one of the grooms to keep watch in the death-chamber, in company with Stephen Hargraves, the softy; and, after bidding the surgeon good-night, walked slowly homeward with his friends. The church clock was striking twelve as the three gentlemen left the wood, and passed through the little iron gateway on to the lawn.

"We had better not tell the ladies more than we are obliged to tell them about this business," said John Mellish. as they approached the house, where the lights were still burning in the hall and drawing-room; "we shall only agitate them by letting them know the worst."

"To be sure, to be sure, my boy," answered the colonel. "My poor little Maggie always cries if she hears of anything of this kind; and Lofthouse is almost as big a baby," added the soldier, glancing rather contemptuously at his son-in-law, who had not spoken once during that slow homeward walk.

John Mellish thought very little of the strange disappearance of Captain Prodder. The man had objected to be summoned as a witness perhaps, and had gone. It was only natural. He did not even know his name; he only knew him as the mouth-piece of evil tidings, which had shaken him to the very soul. That this man Conyers — this man of all others, this man toward whom he had conceived a deeply-rooted aversion, an unspoken horror — should have perished mysteriously by an unknown hand, was an event so strange and appalling as to deprive him for a time of all power of thought, all capability of reasoning. Who had killed this man — this penniless, good-for-nothing trainer? Who could have had any motive for such a deed? Who— The cold sweat broke out upon his brow in the anguish of the thought.

Who had done this deed?

It was not the work of any poacher. No. It was very well for Colonel Maddison, in his ignorance of antecedent facts, to account for it in that manner; but John Mellish knew that he was wrong. James Conyers had only been at the Park a week. He had had neither time nor opportunity for making himself ob-

noxious; and, beyond that, he was not the man to make himself obnoxious. He was a selfish, indolent rascal, who only loved his own ease, and who would have allowed the young partridges to be wired under his very nose. Who, then, had done this deed?

There was only one person who had any motive for wishing to be rid of this man. One person who, made desperate by some great despair, enmeshed perhaps by some net hellishly contrived by a villain, hopeless of any means of extrication, in a moment of madness, might have—No! In the face of every evidence that earth could offer—against reason, against hearing, eyesight, judgment, and memory— he would say, as he said now, *No!* She was innocent! She was innocent! She had looked in her husband's face, the clear light had shone from her luminous eyes, a stream of electric radiance penetrating straight to his heart—and he had trusted her.

"I 'll trust her at the worst," he thought. "If all living creatures upon this wide earth joined their voices in one great cry of upbraiding, I 'd stand by her to the very end, and defy them."

Aurora and Mrs. Lofthouse had fallen asleep upon opposite sofas; Mrs. Powell was walking softly up and down the long drawing-room, waiting and watching — waiting for a fuller knowledge of this ruin which had come upon her employer's household.

Mrs. Mellish sprang up suddenly at the sound of her husband's step as he entered the drawing-room.

"Oh, John," she cried, running to him and laying her hands upon his broad shoulders, "thank Heaven you are come back! Now tell me all—tell me all, John. I am prepared to hear anything, no matter what. This is no ordinary accident. The man who was hurt—"

Her eyes dilated as she looked at him with a glance of intelligence that plainly said, "I can guess what has happened."

"The man was very seriously hurt, Lolly," her husband answered, quietly.

"What man?"

"The trainer recommended to me by John Pastern."

She looked at him for a few moments in silence.

"He is dead?" she said, after that brief pause.

"He is."

Her head sank forward upon her breast, and she walked away, quietly returning to the sofa from which she had arisen.

"I am very sorry for him," she said; "he was not a good man. I am sorry he was not allowed time to repent of his wickedness."

"You knew him, then?" asked Mrs. Lofthouse, who had expressed unbounded consternation at the trainer's death.

"Yes; he was in my father's service some years ago."

Mr. Lofthouse's carriage had been waiting ever since eleven o'clock, and the rector's wife was only too glad to bid her friends good-night, and to drive away from Mellish Park and its fatal associations; so, though Colonel Maddison would have preferred stopping to smoke another cheroot while he discussed the business with John Mellish, he was fain to submit to feminine authority, and take his seat by his daughter's side in the comfortable landau, which was an open or a close carriage, as the convenience of its proprietor dictated. The vehicle rolled away upon the smooth carriage-drive, the servants closed the hall-doors, and lingered about, whispering to each other, in little groups in the corridors and on the staircases, waiting until their master and mistress should have retired for the night. It was difficult to think that the business of life was to go on just the same though a murder had been done upon the outskirts of the Park, and even the housekeeper, a severe matron at ordinary times, yielded to the common influence, and forgot to drive the maids to their dormitories in the gabled roof.

All was very quiet in the drawing-room where the visitors had left their host and hostess to hug those ugly skeletons which are put away in the presence of company. John Mellish walked slowly up and down the room. Aurora sat staring vacantly at the guttering wax candles in the old-fashioned silver branches, and Mrs. Powell, with her embroidery in full working-order, threaded her needles and snipped away the fragments of her delicate cotton as carefully as if there had been no such thing as crime or trouble in the world, and no higher purpose in life than the achievement of elaborate devices upon French cambric.

She paused now and then to utter some polite commonplace. She regretted such an unpleasant catastrophe, she lamented the disagreeable circumstances of the trainer's death; indeed, she in a manner inferred that Mr. Conyers had shown himself wanting in good taste and respect for his employer by the mode of his death, but the point to which she recurred most frequently was the fact of Aurora's presence in the grounds at the time of the murder.

"I so much regret that you should have been out of doors at the time, my dear Mrs. Mellish," she said, "and, as I should imagine, from the direction which you took on leaving the house, actually near the place where the unfortunate man met his death. It will be so unpleasant for you to have to appear at the inquest."

"Appear at the inquest!" cried John Mellish, stopping suddenly, and turning fiercely upon the placid speaker. "Who says that my wife will have to appear at the inquest?"

"I merely imagined it probable that —"

"Then you'd no business to imagine it, ma'am," retorted Mr. Mellish, with no very great show of politeness. "My wife will not appear. Who should ask her to do so? Who should wish her to do so? What has she to do with to-night's business? or what does she know of it more than you or I, or any one else in this house?"

Mrs. Powell shrugged her shoulders.

"I thought that, from Mrs. Mellish's previous knowledge of this unfortunate person, she might be able to throw some light upon his habits and associations," she suggested, mildly.

"Previous knowledge!" roared John. "What knowledge should Mrs. Mellish have of her father's grooms? What interest should she take in their habits or associations?"

"Stop," said Aurora, rising and laying her hand lightly on her husband's shoulder. "My dear, impetuous John, why do you put yourself into a passion about this business? If they choose to call me as a witness, I will tell all I know about this man's death, which is nothing but that I heard a shot fired while I was in the grounds."

She was very pale, but she spoke with a quiet determination, a calm, resolute defiance of the worst that fate could reserve for her.

"I will tell anything that it is necessary to tell," she said, "I care very little what."

With her hand still upon her husband's shoulder, she rested her head on his breast like some weary child nestling in its only safe shelter.

Mrs. Powell rose, and gathered together her embroidery in a pretty, lady-like receptacle of fragile wicker-work. She glided to the door, selected her candlestick, and paused on the threshold to bid Mr. and Mrs. Mellish good-night.

"I am sure you must need rest after this terrible affair," she simpered, "so I will take the initiative. It is nearly one o'clock. Good-night."

If she had lived in the Thane of Cawdor's family, she would have wished Macbeth and his wife a good night's rest after Duncan's murder, and would have hoped they would sleep well; she would have courtesied and simpered amid the tolling of alarm-bells, the clashing of vengeful swords, and the blood bedabbled visages of the drunken grooms. It must have been the Scottish queen's *companion* who watched with the truckling physician, and played the spy upon her mistress's remorseful wanderings, and told how it was the conscience-stricken lady's habit to do this and thus, no one but a genteel mercenary would have been so sleepless in the dead hours of the night, lying in wait for the revelation of horrible secrets, the muttered clews to deadly mysteries.

"Thank God, she's gone at last!" cried John Mellish, as the door closed very softly and very slowly upon Mrs. Powell. "I hate that woman, Lolly."

Heaven knows I have never called John Mellish a hero; I have never set him up as a model of manly perfection or infallible virtue; and, if he is not faultless, if he has those flaws and blemishes which seem a constituent part of our imperfect clay, I make no apology for him, but trust him to the tender mercies of those who, not being *quite* perfect themselves, will, I am sure, be merciful to him. He hated those who hated his wife, or did her any wrong, however small. He loved those who loved her. In the great power of his wide affection, all self-esteem was annihilated. To love her was to love him; to serve her was to do him treble service; to praise her was to make him vainer than the vainest school-girl. He freely took upon his shoulders every debt that she owed, whether of love or of hate; and he was ready to pay either species of account to the utmost farthing, and with no mean interest upon the sum total. "I hate that woman, Lolly," he repeated, "and I shan't be able to stand her much longer."

Aurora did not answer him. She was silent for some moments, and when she did speak it was evident that Mrs. Powell was very far away from her thoughts.

"My poor John," she said, in a low, soft voice, whose melancholy tenderness went straight to her husband's heart; "my dear, how happy we were together for a little time! How very happy we were, my poor boy!"

"Always, Lolly," he answered, "always, my darling."

"No, no, no," said Aurora, suddenly; "only for a little while. What a horrible fatality has pursued us! what a frightful curse has clung to me! The curse of disobedience, John—the curse of Heaven upon my disobedience. To think that this man should have been sent here, and that he—"

She stopped, shivering violently, and clinging to the faithful breast that sheltered her.

John Mellish quietly led her to her dressing-room, and placed her in the care of her maid.

"Your mistress has been very much agitated by this night's business," he said to the girl; "keep her as quiet as you possibly can."

Mrs. Mellish's bedroom, a comfortable and roomy apartment, with a low ceiling and deep bay-windows, opened into a morning-room, in which it was John's habit to read the newspapers and sporting periodicals, while his wife wrote letters, drew pencil sketches of dogs and horses, or played with her favorite Bow-wow. They had been very childish, and idle, and happy in this pretty chintz-hung chamber; and, going into it to-night in utter desolation of heart, Mr. Mellish felt his sorrows all the more bitterly for the remembrance of those by-gone joys. The shaded lamp was lighted on the morocco-covered writing-table, and glimmered softly on the picture-frames,

caressing the pretty modern paintings, the simple, domestic-story pictures which adorned the subdued gray walls. This wing of the old house had been refurnished for Aurora, and there was not a chair or a table in the room that had not been chosen by John Mellish with a special view to the comfort and the pleasure of his wife. The upholsterer had found him a liberal employer, the painter and the sculptor a noble patron. He had walked about the Royal Academy with a catalogue and a pencil in his hand, choosing all the "pretty" pictures for the beautification of his wife's rooms. A lady in a scarlet riding-habit and three-cornered beaver hat, a white pony, and a pack of greyhounds, a bit of stone terrace and sloping turf, a flower-bed, and a fountain made poor John's idea of a pretty picture; and he had half a dozen variations of such familiar subjects in his spacious mansion. He sat down to-night, and looked hopelessly round the pleasant chamber, wondering whether Aurora and he would ever be happy again — wondering if this dark, mysterious, storm-threatening cloud would ever pass from the horizon of his life, and leave the future bright and clear.

"I have not been good enough," he thought; "I have intoxicated myself with my happiness, and have made no return for it. What am I, that I should have won the woman I love for my wife, while other men are laying down the best desires of their hearts a willing sacrifice, and going out to fight the battle for their fellow-men? What an indolent, good-for-nothing wretch I have been! How blind, how ungrateful, how undeserving!"

John Mellish buried his face in his broad hands, and repented of the carelessly happy life which he had led for one-and-thirty thoughtless years. He had been awakened from his unthinking bliss by a thunder-clap, that had shattered the fairy castle of his happiness, and laid it level with the ground; and in his simple faith he looked into his own life for the cause of the ruin which had overtaken him. Yes, it must be so; he had not deserved his happiness, he had not earned his good fortune. Have you ever thought of this, ye simple country squires, who give blankets and beef to your poor neighbors in the cruel winter-time, who are good and gentle masters, faithful husbands, and tender fathers, and who lounge away your easy lives in the pleasant places of this beautiful earth? Have you ever thought that, when all your good deeds have been gathered together and set in the balance, the sum of them will be very small when set against the benefits you have received? It will be a very small percentage which you will yield your Master for the ten talents intrusted to your care. Remember John Howard, fever-stricken and dying, Mrs. Fry, laboring in criminal prisons, Florence Nightingale, in the bare hospital chambers, in the

close and noxious atmosphere among the dead
and the dying These are the people who
return cent per cent for the gifts intrusted to
them. These are the saints whose good deeds
shine among the stars for ever and ever,
these are the indefatigable workers who, when
the toil and turmoil of the day is done, hear
the Master's voice in the still even-tune wel-
coming them to His rest

John Mellish, looking back at his life, humbly acknowledged that it had been a compar-
atively useless one He had distributed happiness to the people who had come in his way,
but he had never gone out of his way to
make people happy. I dare say that Dives
was a liberal master to his own servants, although he did not trouble himself to look after
the beggar who sat at his gates The Israel-
ite who sought instruction from the lips of
inspiration was willing to do his duty to his
neighbor, but had yet to learn the broad signification of that familiar epithet, and poor
John, like the rich young man, was ready to
serve his Master faithfully, but had yet to
learn the manner of his service.

"If I could save her from the shadow of
sorrow or disgrace, I would start to-morrow
barefoot on a pilgrimage to Jerusalem," he
thought "What is there that I would not
do for her? what sacrifice would seem too
great? what burden too heavy to bear?"

CHAPTER XXVI

AT THE GOLDEN LION

Mr William Dork, the constable, reached
Doncaster at about quarter-past one o'clock
upon the morning after the murder, and drove
straight to the Reindeer. That hotel had
been closed for a couple of hours, and it was
only by the exercise of his authority that Mr
Dork obtained access, and a hearing from the
sleepy landlord The young man who had
driven Mr Prodder was found after considerable difficulty, and came stumbling down the
servants' staircase in a semi-somnolent state
to answer the constable's inquiries He had
driven the seafaring gentleman, whose name
he did not know, direct to the Doncaster Station, in time to catch the mail-train, which
started at 12.30 He had parted with the
gentleman at the door of the station three
minutes before the train started

This was all the information that Mr Dork
could obtain. If he had been a sharp London
detective, he might have made his arrangements for laying hands upon the fugitive sailor
at the first station at which the train stopped,
but being merely a simple rural functionary,
he scratched his stubble head, and stared at
the landlord of the Reindeer in utter mental
bewilderment

"He was in a devil of a hurry, the chap,"

he muttered rather sulkily. "What did he
want to coot away for?"

The young man who had acted as charioteer could not answer this question. He only
knew that the seafaring gentleman had promised him half a sovereign if he caught the
mail-train, and that he had earned his reward

"Well, I suppose it a'n't so very particklar," said Mr Dork, sipping a glass of rum,
which he had ordered for his refreshment
"You'll have to appear to-morrow, and you
can tell nigh as much as t' other chap." he
added, turning to the young man "You was
with him when the shot were fired, and you
warn't far when he found the body You'll
have to appear and give evidence whenever
the inquest 's held I doubt if it'll be to-
morrow, for there won't be much time to give
notice to the coroner."

Mr Dork wrote the young man's name in
his pocket-book, and the landlord vouched
for his being forthcoming when called upon
Having done this much, the constable left
the inn, after drinking another glass of rum,
and refreshing John Mellish's horse with a
handful of oats and a drink of water. He
drove at a brisk pace back to the Park stables,
delivered the horse and gig to the lad who
had waited for his coming, and returned to
his comfortable little dwelling in the village
of Meslingham, about a mile from the Park
gates

I scarcely know how to describe that long,
quiet, miserable day which succeeded the night
of the murder Aurora Mellish lay in a dull
stupor, not able to lift her head from the pillows upon which it rested, scarcely caring to
raise her eyelids from the aching eyes they
sheltered. She was not ill, nor did she affect
to be ill She lay upon the sofa in her dressing-room, attended by her maid, and visited
at intervals by John, who roamed hither and
thither about the house and grounds, talking
to innumerable people, and always coming to
the same conclusion, namely, that the whole
affair was a horrible mystery, and that he
heartily wished the inquest well over —He
had visitors from twenty miles round his house
— for the evil news had spread far and wide
before noon — visitors who came to condole,
and to sympathize, and wonder, and speculate, and ask questions, until they fairly drove
him mad. But he bore all very patiently
He could tell them nothing except that the
business was as dark a mystery to him as it
could be to them, and that he had no hope of
finding any solution to the ghastly enigma.
They one and all asked him the same question, "Had any one a motive for killing this
man?"

How could he answer them? He might
have told them that if twenty persons had had
a powerful motive for killing James Convers,
it was possible that a one-and-twentieth person, who had no motive, might have done the

deed. That species of argument which builds up any hypothesis out of a series of probabilities may, after all, lead very often to false conclusions.

Mr. Mellish did not attempt to argue the question. He was too weary and sick at heart, too anxious for the inquest to be over, and he free to carry Aurora away with him, and turn his back upon the familiar place, which had been hateful to him ever since the trainer had crossed its threshold.

"Yes, my darling," he said to his wife, as he bent over her pillow, "I shall take you away to the south of France directly this business is settled. You shall leave the scene of all past associations, all by-gone annoyances. We will begin the world afresh."

"God grant that we may be able to do so," Aurora answered, gravely. "Ah! my dear, I can not tell you that I am sorry for this man's death. If he had died nearly two years ago, when I thought he did, how much misery he would have saved me!"

Once in the course of that long summer's afternoon Mr. Mellish walked across the Park to the cottage at the north gates. He could not repress a morbid desire to look upon the lifeless clay of the man whose presence had caused him such vague disquietude, such instinctive terror. He found the softy leaning on the gate of the little garden, and one of the grooms standing at the door of the death-chamber.

"The inquest is to be held at the Golden Lion at ten o'clock to-morrow morning," Mr. Mellish said to the men. "You, Hargraves, will be wanted as a witness."

He walked into the darkened chamber. The groom understood what he came for, and silently withdrew the white drapery that covered the trainer's dead face.

Accustomed hands had done their awful duty. The strong limbs had been straightened. The lower jaw, which had dropped in the agony of sudden death, was supported by a linen bandage; the eyelids were closed over the dark violet eyes; and the face, which had been beautiful in life, was even yet more beautiful in the still solemnity of death. The clay which in life had lacked so much in its lack of a beautiful soul to light it from within, found its level in death. The worthless soul was gone, and the physical perfection that remained had lost its only blemish. The harmony of proportion, the exquisitely modelled features, the charms of detail, all were left, and the face which James Conyers carried to the grave was handsomer than that which had smiled insolent defiance upon the world in the trainer's lifetime.

John Mellish stood for some minutes looking gravely at that marble face.

"Poor fellow!" thought the generous-hearted young squire; "it was a hard thing to die so young. I wish he had never come here.

I wish Lolly had confided in me, and let me made a bargain with this man to stop away and keep her secret. Her secret! her father's secret more likely. What secret could she have had that a groom was likely to discover? It may have been some mercantile business, some commercial transaction of Archibald Floyd's, by which the old man fell into his servant's power. It would be only like my glorious Aurora to take the burden upon her own shoulders, and to bear it bravely through every trial."

It was thus that John Mellish had often reasoned upon the mystery which divided him from his wife. He could not bear to impute even the shadow of evil to her. He could not endure to think of her as a poor, helpless woman, entrapped into the power of a mean-spirited hireling, who was only too willing to make his market out of her secrets. He could not tolerate such an idea as this; and he sacrificed poor Archibald Floyd's commercial integrity for the preservation of Aurora's womanly dignity. Ah! how weak and imperfect a passion is this boundless love! How ready to sacrifice others for that one loved object, which *must* be kept spotless in our imaginations, though a hecatomb of her fellow-creatures are to be blackened and befouled for her justification. If Othello could have established Desdemona's purity by the sacrifice of the reputation of every lady in Cyprus, do you think he would have spared the fair inhabitants of the friendly isle? No; he would have branded every one of them with infamy, if he could, by so doing, have rehabilitated the wife he loved. John Mellish *would* not think ill of his wife. He resolutely shut his eyes to all damning evidence. He clung with a desperate tenacity to his belief in her purity, and only clung the more tenaciously as the proofs against her became more numerous.

The inquest was held at a roadside inn within a quarter of a mile of the north gates—a quiet little place, only frequented on market-days by the country people going backward and forward between Doncaster and the villages beyond Meslingham. The coroner and his jury sat in a long bare room, in which the frequenters of the Golden Lion were wont to play bowls in wet weather. The surgeon, Steeve Hargraves, Jarvis, the young man from the Reindeer, William Dork, the constable, and Mr. Mellish were the only witnesses called; but Colonel Maddison and Mr. Lofthouse were both present during the brief proceedings.

The inquiry into the circumstances of the trainer's death occupied a very short time. Nothing was elicited by the brief examination of the witnesses which in any way led to the elucidation of the mystery. John Mellish was the last person interrogated, and he answered the questions put to him with prompt decision.

There was one inquiry, however, which he was unable to answer, although it was a very simple one. Mr Hayward, the coroner, anxious to discover so much of the history of the dead man as might lead eventually to the discovery of his murderer, asked Mr Mellish if his trainer had been a bachelor or a married man.

"I really can not answer that question," said John, "I should imagine that he was a single man, as neither he nor Mr Pastern told me anything to the contrary. Had he been married, he would have brought his wife with him, I should suppose. My trainer, Langley, was married when he entered my service, and his wife and children have occupied the premises over my stables for some years."

"You infer, then, that James Conyers was unmarried?"

"Most decidedly."

"And it is your opinion that he had made no enemies in the neighborhood?"

"It is next to impossible that he could have done so."

"To what cause, then, do you attribute his death?"

"To an unhappy accident. I can account for it in no other way. The path through the wood is used as a public thoroughfare, and the whole of the plantation is known to be infested with poachers. It was past ten o'clock at night when the shot was heard. I should imagine that it was fired by a poacher, whose eyes deceived him in the shadowy light."

The coroner shook his head. "You forget, Mr Mellish," he said, "that the cause of death was not an ordinary gunshot wound. The shot heard was the report of a pistol, and the deceased was killed by a pistol-bullet."

John Mellish was silent. He had spoken in good faith as to his impression respecting the cause of the trainer's death. In the press and hurry, the horror and confusion of the two last days, the smaller details of the awful event had escaped his memory.

"Do you know any one among your servants, Mr Mellish," asked the coroner, "whom you would consider likely to commit an act of violence of this kind? Have you any one of an especially vindictive character in your household?"

"No," answered John, decisively; "I can answer for my servants as I would for myself. They were all strangers to this man. What motive could they possibly have had to seek his death?"

Mr Hayward rubbed his chin, and shook his head reflectively.

"There was this superannuated trainer whom you spoke of just now, Mr Mellish," he said. "I am well aware that the post of trainer in your stables is rather a good thing. A man may save a good deal of money out of his wages and perquisites with such a master

as you. This former trainer may not have liked being superseded by the deceased. He may have felt some animus toward his successor."

"Langley!" cried John Mellish, "he is as good a fellow as ever breathed. He was not superseded; he resigned the active part of his work at his own wish, and he retained his full wages by mine. The poor fellow has been confined to his bed for the last week."

"Humph!" muttered the coroner. "Then you can throw no light upon this business, Mr. Mellish?"

"None whatever. I have written to Mr Pastern, in whose stables the deceased was employed, telling him of the circumstances of the trainer's death, and begging him to forward the information to any relative of the murdered man. I expect an answer by tomorrow's post, and I shall be happy to submit that answer to you."

Prior to the examination of the witnesses, the jurymen had been conducted to the north lodge, where they had beheld the mortal remains of James Conyers. Mr Morton had accompanied them, and had endeavored to explain to them the direction which the bullet had taken, and the manner in which, according to his own idea, the shot must have been fired. The jurymen who had been impanneled to decide upon this awful question were simple agriculturists and petty tradesmen, who grudged the day's lost labor, and who were ready to accept any solution of the mystery which might be suggested to them by the coroner. They hurried back to the Golden Lion, listened deferentially to the evidence and to Mr Hayward's address, retired to an adjoining apartment, where they remained in consultation for the space of about five minutes, and whence they emerged with a very rambling form of decision, which Mr Hayward reduced into a verdict of wilful murder against some person or persons unknown.

Very little had been said about the disappearance of the seafaring man who had carried the tidings of the murder to Mr Mellish's house. Nobody for a moment imagined that the evidence of this missing witness might have thrown some ray of light upon the mystery of the trainer's death. The seafaring man had been engaged in conversation with the young man from the Reindeer at the time when the shot was fired; he was therefore not the actual murderer, and, strangely significant as his hurried flight might have been to the acute intelligence of a well-trained metropolitan police officer, no one among the rustic officials present at the inquest attached any importance to the circumstance. Nor had Aurora's name been once mentioned during the brief proceedings. Nothing had transpired which in any way revealed her previous acquaintance with James Conyers; and John Mellish drew a deep breath, a long sigh of relief, as he left the Golden Lion and walked homeward. Colonel Maddison, Mr. Lofthouse, and two or three other gentlemen lingered on the threshold of the little inn talking to Mr. Hayward, the coroner.

The inquest was terminated; the business was settled; and the mortal remains of James Conyers could be carried to the grave at the pleasure of his late employer. All was over. The mystery of death and the secrets of life would be buried peacefully in the grave of the murdered man, and John Mellish was free to carry his wife away with him whithersoever he would. Free, have I said? No; for ever and for ever the shadow of that bygone mystery would hang like a funeral pall between himself and the woman he loved; for ever and for ever the recollection of that ghastly undiscovered problem would haunt him in sleeping and in waking, in the sunlight and in the darkness. His nobler nature, triumphing again and again over the subtle influences of damning suggestions and doubtful facts, was again and again shaken, although never quite defeated. He fought the battle bravely, though it was a very hard one, and it was to endure, perhaps, to the end of time. That voiceless argument was for ever to be argued; the spirits of Faith and Infidelity were for ever to be warring with each other in that tortured breast until the end of life— until he died, perhaps, with his head lying upon his wife's bosom, with his cheek fanned by her warm breath, but ignorant to the very last of the real nature of that dark something, that nameless and formless horror with which he had wrestled so patiently and so long.

"I 'll take her away with me," he thought; "and when we are divided by a thousand miles of blue water from the scene of her secret, I will fall on my knees before her, and beseech her to confide in me."

He passed by the north lodge with a shudder, and walked straight along the high-road toward the principal entrance of the Park. He was close to the gates when he heard a voice— a strange, suppressed voice, calling feebly to him to stop. He turned round and saw the softy making his way toward him with a slow, shambling run. Of all human beings, except perhaps that one who now lay cold and motionless in the darkened chamber at the north lodge, this Steeve Hargraves was the last whom Mr. Mellish cared to see. He turned with an angry frown upon the softy, who was wiping the perspiration from his pale face with the ragged end of his neck-handkerchief, and panting hoarsely.

"What is the matter?" asked John. "What do you want with me?"

"It 's th' coroner," gasped Stephen Hargraves—"th' coroner and Mr. Lofthouse, th' parson—they want to speak to ye, sir, oop at the Loi-on."

"What about?"

Steeve Hargraves gave a ghastly grin.

"I doant know, sir," he whispered. "It 's hardly loikely they 'd tell me. There 's summat oop, though, I 'll lay, for Mr. Lofthouse was as whoite as ashes, and seemed strangely oopset about summat. Would you be pleased to step oop, and speak to 'un directly, sir? that was my message."

"Yes, yes, I·'ll go," answered John, absently.

He had taken his hat off, and was passing his hand over his hot forehead in a half-bewildered manner. He turned his back upon the softy, and walked rapidly away, retracing his steps in the direction of the roadside inn.

Stephen Hargraves stood staring after him until he was out of sight, and then turned, and walked on slowly toward the turnstile leading into the wood.

"I know what they 've found," he muttered, "and I know what they want with him. He 'll be some time oop there, so I 'll slip across the wood and tell her. Yes"— he paused, rubbing his hands, and laughing a slow, voiceless laugh, which distorted his ugly face, and made him horrible to look upon — yes, it will be nuts for me to tell her."

CHAPTER XXVII.

"MY WIFE! MY WIFE! WHAT WIFE? I HAVE NO WIFE."

The Golden Lion had reassumed its accustomed air of rustic tranquillity when John Mellish returned to it. The jurymen had gone back to their different avocations, glad to have finished the business so easily; the villagers, who had hung about the inn to hear what they could of the proceedings, were all dispersed; and the landlord was eating his dinner, with his wife and family, in the comfortable little bar-parlor. He put down his knife and fork as John entered the sanded bar, and left his meal to receive such a distinguished visitor.

"Mr. Hayward and Mr. Lofthouse are in the coffee-room, sir," he said. "Will you please to step this way?"

He opened the door of a carpeted room, furnished with shining mahogany tables, and adorned by half a dozen gaudily colored prints of the Doncaster meetings, the great match between Voltigeur and Flying Dutchman, and other events which had won celebrity for the northern race-course. The coroner was sitting at the bottom of one of the long tables, with Mr. Lofthouse standing near him. William Dork, the Meslingham constable, stood near the door, with his hat in his hand, and with rather an alarmed expression dimly visible in his ruddy face. Mr. Hayward and Mr. Lofthouse were both very pale.

One rapid glance was enough to show all

this to John Mellish — enough to show him this, and something more . a basin of blood-stained water before the coroner, and an oblong piece of wet paper, which lay under Mr Hayward's clenched hand

"What is the matter ? Why did you send for me ?" he asked

Bewildered and alarmed as he had been by the message which had summoned him hurriedly back to the inn, he was still more so by the confusion evident in the coroner's manner as he answered this question

"Pray sit down, Mr. Mellish,' he said "I — I — sent for you — at — the — advice of Mr Lofthouse, who—who, as a clergyman and a family man, thought it incumbent upon me—"

Reginald Lofthouse laid his hand upon the coroner's arm with a warning gesture. Mr Hayward stopped for a moment, cleared his throat, and then continued speaking, but in an altered tone

"I have had occasion to reprimand William Dork for a breach of duty, which, though I am aware it may have been, as he says, purely unintentional and accidental—"

"It was indeed, sir," muttered the constable, submissively. "If I 'd ha' know'd—"

"The fact is, Mr Mellish, that on the night of the murder, Dork, in examining the clothes of the deceased, discovered a paper, which had been concealed by the unhappy man between the outer material and the lining of his waistcoat. This paper was so stained by the blood in which the breast of the waistcoat was absolutely saturated that Dork was unable to decipher a word of its contents He therefore was quite unaware of the importance of the paper , and, in the hurry and confusion consequent on the very hard duty he has done for the last two days he forgot to produce it at the inquest He had occasion to make some memorandum in his pocket-book almost immediately after the verdict had been given, and this circumstance recalled to his mind the existence of the paper He came immediately to me, and consulted me upon this very awkward business I examined the document, washed away a considerable portion of the stains which had rendered it illegible, and have contrived to decipher the greater part of it '

"The document is of some importance, then ?" John asked

He sat at a little distance from the table, with his head bent, and his fingers rattling nervously against the side of his chair. He chafed horribly at the coroner's pompous slowness He suffered an agony of fear and bewilderment Why had they called him back ? What was this paper ? How could it concern him ?

"Yes," Mr. Hayward answered, "the document is certainly an important one I have shown it to Mr Lofthouse, for the purpose of taking his advice upon the subject I have

not shown it to Dork , but I detained Dork in order that you may hear from him how and where the paper was found, and why it was not produced at the inquest "

"Why should I ask any questions upon the subject ?" cried John, lifting his head suddenly, and looking from the coroner to the clergyman. "How should this paper concern me ?"

"I regret to say that it does concern you very materially, Mr. Mellish," the rector answered, gently

John's angry spirit revolted against that gentleness What right had they to speak to him like this ? Why did they look at him with those grave, pitying faces ? Why did they drop their voices to that horrible tone in which the bearers of evil tidings pave their way to the announcement of some overwhelming calamity ?

"Let me see this paper, then, if it concerns me," John said, very carelessly "Oh, my God!" he thought, "what is this misery that is coming upon me ? What is this hideous avalanche of trouble which is slowly descending to crush me ?"

"You do not wish to hear anything from Dork ?" asked the coroner.

"No, no !" cried John, savagely "I only want to see that paper " He pointed as he spoke to the wet and blood-stained document under Mr Hayward's hand

"You may go, then, Dork," the coroner said, quietly, "and be sure you do not mention this business to any one It is a matter of purely private interest, and has no reference to the murder You will remember ?"

"Yes, sir "

The constable bowed respectfully to the three gentlemen, and left the room He was very glad to be so well out of the business

"They need n't have called me,' he thought (to call, in the Northern patois, is to scold, to abuse) "They need n't have said it was reputi — wat 's its name '—to keep the paper I might have burnt it if I liked, and said naught about it "

"Now," said John, rising and walking to the table as the door closed upon the constable, "now, then, Mr Hayward, let me see this paper. If it concerns me, or any one connected with me, I have a right to see it "

"A right which I will not dispute," the coroner answered, gravely, as he handed the blood-stained document to Mr Mellish "I only beg you to believe in my heart-felt sympathy with you in this—"

"Let me alone '" cried John, waving the speaker away from him as he snatched the paper from his hand, "let me alone ! Can't you see that I 'm nearly mad ?"

He walked to the window, and with his back to the coroner and Mr Lofthouse, examined the blotched and blotted document in his hands He stared for a long time at those blurred and half-illegible lines before he became aware of their full meaning. But at last, at last, the signification of that miserable paper grew clear to him, and with a loud cry of anguish he dropped into the chair from which he had risen, and covered his face with his strong right hand. He held the paper in the left, crumpled and crushed by the convulsive pressure of his grasp.

"My God!" he ejaculated, after that first cry of anguish, "my God! I never thought of this—I never could have imagined this."

Neither the coroner nor the clergyman spoke. What could they say to him. Sympathetic words could have no power to lessen such a grief as this; they would only fret and harass the strong man in his agony; it was better to obey him; it was far better to let him alone.

He rose at last, after a silence that seemed long to the spectators of his grief.

"Gentlemen," he said, in a loud, resolute voice that resounded through the little room, "I give you my solemn word of honor that when Archibald Floyd's daughter married me, she believed this man, James Conyers, to be dead."

He struck his clenched fist upon the table, and looked with proud defiance at the two men. Then, with his left hand, the hand that grasped the blood-stained paper, thrust into his breast, he walked out of the room. He walked out of the room, and out of the house, but not homeward. A grassy lane opposite the Golden Lion led away to a great waste of brown turf called Harper's Common. John Mellish walked slowly along this lane, and out upon this quiet common-land, lonely even in the broad summer daylight. As he closed the five-barred gate at the end of the lane, and emerged upon the open waste, he seemed to shut the door of the world that lay behind him, and to stand alone with his great grief under the low, sunless summer sky. The dreary scene before him, and the gray atmosphere above his head, seemed in strange harmony with his grief. The reedy water-pools, unbroken by a ripple; the barren verdure, burnt a dull grayish brown by the summer sun; the bloomless heather, and the flowerless rushes—all things upon which he looked took a dismal coloring from his own desolation, and seemed to make him the more desolate. The spoiled child of fortune—the popular young squire, who had never been contradicted in nearly two-and-thirty years—the happy husband, whose pride in his wife had touched upon that narrow boundary-line which separates the sublime from the ridiculous—ah! whither had they fled, all these shadows of the happy days that were gone? They had vanished away; they had fallen into the black gulf of the cruel past. The monster who devours his children had taken back these happy ones, and a desolate man was left in their stead—a desolate man, who looked at a broad ditch and a rushy bank a few paces from where he stood, and thought, "Was it I who leaped that dike a month ago to gather forget-me-nots for my wife?"

He asked himself that question, reader, which we must all ask ourselves sometimes. Was he really that creature of the irrevocable past? Even as I write this I can see that common-land of which I write—the low sky, the sunburnt grass, the reedy water-pools, the flat landscape stretching far away on every side *to regions that are strange to me. I can recall every object in that simple scene — the atmosphere of the sunless day, the sounds in the soft summer air, the voices of the people near me; I can recall everything except — *myself*. This miserable *ego* is the one thing that I can not bring back—the one thing that seems strange to me—the one thing that I can scarcely believe in. If I went back to that Northern common-land to-morrow, I should recognize every hillock, every scrap of furze, or patch of heather. The few years that have gone by since I saw it will have made a scarcely perceptible difference in the features of the familiar place. The slow changes of Nature, immutable in her harmonious law, will have done their work according to that unalterable law; but this wretched me has undergone so complete a change that, if you could bring me back that *alter ego* of the past, I should be unable to recognize the strange creature; and yet it is by no volcanic shocks, no rending asunder of rocky masses, no great convulsions, or terrific agonies of Nature, that the change has come about; it is rather by a slow, monotonous wearing away of salient points, an imperceptible adulteration of this or that constituent part, an addition here, and a subtraction there, that the transformation takes place. It is hard to make a man believe in the physiologists, who declare that the hand which uses his pen to-day is not the same hand that guided the quill with which he wrote seven years ago. He finds it very difficult to believe this; but let him take out of some forgotten writing-desk, thrust into a corner of his lumber-room, those letters which he wrote seven years ago, and which were afterward returned to him by the lady to whom they were addressed, and the question which he will ask himself, as he reads the faded lines, will most surely be, "Was it I who wrote this bosh? Was it I who called a lady with white eyelashes 'the guiding star of a lonely life?' Was it I who was 'inexpressibly miserable, with one *s*, and looked 'forward with unutterable anxiety to the party in Onslow Square, at which I once more should look into those soft blue eyes?' What party in Onslow Square? *Non mi recordo.* 'Those soft blue eyes' were garnished with white lashes, and the lady to whom the letters were written jilted me to marry a rich soap-boiler." Even the law takes cognizance of this wonderful transformation. The debt which Smith contracts in 1850 is null and void in 1857. The Smith of '50 may have been an extravagant rogue; the Smith of '57 may be a conscientious man, who would not cheat his creditors of a farthing. Shall Smith the second be called upon to pay the debts of Smith the first? I leave that question to Smith's conscience and the metaphysicians. Surely the same law should hold good in breach of promise of marriage. Smith the first may have adored Miss Brown; Smith the second may detest her. Shall Smith of 1857 be called upon to perform the contract entered into by that other Smith of 1850? The French criminal law goes still farther. The murderer whose crime remains unsuspected for ten years can laugh at the police officers who discover his guilt in the eleventh. Surely this must be because the real murderer is no longer amenable to justice—because the hand that struck the blow, and the brain that plotted the deed, are alike extinct.

Poor John Mellish, with the world of the past crumbled at his feet, looked out at the blank future, and mourned for the people who were dead and gone.

He flung himself at full length upon the stunted grass, and, taking the crumpled paper from his breast, unfolded it and smoothed it out before him.

It was a certificate of marriage — the certificate of a marriage which had been solemnized at the parish church of Dover upon the 2d of July, 1856, between James Conyers, bachelor, rough-rider, of London, son of Joseph Conyers, stage-coachman, and Susan, his wife, and Aurora Floyd, spinster, daughter of Archibald Floyd, banker, of Felden Woods, Kent.

CHAPTER XXVIII.
AURORA'S FLIGHT.

Mrs. Mellish sat in her husband's room on the morning of the inquest, among the guns and fishing-rods, the riding-boots and hunting-whips, and all the paraphernalia of sportsmanship. She sat in a capacious wicker-work arm-chair close to the open window, with her head lying back upon the chintz-covered cushions, and her eyes wandering far away across the lawn and flower-beds toward the winding pathway by which it was likely John Mellish would return from the inquest at the Golden Lion.

She had openly defied Mrs. Powell, and had locked the door of this quiet chamber upon that lady's stereotyped civilities and sympathetic simpering. She had locked the door upon the outer world, and sat alone in the pleasant window the fullest can ...

showering their scented petals upon her lap with every breath of the summer breeze, and the butterflies hovering about her. The old mastiff sat by her side, with his heavy head lying on her lap, and his big dim eyes lifted to her face. She sat alone, I have said; but Heaven knows she was not companionless. Black care and corroding anxiety kept her faithful company, and would not budge from her side. What companions are so adhesive as trouble and sorrow? what associates so tenacious, what friends so watchful and untiring? This wretched girl stood alone in the centre of a sea of troubles, fearful to stretch out her hands to those who loved her, lest she should drag them into that ocean which was rising to overwhelm her.

"Oh, if I could suffer alone," she thought—"if I could suffer all this misery alone, I think I would go through it to the last without complaining; but the shame, the degradation, the anguish will come upon others more heavily than upon me. What will they not suffer? what will they not endure if the wicked madness of my youth should become known to the world?"

Those others of whose possible grief and shame she thought with such cruel torture were her father and John Mellish. Her love for her husband had not lessened by one iota her love for that indulgent father on whom the folly of her girlhood had brought such bitter suffering. Her generous heart was wide enough for both. She had acknowledged no "divided duty," and would have repudiated any encroachment of the new affection upon the old. The great river of her love widened into an ocean, and embraced a new shore with its mighty tide; but that far-away source of childhood, from which affection first sprang in its soft infantine purity, still gushed in crystal beauty from its unsullied spring. She would perhaps scarcely have recognized the coldly-measured affection of mad Lear's youngest daughter—the affection which could divide itself with mathematical precision between father and husband. Surely, love is too pure a sentiment to be so weighed in the balance. Must we subtract something from the original sum when we are called upon to meet a new demand? or has not affection rather some magic power by which it can double its capital at any moment when there is a run upon the bank? When Mrs. John Anderson becomes the mother of six children, she does not say to her husband, "My dear John, I shall be compelled to rob you of six-tenths of my affection in order to provide for the little ones." No; the generous heart of the wife grows larger to meet the claims upon the mother, as the girl's heart expanded with the new affections of the wife. Every pang ... husband's ... her father ... these two in her own mind. She loved them, and was sorry for them, with an equal measure of love and sorrow.

"If—if the truth should be discovered at this inquest," she thought, "I never can see my husband again; I can never look in his face any more. I will run away to the end of the world, and hide myself from him for ever."

She had tried to capitulate with her fate; she had endeavored to escape the full measure of retribution, and she had failed. She had done evil that good might come of it, in the face of that command which says that all such evil-doing shall be wasted sin, useless iniquity. She had deceived John Mellish, in the hope that the veil of deception might never be rent in twain, that the truth might be undiscovered to the end, and the man she loved spared from cruel shame and grief. But the fruits of that foolish seed, sown long ago, in the day of her disobedience, had grown up around her and hedged her in upon every side, and she had been powerless to cut a pathway for herself through the noxious weeds that her own hands had planted.

She sat with her watch in her hand, and her eyes wandered every now and then from the gardens before her to the figures on the dial. John Mellish had left the house at a little after nine o'clock, and it was now nearly two. He had told her that the inquest would be over in a couple of hours, and that he would hurry home directly it was finished and tell her the result. What would be the result of that inquest? What inquiries might be made? what evidence might, by some unhappy accident, be produced to compromise or to betray her? She sat in a dull stupor, waiting to receive her sentence. What would it be? Condemnation or release? If her secret should escape detection — if James Conyers should be allowed to carry the story of his brief married life to the grave, what relief, what release for the wretched girl, whose worst sin had been to mistake a bad man for a good one — the ignorant trustfulness of a child who is ready to accept any shabby pilgrim for an exiled nobleman or a prince in disguise.

It was half-past two when she was startled by the sound of a shambling footstep upon the gravelled pathway underneath the veranda. The footstep slowly shuffled on for a few paces, then paused, then shuffled on again; and at last a face that she hated made itself visible at the angle of the window opposite to that against which she sat. It was the white face of the softy, which was poked cautiously forward a few inches within the window-frame. The mastiff sprang up with a growl, and made as if he would have flown at that ugly leering face, which looked like one of the hideous decorations of a Gothic building; but Aurora caught the animal's collar with both her hands, and dragged him back.

"Be quiet, Bow-wow," she said; "quiet, boy, quiet."

She still held him with one firm hand, soothing him with the other. "What do you want?" she asked, turning upon the softy with a cold, icy grandeur of disdain, which made her look like Nero's wife defying her false accusers. "What do you want with me? Your master is dead, and you have no longer an excuse for coming here. You have been forbidden the house and the grounds. If you forget this another time, I shall request Mr. Mellish to remind you."

She lifted her disengaged hand, and laid it upon the window-sash; she was going to close the window, when Stephen Hargraves stopped her.

"Don't be in such a hoorry," he said; "I want to speak to you. I 've come straight from th' inquest. I thought you might want to know all about it. I coom out o' friendliness, though you did pay into me with th' horsewhip."

Aurora's heart beat tempestuously against her aching breast. Ah! what hard duty that poor heart had done lately; what icy burdens it had borne, what horrible oppression of secrecy and terror had weighed upon it, crushing out all hope and peace! An agony of suspense and dread convulsed that tortured heart as the softy tempted her — tempted her to ask the issue of the inquest, that she might receive from his lips the sentence of life or death. She little knew how much of her secret this man had discovered; but she knew that he hated her, and that he suspected enough to know his power of torturing her.

She lifted her proud head, and looked at him with a steady glance of defiance. "I have told you that your presence is disagreeable," she said. "Stand aside, and let me shut the window."

The softy grinned insolently, and, holding the window-frame with one of his broad hands, put his head into the room. Aurora rose to leave the window; but he laid the other hand upon her wrist, which shrunk instinctively from contact with his hard, horny palm.

"I tell you I 've got summat particklar to say to you," he whispered. "You shall hear all about it. I was one of th' witnesses at th' inquest, and I 've been hangin' about ever since, and I know everything."

Aurora flung her head back disdainfully, and tried to wrench her wrist from that strong grasp.

"Let me go," she said. "You shall suffer for this insolence when Mr. Mellish returns."

"But he won't be back just yet a while," said the softy, grinning. "He 's gone back to the Golden Loi-on. Th' coroner and Mr. Lofthouse, th' parson, sent for him to tell him summat—summat about you!" hissed Stephen Hargraves, with his dry white lips close to Aurora's ear.

"What do you mean?" cried Mrs. Mellish, till writhing in the softy's grasp — still re-training her dog from flying at him with her disengaged hand; "what do you mean?"

"I mean what I say," answered Steeve Hargraves; "I mean that it 's all found out. They know everything; and they 've sent for Mr. Mellish, to tell him. They 've sent for him to tell him what you was to him that 's dead."

A low wail broke from Aurora's lips. She had expected to hear this, perhaps; she had, at any rate, dreaded it; she had only fought against receiving the tidings from this man; but he had conquered her—he had conquered her, as the dogged, obstinate nature, however base, will always conquer the generous and impulsive soul. He had secured his revenge, and had contrived to be the witness of her agony. He released her wrist as he finished speaking, and looked at her — looked at her with an insolently triumphant leer in his small eyes.

She drew herself up, proudly still — proudly and bravely in spite of all, but with her face changed — changed from its former expression of restless pain to the dull blankness of despair.

"They found th' certificate," said the softy. "He 'd carried it about with him sewed up in 's waistco-at."

The certificate! Heaven have pity upon her girlish ignorance! She had never thought of that; she had never remembered that miserable scrap of paper which was the legal evidence of her folly. She had dreaded the presence of that husband who had arisen, as if from the grave, to pursue and torment her, but she had forgotten that other evidence of the parish register, which might also arise against her at any moment. She had feared the finding of something — some letter—some picture — some accidental record among the possessions of the murdered man, but she had never thought of this most conclusive evidence, this most incontrovertible proof. She put her hand to her head, trying to realize the full horror of her position. The certificate of her marriage with her father's groom was in the hands of John Mellish.

"What will he think of me?" she thought. "How would he ever believe me if I were to tell him that I had received what I thought positive evidence of James Conyers' death a year before my second marriage? How could he believe in me? I have deceived him too cruelly to dare to ask his confidence."

She looked about, trying to collect herself, trying to decide upon what she ought to do, and in her bewilderment and agony forgot for a moment the greedy eyes which were gloating upon her misery. But she remembered herself presently, and, turning sternly upon Stephen Hargraves, spoke to him with a voice which was singularly clear and steady.

"You have told me all that you have to tell," she said; "be so good as to get out of the way while I shut the window."

The softy drew back and allowed her to close the sashes; she bolted the window, and drew down the Venetian blind, effectually shutting out her spy, who crept away slowly and reluctantly toward the shrubbery, through which he could make his way safely out of the grounds.

"I 've paid her out," he muttered, as he shambled off under the shelter of the young trees; "I 've paid her out pretty tidy. It 's almost better than money," he said, laughing silently — "it 's almost better than money to pay off them kind of debts."

Aurora seated herself at John Mellish's desk, and wrote a few hurried lines upon a sheet of paper that lay uppermost among letters and bills.

"MY DEAR LOVE," she wrote, "I can not remain here to see you after the discovery which has been made to-day. I am a miserable coward, and I can not meet your altered looks, I can not hear your altered voice. I have no hope that you can have any other feeling for me than contempt and loathing. But on some future day, when I am far away from you, and the bewilderment of my present misery has grown less, I will write, and explain everything. Think of me mercifully if you can; and if you can believe that, in the wicked concealments of the last few weeks, the mainspring of my conduct has been my love for you, you will only believe the truth. God bless you, my best and truest. The pain of leaving you for ever is less than the pain of knowing that you had ceased to love me. Good-by."

She lighted a taper, and sealed the envelope which contained this letter.

"The spies who hate and watch me shall not read this," she thought, as she wrote John's name upon the envelope.

She left the letter upon the desk, and, rising from her seat, looked round the room — looked with a long, lingering gaze, that dwelt on each familiar object. How happy she had been among all that masculine litter! how happy with the man she had believed to be her husband! how innocently happy before the coming down of that horrible storm-cloud which had overwhelmed them both! She turned away with a shudder.

"I have brought disgrace and misery upon all who have loved me," she thought. "If I had been less cowardly — if I had told the truth — all this might have been avoided if I had confessed the truth to Talbot Bulstrode."

She paused at the mention of that name.

"I will go to Talbot," she thought. "He is a good man. I will go to him; I shall have no ...... now in tell...... bir ..." He will advise me ...... t t..... w ...... th discovery ...... r..... p..... tat

Aurora had dimly foreseen this misery when she had spoken to Lucy Bulstrode at Felden; she had dimly foreseen a day in which all would be discovered, and she would fly to Lucy to ask for a shelter.

She looked at her watch.

"A quarter-past three." she said. "There is an express that leaves Doncaster at five. I could walk the distance in the time."

She unlocked the door, and ran up stairs to her own rooms. There was no one in the dressing-room, but her maid was in the bedroom, arranging some dresses in a huge wardrobe.

Aurora selected her plainest bonnet and a large gray cloak, and quietly put them on before the cheval glass in one of the pretty French windows. The maid, busy with her own work, did not take any particular notice of her mistress's actions; for Mrs. Mellish was accustomed to wait upon herself, and disliked any officious attention.

"How pretty the rooms look!" Aurora thought, with a weary sigh; "how simple and countrified! It was for me that the new furniture was chosen, for me that the bath-room and conservatory were built."

She looked through the vista of brightly-carpeted rooms.

Would they ever seem as cheerful as they had once done to their master? Would he still occupy them, or would he lock the doors, and turn his back upon the old house in which he had lived such an untroubled life for nearly two-and-thirty years?

"My poor boy, my poor boy!" she thought. "Why was I ever born to bring such sorrow upon him?"

There was no egotism in her sorrow for his grief. She knew that he had loved her, and she knew that this parting would be the bitterest agony of his life; but in the depth of mortification which her own womanly pride had undergone, she could not look beyond the present shame of the discovery made that day to a future of happiness and release.

"He will believe that I never loved him," she thought. "He will believe that he was the dupe of a designing woman, who wished to regain the position she had lost. What will he not think of me that is base and horrible?"

The face which she saw in the glass was very pale and rigid; the large dark eyes dry and lustrous, the lips drawn tightly down over the white teeth.

"I look like a woman who could cut her throat in such a crisis as this," she said. "How often I have wondered at the desperate deeds done by women! I shall never wonder again."

She unlocked her dressing-case, and took a couple of bank-notes and some loose gold from one of the drawers. She put these in her purse, gathered her cloak about her, and walked toward the door.

She paused on the threshold to speak to her maid, who was still busy in the inner room.

"I am going into the garden, Parsons," she said; "tell Mr. Mellish that there is a letter for him in his study."

The room in which John kept his boots and racing-accounts was called a "study" by the respectful household.

The dog Bow-wow lifted himself lazily from his tiger-skin rug as Aurora crossed the hall, and came sniffing about her, and endeavored to follow her out of the house. But she ordered him back to his rug, and the submissive animal obeyed her, as he had often done in his youth, when his young mistress used to throw her doll into the water at Felden, and send the faithful mastiff to rescue that fair-haired waxen favorite. He obeyed her now, but a little reluctantly; and he watched her suspiciously as she descended the flight of steps before the door.

She walked at a rapid pace across the lawn, and into the shrubbery, going steadily southward, though by that means she made her journey longer; for the north lodge lay toward Doncaster. In her way through the shrubbery she met two people, who walked closely side by side, engrossed in a whispering conversation, and who both started and changed countenance at seeing her. These two people were the softy and Mrs. Powell.

"So," she thought, as she passed this strangely-matched pair, "my two enemies are laying their heads together to plot my misery. It is time that I left Mellish Park."

She went out of a little gate leading into some meadows. Beyond these meadows there was a long shady lane that led behind the house to Doncaster. It was a path rarely chosen by any of the household at the Park, as it was the longest way to the town.

Aurora stopped at about a mile from the house which had been her own, and looked back at the picturesque pile of building, half hidden under the luxuriant growth of a couple of centuries.

"Good-by, dear home, in which I was an impostor and a cheat," she said; "good-by for ever and for ever, my own dear love."

While Aurora uttered these few words of passionate farewell, John Mellish lay upon the sun-burnt grass, staring absently at the still water-pools under the gray sky—pitying her, praying for her, and forgiving her from the depth of his honest heart.

CHAPTER XXIX.

JOHN MELLISH FINDS HIS HOME DESOLATE.

The sun was low in the western sky, and distant village clocks had struck seven, when John Mellish walked slowly away from that lonely waste of stunted grass called Harper's Common, and strolled homeward in the peaceful evening.

The Yorkshire squire was still very pale. He walked with his head bent forward upon his breast, and the hand that grasped the crumpled paper thrust into the bosom of his waistcoat; but a hopeful light shone in his eyes, and the rigid lines of his mouth had relaxed into a tender smile — a smile of love and forgiveness. Yes, he had prayed for her, and forgiven her, and he was at peace. He had pleaded her cause a hundred times in the dull quiet of that summer's afternoon, and had excused her, and forgiven her. Not lightly, Heaven is a witness; not without a sharp and cruel struggle, that had rent his heart with tortures undreamed of before.

This revelation of the past was such bitter shame to him — such horrible degradation — such irrevocable infamy. His love, his idol, his empress, his goddess—it was of her he thought. By what hellish witchcraft had she been insnared into the degrading alliance recorded in this miserable scrap of paper? The pride of five unsullied centuries arose, fierce and ungovernable, in the breast of the country gentleman, to resent this outrage upon the woman he loved. O God, had all his glorification of her been the vain boasting of a fool who had not known what he talked about? He was answerable to the world for the past as well as for the present. He had made an altar for his idol, and had cried aloud to all who came near her to kneel down and perform their worship at her shrine, and he was answerable to these people for the purity of their divinity. He could not think of her as less than the idol which his love had made her — perfect, unsullied, unassailable. Disgrace where she was concerned knew in his mind no degrees.

It was not his own humiliation he thought of when his face grew hot as he imagined the talk there would be in the county if this fatal indiscretion of Aurora's youth ever became generally known; it was the thought of her shame that stung him to the heart. He never once disturbed himself with any prevision of the ridicule which was likely to fall upon him.

It was here that John Mellish and Talbot Bulstrode were so widely different in their manner of loving and suffering. Talbot sought a wife who should reflect honor upon himself, and had fallen away from Aurora at the first trial of his faith, shaken with horrible apprehensions of his own danger. But John Mellish had submerged his very identity into that of the woman he loved. She was his faith and his worship, and it was for her glory that he wept in this cruel day of shame. The wrong which he found so hard to forgive was not her wrong against him, but that other and more fatal wrong against her: he had said that his affection was universal, and

partook of all the highest attributes of that sublime self-abnegation which we call Love. The agony which he felt to-day was the agony which Archibald Floyd had suffered years before. It was vicarious torture, endured for Aurora, and not for himself; and, in his struggle against that sorrowful anger which he felt for her folly, every one of her perfections took up arms upon the side of his indignation, and fought against their own mistress. Had she been less beautiful, less queenly, less generous, great, and noble, he might have forgiven her that self-inflicted shame more easily. But she was so perfect; and how could she—how could she?

He unfolded the wretched paper half a dozen times, and read and reread every word of that commonplace legal document, before he could convince himself that it was not some vile forgery, concocted by James Conyers for purposes of extortion. But he prayed for her, and forgave her. He pitied her with more than a mother's tender pity, with more than a sorrowful father's anguish.

"My poor dear!" he said, "my poor dear! she was only a school-girl when this certificate was first written—an innocent child, ready to believe in any lies told her by a villain."

A dark frown obscured the Yorkshireman's brow as he thought this — a frown that would have promised no good to Mr. James Conyers had not the trainer passed out of the reach of all earthly good and evil.

"Will God have mercy upon a wretch like that?" thought John Mellish; "will that man be forgiven for having brought disgrace and misery upon a trusting girl?"

It will perhaps be wondered at that John Mellish, who suffered his servants to rule in his household, and allowed his butler to dictate to him what wines he should drink, who talked freely to his grooms, and bade his trainer sit in his presence — it will be wondered at, perhaps, that this frank, free-spoken, simple-mannered young man should have felt so bitterly the shame of Aurora's unequal marriage. It was a common saying in Doncaster that Squire Mellish, of the Park, had no pride; that he would clap poor folks on the shoulder, and give them good-day as he lounged in the quiet street; that he would sit upon the corn-chandler's counter, slashing his hunting-whip upon those popular tops—about which a legend was current, to the effect that they were always cleaned with Champagne—and discussing the prospects of the September meeting; and that there was not within the three Ridings a better landlord or a nobler-hearted gentleman. And all this was perfectly true. John Mellish was entirely without personal pride; but there was another pride, which was wholly inseparable from his education and position, and this was the pride of caste. He was strictly conservative and, ... again he was ready to talk to his groom, ... the soldier, or his trusted retainer the groom, as freely as he would have held converse with his equals, he would have opposed all the strength of his authority against the saddler had that honest tradesman attempted to stand for his native town, and would have annihilated the groom with one angry flash of his bright blue eyes had the servant infringed by so much as an inch upon the broad extent of territory that separated him from his master.

The struggle was finished before John Mellish arose from the brown turf, and turned toward the home which he had left early that morning, ignorant of the great trouble that was to fall upon him, and only dimly conscious of some dark foreboding of the coming of an unknown horror. The struggle was over, and there was now only hope in his heart—the hope of clasping his wife to his breast, and comforting her for all the past. However bitterly he might feel the humiliation of this madness of her ignorant girlhood, it was not for him to remind her of it; his duty was to confront the world's slander or the world's ridicule, and oppose his own breast to the storm, while she was shielded by the great shelter of his love. His heart yearned for some peaceful foreign land, in which his idol would be far away from all who could tell her secret, and where she might reign once more glorious and unapproachable. He was ready to impose any cheat upon the world, in his greediness of praise and worship for her—for her. How tenderly he thought of her, walking slowly homeward in that tranquil evening? He thought of her waiting to hear from him the issue of the inquest, and he reproached himself for his neglect when he remembered how long he had been absent.

"But my darling will scarcely be uneasy," he thought; "she will hear all about the inquest from some one or other, and she will think that I have gone into Doncaster on business. She will know nothing of the finding of this detestable certificate. No one need know of it. Lofthouse and Hayward are honorable men, and they will keep my poor girl's secret; they will keep the secret of her foolish youth—my poor, poor girl!"

He longed for that moment which he fancied so near—the moment in which he should fold her in his arms, and say, "My dearest one, be at peace; there is no longer any secret between us. Henceforth your sorrows are my sorrows, and it is hard if I can not help you to carry the load lightly. We are one, my dear. For the first time since our wedding-day, we are truly united."

He expected to find Aurora in his own room, for she had declared her intention of sitting there all day; and he ran across the broad lawn to the rose-shadowed veranda that sheltered his favorite retreat. The blind was drawn down and the window bolted, as Aurora had bolted it in her wish to exclude Mr.

Stephen Hargraves. He knocked at the window, but there was no answer.

"Lolly has grown tired of waiting," he thought.

The second dinner-bell rang in the hall while Mr. Mellish lingered outside this darkened window. The commonplace sound reminded him of his social duties.

"I must wait till dinner is over, I suppose, before I talk to my darling," he thought. "I must go through all the usual business, for the edification of Mrs. Powell and the servants, before I can take my darling to my breast, and set her mind at ease for ever."

John Mellish submitted himself to the indisputable force of those ceremonial laws which we have made our masters, and he was prepared to eat a dinner for which he had no appetite, and wait two hours for that moment for whose coming his soul yearned, rather than provoke Mrs. Powell's curiosity by any deviation from the common course of events.

The windows of the drawing-room were open, and he saw the glimmer of a pale muslin dress at one of them. It belonged to Mrs. Powell, who was sitting in a contemplative attitude, gazing at the evening sky.

She was not thinking of that western glory of pale crimson and shining gold. She was thinking that if John Mellish cast off the wife who had deceived him, and who had never legally been his wife, the Yorkshire mansion would be a fine place to live in; a fine place for a housekeeper who knew how to obtain influence over her master, and who had the secret of his married life and of his wife's disgrace to help her on to power.

"He 's such a blind, besotted fool about her," thought the ensign's widow, "that if he breaks with her to-morrow, he 'll go on loving her just the same, and he 'll do anything to keep her secret. Let it work which way it will, they 're in my power—they 're both in my power; and I 'm no longer a poor dependent, to be sent away, at a quarter's notice, when it pleases them to be tired of me."

The bread of dependence is not a pleasant diet, but there are many ways of eating the same food. Mrs. Powell's habit was to receive all favors grudgingly, as she would have given, had it been her lot to give instead of to receive. She measured others by her own narrow gauge, and was powerless to comprehend or believe in the frank impulses of a generous nature. She knew that she was a useless member of Poor John's household, and that the young squire could have easily dispensed with her presence. She knew, in short, that she was retained by reason of Aurora's pity for her friendlessness; and, having neither gratitude nor kindly feelings to give in return for her comfortable shelter, she resented her own poverty of nature, and hated her entertainers for their generosity. It is a property of these narrow natures so to resent the attributes they can envy, but can not even understand; and Mrs. Powell had been far more at ease in households in which she had been treated as a lady-like drudge than she had ever been at Mellish Park, where she was received as an equal and a guest. She had eaten the bitter bread upon which she had lived so long in a bitter spirit, that her whole nature had turned to gall from the influence of that disagreeable diet. A moderately generous person can bestow a favor, and bestow it well; but to receive a boon with perfect grace requires a far nobler and more generous nature.

John Mellish approached the open window at which the ensign's widow was seated, and looked into the room. Aurora was not there. The long saloon seemed empty and desolate. The decorations of the temple looked cold and dreary, for the deity was absent.

"No one here!" exclaimed Mr. Mellish, disconsolately.

"No one but me," murmured Mrs. Powell, with an accent of mild deprecation.

"But where is my wife, ma'am?"

He said those two small words, "my wife," with such a tone of resolute defiance that Mrs. Powell looked at him as he spoke, and thought, "He has seen the certificate."

"Where is Aurora?" repeated John.

"I believe that Mrs. Mellish has gone out."

"Gone out! where?"

"You forget, sir," said the ensign's widow, reproachfully — "you appear to forget your special request that I should abstain from all supervision of Mrs. Mellish's arrangements. Prior to that request, which I may venture to suggest was unnecessarily emphatic, I had certainly considered myself as the humble individual chosen by Miss Floyd's aunt, and invested by her with a species of authority over the young lady's actions, in some manner responsible for—"

John Mellish chafed horribly under the merciless stream of long words which Mrs. Powell poured upon his head.

"Talk about that at another time, for Heaven's sake, ma'am," he said, impatiently. "I only want to know where my wife is. Two words will tell me that, I suppose."

"I am sorry to say that I am unable to afford you any information upon that subject," answered Mrs. Powell; "Mrs. Mellish quitted the house at about half-past three o'clock, dressed for walking. I have not seen her since."

Heaven forgive Aurora for the trouble it had been her lot to bring upon those who best loved her. John's heart grew sick with terror at this first failure of his hope. He had pictured her waiting to receive him, ready to fall upon his breast in answer to his passionate cry, "Aurora, come! come, dear love! the secret has been discovered, and is forgiven."

"Somebody knows where my wife has gone,

10

I suppose, Mrs. Powell?" he said, fiercely, turning upon the ensign's widow in his wrathful sense of disappointment and alarm. He was only a big child after all, with a child's alternate hopefulness and despair; with a child's passionate devotion for those he loved, and ignorant terror of danger to those beloved ones.

"Mrs. Mellish may have made a confidante of Parsons," replied the ensign's widow, "but she certainly did not enlighten me as to her intended movements. Shall I ring the bell for Parsons?"

"If you please."

John Mellish stood upon the threshold of the French window, not caring to enter the handsome chamber of which he was the master. Why should he go into the house? It was no home for him without the woman who had made it so dear and sacred — dear even in the darkest hour of sorrow and anxiety, sacred even in despite of the trouble his love had brought upon him.

The maid Parsons appeared in answer to a message sent by Mrs. Powell, and John strode into the room, and interrogated her sharply as to the departure of her mistress.

The girl could tell very little, except that Mrs. Mellish had said that she was going into the garden, and that she had left a letter in the study for the master of the house. Perhaps Mrs. Powell was even better aware of the existence of this letter than the abigail herself. She had crept stealthily into John's room after her interview with the softy and her chance encounter with Aurora. She had found the letter lying on the table, sealed with a crest and monogram that were engraved upon a bloodstone worn by Mrs. Mellish among the trinkets on her watch-chain. It was not possible, therefore, to manipulate this letter with any safety, and Mrs. Powell had contented herself by guessing darkly at its contents. The softy had told her of the fatal discovery of the morning, and she instinctively comprehended the meaning of that sealed letter. It was a letter of explanation and farewell, perhaps — perhaps only of farewell.

John strode along the corridor that led to his favorite room. The chamber was dimly lighted by the yellow evening sunlight which streamed from between the Venetian blinds and drew golden bars upon the matted floor. But even in that dusky and uncertain light he saw the white patch upon the table, and sprang with tigerish haste upon the letter his wife had left for him.

He drew up the Venetian blind, and stood in the embrasure of the window, with the evening sunlight upon his face, reading Aurora's letter. There was neither anger nor alarm visible in his face as he read — only supreme love and supreme compassion.

"My poor darling! my poor girl! How

could she think that there could ever be such a word as good-by between us! Does she think so lightly of my love as to believe that it could fail her now, when she wants it most? Why, if that man had lived," he thought, his face darkening with the memory of that unburied clay which yet lay in the still chamber at the north lodge — " if that man had lived, and had claimed her, and carried her away from me by the right of the paper in my breast, I would have clung to her still; I would have followed wherever he went, and would have lived near him, that she might have known where to look for a defender from every wrong; I would have been his servant, the willing servant and contented hanger-on of a boor, if I could have served her by enduring his insolence. So, my dear, my dear," murmured the young squire, with a tender smile, " it was worse than foolish to write this letter to me, and even more useless than it was cruel to run away from the man who would follow you to the farthest end of this wide world."

He put the letter into his pocket, and took his hat from the table. He was ready to start — he scarcely knew for what destination; for the end of the world, perhaps — in his search for the woman he loved. But he was going to Felden Woods before beginning the longer journey, as he fully believed that Aurora would fly to her father in her foolish terror.

" To think that anything could ever happen to change or lessen my love for her," he said: " foolish girl! foolish girl!"

He rang for his servant, and ordered the hasty packing of his smallest portmanteau. He was going to town for a day or two, and he was going alone. He looked at his watch; it was only a quarter after eight, and the mail left Doncaster at half-past twelve. There was plenty of time, therefore; a great deal too much time for the feverish impatience of Mr. Mellish, who would have chartered a special engine to convey him, had the railway officials been willing. There were four long hours during which he must wait, wearing out his heart in his anxiety to follow the woman he loved — to take her to his breast, and comfort and shelter her — to tell her that true love knows neither decrease nor change. He ordered the dog-cart to be got ready for him at eleven o'clock. There was a slow train that left Doncaster at ten; but, as it reached London only ten minutes before the mail, it was scarcely desirable as a conveyance. Yet, after the hour had passed for its starting, Mr. Mellish reproached himself bitterly for that lost ten minutes, and was tormented by a fancy that, through the loss of those very ten minutes, he should miss the chance of an immediate meeting with Aurora.

It was nine o'clock before he remembered the necessity of making some pretence of sitting down to dinner. He took his place at the end of the long table, and sent for Mrs. Powell, who appeared in answer to his summons, and seated herself with a well-bred affectation of not knowing that the dinner had been put off for an hour and a half.

" I 'm sorry I 've kept you so long, Mrs. Powell," he said, as he sent the ensign's widow a ladleful of clear soup, that was of the temperature of lemonade. " The truth is, that I — I — find I shall be compelled to run up to town by the mail."

" Upon no unpleasant business, I hope?"

" Oh, dear, no; not at all. Mrs. Mellish has gone up to her father's place, and — and — has requested me to follow her," added John, telling a lie with considerable awkwardness, but with no very great remorse. He did not speak again during dinner. He ate anything that his servants put before him, and took a good deal of wine; but he ate and drank alike unconsciously, and when the cloth had been removed, and he was left alone with Mrs. Powell, he sat staring at the reflection of the wax candles in the depths of the mahogany. It was only when the lady gave a little ceremonial cough, and rose with the intention of simpering out of the room, that he roused himself from his long reverie, and looked up suddenly.

" Don't go just this moment, if you please, Mrs. Powell," he said. " If you 'll sit down again for a few minutes, I shall be glad. I wished to say a word or two to you before I leave Mellish."

He rose as he spoke, and pointed to a chair. Mrs. Powell seated herself, and looked at him earnestly, with an eager, viperish earnestness, and a nervous movement of her thin lips.

" When you came here, Mrs. Powell," said John, gravely, " you came as my wife's guest and as my wife's friend. I need scarcely say that you could have had no better claim upon my friendship and hospitality. If you had brought a regiment of dragoons with you as the condition of your visit, they would have been welcome, for I believed that your coming would give pleasure to my poor girl. If my wife had been indebted to you for any word of kindness, for any look of affection, I would have repaid that debt a thousand-fold, had it lain in my power to do so by any service, however difficult. You would have lost nothing by your love for my poor motherless girl if any devotion of mine could have recompensed you for that tenderness. It was only reasonable that I should look to you as the natural friend and counsellor of my darling, and I did so honestly and confidently. Forgive me if I tell you that I very soon discovered how much I had been mistaken in entertaining such a hope. I soon saw that you were no friend to my wife."

" Mr. Mellish!"

" Oh, my dear madam, you think because I

keep hunting-boots and guns in the room I
call my study, and because I remember no
more of the Latin that my tutor crammed into
my head than the first line of the Eton Syn-
tax — you think, because I 'm not clever, that
I must needs be a fool. That 's your mistake,
Mrs. Powell; I 'm not clever enough to be a
fool, and I 've just sufficient perception to see
any danger that assails those I love. You
don't like my wife; you grudge her her youth,
and her beauty, and my foolish love for her;
and you 've watched, and listened, and plotted — in a lady-like way, of course — to do
her some evil. Forgive me if I speak plainly.
Where Aurora is concerned, I feel very
strongly. To hurt her little finger is to torture my whole body. To stab her once is to
stab me a hundred times. I have no wish to
be discourteous to a lady; I am only sorry
that you have been unable to love a poor girl
who has rarely failed to win friends among
those who have known her. Let us part
without animosity, but let us understand each
other for the first time. You do not like us,
and it is better that we should part before you
learn to hate us."

The ensign's widow waited in utter stupefaction until Mr. Mellish stopped, from want
of breath, perhaps, rather than from want of
words.

All her viperish nature rose in white defiance of him, as he walked up and down the
room, chafing himself into a fury with his recollection of the wrong she had done him in
not loving his wife.

"You are perhaps aware, Mr. Mellish," she
said, after an awful pause, "that under such
circumstances the annual stipend due to me
for my services can not be expected to cease
at your caprice; and that, although you may
turn me out of doors"—Mrs. Powell descended to this very commonplace location, and
stooped to the vernacular in her desire to be
spiteful—"you must understand that you will
be liable for my salary until the expiration
of—"

"Oh, pray do not imagine that I shall repu-
diate any claim you may make upon me, Mrs.
Powell," said John, eagerly; "Heaven knows
it has been no pleasure to me to speak as
plainly as I have spoken to-night. I will
write a check for any amount you may consider proper as compensation for this change
in our arrangements. I might have been more
polite, perhaps; I might have told you that
my wife and I think of travelling on the Continent, and that we are, therefore, breaking
up our household. I have preferred telling
you the plain truth. Forgive me if I have
wounded you."

Mrs. Powell rose, pale, menacing, terrible—
terrible in the intensity of her feeble wrath,
and in the consciousness that she had power
to stab the heart of the man who had affront-
ed her.

"You have merely anticipated my own intention, Mr. Mellish," she said. "I could not
possibly have remained a member of your
household after the very unpleasant circumstances that have lately transpired. My worst
wish is, that you may find yourself involved
in no greater trouble through your connection
with Mr. Floyd's daughter. Let me add one
word of warning before I have the honor of
wishing you good-evening. Malicious people
might be tempted to smile at your enthusiastic
mention of your 'wife,' remembering that the
person to whom you allude is Aurora Conyers,
the widow of your groom, and that she has
never possessed any legal claim to the title
you bestow upon her."

If Mrs. Powell had been a man, she would
have found her head in contact with the Tur-
key carpet of John's dining-room before she
could have concluded this speech; as she was
a woman, John Mellish stood looking her full
in the face, waiting till she had finished speaking. But he bore the stab she inflicted without flinching under its cruel pain, and he robbed her of the gratification she had hoped for.
He did not let her see his anguish.

"If Lofthouse has told her the secret," he
cried, when the door had closed upon Mrs.
Powell, "I 'll horsewhip him in the church."

CHAPTER XXX.

AN UNEXPECTED VISITOR.

Aurora found a civil railway official at the
Doncaster station, who was ready to take a
ticket for her, and find her a comfortable seat
in an empty carriage; but before the train
started a couple of sturdy farmers took their
seats upon the spring cushions opposite Mrs.
Mellish. They were wealthy gentlemen, who
farmed their own land, and travelled express;
but they brought a powerful odor of the
stable-yard into the carriage, and they talked
with that honest Northern twang which always has a friendly sound to the writer of
this story. Aurora, with her veil drawn over
her pale face, attracted very little of their attention. They talked of farming-stock and
horse-racing, and looked out of the window
every now and then to shrug their shoulders
at somebody else's agriculture.

I believe they were acquainted with the
capabilities of every acre of land between
Doncaster and Harrow, and knew how it
might have been made "worth ten shillin' an
acre more than it was, too, sir," as they perpetually informed each other.

How wearisome their talk must have seemed to the poor lonely creature who was running away from the man she loved—from the
man who loved her, and would love to the end
of time.

"I did n't mean what I wrote," she thought.

"My poor boy would never love me less. His great heart is made up of unselfish love and generous devotion. But he would be sorry for me; he would be so sorry! He could never be proud of me again; he could never boast of me any more. He would be always resenting some insult, or imagining some slight. It would be too painful for him. He would see his wife pointed at as the woman who had married her groom. He would be embroiled in a hundred quarrels, a hundred miseries. I will make the only return that I can ever make to him for his goodness to me—I will give him up, and go away and hide myself from him for ever."

She tried to imagine what John's life would be without her. She tried to think of him in some future time, when he should have worn out his grief, and reconciled himself to her loss. But she could not, she could not! She could not endure any image of *him* in which he was separated from his love for her.

"How should I ever think of him without thinking of his love for me?" she thought. "He loved me from the first moment in which he saw me. I have never known him except as a lover—generous, pure, and true."

And in this mind Aurora watched the smaller stations, which looked like mere streaks of whitened wood-work as the express tore past them, though every one of them was a mile-stone upon the long road which was separating her from the man she loved.

Ah! careless wives, who think it a small thing, perhaps, that your husbands are honest and generous, constant and true, and who are apt to grumble because your next-door neighbors have started a carriage, while you are fain to be content with eighteen-penny airings in vehicles procured at the nearest cab-stand, stop and think of this wretched girl, who in this hour of desolation recalled a thousand little wrongs she had done to her husband, and would have laid herself under his feet to be walked over by him could she have thus atoned for her petty tyrannies, her petty caprices. Think of her in her loneliness, with her heart yearning to go back to the man she loved, and with her love arrayed against herself, and pleading for him. She changed her mind a hundred times during that four hours' journey, sometimes thinking that she would go back by the next train, and then again remembering that her first impulse had been, perhaps, after all, only too correct, and that John Mellish's heart had turned against her in the cruel humiliation of that morning's discovery.

Have you ever tried to imagine the anger of a person whom you have never seen angry? Have you ever called up the image of a face that has never looked on you except in love and gentleness, and invested that familiar countenance with the blank sternness of estrangement? Aurora did this. She acted over and over again in her weary brain the scene that might have taken place between her husband and herself. She remembered that scene in the hackneyed stage-play, which everybody affects to ridicule, and secretly weeps at. She remembered Mrs. Haller and the Stranger, the children, the countess, the cottage, the jewels, the parchments, and all the old familiar properties of that well-known fifth act in the simple social tragedy, and she pictured to herself John Mellish retiring into some distant country with his rheumatic trainer Langley, and becoming a misanthropical hermit, after the manner of the injured German.

What was her life to be henceforth? She shut her eyes upon that blank future.

"I will go back to my father," she thought; "I will go back to him again, as I went before. But this time there shall be no falsehoods, no equivocations, and this time nothing shall tempt me to leave him again."

Amid all her perplexities, she clung to the thought that Lucy and Talbot would help her. She would appeal to passionless Talbot Bulstrode in behalf of her poor heart-broken John.

"Talbot will tell me what is right and honorable to be done," she thought. "I will hold by what he says. He shall be the arbiter of my future."

I do not believe that Aurora had ever entertained any very passionate devotion for the handsome Cornishman, but it is very certain that she had always respected him. It may be that any love she had felt for him had grown out of that very respect, and that her reverence for his character was made all the greater by the contrast between him and the base-born schemer for whom her youth had been sacrificed. She had submitted to the decree which had separated her from her affianced lover, for she had believed in its justice; and she was ready now to submit to any decision pronounced by the man in whose sense of honor she had unbounded confidence.

She thought of all these things again, and again, and again, while the farmers talked of sheep and turnips, of Thorley's food, Swedes, and beans, and corn, and clover, and of mysterious diseases, which they discussed gravely, under such terms as "red gum," "finger and toe," etc. They alternated this talk with a dash of turf scandal; and even in the all-absorbing perplexities of her domestic sorrows Mrs. Mellish could have turned fiercely upon these innocent farmers when they pooh-poohed John's stable, and made light of the reputation of her namesake the bay filly, and declared that no horse that came out of the squire's stables was ever anything better than a plater or a screw.

The journey came to an end, only too quickly it seemed to Aurora—too quickly, for every mile widened the gulf she had set between herself and the home she loved, every moment only brought the realization of her loss more fully home to her mind

"I will abide by Talbot Bulstrode's advice," she kept saying to herself, indeed, this thought was the only reed to which she clung in her trouble. She was not a strong-minded woman. She had the generous, impulsive nature which naturally turns to others for help and comfort. Secretiveness had no part in her organization, and the one concealment of her life had been a perpetual pain and grief to her.

It was past eight o'clock when she found herself alone amid the bustle and confusion of the King's Cross terminus. She sent a porter for a cab, and ordered the man to drive to Half-Moon street. It was only a few days since she had met Lucy and Talbot at Felden Woods, and she knew that Mr. Bulstrode and his wife were detained in town, waiting for the prorogation of the House.

It was Saturday evening, and therefore a holiday for the young advocate of the Cornish miners and their rights; but Talbot spent his leisure among Blue-books and Parliamentary Minutes, and poor Lucy, who might have been shining, a pale star, at some crowded *conversazione*, was compelled to forego the pleasure of struggling upon the staircase of one of those wise individuals who insist upon inviting their acquaintances to pack themselves into the smallest given space consistent with the preservation of life, and trample upon each other's lace flounces and varnished boots with smiling equanimity. Perhaps, in the universal fitness of things, even these fashionable evenings have a certain solemn purpose, deeply hidden under considerable surface-frivolity. It may be that they serve as moral gymnasia, in which the thews and sinews of social amenity are racked and tortured, with a view to their increased power of endurance. It is good for a man to have his favorite corn trodden upon, and yet be compelled to smile under the torture; and a woman may learn her first great lesson in fortitude from the destruction of fifty guineas' worth of Mechlin, and the necessity of assuming the destroyer that she is rather gratified than otherwise by the sacrifice. *Noblesse oblige*. It is good to "suffer and be strong." Cold coffee and tepid ice-cream may not be the most strengthening or delightful of food, but there may be a moral diet provided at these social gatherings which is not without its usefulness.

Lucy willingly abandoned her own delights, for she had that lady-like appreciation of society which had been a part of her education. Her placid nature knew no abnormal tendencies. She liked the amusements that other girls of her position liked. She had none of the eccentric predilections which had been so fatal to her cousin. She was not like that lovely and illustrious Spanish lady who is said to love the *cirque* better than the opera, and to have a more intense appreciation of a series of flying plunges through tissue-paper-covered hoops than of the most elaborate *fioriture* of tenor or soprano. She gave up something, therefore, in resigning the stereotyped gayeties of the London season. But, Heaven knows, it was very pleasant to her to make the sacrifice. Her inclinations were fatted lambs, which she offered willingly upon the altar of her idol. She was never happier than when sitting by her husband's side, making extracts from the Blue-books, to be quoted in some pamphlet that he was writing, or if she was ever happier, it was only when she sat in the ladies' gallery, straining her eyes athwart the floriated iron fretwork, which screened her from any wandering glances of distracted members, in her vain efforts to see her husband in his place on the government benches, and very rarely seeing more than the crown of Mr. Bulstrode's hat.

She sat by Talbot's side upon this evening, busy with some petty needle-work, and listening with patient attention to her husband's perusal of the proof-sheets of his last pamphlet. It was a noble specimen of the stately and ponderous style of writing, and it abounded in crushing arguments and magnificent climaxes, which utterly annihilated somebody (Lucy did n't exactly make out who), and most incontrovertibly established something, though Mrs. Bulstrode could n't quite understand what. It was enough for her that he had written that wonderful composition, and that it was his rich baritone voice that rolled out the studied Johnsonianisms. If he had pleased to read Greek to her, she would have thought it pleasant to listen. Indeed, there were pet passages of Homer which Mr. Bulstrode now and then loved to recite to his wife, and which the little hypocrite pretended to admire. No cloud had darkened the calm heaven of Lucy's married life. She loved and was beloved. It was a part of her nature to love in a reverential attitude, and she had no wish to approach nearer to her idol. To sit at her sultan's feet, and replenish the rose-water in his *chibouque*, to watch him while he slept, and wave the *punkah* above his seraphic head, to love, and admire, and pray for him, made up the sum of her heart's desire.

It was close upon nine o'clock when Mr. Bulstrode was interrupted in the very crowning sentence of his peroration by a double knock at the street-door. The houses in Half-Moon street are small, and Talbot flung down his proof-sheet with a gesture expressive of considerable irritation. Lucy looked up, half sympathizingly, half apologetically, at her lord and master. She held herself in a manner responsible for his ease and comfort.

"Who can it be, dear?" she murmured, "at such a time—"

"Some annoyance or other, I dare say, my dear," answered Talbot. "But, whoever it is, I won't see them to-night. I suppose, Lucy, I 've given you a pretty fair idea of the effect of this upon my honorable friend, the member for—"

Before Mr. Bulstrode could name the borough of which his honorable friend was the representative, a servant announced that Mrs. Mellish was waiting below to see the master of the house.

"Aurora!" exclaimed Lucy, starting from her seat and dropping the fairy implements of her work in a little shower upon the carpet; "Aurora!" It can't be, surely? Why, Talbot, she only went back to Yorkshire a few days ago."

"Mr. and Mrs. Mellish are both below, I suppose?" Mr. Bulstrode said to the servant.

"No, sir; Mrs. Mellish came alone in a cab from the station, I believe. Mrs. Mellish is in the library, sir. I asked her to walk up stairs, but she requested to see you alone, sir, if you please."

"I 'll come directly," answered Talbot. "Tell Mrs. Mellish I will be with her immediately."

The door closed upon the servant, and Lucy ran toward it, eager to hurry to her cousin.

"Poor Aurora," she said; "there must be something wrong, surely. Uncle Archibald has been taken ill, perhaps; he was not looking well when we left Felden. I 'll go to her, Talbot; I 'm sure she 'd like to see me first."

"No, Lucy, no," answered Mr. Bulstrode, laying his hand upon the door, and standing between it and his wife; "I had rather you did n't see your cousin until I have seen her. It will be better for me to see her first." His face was very grave, and his manner almost stern as he said this. Lucy shrank from him as if he had wounded her. She understood him very vaguely, it is true, but she understood that he had some doubt or suspicion of her cousin, and, for the first time in his life, Mr. Bulstrode saw an angry light kindled in his wife's blue eyes.

"Why should you prevent my seeing Aurora?" Lucy asked; "she is the best and dearest girl in the world. Why should n't I see her?"

Talbot Bulstrode stared in blank amazement at his mutinous wife.

"Be reasonable, my dear Lucy," he answered very mildly; "I hope always to be able to respect your cousin—as much as I respect you. But if Mrs. Mellish leaves her husband in Yorkshire, and comes to London without his permission—for he would never permit her to come alone—she must, explain to me why she does so before I can suffer my wife to receive her."

Poor Lucy's fair head drooped under this reproof.

She remembered her last conversation with her cousin—that conversation in which Aurora had spoken of some far-off day of trouble that might bring her to ask for comfort and shelter in Half-Moon street. Had the day of trouble come already?

"Was it wrong of Aurora to come alone, Talbot, dear?" Lucy asked, meekly.

"Was it wrong?" repeated Mr. Bulstrode, fiercely. "Would it be wrong for you to go tearing from here to Cornwall, child?"

He was irritated by the mere imagination of such an outrage, and he looked at Lucy as if he half suspected her of some such intention.

"But Aurora may have had some very particular reason, dear?" pleaded his wife.

"I can not imagine any reason powerful enough to justify such a proceeding," answered Talbot; "but I shall be better able to judge of that when I 've heard what Mrs. Mellish has to say. Stay here, Lucy, till I send for you."

"Yes, Talbot."

She obeyed as submissively as a child; but she lingered near the door, after her husband had closed it upon her, with a mournful yearning in her heart. She wanted to go to her cousin, and comfort her, if she had need of comfort. She dreaded the effect of her husband's cold and passionless manner upon Aurora's impressionable nature.

Mr. Bulstrode went down to the library to receive his kinswoman. It would have been strange if he had failed to remember that Christmas evening nearly two years before, upon which he had gone down to the shadowy room at Felden, with every hope of his heart crushed, to ask for comfort from the woman he loved. It would have been strange if, in the brief interval that elapsed between his leaving the drawing-room and entering the library, his mind had not flown back to that day of desolation. If there was any infidelity to Lucy in that sharp thrill of pain that pierced his heart as the old memory came back, the sin was as short-lived as the agony which it brought with it. He was able now to say, in all singleness of heart, "I made a wise choice, and I shall never repent of having made it."

The library was a small apartment at the back of the dining-room. It was dimly lighted, for Aurora had lowered the lamp. She did not want Mr. Bulstrode to see her face.

"My dear Mrs. Mellish," said Talbot, gravely, "I am so surprised at this visit that I scarcely know how to say I am glad to see you. I fear something must have happened to cause your travelling alone. John is ill, perhaps, or—"

He might have said much more if Aurora had not interrupted him by casting herself upon her knees before him, and looking up at him with a pale, agonized face, that seemed almost ghastly in the dim lamplight.

It was impossible to describe the look of horror that came over Talbot Bulstrode's face as she did this. It was the Felden scene over again. He came to her in the hope that she would justify herself, and she tacitly acknowledged her humiliation.

She was a guilty woman, then — a guilty creature whom it would be his painful duty to cast out of that pure household. She was a poor, lost, polluted wretch, who must not be admitted into the holy atmosphere of a Christian gentleman's home.

"Mrs Mellish! Mrs Mellish!" he cried, "what is the meaning of this? Why do you give me this horrible pain again? Why do you insist upon humiliating yourself and me by such a scene as this?"

"Oh, Talbot, Talbot!" answered Aurora, "I come to you because you are good and honorable. I am a desolate, wretched woman, and I want your help — I want your advice. I will abide by it; I will, Talbot Bulstrode, so help me Heaven!"

Her voice was broken by her sobs. In her passionate grief and confusion she forgot that it was just possible such an appeal as this might be rather bewildering in its effect upon Talbot. But perhaps, even amid his bewilderment, the young Cornishman saw, or fancied he saw, something in Aurora's manner which had no fellowship with guilt, or with such guilt as he had at first dreaded. I imagine that it must have been so, for his voice was softer and his manner kinder when he next addressed her.

"Aurora," he said, "for pity's sake be calm. Why have you left Mellish? What is the business in which I can help or advise you? Be calm, my dear girl, and I will try and understand you. God knows how much I wish to be a friend to you, for I stand in a brother's place, you know, my dear, and demand a brother's right to question your actions. I am sorry you came up to town alone, because such a step was calculated to compromise you, but if you will be calm, and tell me why you came, I may be able to understand your motives. Come, Aurora, try and be calm."

She was still on her knees, sobbing hysterically. Talbot would have summoned his wife to her assistance, but he could not bear to see the two women associated until he had discovered the cause of Aurora's agitation.

He poured some water into a glass, and gave it her. He placed her in an easy-chair near the open window, and then walked up and down the room until she had recovered herself.

"Talbot Bulstrode," she said, quietly, after a long pause. "I want you to help me in the crisis of my life. I must be candid with you, therefore, and tell you that which I would have died rather than tell you two years ago. You remember the night upon which you left Felden?"

"Remember it? Yes, yes."

"The secret which separated us then, Talbot, was the one secret of my life—the secret of my disobedience, the secret of my father's sorrow. You asked me to give you an account of that one year which was missing out of the history of my life. I could not do so, Talbot, *I would not!* My pride revolted against the horrible humiliation. If you had discovered the secret yourself, and had accused me of the disgraceful truth, I would have attempted no denial, but with my own lips to utter the hateful story—no, no, I could have borne anything better than that. But now that my secret is common property, in the keeping of police officers and stable-boys, I can afford to tell you all. When I left the school in the Rue Saint Dominique, I ran away to marry my father's groom!"

"Aurora!"

Talbot Bulstrode dropped into the chair nearest him, and sat blankly staring at his wife's cousin. Was this the secret humiliation which had prostrated her at his feet in the chamber at Felden Woods?

"Oh, Talbot, how could I have told you this? How can I tell you now why I did this mad and wicked thing, blighting the happiness of my youth by my own act, and bringing shame and grief upon my father? I had no romantic, overwhelming love for this man. I can not plead the excuses which some women urge for their madness. I had only a school-girl's sentimental fancy for his dashing manner, only a school-girl's frivolous admiration of his handsome face. I married him because he had dark blue eyes, and long eyelashes, and white teeth, and brown hair. He had insinuated himself into a kind of intimacy with me by bringing me all the empty gossip of the race-course, by extra attention to my favorite horses, by rearing a litter of puppies for me. All these things brought about associations between us; he was always my companion in my rides, and he contrived before long to tell me his story. Bah! why should I weary you with it?" cried Aurora, scornfully. "He was a prince in disguise, of course; he was a gentleman's son, his father had kept his hunters, he was at war with fortune; he had been ill used and trampled down in the battle of life. His talk was something to this effect, and I believed him. Why should I disbelieve him? I had lived all my life in an atmosphere of truth. My governess and I talked perpetually of the groom's romantic story. She was a silly woman, and encouraged my folly, out of mere stupidity, I believe, and with no suspicion of the mischief she was doing. We criticised the groom's handsome face, his white hands, his aristocratic manners. I mistook insolence for aristocracy, Heaven help me! And, as we saw scarcely any society at that time, I compared my father's groom with the few guests who came to Felden, and the town-bred impostor profited by comparison with rustic gentlemen. Why should I stay to account to you for my folly, Talbot Bulstrode? I could never succeed in doing so, though I talked for a week; I can not account to myself for my madness. I can only look back to that horrible time, and wonder why I was mad."

"My poor Aurora! my poor Aurora!"

He spoke in the pitying tone with which he might have comforted her had she been a child. He was thinking of her in her childish ignorance, exposed to the insidious advances of an unscrupulous schemer, and his heart bled for the motherless girl.

"My father found some letters written by this man, and discovered that his daughter had affianced herself to his groom. He made this discovery while I was out riding with James Conyers — the groom's name was Conyers — and when I came home there was a fearful scene between us. I was mad enough and wicked enough to defend my conduct, and to reproach my father with the illiberality of his sentiments. I went even farther: I reminded him that the house of Floyd and Floyd had had a very humble origin. He took me to Paris upon the following day. I thought myself cruelly treated. I revolted against the ceremonial monotony of the *pension;* I hated the studies, which were ten times more difficult than anything I had ever experienced with my governess; I suffered terribly from the conventual seclusion, for I had been used to perfect freedom among the country roads round Felden ; and, amid all this, the groom pursued me with letters and messages, for he had followed me to Paris, and spent his money recklessly in bribing the servants and hangers-on of the school. He was playing for a high stake, and he played so desperately that he won. I ran away from school, and married him at Dover, within eight or nine hours of my escape from the Rue Saint Dominique."

She buried her face in her hands, and was silent for some time.

"Heaven have pity upon my wretched ignorance!" she said at last; "the illusion under which I had married this man ended in about a week. At the end of that time I discovered that I was the victim of a mercenary wretch, who meant to use me to the uttermost as a means of wringing money from my father. For some time I submitted, and my father paid, and paid dearly, for his daughter's folly; but he refused to receive the man I had married, or to see me until I separated myself from that man. He offered the groom an income on the condition of his going to Australia, and resigning all association with me for ever. But the man had a higher game to play. He wanted to bring about a reconciliation with my father, and he thought that in due time that tender father's resolution

would have yielded to the force of his love. It was little better than a year after our marriage that I made a discovery that transformed me in one moment from a girl into a woman — a revengeful woman, perhaps, Mr. Bulstrode. I discovered that I had been wronged, deceived, and outraged by a wretch who laughed at my ignorant confidence in him. I had learned to hate the man long before this occurred; I had learned to despise his shallow trickeries, his insolent pretensions; but I do not think I felt his deeper infamy the less keenly for that. We were travelling in the south of France, my husband playing the great gentleman upon my father's money, when this discovery was made by me — or not by me; for it was forced upon me by a woman who knew my story and pitied me. Within half an hour of obtaining this knowledge, I acted upon it. I wrote to James Conyers, telling him I had discovered that which gave me the right to call upon the law to release me from him; and if I refrained from doing so, it was for my father's sake, and not for his. I told him that so long as he left me unmolested, and kept my secret, I would remit him money from time to time. I told him that I left him to the associations he had chosen for himself, and that my only prayer was that God, in His mercy, might grant me complete forgetfulness of him. I left this letter for him with the *concierge,* and quitted the hotel in such a manner as to prevent his obtaining any trace of the way I had gone. I stopped in Paris for a few days, waiting for a reply to a letter I had written to my father, telling him that James Conyers was dead. Perhaps that was the worst sin of my life, Talbot. I deceived my father; but I believed that I was doing a wise and merciful thing in setting his mind at rest. He would have never been happy so long as he had believed the man lived. You understand all now, Talbot," she said mournfully. "You remember the morning at Brighton ?"

"Yes, yes; and the newspaper with the marked paragraph—the report of the jockey's death."

"That report was false, Talbot Bulstrode," cried Aurora. "James Conyers was not killed."

Talbot's face grew suddenly pale. He began to understand something of the nature of that trouble which had brought Aurora to him.

"What! he was still living, then ?" he said, anxiously.

"Yes; until the night before last ?"

"But where — where has he been all this time ?"

"During the last ten days at Mellish Park."

She told him the terrible story of the murder. The trainer's death had not yet been reported in the London papers. She told him the dreadful story ; and then, looking up at him with an earnest, imploring face, as she might have done had he been indeed her brother, she entreated him to help and counsel her in this terrible hour of need

' Teach me how to do what is best for my dear love,' she said. ' Don't think of me or my happiness, Talbot, think only of him I will make any sacrifice, I will submit to anything I want to atone to my poor dear for all the misery I have brought upon him."

Talbot Bulstrode did not make any reply to this earnest appeal The administrative powers of his mind were at work; he was busy summing up facts, and setting them before him, in order to grapple with them fairly, and he had no attention to waste upon sentiment or emotion He was walking up and down the room, with his eyebrows knitted sternly over his cold gray eyes and his head bent

"How many people know this secret, Aurora?" he asked, presently

"I can't tell you that; but I fear it must be very generally known," answered Mrs Mellish, with a shuddering recollection of the softy's insolence "I heard of the discovery that had been made from a hanger-on of the stables, a man who hates me — a man whom I — had a misunderstanding with"

' Have you any idea who it was that shot this Conyers?"

"No, not the least idea."

"You do not even guess at any one ?"

"No"

Talbot took a few more turns up and down the small apartment, in evident trouble and perplexity of mind He left the room presently, and called at the foot of the staircase

"Lucy, my dear, come down to your cousin"

I 'm afraid Mrs Bulstrode must have been lurking somewhere about the outside of the drawing-room door, for she flew down the stairs at the sound of the strong voice, and was by her husband's side two or three seconds after he had spoken

"Oh, Talbot," she said, "how long you have been ! I thought you would never send for me What has been the matter with my poor darling ?"

"Go in to her, and comfort her, my dear," Mr Bulstrode answered, gravely, "she has had enough trouble, Heaven knows, poor girl Don't ask her any questions, Lucy, but make her as comfortable as you can, and give her the best room you can find for her. She will stay with us as long as she remains in town."

"Dear, dear Talbot," murmured the young Cornishman's grateful worshipper, "how kind you are !"

"Kind !" cried Mr Bulstrode, "she has need of friends, Lucy, and, God knows, I will act the brother's part toward her, faithfully and bravely Yes, bravely," he added, raising his head with an almost defiant gesture as he slowly ascended the stairs

What was the dark cloud which he saw brooding so fatally over the far horizon ? He dared not think of what it was — he dared not even acknowledge its presence, but there was a sense of trouble and horror in his breast that told him the shadow was there

Lucy Bulstrode ran into the library, and flung herself upon her cousin's breast, and wept with her She did not ask the nature of the sorrow which had brought Aurora an unexpected and uninvited guest to that modest little dwelling-house She only knew that her cousin was in trouble, and, that it was her happy privilege to offer her shelter and consolation She would have fought a sturdy battle in defence of this privilege, but she adored her husband for the generosity which had granted it to her without a struggle For the first time in her life, poor, gentle Lucy took a new position with her cousin It was her turn to protect Aurora, it was her turn to display a pretty motherly tenderness for the desolate creature whose aching head rested on her bosom

The West-End clocks were striking three, in the dead middle of the night, when Mrs Mellish fell into a feverish slumber, even in her sleep repeating again and again, "My poor John ! my poor, dear love ! what will become of him ! my own faithful darling !"

CHAPTER XXXI

TALBOT BULSTRODE'S ADVICE

Talbot Bulstrode went out early upon the quiet Sunday morning after Aurora's arrival, and walked down to the Telegraph Company's Office at Charing Cross, whence he despatched a message to Mr John Mellish. It was a very brief message, only telling Mr Mellish to come to town without delay, and that he would find Aurora in Half-Moon street. Mr Bulstrode walked quietly homeward in the morning sunshine after having performed this duty Even the London streets were bright and dewy in that early sunlight, for it was only a little after seven o'clock, and the fresh morning breezes came sweeping over the house-tops, bringing health and purity from Shooter's Hill and Highgate, Streatham and Barnsbury, Richmond and Hampstead The white morning mists were slowly melting from the worn grass in the Green Park; and weary creatures, who had had no better shelter than the quiet sky, were creeping away to find such wretched resting-places as they might, in that free city, in which to sit for an unreasonable time upon a door-step, or to ask a rich citizen for the price of a loaf, is to commit an indictable offence

Surely it was impossible for any young legislator not quite worn out by a life-long struggle with the time which was never meant to be set right — surely it was impossible for any fresh-hearted, prosperous young Liberal to walk through those quiet streets without thinking of these things. Talbot Bulstrode thought very earnestly and very mournfully. To what end were his labors, after all ? He was fighting for a handful of Cornish miners; doing battle with the rampant spirit of circumlocution for the sake of a few benighted wretches, buried in the darkness of a black abyss of ignorance a hundred times deeper and darker than the material obscurities in which they labored. He was working his best and his hardest that these men might be taught, in some easy, unambitious manner, the simplest elements of Christian love and Christian duty. He was working for these poor far-away creatures, in their forgotten corner of the earth ; and here, around and about him, was ignorance more terrible, because, hand in hand with ignorance of all good, there was the fatal experience of all evil. The simple Cornish miner who uses his pickaxe in the region of his friend's skull when he wishes to enforce an argument, does so because he knows no other species of emphasis. But in the London universities of crime, knavery, and vice, and violence, and sin matriculate and graduate day by day, to take their degrees in the felon's dock or on the scaffold. How could he be otherwise than sorrowful, thinking of these things ? Were Sodom and Gomorrah worse than this city, in which there were yet so many good and earnest men laboring patiently day by day, and taking little rest ? Was the great accumulation of evil so heavy that it rolled for ever back upon these untiring Sisyphuses ? Or did they make some imperceptible advance toward the mountain-top, despite of all discouragement?

With this weary question debating itself in his brain, Mr. Bulstrode walked along Piccadilly toward the comfortable bachelor's quarters, whose most commonplace attributes Lucy had turned to favor and to prettiness; but at the door of the Gloucester Coffee-house Talbot paused to stare absently at a nervous-looking chestnut mare, who insisted upon going through several lively performances upon her hind legs, very much to the annoyance of an unshaven ostler, and not particularly to the advantage of a smart little dog-cart to which she was harnessed.

"You need n't pull her mouth to pieces, my man," cried a voice from the doorway of the hotel; "use her gently, and she 'll soon quiet herself. Steady, my girl, steady !" added the owner of this voice, walking to the dog-cart as he spoke.

Talbot had good reason to stop short, for this gentleman was Mr. John Mellish, whose pale face, and loose, disordered hair betokened a sleepless night.

He was going to spring into the dog-cart when his old friend tapped him on the shoulder.

"This is rather a lucky accident, John, for you 're the very person I want to see," said Mr. Bulstrode. "I 've just telegraphed to you."

John Mellish stared with a blank face.

"Don't hinder me, please,' he said; I 'll talk to you by and by. I 'll call upon you in a day or two. I 'm just off to Felden. I 've only been in town an hour and a half, and should have gone down before if I had not been afraid of knocking up the family."

He made another attempt to get into the vehicle, but Talbot caught him by the arm.

"You need n't go to Felden," he said; your wife 's much nearer."

"Eh ?"

"She 's at my house. Come and have some breakfast."

There was no shadow upon Talbot Bulstrode's mind as his old school-fellow caught him by the hand, and nearly dislocated his wrist in a paroxysm of joy and gratitude. It was impossible for him to look beyond that sudden burst of sunshine upon John's face. If Mr. Mellish had been separated from his wife for ten years, and had just returned from the Antipodes for the sole purpose of seeing her again, he could scarcely have appeared more delighted at the prospect of a speedy meeting.

"Aurora here !" he said; "at your house ? My dear old fellow, you can't mean it. But, of course, I ought to have known she 'd come to you. She could n't have done anything better or wiser, after having been so foolish as to doubt me."

"She came to me for advice, John. She wanted me to advise her how to act for your happiness — yours, you great Yorkshireman, and not her own."

"Bless her noble heart !" cried Mr. Mellish, huskily. "And you told her —"

"I told her nothing, my dear fellow ; but I tell you to take your lawyer down to Doctor's Commons with you to-morrow morning, get a new license, and marry your wife for the second time, in some quiet little out-of-the-way church in the city."

Aurora had risen very early upon that peaceful Sunday morning. The few hours of feverish and fitful sleep had brought very little comfort to her. She stood with her weary head leaning against the window-frame, and looked hopelessly out into the empty London street. She looked out into the desolate beginning of a new life, the blank uncertainty of an unknown future. All the minor miseries peculiar to a toilet in a strange room were doubly miserable to her. Lucy had brought the poor luggageless traveller all the paraphernalia of the toilet-table, and had arranged everything with her own busy hands. But the most insignificant trifle that Aurora touch-

ed in her cousin's chamber brought back the
memory of some costly toy chosen for her
by her husband She had travelled in her
white morning-dress, and the soft lace and
muslin were none the fresher for her journey,
but as two of Lucy's dresses joined together
would have scarcely fitted her stately cousin,
Mrs. Mellish was fain to be content with her
limp muslin What did it matter? The loving eyes which noted every shred of ribbon,
every morsel of lace, every fold of her garments, were, perhaps, never to look upon her
again. She twisted her hair into a careless
mass at the back of her head, and had completed her toilet when Lucy came to the
door, tenderly anxious to know how she had
slept.

'I will abide by Talbot's decision," she repeated to herself again and again "If he
says it is best for my dear that we should
part, I will go away for ever I will ask my
father to take me far away, and my poor darling shall not even know where I have gone.
I will be true in what I do, and will do it
thoroughly."

She looked to Talbot Bulstrode as a wise
judge, to whose sentence she would be willing to submit. Perhaps she did this because
her own heart kept for ever repeating. "Go
back to the man who loves you. Go back, go
back! There is no wrong you can do him so
bitter as to desert him There is no unhappiness you can bring upon him equal to the
unhappiness of losing you Let me be your
guide. Go back, go back!"

But this selfish monitor must not be listened
to How bitterly this poor girl, so old in experience of sorrow, remembered the selfish
sin of her mad marriage! She had refused to
sacrifice a school-girl's foolish delusion, she
had disobeyed the father who had given her
seventeen years of patient love and devotion,
and she looked at all the misery of her youth
as the fatal growth of this evil seed, so rebel-
liously sown Surely such a lesson was not
to be altogether unheeded! Surely it was
powerful enough to teach her the duty of
sacrifice! It was this thought that steeled
her against the pleadings of her own affection It was for this that she looked to Talbot Bulstrode as the arbiter of her future
Had she been a Roman Catholic, she would
have gone to her confessor, and appealed to a
priest—who, having no social ties of his own
must, of course, be the best judge of all the
duties involved in domestic relations — for
comfort and succor, but, being of another
faith, she went to the man whom she most respected, and who, being a husband himself,
might, as she thought, be able to comprehend
the duty that was due to her husband

She went down stairs with Lucy into a little
inner room upon the drawing-room floor   a
snug apartment, opening into a nite on a conservatory It was Mr and Mrs Bulstrode's

habit to breakfast in this cosy little chamber
rather than in that awful temple of slippery
morocco, funereal bronze, and ghastly mahogany, which upholsterers insist upon as the
only legitimate place in which an Englishman may take his meals. Lucy loved to sit
opposite her husband at the small round table,
and minister to his morning appetite from her
pretty breakfast equipage of silver and china
She knew — to the smallest weight employed
at Apothecaries' Hall, I think — how much
sugar Mr Bulstrode liked in his tea. She
poured the cream into his cup as carefully as
if she had been making up a prescription He
took the simple beverage in a great shallow
breakfast-cup of fragile turquoise Sevres, that
had cost seven guineas, and had been made
for Madame du Barry, the rococo merchant
had told Talbot. (Had his customer been a
lady, I fear Marie Antoinette would have
been described as the original possessor of
the porcelain) Mrs Bulstrode loved to minister to her husband She picked the bloated
livers of martyred geese out of the Strasburgh
pies for his delectation, she spread the butter
upon his dry toast and pampered and waited
on him, serving him as only such women serve
their idols But this morning she had her
cousin's sorrows to comfort, and she established Aurora in a capacious chintz-covered easy-
chair on the threshold of the conservatory,
and seated herself at her feet

"My poor, pale darling," she said, tenderly,
' what can I do to bring the roses back to
your cheeks?"

"Love me, and pity me, dear," Aurora answered, gravely, "but don't ask me any questions "

The two women sat thus for some time,
Aurora's handsome head bent over Lucy's
fair face, and her hand clasped in both Lucy's
hands They talked very little, and only
spoke then of indifferent matters, or of Lucy's
happiness and Talbot's parliamentary career.
The little clock over the chimney-piece struck
the quarter before eight, they were very
early, these unfashionable people, and a minute afterward Mrs Bulstrode heard her husband's step upon the stairs, returning from
his ante-breakfast walk It was his habit to
take a constitutional stroll in the Green Park
now and then, so Lucy had thought nothing
of this early excursion

"Talbot has let himself in with his latch-
key," said Mrs Bulstrode, "and I may pour
out the tea, Aurora But listen, dear, I
think there 's some one with him '

There was no need to bid Aurora listen,
she had started from her low seat, and stood
erect and motionless, breathing in a quick,
agitated manner, and looking toward the
door Besides Talbot Bulstrode's step there
was another, quicker and heavier—a step
she knew so well.

The door was opened, and Talbot entered

the room, followed by a visitor, who pushed aside his host with very little attention to the laws of civilized society, and, indeed, nearly drove Mr. Bulstrode backward into a gilded basket of flowers. But this stalwart John Mellish had no intention of being unmannerly or brutal. He pushed aside his friend only as he would have pushed, or tried to push, aside a regiment of soldiers with fixed bayonets, or a Lancaster gun, or a raging ocean, or any other impediment that had come between him and Aurora. He had her in his arms before she could even cry his name aloud in her glad surprise, and in another moment she was sobbing on his breast.

"My darling! my pet! my own!" he cried, smoothing her dark hair with his broad hand, and blessing her, and weeping over her—"my own love! How could you do this? how could you wrong me so much? My own precious darling! had you learned to know me no better than *this* in all our happy married life?"

"I came to ask Talbot's advice, John," she said, earnestly, "and I mean to abide by it, however cruel it may seem."

Mr. Bulstrode smiled gravely as he watched these two foolish people. He was very much pleased with his part in the little domestic drama, and he contemplated them with a sublime consciousness of being the author of all this happiness; for they were happy. The poet has said, there are some moments — very rare, very precious, very brief — which stand by themselves, and have their perfect fulness of joy within their own fleeting span, taking nothing from the past, demanding nothing of the future. Had John and Aurora known that they were to be separated by the breadth of Europe for the remainder of their several lives, they would not the less have wept joyful tears at the pure blissfulness of this meeting.

"You asked me for my advice, Aurora," said Talbot, "and I bring it to you. Let the past die with the man who died the other night. The future is not yours to dispose of; it belongs to your husband, John Mellish."

Having delivered himself of these oracular sentences, Mr. Bulstrode seated himself at the breakfast-table, and looked into the mysterious and cavernous interior of a raised pie with such an intent gaze that it seemed as if he never meant to look out of it. He devoted so many minutes to this serious contemplation that by the time he looked up again Aurora had become quite calm, while Mr. Mellish affected an unnatural gayety, and exhibited no stronger sign of past emotion than a certain inflamed appearance in the region of his eyelids.

But this stalwart, devoted, impressionable Yorkshireman ate a most extraordinary repast in honor of this reunion. He spread mustard on his muffins. He poured Worcester sauce into his coffee, and cream over his deviled cutlets. He showed his gratitude to Lucy by loading her plate with comestibles she did n't want. He talked perpetually, and devoured incongruous viands in utter absence of mind. He shook hands with Talbot so many times across the breakfast-table that he exposed the lives or limbs of the whole party to imminent peril from the boiling water in the urn. He threw himself into a paroxysm of coughing, and made himself scarlet in the face by an injudicious use of Cayenne pepper; and he exhibited himself altogether in such an imbecile light, that Talbot Bulstrode was compelled to have recourse to all sorts of expedients to keep the servants out of the room during the progress of that rather noisy and bewildering repast.

The Sunday papers were brought to the master of the house before breakfast was over; and while John talked, ate, and gesticulated, Mr. Bulstrode hid himself behind the open leaves of the *Weekly Dispatch*, reading a paragraph that appeared in that journal.

This paragraph gave a brief account of the murder and the inquest at Mellish, and wound up by that rather stereotyped sentence, in which the public are informed that "the local police are giving unremitting attention to the affair, and we think we may venture to affirm that they have obtained a clew which will most probably lead to the early discovery of the guilty party."

Talbot Bulstrode, with the newspaper still before his face, sat for some little time frowning darkly at the page upon which this paragraph appeared. The horrible shadow, whose nature he would not acknowledge even to himself, once more lowered upon the horizon which had just seemed so bright and clear.

"I would give a thousand pounds," he thought, "if I could find the murderer of this man."

CHAPTER XXXII.

ON THE WATCH.

Very soon after breakfast upon that happy Sabbath of reunion and contentment, John Mellish drove Aurora to Felden Woods. It was necessary that Archibald Floyd should hear the story of the trainer's death from the lips of his own children, before newspaper paragraphs terrified him with some imperfect outline of the truth.

The dashing phaeton in which Mr. Bulstrode was in the habit of driving his wife was brought to the door as the church-bells were calling devout citizens to their morning duties, and at that unseemly hour John Mellish smacked his whip, and dashed off in the direction of Westminster Bridge.

Talbot Bulstrode's horses soon left London behind them, and before long the phaeton was driving upon the trim park-like roads, overshadowed by luxuriant foliage, and bordered here and there by exquisitely-ordered gardens and rustic villas, that glittered whitely in the sunshine. The holy peace of the quiet Sabbath was upon every object that they passed, even upon the leaves and flowers, as it seemed to Aurora. The birds sang subdued and murmuring harmonies; the light summer breeze scarcely stirred the deep grass on which the lazy cattle stood to watch the phaeton dash by.

Ah! how happy Aurora was, seated by the side of the man whose love had outlasted every trial! How happy now that the dark wall that had divided them was shattered, and they were indeed united! John Mellish was as tender and pitying toward her as a mother to her forgiven child. He asked no explanations; he sought to know nothing of the past. He was content to believe that she had been foolish and mistaken, and that the mistake and folly of her life would be buried in the grave of the murdered trainer.

The lodge-keeper at Felden Woods exclaimed as he opened the gates to his master's daughter. He was an old man, and he had opened the same gates more than twenty years before, when the banker's dark-eyed bride had first entered her husband's mansion.

Archibald Floyd welcomed his children heartily. How could he ever be otherwise than unutterably happy in the presence of his darling, however often she might come, with whatever eccentricity she might time her visits?

Mrs. Mellish led her father into his study.

"I must speak to you alone, papa," she said, "but John knows all I have to say. There are no secrets between us now. There never will be again."

Aurora had a painful story to tell her father, for she had to confess to him that she had deceived him upon the occasion of her return to Felden after her parting with James Conyers.

"I told you a story, father," she said, "when I told you that my husband was dead. But, Heaven knows, I believed that I should be forgiven the sin of that falsehood, for I thought that it would spare you grief and trouble of mind, and surely anything would have been justifiable that could have done that. I suppose good never can come out of evil, for I have been bitterly punished for my sin. I received a newspaper within a few months of my return in which there was a paragraph describing the death of James Conyers. The paragraph was not correct, for the man had escaped with his life, and when I married John Mellish, my first husband was alive."

Archibald Floyd uttered a cry of despair, and half rose from his easy-chair, but Aurora knelt upon the ground by his side, with her arms about him, soothing and comforting him.

"It is all over now, dear father," she said,

"it is all over. The man is dead. I will tell you how he died by and by. It is all over. John knows all; and I am to marry him again. Talbot Bulstrode says that it is necessary, as our marriage was not legal. My own dear father, there is to be no more secrecy, no more unhappiness,—only love, and peace, and union for all of us."

She told the old man the story of the trainer's death, dwelling very little upon the particulars, and telling nothing of her own doings that night, except that she had been in the wood at the time of the murder, and that she had heard the pistol fired.

It was not a pleasant story, this story of murder, and violence, and treachery within the boundary of his daughter's home. Even amid Aurora's assurances that all sorrow was past, that doubt and uncertainty were to vanish away before security and peace, Archibald Floyd could not control this feeling. He was restless and uneasy in spite of himself. He took John Mellish out upon the terrace in the afternoon sunshine, while Aurora lay asleep upon one of the sofas in the long drawing-room, and talked to him of the trainer's death as they walked up and down. There was nothing to be elicited from the young squire that threw any light upon the catastrophe, and Archibald Floyd tried in vain to find any issue out of the darkness of the mystery.

"Can you imagine any one having any motive for getting rid of this man?" the banker asked.

John shrugged his shoulders. He had been asked this question so often before, and had been always obliged to give the same reply.

No, he knew of no motive which any one about Mellish could be likely to have.

"Had the man any money about him?" asked Mr. Floyd.

"Goodness knows whether he had or not," John answered, carelessly, "but I should think it was n't likely he had much. He had been out of a situation, I believe, for some time before he came to me, and he had spent a good many months in a Prussian hospital. I don't suppose he was worth robbing."

The banker remembered the two thousand pounds which he had given to his daughter. What had Aurora done with that money? Had she known of the trainer's existence when she asked for it? and had she wanted it for him? She had not explained this in her hurried story of the murder, and how could he press her upon so painful a subject? Why should he not accept her own assurance that all was over, and that nothing remained but peace.

Archibald Floyd and his children spent a tranquil day together, not talking much, for Aurora was completely worn out by the fatigue and excitement she had undergone. What had her life been but agitation and terror since the day upon which Mr. John

Pastern's letter had come to Mellish to tell her of the existence of her first husband? She slept through the best part of the day, lying upon a sofa, and with John Mellish sitting by her side keeping watch over her. She slept while the bells of Beckenham church summoned the parishioners to afternoon service, and while her father went to assist in those quiet devotions, and to kneel on his hassock in the old square pew, and pray for the peace of his beloved child. Heaven knows how earnestly the old man prayed for his daughter's happiness, and how she filled his thoughts; not distracting him from more sacred thoughts, but blending her image with his worship in alternate prayer and thanksgiving. Those who watched him as he sat, with the sunshine on his gray head, listening reverentially to the sermon, little knew how much trouble had been mingled with the great prosperity of his life. They pointed him out respectfully to strangers as a man whose signature across a slip of paper could make that oblong morsel of beaten rag into an incalculable sum of money; a man who stood upon a golden pinnacle with the Rothschilds, and Montefiores, and Couttses; who could afford to pay the national debt any morning that the whim seized him; and who was yet a plain man, and simple as a child, as anybody might see, the admiring parishioners would add, as the banker came out of church shaking hands right and left, and nodding to the charity children.

I 'm afraid the children dropped lower courtesies in the pathway of Mr. Floyd than even before the Vicar of Beckenham; for they had learned to associate the image of the banker with buns and tea, with sixpences and oranges, gambols on the smooth lawn at Felden, and jovial feasts in monster tents to the music of clashing brass bands, and with even greater treats in the way of excursions to a Crystal Palace on a hill, an enchanted fairyland of wonders, from which it was delicious to return in the dewy evening, singing hymns of rejoicing that shook the vans in which they travelled.

The banker had distributed happiness right and left; but the money which might have paid the national debt had been impotent to save the life of the dark-eyed woman he had loved so tenderly, or to spare him one pang of uneasiness about his idolized child. Had not that all-powerful wealth been rather the primary cause of his daughter's trouble, since it had cast her, young, inexperienced, and trusting, a prey into the mercenary hands of a bad man, who would not have cared to persecute her but for the money that had made her such a golden prize for any adventurer who might please to essay the hazard of winning her?

With the memory of these things always in his mind, it was scarcely strange that Archibald Floyd should bear the burden of his riches meekly and fearfully, knowing that,

whatever he might be in the Stock Exchange, he was in the sight of Heaven only a feeble old man, very assailable by suffering, very liable to sorrow, and humbly dependent on the mercy of the Hand that is alone powerful to spare or to afflict, as seemeth good to Him who guides it.

Aurora awoke out of her long sleep while her father was at church. She awoke to find her husband watching her; the Sunday papers lying forgotten on his knee, and his honest eyes fixed on the face he loved.

"My own dear John," she said, as she lifted her head from the pillows, supporting herself upon her elbow, and stretching out one hand to Mr. Mellish, "my own dear boy, how happy we are together now! Will anything ever come to break our happiness again, my dear? Can Heaven be so cruel as to afflict us any more?"

The banker's daughter, in the sovereign vitality of her nature, had rebelled against sorrow as a strange and unnatural part of her life. She had demanded happiness almost as a right; she had wondered at her afflictions, and been unable to understand why she should be thus afflicted. There are natures which accept suffering with patient meekness, and acknowledge the justice by which they suffer; but Aurora had never done this. Her joyous soul had revolted against sorrow, and she arose now in the intense relief which she felt in her release from the bonds that had been so hateful to her, and challenged Providence with her claim to be happy for evermore.

John Mellish thought very seriously upon this matter. He could not forget the night of the murder—the night upon which he had sat alone in his wife's chamber pondering upon his unworthiness.

"Do you think we deserve to be happy, Lolly?" he said, presently. "Don't mistake me, my darling. I know that you're the best and brightest of living creatures — tenderhearted, loving, generous, and true. But do you think we take life quite seriously enough, Lolly, dear? I 'm sometimes afraid that we 're too much like the careless children in the pretty childish allegory, who played about among the flowers on the smooth grass in the beautiful garden until it was too late to set out upon the long journey on the dark road which would have led them to Paradise. What shall we do, my darling, to deserve the blessings God has given us so freely — the blessings of youth and strength, and love and wealth? What shall we do, dear? I don't want to turn Mellish into a Philanstery exactly, nor to give up my racing-stud if I can help it," John said, reflectively; "but I want to do something, Lolly, to prove that I am grateful to Providence. Shall we build a lot of schools, or a church, or almshouses, or something of that sort? Lofthouse would like me to put up a painted window in Mellish urch, and a new pulpit with a patent sound-g-board, but I can't see that painted win-ws and sounding-boards do much good in general way I want to do something, urora, to prove my gratitude to the Provi-nce that has given me the loveliest and best women for my true-hearted wife"

The banker's daughter smiled almost mourn-lly upon her devoted husband.

"Have I been such a blessing to you, John," e said, "that you should be grateful for me? ave I not brought you far more sorrow than ppiness, my poor dear?"

"No," shouted Mr Mellish emphatically. The sorrow you have brought me has been thing to the joy I have felt in your love. y own dearest girl, to be sitting here by your le to-day, and to hear you tell me that you ve me, is enough happiness to set against all e trouble of mind that I have endured since e man that is dead came to Mellish"

I hope my poor John Mellish will be for-ven if he talked a great deal of nonsense to e wife he loved He had been her lover om the first moment in which he had seen r, darkly beautiful, upon the gusty Brighton arade, and he was her lover still No shadow contempt had ever grown out of his famili-rity with her And, indeed, I am disposed take objection to that old proverb, or at least believe that contempt is only engendered familiarity with things which are in them-lves base and spurious. The priest who is miliar with the altar learns no contempt for s sacred images, but it is rather the ignorant cophyte who sneers and sniggers at things hich he can not understand. The artist be-omes only more reverent as toil and study ake him more familiar with his art, its ernal sublimity grows upon him, and he orships the far-away Goddess of Perfection humbly when he drops his brush or his hisel after a life of patient labor as he did hen first he ground color or pointed rough locks of marble for his master And I can ot believe that a good man's respect for the oman he loves can be lessened by that sweet nd every-day familiarity in which a hundred ousehold virtues and gentle beauties—never reamed of in the ball-rooms where he first anced with an unknown idol in gauzy robes nd glimmering jewels—grow upon him, until e confesses that the wife of ten years stand-g is even ten times dearer than the bride of week's honeymoon

Archibald Floyd came back from church, nd found his two children sitting side by side one of the broad windows, watching for his rrival, and whispering together like lovers, s I have said they were.

They dined pleasantly together later in the vening, and a little after dark the phaeton vas brought round to the terrace-steps and Aurora kissed her father as she wished him ood-night

"You will come up to town, and be present at the marriage, sir, I know," John whispered, as he took his father-in-law's hand "Talbot Bulstrode will arrange all about it It is to take place at some out-of-the-way little church in the city Nobody will be any the wiser, and Aurora and I will go back to Mellish as quietly as possible There's only Lofthouse and Hayward know the secret of the certifi-cate, and they—"

John Mellish stopped suddenly He re-membered Mrs Powell's parting sting *She* knew the secret But how could she have come by that knowledge? It was impossible that either Lofthouse or Hayward could have told her They were both honorable men, and they had pledged themselves to be silent

Archibald Floyd did not observe his son-in-law's embarrassment, and the phaeton drove away, leaving the old man standing on the terrace-steps looking after his daughter

"I must shut up this place," he thought, "and go to Mellish to finish my days I can not endure these separations, I can not bear this suspense It is a pitiful sham, my keep-ing house, and living in all this dreary gran-deur I'll shut up the place, and ask my daughter to give me a quiet corner in her Yorkshire home, and a grave in the parish church-yard"

The lodge-keeper turned out of his com-fortable Gothic habitation to open the clank-ing iron gates for the phaeton; but John drew up his horses before they dashed into the road, for he saw that the man wanted to speak to him

"What is it, Forbes?" he asked

"Oh, it's nothing particular, sir," said the man, 'and perhaps I ought n't to trouble you about it; but did you expect any one down to-day, sir?"

"Expect any one here? no'" exclaimed John

"There's been a person inquirin', sir, this afternoon—two persons, I may say, in a shay-cart—but one of 'em asked particular if you was here, sir, and if Mrs Mellish was here, and when I said yes, you was, the gent says it was n't worth troublin' you about, the busi-ness as he'd come upon, and as he'd call another time And he asked me what time you'd be likely to be leavin' the Woods, and I said I made no doubt you'd stay to dinner up at the house So he says 'All right' and drives off'

"He left no message, then?"

"No, sir. He said nothin more than what I've told you"

"Then his business could have been of no great importance, Forbes," answered John, laughing "So we need n't worry our heads about him Good-night."

Mr Mel. . , . . . ve d'ng piece . . . . nd, gave Talbot's . . . . and the phaeton rolled off

Loudonward over the crisp gravel of the well-kept Beckenham roads.

"Who could the man have been?" Aurora asked, as they left the gates.

"Goodness knows, my dear," John answered, carelessly. "Somebody on racing business, perhaps."

Racing business seems to be in itself such a mysterious business that it is no strange thing for mysterious people to be always turning up in relation to it. Aurora, therefore, was content to accept this explanation, but not without some degree of wonderment.

"I can't understand the man coming to Felden after you, John," she said. "How could he know that you were to be there to-day?"

"Ah! how indeed, Lolly?" returned Mr. Mellish. "He chanced it, I suppose. A sharp customer, no doubt; wants to sell a horse, I dare say, and heard I did n't mind giving a good price for a good thing."

Mr. Mellish might have gone even farther than this, for there were many *horsey* gentlemen in his neighborhood, past masters in the art they practised, who were wont to say that the young squire, judiciously manipulated, might be induced to give a remarkably good price for a very bad thing, and there were many broken-down, slim-legged horses in the Mellish stables that bore witness to the same fact. Those needy *chevaliers d'esprit*, who think that Burke's landed gentry were created by Providence and endowed with the goods of this world for their especial benefit, just as pigeons are made plump and nice eating for the delectation of hawks, drove a wholesale trade upon the young man's frank simplicity and hearty belief in his fellow-creatures. I think it is Eliza Cook who says, "It is better to trust and be deceived, than own the mean, poor spirit that betrays;" and if there is any happiness in being "done," poor John enjoyed that fleeting delight pretty frequently.

There was a turn in the road between Beckenham and Norwood; and as the phaeton swept round, a chaise or dog-cart, a shabby vehicle enough, with a rakish-looking horse, drove close up, and the man who was driving asked the squire to put him in the nearest way to London. The vehicle had been behind them all the way from Felden, but had kept at a very respectful distance until now.

"Do you want to get to the city or the West End?" John asked.

"The West End."

"Then you can't do better than follow us," answered Mr. Mellish; "the road's clean enough, and your horse seems a good one to go. You can keep us in sight, I suppose?"

"Yes, sir, and thank ye."

"All right, then."

Talbot Bulstrode's thorough-breds dashed off, but the rakish-looking horse kept his ground behind them. He had something of the insolent, off-hand assurance of a butcher's horse, accustomed to whirl a bare-headed, blue-coated master through the sharp morning air.

"I was right, Lolly," Mr. Mellish said, as he left the dog-cart behind.

"How do you mean, dear?" asked Aurora.

"The man who spoke to us just now is the man who has been inquiring for me at Felden. He 's a Yorkshireman."

"A Yorkshireman!"

"Yes; did n't you hear the North-country twang?"

No; she had not listened to the man, nor heeded him. How should she think of anything but her newborn happiness — the newborn confidence between herself and the husband she loved?

Do not think her hard-hearted or cruel if she forgot that it was the death of a fellow-creature, a sinful man stricken down in the prime of youth and health, that had given her this welcome release. She had suffered so much that the release could not be otherwise than welcome, let it come how it might.

Her nature, frank and open as the day, had been dwarfed and crippled by the secret that had blighted her life. Can it be wondered, then, that she rejoiced now that all need of secrecy was over, and this generous spirit might expand as it pleased?

It was past ten when the phaeton turned into Half-Moon street. The men in the dog-cart had followed John's directions to the letter, for it was only in Piccadilly that Mr. Mellish had lost sight of them among other vehicles travelling backward and forward on the lamplit thoroughfare.

Talbot and Lucy received their visitors in one of the pretty little drawing-rooms. The young husband and wife had spent a quiet day together; going to church in the morning and afternoon, dining alone, and sitting in the twilight, talking happily and confidentially. Mr. Bulstrode was no Sabbath-breaker; and John Mellish had reason to consider himself a peculiarly privileged person, inasmuch as the thorough-breds had been permitted to leave their stables for his service, to say nothing of the groom, who had been absent from his hard seat in the servants' pew at a fashionable chapel in order that he might accompany John and Aurora to Felden.

The little party sat up rather late, Aurora and Lucy talking affectionately together, side by side, upon a sofa in the shadow of the room, while the two men lounged in the open window. John told his host the history of the day, and in doing so casually mentioned the man who had asked him the way to London.

Strange to say, Talbot Bulstrode seemed

especially interested in this part of the story. He asked several questions about the men. He asked what they wore like; what was said by either of them; and made many other inquiries, which seemed equally trivial.

"Then they followed you into town, John?" he said, finally.

"Yes; I only lost sight of them in Piccadilly, five minutes before I turned the corner of the street."

"Do you think they had any motive in following you?" asked Talbot.

"Well, I fancy so; they're on the look-out for information, I expect. The man who spoke to me looked something like a tout. I've heard that Lord Stamford's rather anxious about my West-Australian colt, the Pork Butcher. Perhaps his people have set these men to work to find out if I'm going to run him in the Leger."

Talbot Bulstrode smiled bitterly, almost mournfully, at the vanity of horseflesh. It was painful to see this light-hearted young squire looking in such ignorant hopefulness toward a horizon upon which graver and more thoughtful men could see a dreadful shadow lowering. Mr. Bulstrode was standing close to the balcony; he stepped out among the china boxes of mignonette, and looked down into the quiet street. A man was leaning against a lamp-post some few paces from Talbot's house, smoking a cigar, and with his face turned toward the balcony. He finished his cigar deliberately, threw the end into the road, and walked away while Talbot kept watch; but Mr. Bulstrode did not leave his post of observation, and about a quarter of an hour afterward he saw the same man lounging slowly along the pavement upon the other side of the street. John, who sat within the shadow of the window-curtains, lolling against them, and creasing their delicate folds with the heavy pressure of his broad back, was utterly unconscious of all this.

Early the next morning Mr. Bulstrode and Mr. Mellish took a Hansom cab, and rattled down to Doctor's Commons, where, for the second time in his life, John gave himself up to be fought for by white-aproned ecclesiastical touts, and eventually obtained the Archbishop of Canterbury's gracious sanction of his marriage with Aurora, widow of James Conyers, only daughter of Archibald Floyd, banker. From Doctor's Commons the two gentlemen drove to a certain quiet, out-of-the-way church, within the sound of Bow bells, but so completely hidden among piles of warehouses, top-heavy chimneys, sloping roofs, and other eccentricities of masonry, that any unhappy bridegroom who had appointed to be married there was likely enough to spend the whole of the wedding-day in futile endeavors to find the church-door. Here John discovered a mouldy clerk, who was fetched from some habitation in the

neighborhood with considerable difficulty by a boy, who volunteered to accomplish anything under heaven for a certain copper consideration; and to this clerk Mr. Mellish gave notice of a marriage which was to take place upon the following day, by special license.

"I'll take my second marriage certificate back with me," John said, as he left the church, "and then I should like to see who'll dare to look me in the face, and tell me that my darling is not my own lawfully-wedded wife."

He was thinking of Mrs. Powell as he said this. He was thinking of the pale, spiteful eyes that had looked at him, and of the woman's tongue that had stabbed him with all a little nature's great capacity for hate. He would be able to defy her now; he would be able to defy every creature in the world who dared to breathe a syllable against his beloved wife.

Early the next morning the marriage took place. Archibald Floyd, Talbot Bulstrode, and Lucy were the only witnesses—that is to say, the only witnesses with the exception of the clerk and the pew-opener, and a couple of men who lounged into the church when the ceremony was half over, and slouched about one of the side aisles, looking at the monuments, and talking to each other in whispers, until the parson took off his surplice, and John came out of the vestry with his wife upon his arm.

Mr. and Mrs. Mellish did not return to Half-Moon street; they drove straight to the Great Northern Station, whence they started by the afternoon express for Doncaster. John was anxious to return; for remember that he had left his household under very peculiar circumstances, and strange reports might have arisen in his absence.

The young squire would perhaps scarcely have thought of this had not the idea been suggested to him by Talbot Bulstrode, who particularly urged upon him the expediency of returning immediately.

"Go back, John," said Mr. Bulstrode, "without an hour's unnecessary delay. If by any chance there should be some farther disturbance about this murder, it will be much better for you, and Aurora too, to be on the spot. I will come down to Mellish myself in a day or two, and will bring Lucy with me, if you will allow me."

"Allow you, my dear Talbot!"

"I will come, then. Good-by, and God bless you! Take care of your wife."

CHAPTER XXXIII.

CAPTAIN PRODDER GOES BACK TO DONCASTER.

Mr. Samuel Prodder, returning to London, after having played his insignificant part in

11

the tragedy at Felden Woods, found that city singularly dull and gloomy. He put up at some dismal boarding-house, situated amid a mazy labyrinth of brick and mortar between the Tower and Wapping, and having relations with another boarding-house in Liverpool. He took up his abode at this place, in which he was known and respected. He drank rum and water, and played cribbage with other seamen, made after the same pattern as himself. He even went to an East-End theatre upon the Saturday night after the murder, and sat out the representation of a nautical drama, which he would have been glad to have believed in, had it not promulgated such wild theories in the science of navigation, and exhibited such extraordinary experiments in the manœuvring of the man-of-war upon which the action of the play took place as to cause the captain's hair to stand on end in the intensity of his wonder. The things people did upon that ship curdled Samuel Prodder's blood, as he sat in the lonely grandeur of the eighteen-penny boxes. It was quite a common thing for them to walk unhesitatingly through the bulwarks, and disappear in what ought to have been the sea. The extent of browbeating and humiliation borne by the captain of that noble vessel; the amount of authority exercised by a sailor with loose legs; the agonies of sea-sickness, represented by a comic countryman, who had no particular business on board the gallant bark; the proportion of hornpipe-dancing and nautical ballad-singing gone through as compared to the work that was done, all combined to impress poor Samuel with such a novel view of her majesty's naval service that he was very glad when the captain who had been browbeaten suddenly repented of all his sins — not without a sharp reminder from the prompter, who informed the *dramatis personœ* that it was *past* twelve, and they 'd better cut it short — joined the hands of the contumacious sailor and a young lady in white muslin, and begged them to be happy.

It was in vain that the captain sought distraction from the one idea upon which he had perpetually brooded since the night of his visit to Mellish Park. He would be wanted in Yorkshire to tell what he knew of the dark history of that fatal night. He would be called upon to declare at what hour he had entered the wood, whom he had met there, what he had seen and heard there. They would extort from him that which he would have died rather than tell. They would cross-examine, and bewilder, and torment him, until he told them everything — until he repeated, syllable by syllable, the passionate words that had been said — until he told them how, within a quarter of an hour of the firing of the pistol, he had been the witness of a desperate scene between his niece and the murdered man — a scene in which concentrated hate, vengeful fury, illimitable disdain and detestation had been expressed by her — by her alone: the man had been calm and moderate enough. It was she who had been angry; it was she who had given loud utterance to her hate.

Now, by reason of one of those strange inconsistencies common to weak human nature, the captain, though possessed night and day by a blind terror of being suddenly pounced upon by the minions of the law, and compelled to betray his niece's secret, could not rest in his safe retreat amid the labyrinths of Wapping, but must needs pine to return to the scene of the murder. He wanted to know the result of the inquest. The Sunday papers gave a very meagre account, only hinting darkly at suspected parties. He wanted to ascertain for himself what had happened at the inquest, and whether his absence had given rise to suspicion. He wanted to see his niece again — to see her in the daylight, undisturbed by passion. He wanted to see this beautiful tigress in her calmer moods, if she ever had any calmer moods. Heaven knows the simple merchant-captain was wellnigh distracted as he thought of his sister Eliza's child, and the awful circumstances of his first and only meeting with her.

Was she — that which he feared people might be led to think her if they heard the story of that scene in the wood? No, no, no! She was his sister's child—the child of that merry, impetuous little girl who had worn a pinafore and played hop-scotch. He remembered his sister flying into a rage with one Tommy Barnes for unfair practices in that very game, and upbraiding him almost as passionately as Aurora had upbraided the dead man. But if Tommy Barnes had been found strangled by a skipping-rope, or shot dead from a pea-shooter in the next street a quarter of an hour afterward, would Eliza's brother have thought that she must needs be guilty of the boy's murder? The captain had gone so far as to reason thus in his trouble of mind. His sister Eliza's child would be likely to be passionate and impetuous, but his sister Eliza's child would be a generous, warm-hearted creature, incapable of any cruelty in either thought or deed. He remembered his sister Eliza boxing his ears on the occasion of his gouging out the eyes of her wax doll, but he remembered the same dark-eyed sister sobbing piteously at the spectacle of a lamb that a heartless butcher was dragging to the slaughter-house.

But the more seriously Captain Prodder revolved this question in his mind, the more decidedly his inclination pointed to Doncaster; and early upon that very morning on which the quiet marriage had taken place in the obscure city church he repaired to a magnificent Israelitish temple of fashion in the Minories, and there ordered a suit of such clothes as were most affected by elegant landsmen. The Israelitish salesman recommended something light and lively in the fancy-check line; and Mr. Prodder, submitting to that authority as beyond all question, invested himself in a suit which he had contemplated solemnly athwart a vast expanse of plate-glass before entering the temple of the Graces. It was "our aristocratic tourist," at seventy-seven shillings and sixpence, and was made of a fleecy and rather powdery-looking cloth, in which the hues of baked and unbaked bricks predominated over a more delicate hearth-stone tint, which latter the shopman had declared to be a color that West-End tailors had vainly striven to emulate.

The captain, dressed in "our aristocratic tourist," which suit was of the ultra cut-away and peg-toppy order, and with his sleeves and trowsers inflated by any chance summer's breeze, had perhaps more of the appearance of a tombola than is quite in accordance with a strictly artistic view of the human figure. In his desire to make himself utterly irrecognizable as the seafaring man who had carried the tidings of the murder to Mellish Park, the captain had tortured himself by substituting a tight circular collar and a wisp of purple ribbon for the honest half-yard of snowy linen which it had been his habit to wear turned over the loose collar of his blue coat. He suffered acute agonies from this modern device, but he bore them bravely; and he went straight from the tailor's to the Great Northern Railway Station, where he took his ticket for Doncaster. He meant to visit that town as an aristocratic tourist; he would keep himself aloof from the neighborhood of Mellish Park, but he would be sure to hear the result of the inquest, and he would be able to ascertain for himself whether any trouble had come upon his sister's child.

The sea-captain did not travel by that express which carried Mr. and Mrs. Mellish to Doncaster, but by an earlier and a slower train, which lumbered quietly along the road, conveying inferior persons, to whom time was not measured by a golden standard, and 'who smoked, and slept, and ate, and drank resignedly enough through the eight or nine hours journey.

It was dusk when Samuel Prodder reached the quiet racing-town from which he had fled away in the dead of the night so short a time before. He left the station, and made his way to the market-place, and from the market-place he struck into a narrow lane that led him to an obscure street upon the outskirts of the town. He had a great terror of being led by some unhappy accident into the neighborhood of the "Reindeer," lest he should be recognized by some hanger-on of that hotel.

Half-way between the beginning of the straggling street and the point at which it dwindled and shrank away into a country lane, the captain found a little public-house called the "Crooked Rabbit"—such an obscure and out-of-the-way place of entertainment that poor Samuel thought himself safe in seeking for rest and refreshment within its dingy walls. There was a framed and glazed legend of "good beds" hanging behind an opaque window-pane—beds for which the landlord of the "Crooked Rabbit" was in the habit of asking and receiving almost fabulous prices during the great Leger week. But there seemed little enough doing at the humble tavern just now, and Captain Prodder walked boldly in, ordered a steak and a pint of ale, with a glass of rum and water, hot, to follow, at the bar, and engaged one of the good beds for his accommodation. The landlord, who was a fat man, lounged with his back against the bar, reading the sporting news in the *Manchester Guardian*; and it was the landlady who took Mr. Prodder's orders, and showed him the way into an awkwardly-shaped parlor, which was much below the rest of the house, and into which the uninitiated visitor was apt to precipitate himself head foremost, as into a well or pit. There were several small mahogany tables in this room, all adorned with sticky arabesques formed by the wet impressions of the bottom rims of pewter pots; there were so many spittoons that it was almost impossible to walk from one end of the room to the other without taking unintentional foot-baths of sawdust; there was an old bagatelle-table, the cloth of which had changed from green to dingy yellow, and was frayed and tattered like a poor man's coat; and there was a low window, the sill of which was almost on a level with the pavement of the street.

The merchant-captain threw off his hat, loosened the slip of ribbon and the torturing circular collar supplied him by the Israelitish outfitter, and cast himself into a shining mahogany arm-chair close to this window. The lower panes were shrouded by a crimson curtain, and he lifted this very cautiously, and peered for a few moments into the street. It was lonely enough and quiet enough in the dusky summer's evening. Here and there lights twinkled in a shop-window, and upon one threshold a man stood talking to his neighbor. With one thought always paramount in his mind, it is scarcely strange that Samuel Prodder should fancy these people must necessarily be talking of the murder.

The landlady brought the captain the steak he had ordered, and the tired traveller seated himself at one of the tables, and discussed his simple meal. He had eaten nothing since seven o'clock that morning, and he made very short work of the three-quarters of a pound of meat that had been cooked for him. He finished his beer, drank his rum and water, smoked a pipe, and then, as he had the room still to himself, he made an impromptu couch of Windsor chairs arranged in a row, and, in his own parlance, turned-in upon this rough hammock to take a brief stretch.

He might have set his mind at rest, perhaps, before this, had he chosen. He could have questioned the landlady about the murder at Mellish Park; she was likely to know as much as any one else he might meet at the "Crooked Rabbit." But he had refrained from doing this because he did not wish to draw attention to himself in any way as a person in the smallest degree interested in the murder. How did he know what inquiries had possibly been made for the missing witness? There was perhaps some enormous reward offered for his apprehension, and a word or a look might betray him to the greedy eyes of those upon the watch to obtain it.

Remember that this broad-shouldered seafaring man was as ignorant as a child of all things beyond the deck of his own vessel, and the watery high-roads he had been wont to navigate. Life along-shore was a solemn mystery to him — the law of the British dominions a complication of inscrutable enigmas, only to be spoken of and thought of in a spirit of reverence and wonder. If anybody had told him that he was likely to be seized upon as an accessory before the fact, and hung out of hand for his passive part in the Mellish catastrophe, he would have believed them implicitly. How did he know how many Acts of Parliament his conduct in leaving Doncaster without giving his evidence might come under? It might be high treason, leze-majesty — anything in the world that is unpronounceable and awful — for aught this simple sailor knew to the contrary. But in all this it was not his own safety that Captain Prodder thought of. That was of very little moment to this light-hearted, easy-going sailor. He had perilled his life too often on the high-seas to set any exaggerated value upon it ashore. If they chose to hang an innocent man, they must do their worst; it would be their mistake, not his; and he had a simple, seaman-like faith, rather vague, perhaps, and not very reducible to anything like Thirty-nine Articles, that told him that there were sweet little cherubs sitting up aloft who would take good care that any such sublunary mistake should be rectified in a certain supernal log-book, upon whose pages Samuel Prodder hoped to find himself set down as an honest and active sailor, always humbly obedient to the signals of his Commander.

It was for his niece's sake, then, that the sailor dreaded any discovery of his whereabouts, and it was for her sake that he resolved upon exercising the greatest degree of caution of which his simple nature was capable.

"I won't ask a single question," he thought;

"there's sure to be a pack of lubbers dropping in here by and by, and I shall hear 'em talking about the business as likely as not. These country folks would have nothing to talk about if they did n't overhaul the ship's books of their betters."

The captain slept soundly for upward of an hour, and was awakened at the end of that time by the sound of voices in the room, and the fumes of tobacco. The gas was flaring high in the low-roofed parlor when he opened his eyes, and at first he could scarcely distinguish the occupants of the room for the blinding glare of light.

"I won't get up," he thought; "I'll sham asleep for a bit, and see whether they happen to talk about the business."

There were only three men in the room. One of them was the landlord, whom Samuel Prodder had seen reading in the bar; and the other two were shabby-looking men, with by no means too respectable a stamp either upon their persons or their manners. One of them wore a velveteen cut-away coat with big brass buttons, knee-breeches, blue stockings, and high-lows. The other was a pale-faced man, with mutton-chop whiskers, and dressed in a shabby-genteel costume that gave indication of general vagabondage rather than of any particular occupation.

They were talking of horses when Captain Prodder awoke, and the sailor lay for some time listening to a jargon that was utterly unintelligible to him. The men talked of Lord Zetland's lot, of Lord Glasgow's lot, and the Leger, and the Cup, and made offers to bet with each other, and quarrelled about the terms, and never came to an agreement, in a manner that was utterly bewildering to poor Samuel; but he waited patiently, still feigning to be asleep, and not in any way disturbed by the men, who did not condescend to take any notice of him.

"They'll talk of the other business presently," he thought; "they're safe to talk of it."

Mr. Prodder was right.

After discussing the conflicting merits of half the horses in the racing calendar, the three men abandoned the fascinating subject; and the landlord, re-entering the room after having left it to fetch a supply of beer for his guests, asked if either of them had heard if anything new had turned up about that business at Mellish.

"There's a letter in to-day's *Guardian*," he added, before receiving any reply to his question, "and a pretty strong one. It tries to fix the murder upon some one in the house, but it don't exactly name the party. It would n't be safe to do that yet a while, I suppose."

Upon the request of the two men, the landlord of the "Crooked Rabbit" read the letter in the Manchester daily paper. It was a very clever letter, and a spirited one, giving a synopsis of the proceedings at the inquest, and commenting very severely upon the manner in which that investigation had been conducted. Mr. Prodder quailed until the Windsor chairs trembled beneath him as the landlord read one passage, in which it was remarked that the stranger who carried the news of the murder to the house of the victim's employer, the man who had heard the report of the pistol, and had been chiefly instrumental in the finding of the body, had not been forthcoming at the inquest.

"He had disappeared mysteriously and abruptly, and no efforts were made to find him," wrote the correspondent of the *Guardian*. "What assurance can be given for the safety of any man's life when such a crime as the Mellish-Park murder is investigated in this loose and indifferent manner? The catastrophe occurred within the boundary of the Park fence. Let it be discovered whether any person in the Mellish household had a motive for the destruction of James Conyers. The man was a stranger to the neighborhood. He was not likely, therefore, to have made enemies outside the boundary of his employer's estate, but he may have had some secret foe within that limit. Who was he? where did he come from? what were his antecedents and associations? Let each one of these questions be fully sifted, and let a cordon be drawn round the house, and let every creature living in it be held under the surveillance of the law until patient investigation has done its work, and such evidence has been collected as must lead to the detection of the guilty person."

To this effect was the letter which the landlord read in a loud and didactic manner, that was very imposing, though not without a few stumbles over some hard words, and a good deal of slap-dash jumping at others.

Samuel Prodder could make very little of the composition, except that it was perfectly clear he had been missed at the inquest, and his absence commented upon. The landlord and the shabby-genteel man talked long and discursively upon the matter; the man in the velveteen coat, who was evidently a thoroughbred Cockney, and only newly arrived in Doncaster, required to be told the whole story before he was upon a footing with the other two. He was very quiet, and generally spoke between his teeth, rarely taking the unnecessary trouble of removing his short clay pipe from his mouth except when it required refilling. He listened to the story of the murder very intently, keeping one eye upon the speaker and the other upon his pipe, and nodding approvingly now and then in the course of the narrative.

He took his pipe from his mouth when the story was finished, and filled it from a gutta-percha pouch, which had to be turned inside out in some mysterious manner before the tobacco could be extricated from it. While he was packing the loose fragments of shag or bird's-eye neatly into the bowl of the pipe with his stumpy little finger, he said, with supreme carelessness:

"I know'd Jim Conyers."

"Did you, now?" exclaimed the landlord, opening his eyes very wide.

"I know'd him," repeated the man, "as intimate as I know'd my own mother; and when I read of the murder in the newspaper last Sunday, you might have knocked me down with a feather. 'Jim 's got it at last,' I said; for he was one of them coves that goes through the world cock-a-doodling over other people to sich an extent that, when they do drop in for it, there 's not many particular sorry for 'em. He was one of your selfish chaps, this here; and when a chap goes through this life makin' it his leadin' principle to care about nobody, he must n't be surprised if it ends by nobody carin' for him. Yes, I know'd Jim Conyers," added the man, slowly and thoughtfully, "and I know'd him under rather peccoliar circumstances."

The landlord and the other man pricked up their ears at this point of the conversation.

The trainer at Mellish Park had, as we know, risen to popularity from the hour in which he had fallen upon the dewy turf in the wood, shot through the heart.

"If there was n't any partiklar objections," the landlord of the "Crooked Rabbit" said, presently, "I should oncommonly like to hear anything you 've got to tell about the poor chap. There 's a deal of interest took about the matter in Doncaster, and my customers have scarcely talked of anything else since the inquest."

The man in the velveteen coat rubbed his chin, and smoked his pipe reflectively. He was evidently not a very communicative man, but it was also evident that he was rather gratified by the distinction of his position in the little public-house parlor.

This man was no other than Mr. Matthew Harrison, the dog-fancier, Aurora's pensioner, the man who had traded upon her secret, and made himself the last link between herself and the low-born husband she had abandoned.

Samuel Prodder lifted himself from the Windsor chairs at this juncture. He was too much interested in the conversation to be able to simulate sleep any longer. He got up, stretched his legs and arms, made an elaborate show of having just awakened from a profound and refreshing slumber, and asked the landlord of the "Crooked Rabbit" to mix him another glass of that pineapple-rum grog.

The captain lighted his pipe while his host departed upon this errand. The seaman glanced rather inquisitively at Mr. Harrison;

166 AURORA FLOYD.

but he was fain to wait until the conversation took its own course, and offered him a safe opportunity of asking a few questions.

"The pecooliar circumstances under which I know'd James Conyers," pursued the dog-fancier, after having taken his own time, and smoked out half a pipeful of tobacco, to the acute aggravation of his auditory, "was a woman—and a stunner she was, too; one of your regular spitfires, that 'll knock you into the middle of next week if you so much as asks her how she does in a manner she don't approve of. She was a woman, she was, and a handsome one too; but she was more than a match for James, with all his brass. Why, I 've seen her great black eyes flash fire upon him," said Mr. Harrison, looking dreamily before him, as if he could even at that moment see the flashing eyes of which he spoke—"I 've seen her look at him as if she 'd wither him up from off the ground he trod upon with that contempt she felt for him."

Samuel Prodder grew strangely uneasy as he listened to this man's talk of flashing black eyes and angry looks directed at James Conyers. Had he not seen his niece's shining orbs flame fire upon the dead man only a quarter of an hour before he received his death-wound—only so long—Heaven help that wretched girl!—only so long before the man for whom she had expressed unmitigated hate had fallen by the hand of an unknown murderer?

"She must have been a tartar, this young woman of yours," the landlord observed to Mr. Harrison.

"She was a tartar," answered the dog-fancier; "but she was the right sort, too, for all that; and, what 's more, she was a kind friend to me. There 's never a quarter-day goes by that I don't have cause to say so."

He poured out a fresh glass of beer as he spoke, and tossed the liquor down his capacious throat with the muttered sentiment, "Here 's toward her."

Another man had entered the room while Mr. Prodder had sat smoking his pipe and drinking his rum and water—a hump-backed, white-faced man, who sneaked into the public-house parlor as if he had no right to be there, and seated himself noiselessly at one of the tables.

Samuel Prodder remembered this man. He had seen him through the window in the lighted parlor of the north lodge when the body of James Conyers had been carried into the cottage. It was not likely, however, that the man had seen the captain.

"Why, if it is n't Steeve Hargraves, from the Park!" exclaimed the landlord, as he looked round and recognized the softy; "he 'll be able to tell plenty, I dare say. We 've been talking of the murder, Steeve," he added, in a conciliatory manner.

Mr. Hargraves rubbed his clumsy hands about his head, and looked furtively, yet searchingly, at each member of the little assembly.

"Ay, sure," he said, "folks don't seem to me to talk about aught else. It was bad enough up at the Park, but it seems worse in Doncaster."

"Are you stayin' up town, Steeve?" asked the landlord, who seemed to be upon pretty intimate terms with the late hanger-on of Mellish Park.

"Yes, I 'm stayin' oop town for a bit; I 've been out of place since the business oop there; you know how I was turned out of the house that had sheltered me ever since I was a boy, and you know who did it. Never mind that; I 'm out of place now, but you may draw me a mug of ale; I 've money enough for that."

Samuel Prodder looked at the softy with considerable interest. He had played a small part in the great catastrophe, yet it was scarcely likely that he should be able to throw any light upon the mystery. What was he but a poor half-witted hanger-on of the murdered man, who had lost all by his patron's untimely death?

The softy drank his beer, and sat silent, ungainly, and disagreeable to look upon, among the other men.

"There 's a reg'lar stir in the Manchester papers about this murder, Steeve," the landlord said, by way of opening a conversation; "it don't seem to me as if the business was goin' to be let drop over quietly. There 'll be a second inquest, I reckon, or a examination, or a memorial to the Secretary of State, or summat o' that sort, before long."

The softy's face, expressionless almost always, expressed nothing now but stolid indifference; the stupid indifference of a half-witted ignoramus, to whose impenetrable intellect even the murder of his own master was a far-away and obscure event, not powerful enough to awaken any effort of attention.

"Yes; I 'll lay there 'll be a stir about it before long," the landlord continued. "The papers put it down very strong that the murder must have been done by some one in the house—by some one as had more knowledge of the man, and more reason to be angry against him, than strangers could have. Now you, Hargraves, were living at the place; you must have seen and heard things that other people have n't had the opportunity to hear. What do you think about it?"

Mr. Hargraves scratched his head reflectively.

"The papers are cleverer nor me," he said at last; "it would n't do for a poor fond chap like me to go again' such as them. I think what they think. I think it was some one about the place did it; some one that had good reason to be spiteful against him that 's dead."

An imperceptible shudder passed over the softy's frame as he alluded to the murdered man It was strange with what gusto the other three men discussed the ghastly subject, returning to it persistently in spite of every interruption, and in a manner licking their lips over its gloomiest details. It was surely more strange that they should do this than that Stephen Hargraves should exhibit some reluctance to talk freely upon the dismal topic.

"And who do you think had cause to be spiteful agen him, Steeve?" asked the landlord. "Had him and Mr. Mellish fell out about the management of the stable?"

"Him and Mr Mellish had never had an angry word pass between 'em, as I 've heard of," answered the softy

He laid such a singular emphasis upon the word Mr that the three men looked at him wonderingly, and Captain Prodder took his pipe from his mouth, and grasped the back of a neighboring chair as firmly as if he had entertained serious thoughts of flinging that trifle of furniture at the softy's head

"Who else could it have been, then, as had a spite against the man?" asked some one

Samuel Prodder scarcely knew who it was who spoke for his attention was concentrated upon Stephen Hargraves, and he never once removed his gaze from the white face, and dull, blinking eyes

"Who was it that went to meet him late at night in the north lodge?" whispered the softy. "Who was it that could n't find words that was bad enough for him, or looks that was angry enough for him? Who was it that wrote him a letter — I 've got it, and I mean to keep it, too — askin' of him to be in the wood at such and such a time upon the very night of the murder? Who was it that met him there in the dark—as others could tell as well as me? Who was it that did this?"

No one answered The men looked at each other and at the softy with open mouths, but said nothing Samuel Prodder grasped the topmost bar of the wooden chair still more tightly, and his broad bosom rose and fell beneath his tourist waistcoat like a raging sea; but he sat in the shadow of the queerly-shaped room, and no one noticed him

"Who was it that ran away from her own home, and hid herself after the inquest?" whispered the softy. 'Who was it that was afraid to stop in her own house, but must run away to London without leaving word where she was gone for anybody? Who was it that was seen upon the mornin' before the murder meddlin' with her husband's guns and pistols, and was seen by more than me, as them that saw her will testify when the time comes? Who was this?"

Again there was no answer The raging sea labored still more heavily under Captain Prodder's waistcoat, and his grasp tightened, if it could tighten, on the rail of the chair,

but he uttered no word There was more to come, perhaps, yet, and he might want every chair in the room as instruments with which to appease his vengeance.

"You was talkin', when I just came in, a while ago, of a young woman in connection with Mr. James Conyers, sir," said the softy, turning to Matthew Harrison, "a black-eyed woman, you said, might she have been his wife?"

The dog-fancier started, and deliberated for a few moments before he answered

"Well, in a manner of speaking, she was his wife," he said at last, rather reluctantly.

"She was a bit above him, loike, was n't she?" asked the softy. "She had more money than she knew what to do with, eh?"

The dog-fancier stared at the questioner

"You know who she was, I suppose?" he said, suspiciously.

"I think I do," whispered Stephen Hargraves "She was the daughter of Mr Floyd, the rich banker oop in London; and she married James Conyers, and she got tired of him, and she married our squire while her first husband was alive, and she wrote a letter to him that's dead, askin' of him to meet her upon the night of the murder."

Captain Prodder flung aside the chair. It was too poor a weapon with which to wreak his wrath, and with one bound he sprang upon the softy, seizing the astonished wretch by the throat, and overturning a table, with a heap of crashing glasses and pewter pots, that rolled away into the corners of the room

"It's a lie!" roared the sailor, "you foul-mouthed hound! you know that it 's a lie! Give me something," cried Captain Prodder, "give me something, somebody, and give it quick, that I may pound this man into a mash as soft as a soaked ship's biscuit, for if I use my fists to him I shall murder him, as sure as I stand here It 's my sister Eliza's child you want to slander, is it? You 'd better have kept your mouth shut while you was in her own uncle's company I meant to have kep' quiet here," cried the captain, with a vague recollection that he had betrayed himself and his purpose; "but was I to keep quiet and hear lies told of my own niece? Take care," he added, shaking the softy, till Mr Hargraves' teeth chattered in his head, "or I 'll knock those crooked teeth of yours down your ugly throat, to hinder you from telling any more lies of my dead sister's only child"

"They were n't lies," gasped the softy, doggedly, "I said I 've got the letter, and I have got it. Let me go, and I 'll show it to you"

The sailor released the dirty wisp of cotton neckerchief by which he had held Stephen Hargraves, but he still retained a grasp upon his coat-collar

"Shall I show you the letter?" asked the softy

"Yes"

Mr. Hargraves fumbled in his pockets for some minutes, and ultimately produced a dirty scrap of crumpled paper.

It was the brief scrawl which Aurora had written to James Conyers, telling him to meet her in the wood. The murdered man had thrown it carelessly aside, after reading it, and it had been picked up by Stephen Hargraves.

He would not trust the precious document out of his own clumsy hands, but held it before Captain Prodder for inspection.

The sailor stared at it, anxious, bewildered, fearful; he scarcely knew how to estimate the importance of the wretched scrap of circumstantial evidence. There were the words, certainly, written in a bold, scarcely feminine hand. But these words in themselves proved nothing until it could be proved that his niece had written them.

"How do I know as my sister Eliza's child wrote that?" he asked.

"Ay, sure; but she did, though," answered the softy. "But, coom, let me go now, will you?" he added, with cringing civility; "I did n't know you was her uncle. How was I to know aught about it? I don't want to make any mischief agen Mrs. Mellish, though she 's been no friend to me. I did n't say anything at the inquest, did I? though I might have said as much as I 've said to-night, if it comes to that, and have told no lies. But when folks bother *me* about him that 's dead, and ask this, and that, and t' other, and go on as if I had a right to know all about it, I 'm free to tell my thoughts, I suppose—surely I 'm free to tell my thoughts?"

"I 'll go straight to Mr. Mellish, and tell him what you 've said, you scoundrel!" cried the captain.

"Ay, do," whispered Stephen Hargraves, maliciously; "there 's some of it that 'll be stale news to him, anyhow."

CHAPTER XXXIV.

DISCOVERY OF THE WEAPON WITH WHICH JAMES CONYERS HAD BEEN SLAIN.

Mr. and Mrs. Mellish returned to the house in which they had been so happy; but it is not to be supposed that the pleasant country mansion could be again, all in a moment, the home that it had been before the advent of James Conyers, the trainer, and the tragedy that had so abruptly concluded his brief service.

No; every pang that Aurora had felt, every agony that John had endured, had left a certain impress upon the scene in which it had been suffered. The subtle influences of association hung heavily about the familiar place. We are the slaves of such associations, and we are powerless to stand against their silent force. Scraps of color and patches of gilding upon the walls will bear upon them, as plainly as if they were covered with hieroglyphical inscriptions, the shadows of the thoughts of those who have looked upon them. Transient and chance effects of light or shade will recall the same effects, seen and observed — as Fagin observed the broken spike upon the guarded dock—in some horrible crisis of misery and despair. The commonest household goods and chattels will bear mute witness of your agonies: an easy-chair will say to you, "It was upon me you cast yourself in that paroxysm of rage and grief;" the pattern of a dinner-service may recall to you that fatal day on which you pushed your food untasted from you, and turned your face, like grief-stricken King David, to the wall. The bed you lay upon, the curtains that sheltered you, the pattern of the paper on the walls, the common every-day sounds of the household, coming muffled and far-away to that lonely room in which you hid yourself, all these bear record of your sorrow, and of that hideous double action of the mind which impresses these things most vividly upon you at the very time when it would seem they should be most indifferent.

But every sorrow, every pang of wounded love, or doubt, or jealousy, or despair, is a fact—a fact once, and a fact for ever; to be outlived, but very rarely to be forgotten; leaving such an impress upon our lives as no future joys can quite wear out. The murder has been done, and the hands are red. The sorrow has been suffered; and, however beautiful Happiness may be to us, she can never be the bright virginal creature she once was, for she has passed through the valley of the shadow of death, and we have discovered that she is not immortal.

It is not to be expected, then, that John Mellish and his wife Aurora could feel quite the same in the pretty chambers of the Yorkshire mansion as they had felt before the first shipwreck of their happiness. They had been saved from peril and destruction, and landed, by the mercy of Providence, high and dry upon a shore that seemed to promise them pleasure and security henceforth. But the memory of the tempest was yet new to them; and upon the sands that were so smooth to-day they had seen yesterday the breakers beating with furious menace, and hurrying onward to destroy them.

The funeral of the trainer had not yet taken place, and it was scarcely a pleasant thing for Mr. Mellish to remember that the body of the murdered man still lay, stark and awful, in the oak coffin that stood upon trestles in the rustic chamber at the north lodge.

"I 'll pull that place down, Lolly," said John, as he turned away from an open window, through which he could see the Gothic chimneys of the trainer's late habitation glim-

mering redly above the trees. "I 'll pull the
place down, my pet. The gates are never
used, except by the stable-boys; I 'll knock
them down, and the lodge too, and build some
loose boxes for the brood-mares with the materials. And we 'll go away to the south of
France, darling, and run across to Italy, if
you like, and forget all about this horrid
business."

"The funeral will take place to-morrow,
John, will it not?" Aurora asked.

"To-morrow, dear! to-morrow is Wednes-
day, you know. It was upon Thursday night
that—"

"Yes, yes," she answered, interrupting him,
"I know—I remember."

She shuddered as she spoke, remembering
the ghastly circumstances of the night to
which he alluded — remembering how the
dead man had stood before her, strong in
health and vitality, and had insolently defied
her hatred. Away from Mellish Park, she
had only remembered that the burden of her
life had been removed from her, and that she
was free. But here—here, upon the scene of
the hideous story—she recollected the manner
of her release, and that memory oppressed
her even more terribly than her old secret,
her only sorrow.

She had never seen or known in this man
who had been murdered one redeeming quality, one generous thought. She had known
him as a liar, a schemer, a low and paltry
swindler, a selfish spendthrift, extravagant to
wantonness upon himself, but meaner than
words could tell toward others ; a profligate,
a traitor, a glutton, a drunkard. This is what
she had found behind her school-girl's fancy
for a handsome face, for violet-tinted eyes,
and soft brown curling hair. Do not call her
hard, then, if sorrow had no part in the shuddering horror she felt as she conjured up the
image of him in his death-hour, and saw the
glazing eyes turned angrily upon her. She
was little more than twenty ; and it had been
her fate always to take the wrong step,
always to be misled by the vague finger-
posts upon life's high-road, and to choose
the longest, and crookedest, and hardest way
toward the goal she sought to reach.

Had she, upon the discovery of the first
husband's infidelity, called the law to her
aid — she was rich enough to command its
utmost help, though Sir Cresswell Cresswell
did not then keep the turnpike upon such a
royal road to divorce as he does now — she
might have freed herself from the hateful
chains so foolishly linked together, and might
have defied this dead man to torment or
assail her.

But she had chosen to follow the counsel of
expediency, and it had led her upon the
crooked way through which I have striven to
follow her. I feel that there is much need of
apology for her. Her own hands had sown

the dragon's teeth, from whose evil seed had
sprung up armed men strong enough to rend
and devour her. But then, if she had been
faultless, she could not have been the heroine
of this story; for I think some wise man of
old remarked that the perfect women were
those who left no histories behind them, but
went through life upon such a tranquil course
of quiet well-doing as left no footprints on the
sands of time ; only mute records hidden here
and there, deep in the grateful hearts of those
who had been blessed by them.

The presence of the dead man within the
boundary of Mellish Park made itself felt
throughout the household that had once been
such a jovial one. The excitement of the
catastrophe had passed away, and only the
dull gloom remained — a sense of oppression
not to be cast aside. It was felt in the servants' hall as well as in Aurora's luxurious
apartments. It was felt by the butler as well
as by the master. No worse deed of violence
than the slaughter of an unhappy stag, who
had rushed for a last refuge to the Mellish
flower-garden, and had been run down by
furious hounds upon the velvet lawn, had
ever before been done within the boundary
of the young squire's home. The house was
an old one, and had stood, gray and ivy-
shrouded, through the perilous days of civil
war. There were secret passages, in which
loyal squires of Mellish had hidden from
ferocious Roundheads bent upon riot and
plunder. There were broad hearth-stones,
upon which sturdy blows had been given and
exchanged by strong men in leathern jerkins
and clumsy iron-heeled boots; but the Roy-
alist Mellish had always ultimately escaped—
up a chimney, or down a cellar, or behind a
curtain of tapestry ; and the wicked Praise-
the-Lord Thompsons and Smiter-of-the-Philis-
tines Joneses had departed after plundering
the plate-chest and emptying the wine-bar-
rels. There had never before been set upon
the place in which John Mellish had first seen
the light the red hand of MURDER.

It was not strange, then, that the servants
sat long over their meals, and talked in
solemn whispers of the events of the past
week. There was more than the murder to
talk about. There was the flight of Mrs.
Mellish from beneath her husband's roof
upon the very day of the inquest. It was
all very well for John to give out that his
wife had gone up to town upon a visit to her
cousin, Mrs. Bulstrode. Such ladies as Mrs.
Mellish do not go upon visits without escort,
without a word of notice, without the poorest
pretence of bag and baggage. No; the mistress of Mellish Park had fled away from her
home under the influence of some sudden
panic. Had not Mrs. Powell said as much, or
hinted as much ? for when did the lady-like
creature ever vulgarize her opinions by stating them plainly ? The matter was obvious.

Mr. Mellish had taken, no doubt, the wisest course; he had pursued his wife, and brought her back, and had done his best to hush up the matter; but Aurora's departure had been a flight—a sudden and unpremeditated flight.

The lady's maid — ah! how many handsome dresses, given to her by a generous mistress, lay neatly folded in the girl's boxes on the second story!—told how Aurora had come to her room, pale and wild-looking, and had dressed herself unassisted for that hurried journey upon the day of the inquest. The girl liked her mistress, loved her, perhaps; for Aurora had a wondrous and almost dangerous faculty for winning the love of those who came near her; but it was so pleasant to have something to say about this all-absorbing topic, and to be able to make one's self a feature in the solemn conclave. At first they had talked only of the murdered man, speculating upon his life and history, and building up a dozen theoretical views of the murder. But the tide had turned now, and they talked of their mistress; not connecting her in any positive or openly-expressed manner with the murder, but commenting upon the strangeness of her conduct, and dwelling much upon those singular coincidences by which she had happened to be roaming in the dark upon the night of the catastrophe, and to run away from her home upon the day of the inquest.

"It *was* odd, you know," the cook said; "and them black-eyed women are generally regular spirity ones. *I* should n't like to offend Master John's wife. Do you remember how she paid into t' softy?"

"But there was nought o' sort between her and the trainer, was there?" asked some one.

"I don't know about that. But softy said she hated him like poison, and that there was no love lost between 'em."

But why should Aurora have hated the dead man? The ensign's widow had left the sting of her venom behind her, and had suggested to these servants, by hints and innuendoes, something so far more base and hideous than the truth that I will not sully these pages by recording it. But Mrs. Powell had of course done this foul thing without the utterance of one ugly word that could have told against her gentility, had it been repeated aloud in a crowded drawing-room. She had only shrugged her shoulders, and lifted her straw-colored eyebrows, and sighed half regretfully, half deprecatingly; but she had blasted the character of the woman she hated as shamefully as if she had uttered a libel too gross for Holywell street. She had done a wrong that could only be undone by the exhibition of the blood-stained certificate in John's keeping, and the revelation of the whole story connected with that fatal scrap of paper. She had done this before packing her boxes; and she had gone away from the house that had sheltered her well pleased at having done this wrong, and comforting herself yet farther by the intention of doing more mischief through the medium of the penny-post.

It is not to be supposed that the Manchester paper, which had caused so serious a discussion in the humble parlor of the "Crooked Rabbit," had been overlooked in the servants' hall at Mellish. The Manchester journals were regularly forwarded to the young squire from the metropolis of cotton-spinning and horse-racing, and the mysterious letter in the *Guardian* had been read and commented upon. Every creature in that household, from the fat housekeeper who had kept the keys of the store-room through nearly three generations, to the rheumatic trainer, Langley, had a certain interest in the awful question. A nervous footman turned pale as that passage was read which declared that the murder had been committed by some member of the household; but I think there were some younger and more adventurous spirits—especially a pretty housemaid, who had seen the thrilling drama of *Susan Hopley* performed at the Doncaster Theatre during the spring meeting — who would have rather liked to be accused of the crime, and to emerge spotless and triumphant from the judicial ordeal, through the evidence of an idiot, or a magpie, or a ghost, or some other witness common and popular in criminal courts.

Did Aurora know anything of all this? No; she only knew that a dull and heavy sense of oppression in her own breast made the very summer atmosphere floating in at the open windows seem stifling and poisonous; that the house, which had once been so dear to her, was as painfully and perpetually haunted by the ghastly presence of the murdered man as if the dead trainer had stalked palpably about the corridors wrapped in a blood-stained winding-sheet.

She dined with her husband alone in the great dining-room. Many people had called during the two days that Mr. and Mrs. Mellish had been absent; among others, the rector, Mr. Lofthouse, and the coroner, Mr. Hayward.

"Lofthouse and Hayward will guess why we went away," John thought, as he tossed the cards over in the basket; "they will guess that I have taken the proper steps to make my marriage legal, and to make my darling quite my own."

They were very silent at dinner, for the presence of the servants sealed their lips upon the topic that was uppermost in their minds. John looked anxiously at his wife every now and then, for he saw that her face had grown paler since her arrival at Mellish; but he waited until they were alone before he spoke.

"My darling," he said, as the door closed behind the butler and his subordinate, "I am sure you are ill. This business has been too much for you."

"It is the air of this house that seems to oppress me, John," answered Aurora. "I had forgotten all about this dreadful business while I was away. Now that I come back, and find that the time which has been so long to me—so long in misery and anxiety, and so long in joy, my own dear love, through you—is in reality only a few days, and that the murdered man still lies near us, I—I shall be better when—when the funeral is over, John."

"My poor darling, I was a fool to bring you back. I should never have done so but for Talbot's advice. He urged me so strongly to come back directly. He said that if there should be any disturbance about the murder, we ought to be upon the spot."

"Disturbance! What disturbance?" cried Aurora.

Her face blanched as she spoke, and her heart sank within her. What farther disturbance could there be? Was the ghastly business as yet unfinished then? She knew—alas! only too well—that there could be no investigation of this matter which would not bring her name before the world linked with the name of the dead man. How much she had endured in order to keep that shameful secret from the world! How much she had sacrificed in the hope of saving her father from humiliation! And now, at the last, when she had thought that the dark chapter of her life was finished, the hateful page blotted out—now, at the very last, there was a probability of some new disturbance which would bring her name and her history into every newspaper in England.

"Oh, John, John!" she cried, bursting into a passion of hysterical sobs, and covering her face with her clasped hands, "am I never to hear the last of this? Am I never, never, never to be released from the consequences of my miserable folly?"

The butler entered the room as she said this; she rose hurriedly, and walked to one of the windows, in order to conceal her face from the man.

"I beg your pardon, sir," the old servant said, "but they 've found something in the Park, and I thought perhaps you might like to know—"

"They 've found something? What," exclaimed John, utterly bewildered between his agitation at the sight of his wife's grief and his endeavor to understand the man.

"A pistol, sir. One of the stable-lads found it just now. He went to the wood with another boy to look at the place where—the—the man was shot, and he 's brought back a pistol he found there. It was close against the water, but hid away among the weeds and rushes. Whoever threw it there, thought, no doubt, to throw it in the pond; but Jim, that 's one of the boys, fancied he saw something glitter, and sure enough it was the band of a pistol; and I think it must be the one that the trainer was shot with, Mr. John."

"A pistol!" cried Mr. Mellish; "let me see it."

His servant handed him the weapon. It was small enough for a toy, but none the less deadly in a skilful hand. It was a rich man's fancy, deftly carried out by some cunning gunsmith, and enriched by elaborate inlaid work of purple steel and tarnished silver. It was rusty, from exposure to rain and dew; but Mr. Mellish knew the pistol well, for it was his own.

It was his own; one of his pet playthings; and it had been kept in the room which was only entered by privileged persons—the room in which his wife had busied herself upon the day of the murder with the rearrangement of his guns.

CHAPTER XXXV.

UNDER A CLOUD.

Talbot Bulstrode and his wife came to Mellish Park a few days after the return of John and Aurora. Lucy was pleased to come to her cousin—pleased to be allowed to love her without reservation—grateful to her husband for his gracious goodness in setting no barrier between her and the friend she loved.

And Talbot—who shall tell the thoughts that were busy in his mind, as he sat in a corner of the first-class carriage, to all outward appearance engrossed in the perusal of a *Times* leader?

I wonder how much of the Thunderer's noble Saxon-English Mr. Bulstrode comprehended that morning? The broad white paper on which the *Times* is printed serves as a convenient screen for a man's face. Heaven knows what agonies have been sometimes endured behind that printed mass. A woman, married, and a happy mother, glances carelessly enough at the Births, and Marriages, and Deaths, and reads, perhaps, that the man she loved, and parted with, and broke her heart for fifteen or twenty years before, has fallen shot through the heart, far away upon an Indian battle-field. She holds the paper firmly enough before her face, and her husband goes on with his breakfast, and stirs his coffee, or breaks his egg, while she suffers her agony—while the comfortable breakfast-table darkens and goes away from her, and the long-ago day comes back upon which the cruel ship left Southampton, and the hard voices of well-meaning friends held forth monotonously upon the folly of improvident marriages. Would it not be better, by the by, for wives to make a practice of telling their husbands all the sentimental little stories connected with the prematrimonial era? Would it not be wiser to gossip freely about Charles' dark eyes and mustache, and to hope that the poor fellow is getting on well in the Indian service, than to keep a skeleton, in the shape of a phantom ensign in the 87th, hidden away in some dark chamber of the feminine memory?

But other than womanly agonies are suffered behind the *Times*. The husband reads bad news of the railway company in whose shares he has so rashly invested that money which his wife believes safely lodged in the jog-trot, three-per-cent-yielding Consols. The dashing son, with Newmarket tendencies, reads evil tidings of the horse he has backed so boldly, perhaps at the advice of a Manchester prophet, who warranted putting his friends in the way of winning a hatful of money for the small consideration of three and sixpence in postage stamps. Visions of a wall that it will not be very easy to square; of a black-list of play or pay engagements; of a crowd of angry bookmen clamorous for their dues, and not slow to hint at handy horse-ponds, and possible tar and feathers, for defaulting swells and sneaking welshers—all these things flit across the disorganized brain of the young man, while his sisters are entreating to be told whether the *Crown Diamonds* is to be performed that night, and if "dear Miss Pyne" will warble Rode's air before the curtain falls. The friendly screen hides his face; and by the time he has looked for the Covent Garden advertisements, and given the required information, he is able to set the paper down, and proceed calmly with his breakfast, pondering ways and means as he does so.

Lucy Bulstrode read a High-Church novel, while her husband sat with the *Times* before his face, thinking of all that had happened to him since he had first met the banker's daughter. How far away that old love-story seemed to have receded since the quiet domestic happiness of his life had begun in his marriage with Lucy! He had never been false, in the remotest shadow of a thought, to his second love; but, now that he knew the secret of Aurora's life, he could but look back and wonder how he should have borne that cruel revelation if John's fate had been his; if he had trusted the woman he loved in spite of the world, in spite of her own strange words, which had so terribly strengthened his worst fear, so cruelly redoubled his darkest doubts.

"Poor girl," he thought; "it was scarcely strange that she should shrink from telling that humiliating story. I was not tender enough. I confronted her in my obstinate and pitiless pride. I thought of myself rather than of her and of her sorrow. I was barbarous and ungentlemanly; and then I wondered that she refused to confide in me."

Talbot Bulstrode, reasoning after the fact, saw the weak points of his conduct with a preternatural clearness of vision, and could not repress a sharp pang of regret that he had not acted more generously. There was no infidelity to Lucy in this thought. He would not have exchanged his devoted little wife for the black-browed divinity of the past, though an all-powerful fairy had stood at his side ready to cancel his nuptials, and tie a fresh knot between him and Aurora. But he was a gentleman, and he felt that he had grievously wronged, insulted, and humiliated a woman whose worst fault had been the trusting folly of an innocent girl.

"I left her on the ground in that room at Felden," he thought—"kneeling on the ground, with her beautiful head bowed down before me. O my God, can I ever forget the agony of that moment? Can I ever forget what it cost me to do what I thought was right?"

The cold perspiration broke out upon his forehead as he remembered that by-gone pain, as it may do with a cowardly person who recalls too vividly the taking out of a three-pronged double tooth, or the cutting off of a limb.

"John Mellish was ten times wiser than I," thought Mr. Bulstrode; "he trusted to his instinct, and recognized a true woman when he met her. I used to despise him at Rugby because he couldn't construe Cicero. I never thought he'd live to be wiser than me."

Talbot Bulstrode folded the *Times* newspaper, and laid it down in the empty seat beside him. Lucy shut the third volume of her novel. How should she care to read when it pleased her husband to desist from reading?

"Lucy," said Mr. Bulstrode, taking his wife's hand (they had the carriage to themselves, a piece of good fortune which often happens to travellers who give the guard half a crown), "Lucy, I once did your cousin a great wrong; I want to atone for it now. If any trouble, which no one yet foresees, should come upon her, I want to be her friend. Do you think I am right in wishing this, dear?"

"Right, Talbot?"

Mrs. Bulstrode could only repeat the word in unmitigated surprise. When did she ever think him anything but the truest, and wisest, and most perfect of created beings?

Everything seemed very quiet at Mellish when the visitors arrived. There was no one in the drawing-room, nor in the smaller room within the drawing room; the Venetians were closed, for the day was close and sultry; there were vases of fresh flowers upon the tables, but there were no open books, no litter of frivolous needle-work or drawing materials, to indicate Aurora's presence.

"Mr. and Mrs. Mellish expected you by the later train, I believe sir," the servant said, as he ushered Talbot and his wife into the drawing-room.

"Shall I go and look for Aurora?" Lucy said to her husband. "She is in the morning-room, I dare say."

Talbot suggested that it would be better, perhaps, to wait till Mrs. Mellish came to them. So Lucy was fain to remain where he was. She went to one of the open windows, and pushed the shutters apart. The blazing sunshine burst into the room, and drowned it in light. The smooth lawn was aflame with scarlet geraniums and standard roses, and all manner of gaudily-colored blossoms; but Mrs. Bulstrode looked beyond this vividly-tinted *parterre* to the thick woods, that loomed darkly purple against the glowing sky.

It was in that very wood that her husband had declared his love for her; the same wood that had since been outraged by violence and murder.

"The — the man is buried, I suppose, Talbot?" she said to her husband.

"I believe so, my dear."

"I should never care to live in this place again, if I were Aurora."

The door opened before Mrs. Bulstrode had finished speaking, and the mistress of the house came toward them. She welcomed them affectionately and kindly, taking Lucy in her arms, and greeting her very tenderly; but Talbot saw that she had changed terribly within the few days that had passed since her return to Yorkshire, and his heart sank as he observed her pale face and the dark circles about her hollow eyes.

Could she have heard — Could anybody have given her reason to suppose—

"You are not well, Mrs. Mellish," he said, as he took her hand.

"No, not very well. This oppressive weather makes my head ache."

"I am sorry to see you looking ill. Where shall I find John?" asked Mr. Bulstrode.

Aurora's pale face flushed suddenly.

"I—I—don't know," she stammered. "He is not in the house; he has gone out — to the stables—or to the farm, I think. I'll send for him."

"No, no," Talbot said, intercepting her hand on its way to the bell. "I'll go and look for him. Lucy will be glad of a chat with you, I dare say, Aurora, and will not be sorry to get rid of me."

Lucy, with her arm about her cousin's waist, assented to this arrangement. She was grieved to see the change in Aurora's looks, the unnatural constraint of her manner.

Mr. Bulstrode walked away, hugging himself upon having done a very wise thing.

"Lucy is a great deal more likely to find out what is the matter than I am," he thought. "There is a sort of freemasonry between women, an electric affinity, which a man's presence always destroys. How deathly pale Aurora looks! Can it be possible that the trouble I expected has come so soon?"

He went to the stables, but not so much to look for John Mellish as in the hope of finding somebody intelligent enough to furnish him with a better account of the murder than any he had yet heard.

"Some one else, as well as Aurora, must have had a reason for wishing to get rid of this man," he thought. "There must have been some motive—revenge, gain—something which no one has yet fathomed."

He went into the stable-yard; but he had no opportunity of making his investigation, for John Mellish was standing in a listless attitude before a small forge, watching the shoeing of one of his horses. The young squire looked up with a start as he recognized Talbot, and gave him his hand, with a few straggling words of welcome. Even in that moment Mr. Bulstrode saw that there was perhaps a greater change in John's appearance than in that of Aurora. The Yorkshireman's blue eyes had lost their brightness, his step its elasticity; his face seemed sunken and haggard, and he evidently avoided meeting Talbot's eye. He lounged listlessly away from the forge, walking at his guest's side, in the direction of the stable-gates; but he had the air of a man who neither knows nor cares whither he is going.

"Shall we go to the house?" he said. "You must want some luncheon after your journey." He looked at his watch as he said this. It was half-past three, an hour after the usual time for luncheon at Mellish.

"I've been in the stables all the morning," he said. "We're busy making our preparations for the York Summer."

"What horses do you run?" Mr. Bulstrode asked, politely affecting to be interested in a subject that was utterly indifferent to him, in the hope that stable-talk might rouse John from his listless apathy.

"What horses?" repeated Mr. Mellish, vaguely. "I—I hardly know. Langley manages all that for me, you know; and —I —I forget the names of the horses he proposed, and—"

Talbot Bulstrode turned suddenly upon his friend, and looked him full in the face. They had left the stables by this time, and were in a shady pathway that led through a shrubbery toward the house.

"John Mellish," he said, "this is not fair toward an old friend. You have something on your mind, and you are trying to hide it from me."

The squire turned away his head.

"I have something on my mind, Talbot," he said, quietly. "If you could help me, I'd ask your help more than any man's. But you can't, you can't!"

"But suppose I think I *can* help you?" cried Mr. Bulstrode. "Suppose I mean to try and do so, whether you will or no? I think I can guess what your trouble is, John, but I thought you were a braver man than to give way under it; I thought you were just

the sort of man to struggle through it nobly
and bravely, and to get the better of it by
your own strength of will."

"What do you mean?" exclaimed John
Mellish. "You can guess—you know—you
thought! Have you no mercy upon me, Talbot Bulstrode? Can't you see that I'm almost mad, and that this is no time for you to
force your sympathy upon me? Do you want
me to betray myself? Do you want me to
betray—'

He stopped suddenly, as if the words had
choked him, and, passionately stamping his
foot upon the ground, walked on hurriedly,
with his friend still by his side.

The dining-room looked dreary enough
when the two men entered it, although the
table gave promise of a very substantial luncheon; but there was no one to welcome them,
or to officiate at the banquet.

John seated himself wearily in a chair at
the bottom of the table.

"You had better go and see if Mrs. Bulstrode and your mistress are coming to luncheon," he said to a servant, who left the room
with his master's message, and returned three
minutes afterward to say that the ladies were
not coming.

The ladies were seated side by side upon a
low sofa in Aurora's morning-room. Mrs. Mellish sat with her head upon her cousin's shoulder. She had never had a sister, remember,
and gentle Lucy stood in place of that near
and tender comforter. Talbot was perfectly
right; Lucy had accomplished that which he
would have failed to bring about. She had
found the key to her cousin's unhappiness.

"Ceased to love you, dear!" exclaimed Mrs.
Bulstrode, echoing the words that Aurora had
last spoken. "Impossible!"

"It is true, Lucy," Mrs. Mellish answered,
despairingly. "He has ceased to love me.
There is a black cloud between us now, now
that all secrets are done away with. It is
very bitter for me to bear, Lucy, for I thought
we should be so happy and united. But—
but it is only natural. He feels the degradation so much. How can he look at me without remembering who and what I am? The
widow of his groom! Can I wonder that he
avoids me?"

"Avoids you, dear!"

"Yes, avoids me. We have scarcely spoken
a dozen words to each other since the night
of our return. He was so good to me, so tender and devoted during the journey home,
telling me again and again that this discovery
had not lessened his love, that all the trial and
horror of the past few days had only shown
him the great strength of his affection; but on
the night of our return, Lucy, he changed—
changed suddenly and inexplicably; and now
I feel that there is a gulf between us that can
never be passed again. He is alienated from
me for ever."

"Aurora, all this is impossible," remonstrated Lucy. "It is your own morbid fancy,
darling."

"My fancy!" cried Aurora, bitterly. "Ah!
Lucy, you can not know how much I love my
husband, if you think that I could be deceived
in one look or tone of his. Is it my fancy that
he averts his eyes when he speaks to me? Is
it my fancy that his voice changes when he
pronounces my name? Is it my fancy that
he roams about the house like a ghost, and
paces up and down his room half the night
through? If these things are my fancy, Heav-
en have mercy upon me, Lucy, for I must be
going mad."

Mrs. Bulstrode started as she looked at her
cousin. Could it be possible that all the
trouble and confusion of the past week or
two had indeed unsettled this poor girl's intellect?

"My poor Aurora," she murmured, smoothing the heavy hair away from her cousin's
tearful eyes, "my poor darling, how is it possible that John should change toward you?
He loved you so dearly, so devotedly; surely
nothing could alienate him from you."

"I used to think so, Lucy," Aurora murmured in a low, heart-broken voice; "I used
to think nothing could ever come to part us.
He said he would follow me to the uttermost
end of the world; he said that no obstacle on
earth should ever separate us; and now—"

She could not finish the sentence, for she
broke into convulsive sobs, and hid her face
upon her cousin's shoulder, staining Mrs. Bulstrode's pretty silk dress with her hot tears.

"Oh, my love, my love," she cried, piteously, "why did n't I run away and hide myself
from you? why did n't I trust to my first instinct, and run away from you for ever? Any
suffering would be better than this—any suffering would be better than this!"

Her passionate grief merged into a fit of
hysterical weeping, in which she was no longer
mistress of herself. She had suffered for the
past few days more bitterly than she had ever
suffered yet. Lucy understood all that. She
was one of those people whose tenderness instinctively comprehends the griefs of others.
She knew how to treat her cousin; and in less
than an hour after this emotional outbreak
Aurora was lying on her bed, pale and exhausted, but sleeping peacefully. She had
carried the burden of her sorrow in silence
during the past few days, and had spent sleepless nights in brooding over her trouble. Her
conversation with Lucy had unconsciously relieved her, and she slumbered calmly after
the storm. Lucy sat by the bed watching the
sleeper for some time, and then stole on tiptoe from the room.

She went, of course, to tell her husband all
that had passed, and to take counsel from his
sublime wisdom.

She found Talbot in the drawing-room

done; he had eaten a dreary luncheon in John's company, and had been hastily left by his host immediately after the meal. There had been no sound of carriage-wheels upon the gravelled drive all that morning; there had been no callers at Mellish since John's return; for a horrible scandal had spread itself throughout the length and breadth of the county, and those who spoke of the young squire and his wife talked in solemn undertones, and gravely demanded of each other whether some serious step should not be taken about the business which was uppermost in everybody's mind.

Lucy told Talbot all that Aurora had said to her. This was no breach of confidence in the young wife's code of morality; for were not she and her husband immutably one, and how *could* she have any secret from him?

"I thought so!" Mr. Bulstrode said, when Lucy had finished her story.

"You thought what, dear?"

"That the breach between John and Aurora was a serious one. Don't look so sorrowful, my darling. It must be our business to reunite these divided lovers. You shall comfort Aurora, Lucy, and I'll look after John."

Talbot Bulstrode kissed his little wife, and went straight away upon his friendly errand. He found John Mellish in his own room—the room in which Aurora had written to him upon the day of her flight—the room from which the murderous weapon had been stolen by some unknown hand. John had hidden the rusty pistol in one of the locked drawers of his Davenport; but it was not to be supposed that the fact of its discovery could be locked up or hidden away. *That* had been fully discussed in the servants' hall; and who shall doubt that it had travelled farther, percolating through some of those sinuous channels which lead away from every household?

"I want you to come for a walk with me, Mr. John Mellish," said Talbot, imperatively; "so put on your hat, and come into the Park. You are the most agreeable gentleman I ever had the honor to visit, and the attention you pay your guests is really something remarkable."

Mr. Mellish made no reply to this speech. He stood before his friend pale, silent, and sullen. He was no more like the hearty Yorkshire squire whom we have known than he was like Viscount Palmerston or Lord Clyde. He was transformed out of himself by some great trouble that was preying upon his mind, and, being of a transparent and childishly truthful disposition, was unable to disguise his anguish.

"John, John," cried Talbot, "we were little boys together at Rugby, and have backed each other in a dozen childish fights. Is it kind of you to withhold your friendship from me now, when I have come here on purpose to be a friend to you—to you and to Aurora?"

John Mellish turned away his head as his friend mentioned that familiar name, and the gesture was not lost upon Mr Bulstrode.

"John, why do you refuse to trust me?"

"I don't refuse. I—why did you come to this accursed house?" cried John Mellish, passionately; "why did you come here, Talbot Bulstrode? You don't know the blight that is upon this place, and those who live in it, or you would have no more come here than you would willingly go to a plague-stricken city. Do you know that since I came back from London not a creature has called at this house? Do you know that when I am I—and —my wife—went to church on Sunday, the people we knew sneaked away from our path as if we had just recovered from typhus fever? Do you know that the cursed gaping rabble come from Doncaster to stare over the Park palings, and that this house is a show to half the West Riding? Why do you come here? You will be stared at, and grinned at, and scandalized—you, who— Go back to London to-night, Talbot, if you don't want to drive me mad."

"Not till you trust me with your troubles, John," answered Mr. Bulstrode, firmly. "Put on your hat, and come out with me. I want you to show me the spot where the murder was done."

"You may get some one else to show it you," muttered John, sullenly; "I'll not go there!"

"John Mellish," cried Talbot, suddenly, "am I to think you a coward and a fool? By the Heaven that's above me, I shall think so if you persist in this nonsense. Come out into the Park with me; I have the claim of past friendship upon you, and I'll not have that claim set aside by any folly of yours."

The two men went out upon the lawn, John complying moodily enough with his friend's request, and walked silently across the Park toward that portion of the wood in which James Conyers had met his death. They had reached one of the loneliest and shadiest avenues in this wood, and were, in fact, close against the spot from which Samuel Prodder had watched his niece and her companion on the night of the murder, when Talbot stopped suddenly, and laid his hand on the squire's shoulder.

"John," he said, in a determined tone, "before we go to look at the place where this bad man died, you must tell me your trouble."

Mr. Mellish drew himself up proudly, and looked at the speaker with gloomy defiance lowering upon his face.

"I will tell no man that which I do not choose to tell," he said, firmly; and then, with a sudden change that was terrible to see, he cried impetuously, "Why do you torment me, Talbot? I tell you that I can't trust you—I can't trust any one upon earth. If—if I told you — the horrible thought that — if I told you, it would be your duty to — I — Talbot, Talbot, have pity upon me — let me alone — go away from me — I —"

Stamping furiously, as if he would have trampled down the cowardly despair for which he despised himself, and beating his forehead with his clenched fists, John Mellish turned away from his friend, and, leaning against the gnarled branch of a great oak, wept aloud. Talbot Bulstrode waited till the paroxysm had passed away before he spoke again; but when his friend had grown calmer, he linked his arm about him, and drew him away almost as tenderly as if the big Yorkshireman had been some sorrowing woman, sorely in need of manly help and comfort.

"John, John," he said gravely, "thank God for this; thank God for anything that breaks the ice between us. I know what your trouble is, poor old friend, and I know that you have no cause for it. Hold up your head, man, and look forward to a happy future. I know the black thought that has been gnawing at your poor, foolish, manly, heart; *you think that Aurora murdered the groom!*"

John Mellish started, shuddering convulsively.

"No, no," he gasped; "who said so — who said — "

"You think this, John," continued Talbot Bulstrode, "and you do her the most grievous wrong that ever yet was done to woman — a more shameful wrong than I committed when I thought that Aurora Floyd had been guilty of some base intrigue."

"You don't know — " stammered John.

"I don't know! I know all, and foresaw trouble for you before *you* saw the cloud that was in the sky. But I never dreamed of this. I thought the foolish country-people would suspect your wife, as it always pleases people to try and fix a crime upon the person in whom that crime would be more particularly atrocious. I was prepared for this; but to think that you — you, John, who should have learned to know your wife by this time — to think that you should suspect the woman you have loved of a foul and treacherous murder!"

"How do we know that the—that the man was murdered?" cried John, vehemently. "Who says that the deed was treacherously done? He may have goaded her beyond endurance, insulted her generous pride, stung her to the very quick, and in the madness of her passion — having that wretched pistol in her possession — she may — "

"Stop!" interrupted Talbot. "What pistol? You told me the weapon had not been found."

"It was found upon the night of our return."

"Yes; but why do you associate this weapon with Aurora? What do you mean by saying that the pistol was in her possession?"

"Because — O my God! Talbot, why do you wring these things from me?"

"For your own good, and for the justification of an innocent woman, so help me Heaven!" answered Mr. Bulstrode. "Do not be afraid to be candid with me, John. Nothing would ever make me believe Aurora Mellish guilty of this crime."

The Yorkshireman turned suddenly toward his friend, and, leaning upon Talbot Bulstrode's shoulder, wept for the second time during that woodland ramble.

"May God in heaven bless you for this, Talbot!" he cried, passionately. "Ah! my love, my dear, what a wretch I have been to you! but Heaven is my witness that, even in my worst agony of doubt and horror, my love has never lessened. It never could, it never could!"

"John, old fellow," said Mr. Bulstrode, cheerfully, "perhaps, instead of talking this nonsense (which leaves me entirely in the dark as to everything that has happened since you left London), you will do me the favor to enlighten me as to the cause of these foolish suspicions."

They had reached the ruined summer-house, and the pool of stagnant water on the margin of which James Conyers had met with his death. Mr. Bulstrode seated himself upon a pile of broken timber, while John Mellish paced up and down the smooth patch of turf between the summer-house and the water, and told, disjointedly enough, the story of the finding of the pistol which had been taken out of his room.

"I saw that pistol upon the day of the murder," said he. "I took particular notice of it; for I was cleaning my guns that morning, and I left them all in confusion while I went down to the lodge to see the trainer. When I came back — I — ".

"Well, what then?"

"Aurora had been setting my guns in order."

"You argue, therefore, that your wife took the pistol?"

John looked piteously at his friend; but Talbot's grave smile reassured him.

"No one else had permission to go into the room," he answered. "I keep my papers and accounts there, you know, and it's an understood thing that none of the servants are allowed to go there except when they clean the room."

"To be sure! But the room is not locked, I suppose?"

"Locked! of course not."

"And the windows, which open to the ground, are sometimes left open, I dare say?"

"Almost always, in such weather as this."

"Then, my dear John, it may be just possible that some one who had not permission to enter the room did nevertheless enter it for the purpose of abstracting this pistol. Have you asked Aurora why she took upon herself to rearrange your guns? She had never done such a thing before, I suppose?"

"Oh, yes, very often I 'm rather in the habit of leaving them about after cleaning them, and my darling understands all about them as well as I do. She has often put them away for me."

"Then there was nothing particular in her doing so upon the day of the murder. Have you asked her how long she was in your room, and whether she can remember seeing this particular pistol among others?"

"Ask her!" exclaimed John, "how could I ask her when —"

"When you had been mad enough to suspect her. No, my poor old friend, you made the same mistake that I committed at Felden. You presupposed the guilt of the woman you loved, and you were too great a coward to investigate the evidence upon which your suspicions were built. Had I been wise enough, instead of blindly questioning this poor, bewildered girl, to tell her plainly what it was that I suspected, the incontrovertible truth would have flashed out of her angry eyes, and one indignant denial would have told me how basely I had wronged her. You shall not make the mistake that I made, John. You must go frankly and fearlessly to the wife you love, tell her of the suspicion that overclouds her fame, and implore her to help you to the uttermost of her power in unravelling the mystery of this man's death. The assassin *must* be found, John, for, so long as he remains undiscovered, you and your wife will be the victims of every penny-a-liner who finds himself at a loss for a paragraph."

"Yes," Mr Mellish answered bitterly, "the papers have been hard at it already; and there 's been a fellow hanging about the place for the last few days whom I 've had a very strong inclination to thrash. Some reporter, I suppose, come to pick up information."

"I suppose so," Talbot answered, thoughtfully, "what sort of a man was he?"

"A decent-looking fellow enough, but a Londoner, I fancy, and — stay!" exclaimed John, suddenly, "there 's a man coming toward us from the turnstile, and, unless I 'm considerably mistaken, it 's the very fellow."

Mr Mellish was right.

The wood was free to any foot-passenger who pleased to avail himself of the pleasant shelter of spreading beeches, and the smooth carpet of mossy turf, rather than tramp wearily upon the dusty highway.

The stranger advancing from the turnstile was a decent-looking person, dressed in dark, tight-fitting clothes, and making no unnecessary or ostentatious display of linen, for his coat was buttoned tightly to the chin. He

looked at Talbot and John as he passed them, not insolently, or even inquisitively, but with one brightly rapid and searching glance, which seemed to take in the most minute details in the appearance of both gentlemen. Then, walking on a few paces, he stopped, and looked thoughtfully at the pond, and the bank above it.

"This is the place, I think, gentlemen?" he said, in a frank and rather free-and-easy manner.

Talbot returned his look with interest.

"If you mean the place where the murder was committed, it is," he said.

"Ah! I understood so," answered the stranger, by no means abashed.

He looked at the bank, regarding it, now from one point, now from another, like some skilful upholsterer taking the measure of a piece of furniture. Then, walking slowly round the pond, he seemed to plumb the depth of the stagnant water with his small gray eyes.

Talbot Bulstrode watched the man as he took this mental photograph of the place. There was a business-like composure in his manner which was entirely different to the eager curiosity of a scandal-monger and a busybody.

Mr Bulstrode rose as the man walked away, and went slowly after him.

"Stop where you are, John," he said, as he left his companion, "I 'll find out who this fellow is."

He walked on, and overtook the stranger at about a hundred yards from the pond.

"I want to have a few words with you before you leave the Park, my friend," he said, quietly, "unless I am very much mistaken, you are a member of the detective police, and come here with credentials from Scotland Yard."

The man shook his head with a quiet smile.

"I 'm not obliged to tell everybody my business," he answered, coolly; "this footpath is a public thoroughfare, I believe?"

"Listen to me, my good fellow," said Mr Bulstrode. "It may serve your purpose to beat about the bush, but I have no reason to do so, and therefore may as well come to the point at once. If you are sent here for the purpose of discovering the murderer of James Conyers, you can be more welcome to no one than to the master of that house."

He pointed to the Gothic chimneys as he spoke.

"If those who employ you have promised you a liberal reward, Mr Mellish will willingly treble the amount they may have offered you. He would not give you cause to complain of his liberality should you succeed in accomplishing the purpose of your errand. If you think you will gain anything by underhand measures, and by keeping yourself dark, you are very much mistaken; for no one can be

12

better able or more willing to give you assistance in this than Mr. and Mrs. Mellish."

The detective—for he had tacitly admitted the fact of his profession — looked doubtfully at Talbot Bulstrode.

"You 're a lawyer, I suppose ?" he said.

"I am Mr. Talbot Bulstrode, member for Penruthy, and the husband of Mrs. Mellish's first cousin."

The detective bowed.

"My name is Joseph Grimstone, of Scotland Yard and Ball's Pond," he said; "and I certainly see no objection to our working together. If Mr. Mellish is prepared to act on the square, I 'm prepared to act with him, and to accept any reward his generosity may offer. But if he or any friend of his wants to hoodwink Joseph Grimstone, he 'd better think twice about the game before he tries it on—that 's all."

Mr. Bulstrode took no notice of this threat, but looked at his watch before replying to the detective.

"It 's a quarter-past six," he said. "Mr. Mellish dines at seven. Can you call at the house, say at nine, this evening ? You shall then have all the assistance it is in our power to give you."

"Certainly, sir. At nine this evening."

"We shall be prepared to receive you. Good-afternoon."

Mr. Grimstone touched his hat, and strolled quietly away under the shadow of the beeches, while Talbot Bulstrode walked back to rejoin his friend.

It may be as well to take this opportunity of stating the reason of the detective's early appearance at Mellish Park. Upon the day of the inquest, and consequently the next day but one after the murder, two anonymous letters, worded in the same manner, and written by the same hand, were received respectively by the head of the Doncaster constabulary and by the chief of the Scotland-Yard detective confederacy.

These anonymous communications—written in a hand which, in spite of all attempt at disguise, still retained the spidery peculiarities of feminine calligraphy —pointed, by a sinuous and inductive process of reasoning, at Aurora Mellish as the murderess of James Conyers. I need scarcely say that the writer was no other than Mrs. Powell. She has disappeared for ever from my story, and I have no wish to blacken a character which can ill afford to be slandered. The ensign's widow actually believed in the guilt of her beautiful patroness. It is so easy for an envious woman to believe horrible things of the more prosperous sister whom she hates.

CHAPTER XXXVI.

REUNION.

"We are on the verge of a precipice," Talbot Bulstrode thought, as he prepared for dinner in the comfortable dressing-room allotted to him at Mellish —"we are on the verge of a precipice, and nothing but a bold grapple with the worst can save us. Any reticence, any attempt at keeping back suspicious facts, or hushing up awkward coincidences, would be fatal to us. If John had made away with this pistol with which the deed was done, he would have inevitably fixed a most fearful suspicion upon his wife. Thank God I came here to-day! We must look matters straight in the face, and our first step must be to secure Aurora's help. So long as she is silent as to her share in the events of that day and night, there is a link missing in the chain, and we are all at sea. John must speak to her to-night; or perhaps it will be better for me to speak."

Mr. Bulstrode went down to the drawing-room, where he found his friend pacing up and down, solitary and wretched.

"The ladies are going to dine up stairs," said Mr. Mellish, as Talbot joined him. "I have just had a message to say so. Why does she avoid me, Talbot? Why does my wife avoid me like this? We have scarcely spoken to each other for days."

"Shall I tell you why, you foolish John ?" answered Mr. Bulstrode. "Your wife avoids you because you have chosen to alienate yourself from her, and because she thinks, poor girl, that she has lost your affection. She fancies that the discovery of her first marriage has caused a revulsion of feeling, and that you no longer love her."

"No longer love her!" cried John. "O my God! she ought to know that, if I could give my life for her fifty times over, I would do it, to save her one pang. I would do it, so help me Heaven, though she was the guiltiest wretch that had ever crawled the earth!"

"But no one asks you to do anything of the kind," said Mr. Bulstrode. "You are only requested to be reasonable and patient, to put a proper trust in Providence, and to be guided by people who are rather less impetuous than your ungovernable self."

"I will do what you like, Talbot; I will do what you like."

Mr. Mellish pressed his friend's hand. Had he ever thought, when he had seen Talbot an accepted lover at Felden, and had hated him with a savage and wild Indian-like fury, that he would come to be thus humbly grateful to him — thus pitifully dependent upon his superior wisdom? He wrung the young politician's hand, and promised to be as submissive as a child beneath his guidance.

In compliance, therefore, with Talbot's command, he ate a few morsels of fish, and drank a couple of glasses of sherry, and, having thus gone through a show of dining, he went with Mr Bulstrode to seek Aurora.

She was sitting with her cousin in the morning-room, looking terribly pale in the dim dusk of the August evening—pale and shadowy in her loose white muslin dress. She had only lately risen, after a long feverish slumber, and had pretended to dine out of courtesy to her guest. Lucy had tried in vain to comfort her cousin. This passionate, impetuous, spoiled child of fortune and affection refused all consolation, crying out again and again that she had lost her husband's love, and that there was nothing left for her upon earth.

But in the very midst of one of these desponding speeches she sprang up from her seat, erect and trembling, with her parted lips quivering and her dark eyes dilated, startled by the sound of a familiar step, which within the last few days had been seldom heard in the corridor outside her room. She tried to speak, but her voice failed her; and in another moment the door had been dashed open by a strong hand, and her husband stood in the room holding out his arms and calling to her.

"Aurora! Aurora! my own dear love, my own poor darling!"

She was folded to his breast before she knew that Talbot Bulstrode stood close behind him.

"My own darling," John said, "my own dearest, you can not tell how cruelly I have wronged you. But oh, my love, the wrong has brought unendurable torture with it. My poor, guiltless girl! how could I—how could I— But I was mad, and it was only when Talbot—"

Aurora lifted her head from her husband's breast, and looked wonderingly into his face, utterly unable to guess the meaning of these broken sentences.

Talbot laid his hand upon his friend's shoulder. "You will frighten your wife if you go on in this manner, John," he said, quietly. "You must n't take any notice of his agitation, my dear Mrs Mellish. There is no cause, believe me, for all this outcry. Will you sit down by Lucy and compose yourself? It is eight o'clock, and between this and nine we have some serious business to settle."

"Serious business" repeated Aurora, vaguely. She was intoxicated by her sudden happiness. She had no wish to ask any explanation of the mystery of the past few days. It was all over, and her faithful husband loved her as devotedly and tenderly as ever. How could she wish to know more than this?

She seated herself at Lucy's side, in obedience to Talbot, but she still held her husband's hand, she still looked in his face for the moment most supremely unconscious that the scheme of creation included anything beyond this stalwart Yorkshireman.

Talbot Bulstrode lighted the lamp upon Aurora's writing-table—a shaded lamp, which only dimly illuminated the twilight room—and then, taking his seat near it, said gravely.

"My dear Mrs. Mellish, I shall be compelled to say something which I fear may inflict a terrible shock upon you. But this is no time for reservation—scarcely a time for ordinary delicacy. Will you trust in the love and friendship of those who are around you, and promise to bear this new trial bravely? I believe and hope that it will be a very brief one."

Aurora looked wonderingly at her husband, not at Talbot.

"A new trial?" she said, inquiringly.

"You know that the murderer of James Conyers has not yet been discovered?" said Mr Bulstrode.

"Yes, yes, but what of that?"

"My dear Mrs. Mellish, my dear Aurora, the world is apt to take a morbid delight in horrible ideas. There are some people who think that you are guilty of this crime!"

"I!"

She rose suddenly from her low seat, and turned her face toward the lamplight with a look of such blank amazement, such utter wonder and bewilderment, that, had Talbot Bulstrode until that moment believed her guilty, he must thenceforth and for ever have been firmly convinced of her innocence.

"I!" she repeated.

Then turning to her husband, with a sudden alteration in her face, that blank amazement changing to a look of sorrow, mingled with reproachful wonder, she said, in a low voice

"You thought this of me, John, you thought this!"

John Mellish bowed his head before her.

"I did, my dear," he murmured, "God forgive me for my wicked folly, I did think this, Aurora. But I pitied you, and was sorry for you, my own dear love, and when I thought it most, I would have died to save you from shame or sorrow. My love has never changed, Aurora, my love has never changed."

She gave him her hand, and once more resumed her seat. She sat for some moments in silence, as if trying to collect her thoughts, and to understand the meaning of this strange scene.

"Who suspects me of this crime?" she said, presently. "Has any one else suspected me? Any one besides—my husband?"

"I can scarcely tell you, my dear Mrs Mellish," answered Talbot, "when an event of this kind takes place, it is very difficult to say who may or may not be suspected. Different persons set up different theories: one man writes to a newspaper to declare that, in his opinion, the crime was committed by some person within the house, another man writes as positively to another paper, asserting that the murderer was undoubtedly a stranger. Each man brings forward a mass of suppositious evidence in favor of his own argument, and each thinks a great deal more of proving his own cleverness than of furthering the ends of justice. No shadow of slander must rest upon this house, or upon those who live in it. It is necessary, therefore, imperatively necessary, that the real murderer should be found. A London detective is already at work. These men are very clever; some insignificant circumstance, forgotten by those most interested in discovering the truth, would be often enough to set a detective on the right track. This man is coming here at nine o'clock, and we are to give him all the assistance we can. Will you help us, Aurora?"

"Help you? How?"

"By telling us all you know of the night of the murder. Why were you in the wood that night?"

"I was there to meet the dead man."

"For what purpose?"

Aurora was silent for some moments, and then, looking up with a bold, half-defiant glance, she said suddenly:

"Talbot Bulstrode, before you blame or despise me, remember how the tie that bound me to this man had been broken. The law would have set me free from him if I had been brave enough to appeal to the law; and was I to suffer all my life because of the mistake I had made in not demanding a release from the man whose gross infidelity entitled me to be divorced from him? Heaven knows I had borne with him patiently enough. I had endured his vulgarity, his insolence, his presumption; I had gone penniless while he spent my father's money in a gambling-booth on a race-course, and dinnerless while he drank Champagne with cheats and reprobates. Remember this when you blame me most. I went into the wood that night to meet him for the last time upon this earth. He had promised me that he would emigrate to Australia upon the payment of a certain sum of money."

"And you went that night to pay it to him?" cried Talbot, eagerly.

"I did. He was insolent, as he always was; for he hated me for having discovered that which shut him out from all claim upon my fortune. He hated himself for his folly in not having played his cards better. Angry words passed between us; but it ended in his declaring his intention of starting for Liverpool early the next morning, and—"

"You gave him the money?"

"Yes."

"But tell me—tell me, Aurora," cried Talbot, almost too eager to find words, "how long had you left him when you heard the report of the pistol?"

"Not more than ten minutes."

"John Mellish," exclaimed Mr. Bulstrode, "was there any money found upon the person of the murdered man?"

"No—yes; I believe there was a little silver," Mr. Mellish answered, vaguely.

"A little silver!" cried Talbot, contemptuously. "Aurora, what was the sum you gave James Conyers upon the night of his death?"

"Two thousand pounds."

"In a check?"

"No, in notes."

"And that money has never been heard of since?"

No; John Mellish declared that he had never heard of it.

"Thank God!" exclaimed Mr. Bulstrode; "we shall find the murderer."

"What do you mean?" asked John.

"Whoever killed James Conyers, killed him in order to rob him of the money that he had upon him at the time of his death."

"But who could have known of the money?" asked Aurora.

"Anybody; the pathway through the wood is a public thoroughfare. Your conversation with the murdered man may have been overheard. You talked about the money, I suppose?"

"Yes."

"Thank God, thank God! Ask your wife's pardon for the cruel wrong you have done her, John, and then come down stairs with me. It's past nine, and I dare say Mr. Grimstone is waiting for us. But stay—one word, Aurora. The pistol with which this man was killed was taken from this house—from John's room. Did you know that?"

"No; how should I know it?" Mrs. Mellish asked, naively.

"That fact is against the theory of the murder having been committed by a stranger. Is there any one of the servants whom you could suspect of such a crime, John?"

"No," answered Mr. Mellish, decisively, "not one."

"And yet the person who committed the murder must have been the person who stole your pistol. You, John, declare that very pistol to have been in your possession upon the morning before the murder?"

"Most certainly."

"You put John's guns back into their places upon that morning, Aurora," said Mr. Bulstrode; "do you remember seeing that particular pistol?"

"No," Mrs. Mellish answered; "I should not have known it from the others."

"You did not find any of the servants in the room that morning?"

"Oh, no," Aurora answered immediately; "Mrs. Powell came into the room while I was there. She was always following me about, and I suppose she had heard me talking to—"

" Talking to whom ?"

" To James Conyers' hanger-on and messenger, Stephen Hargraves — the softy, as they call him '

" You were talking to him ? Then this Stephen Hargraves was in the room that morning ?"

" Yes, he brought me a message from the murdered man and took back my answer "

" Was he alone in the room ?"

" Yes; I found him there when I went in expecting to find John I dislike the man — unjustly, perhaps, for he is a poor, half-witted creature, who, I dare say, scarcely knows right from wrong, and I was angry at seeing him He must have come in through the window "

A servant entered the room at this moment He came to say that Mr Grimstone had been waiting below for some time, and was anxious to see Mr. Bulstrode

Talbot and John went down stairs together. They found Mr Joseph Grimstone sitting at a table in the comfortable room that had lately been sacred to Mrs Powell, with the shaded lamp drawn close to his elbow, and a greasy little memorandum-book open before him He was thoughtfully employed making notes in this memorandum-book with a stumpy morsel of lead-pencil — when do these sort of people begin their pencils, and how is it that they always seem to have arrived at the stump ' — when the two gentlemen entered

John Mellish leaned against the mantle-piece, and covered his face with his hand For any practical purpose, he might as well have been in his own room He knew nothing of Talbot's reasons for this interview with the detective officer He had no shadowy idea, no growing suspicion shaping itself slowly out of the confusion and obscurity, of the identity of the murderer. He only knew that his Aurora was innocent, that she had indignantly refuted his base suspicion, and that he had seen the truth, radiant as the light of inspiration, shining out of her beautiful face

Mr Bulstrode rang, and ordered a bottle of sherry for the delectation of the detective, and then, in a careful and business-like manner, he recited all that he had been able to discover upon the subject of the murder Joseph Grimstone listened very quietly, following Talbot Bulstrode with a shining track of lead-pencil hieroglyphics over the greasy paper, just as Tom Thumb strewed crumbs of bread in the forest pathway with a view to his homeward guidance. The detective only looked up now and then to drink a glass of sherry, and smack his lips with the quiet approval of a connoisseur When Talbot had told all that he had to tell, Mr Grimstone thrust the memorandum-book into a very tight breast-pocket, and, taking his hat from under the chair upon which he had been seated, prepared to depart.

" If this information about the money is quite correct," he said, " I think I can see

my way through the affair — that is, if we can have the numbers of the notes I can't stir a peg without the numbers of the notes "

Talbot's countenance fell Here was a death-blow Was it likely that Aurora, that impetuous and unbusiness-like girl, had taken the numbers of the notes which, in utter scorn and loathing, she had flung as a last bribe to the man she hated ?

" I 'll go and make inquiries of Mrs Mellish," he said, " but I fear it is scarcely likely that I shall get the information you want "

He left the room, but five minutes afterward returned triumphant.

" Mrs Mellish had the notes from her father," he said " Mr. Floyd took a list of the numbers before he gave his daughter the money."

" Then, if you 'll be so good as to drop Mr Floyd a line, asking for that list by a return of post, I shall know how to act,' replied the detective " I have n't been idle this afternoon, gentlemen, any more than you I went back after I parted with you, Mr. Bulstrode, and had another look at the pond. I found something to pay me for my trouble "

He took from his waistcoat-pocket a small object, which he held between his finger and thumb

Talbot and John looked intently at this dingy object, but could make nothing out of it. It seemed to be a mere disk of rusty metal

" It 's neither more nor less than a brass button," the detective said, with a smile of quiet superiority; " maker's name Crosby, Birmingham There 's marks upon it which seem oncommon like blood; and, unless I 'm very much mistaken, it 'll be found to fit pretty correct into the barrel of your pistol, Mr Mellish So what we 've got to do is to find a gentleman wearin' or havin' in his possession a waistcoat with buttons by Crosby, Birmingham, and one button missin', and if we happen to find the same gentleman changin' one of the notes that Mr. Floyd took the numbers of, I don't think we shall be very far off layin' our hands on the man we want "

With which oracular speech Mr Grimstone departed, charged with a commission to proceed forthwith to Doncaster, to order the immediate printing and circulating of a hundred bills, offering a reward of £200 for such information as would lead to the apprehension of the murderer of James Conyers — this reward to be given by Mr Mellish, and to be over and above any reward offered by the government.

CHAPTER XXXVII

THE BRASS BUTTON, BY CROSBY, BIRMINGHAM

Mr Matthew Harrison and Captain Prodder were both accommodated with suitable entertainment at the sign of the " Crooked

Rabbit;" but while the dog-fancier appeared to have ample employment in the neighborhood — employment of a mysterious nature, which kept him on the tramp all day, and sent him home at sunset, tired and hungry, to his hostelry — the sailor, having nothing whatever to do, and a great burden of care upon his mind, found the time hang very heavily upon his hands, although, being naturally of a social and genial temper, he made himself very much at home in his strange quarters. From Mr. Harrison the captain obtained much information respecting the secret of all the sorrow that had befallen his niece. The dog-fancier had known James Conyers from his boyhood; had known his father, the "swell" coachman of a Brighton Highflyer, or Sky-rocket, or Electric, and the associate of the noblemen and gentlemen of that princely era, in which it was the right thing for the youthful aristocracy to imitate the manners of Mr. Samuel Weller, senior. Matthew Harrison had known the trainer in his brief and stormy married life, and had accompanied Aurora's first husband as a humble dependent and hanger-on in that foreign travel which had been paid for out of Archibald Floyd's check-book. The honest captain's blood boiled as he heard that shameful story of treachery and extortion practised upon an ignorant school-girl. Oh, that he had been by to avenge those outrages upon the child of the dark-eyed sister he had loved! His rage against the undiscovered murderer of the dead man was redoubled when he remembered how comfortably James Conyers had escaped from his vengeance.

Mr. Stephen Hargraves, the softy, took good care to keep out of the way of the "Crooked Rabbit," having no wish to encounter Captain Prodder a second time; but he still hung about the Town of Doncaster, where he had a lodging up a wretched alley, hidden away behind one of the back streets — a species of lair common to every large town, and only to be found by the inhabitants of the locality.

The softy had been born and bred, and had lived his life in such a narrow radius, that the uprooting of one of the oaks in Mellish Park could scarcely be a slower or more painful operation than the severing of those ties of custom which held the boorish hanger-on to the neighborhood of the household in which he had so long been an inmate. But, now that his occupation at Mellish was for ever gone, and his patron, the trainer, dead, he was alone in the world, and had need to look out for a fresh situation.

But he seemed rather slow to do this. He was not a very prepossessing person, it must be remembered, and there were not very many services for which he was fitted. Although upward of forty years of age, he was generally rather loosely described as a young man who understood all about horses, and this qualification was usually sufficient to procure for any individual whatever some kind of employment in the neighborhood of Doncaster. The softy seemed, however, rather to keep aloof from the people who knew and could have recommended him; and when asked why he did not seek a situation, gave evasive answers, and muttered something to the effect that he had saved a little bit of money at Mellish Park, and had no need to come upon the parish if he was out of work for a week or two.

John Mellish was so well known as a generous paymaster, that this was a matter of surprise to no one. Steevé Hargraves had no doubt had pretty pickings in that liberal household. So the softy went his way unquestioned, hanging about the town in a lounging, uncomfortable manner, sitting in some public-house tap-room half the day and night, drinking his meagre liquor in a sullen and unsocial style peculiar to himself, and consorting with no one.

He made his appearance at the railway station one day, and groped helplessly through all the time-tables pasted against the walls; but he could make nothing of them unaided, and was at last compelled to appeal to a good-tempered-looking official who was busy on the platform.

"I want th' Liverpool trayuns," he said, "and I can't find nowght about 'em here."

The official knew Mr. Hargraves, and looked at him with a stare of open wonder.

"My word! Steevé," he said, laughing, "what takes you to Liverpool? I thought you'd never been farther than York in your life."

"Maybe I have n't," the softy answered, sulkily; "but that's no reason I should n't go now. I've heard of a situation at Liverpool, as I think 'll suit me."

"Not better than the place you had with Mr. Mellish."

"Perhaps not," muttered Mr. Hargraves, with a frown darkening over his ugly face; "but Mellish Park be no pleace for me now, and arn't been for a long time past."

The railway official laughed.

The story of Aurora's chastisement of the half-witted groom was pretty well known among the towns-people of Doncaster, and I am sorry to say there were very few members of that sporting community who did not admire the mistress of Mellish Park something more by reason of this little incident in her history.

Mr. Hargraves received the desired information about the railway route between Doncaster and Liverpool, and then left the station.

A shabby-looking little man, who had also been making some inquiries of the same official who had talked to the softy, and had consequently heard the above brief dialogue, followed Stephen Hargraves from the station into the town Indeed, had it not been that the softy was unusually slow of perception, he might have discovered that upon this particular day the same shabby-looking little man generally happened to be hanging about any and every place to which he, Mr Hargraves, betook himself But the cast-off retainer of Mellish Park did not trouble himself with any such misgivings His narrow intellect, never wide enough to take in many subjects at a time, was fully absorbed by other considerations; and he loitered about with a gloomy and preoccupied expression on his face that by no means enhanced his personal attractions.

It is not to be supposed that Mr. Joseph Grimstone let the grass grow under his feet after his interview with John Mellish and Talbot Bulstrode He had heard enough to make his course pretty clear to him, and he went to work quietly and sagaciously to win the reward offered to him

There was not a tailor's shop in Doncaster or its vicinity into which the detective did not make his way There was not a garment *confectionnée* by any of the civil purveyors upon whom he intruded that Mr Grimstone did not examine not a drawer of odds and ends which he did not ransack, in his search for buttons by 'Crosby, maker, Birmingham" But for a long time he made his inquisition in vain Before the day succeeding that of Talbot's arrival at Mellish was over, the detective had visited every tailor or clothier in the neighborhood of the racing metropolis of the north, but no traces of " Crosby, maker, Birmingham," had he been able to find Brass waistcoat-buttons are not particularly affected by the leaders of the fashion in the present day, and Mr Grimstone found almost every variety of fastening upon the waistcoats he examined except that one special style of button, a specimen of which, out of shape and blood-stained, he carried deep in his trowsers-pocket

He was returning to the inn at which he had taken up his abode, and where he was supposed to be a traveller in the Glenfield starch and sugar-plum line, tired and worn out with a day's useless work, when he was attracted by the appearance of some ready-made garments gracefully festooned about the door of a Doncaster pawnbroker, who exhibited silver teaspoons, oil paintings, boots and shoes, dropsical watches, doubtful rings, and remnants of silk and satin in his artistically-arranged window

Mr Grimstone stopped short before the money-lender's portal.

" I won't be beaten," he muttered between his teeth " If this man has got any waistcoats, I 'll have a look at 'em "

He lounged into the shop in a leisurely manner, and asked the proprietor of the establishment if he had anything cheap in the way of fancy waistcoats

Of course the proprietor had everything desirable in that way, and from a kind of grove or arbor of all manner of dry goods at the back of the shop he brought out half a dozen brown-paper parcels, the contents of which he exhibited to Mr Joseph Grimstone

The detective looked at a great many waistcoats, but with no satisfactory result

" You have n't got anything with brass buttons, I suppose ?" he inquired at last

The proprietor shook his head reflectively

" Brass buttons a'n't much worn nowadays," he said , " but I 'll lay I 've got the very thing you want, now I come to think of it I got 'em an uncommon bargain from a traveller for a Birmingham house, who was here at the September meeting three years ago, and lost a hatful of money upon Underhand, and left a lot of things with me, in order to make up what he wanted "

Mr Grimstone pricked up his ears at the sound of " Birmingham " The pawnbroker retired once more to the mysterious caverns at the back of his shop, and, after a considerable search, succeeded in finding what he wanted He brought another brown-paper parcel to the counter, turned the flaming gas a little higher, and exhibited a heap of very gaudy and vulgar-looking waistcoats, evidently of that species of manufacture which is generally called slop-work.

" These are the goods," he said , " and very tasty and lively things they are, too I had a dozen of 'em , and I 've only got these five left "

Mr. Grimstone had taken up a waistcoat of a flaming check pattern, and was examining it by the light of the gas

Yes, the purpose of his day's work was accomplished at last The back of the brass buttons bore the name of Crosby, Birmingham

" You 've only got five left out of the dozen," said the detective ; " then you 've sold seven ?"

" I have '

" Can you remember who you sold 'em to ?"

The pawnbroker scratched his head thoughtfully.

" I think I must have sold 'em all to the men at the works," he said " They take their wages once a fortnight, and there 's some of 'em drop in here every other Saturday night to buy something or other, or to take something out of pledge I know I sold four or five that way "

" But can you remember selling one of them to anybody else ?" asked the detective 'I 'm not asking out of curiosity, and I d n't mind standing something handsome by and by, if you can give me the information I want. Think it over, now, and take your time. You could n't have sold 'em all seven to the men from the works."

"No, I did n't," answered the pawnbroker, after a pause. "I remember, now, I sold one of them—a fancy sprig on a purple ground—to Josephs, the baker in the next street; and I sold another—a yellow stripe on a brown ground — to the head gardener at Mellish Park."

Mr. Joseph Grimstone's face flushed hot and red. His day's work had not been wasted. He was bringing the buttons by Crosby of Birmingham very near to where he wanted to bring them.

"You can tell me the gardener's name, I suppose ?" he said to the pawnbroker.

"Yes; his name 's Dawson. He belongs to Doncaster, and he and I were boys together. I should not have remembered selling him the waistcoat, perhaps—for it 's nigh upon a year and a half ago — only he stopped and had a chat with me and my missis the night he bought it."

Mr. Grimstone did not linger much longer in the shop. His interest in the waistcoats was evidently departed. He bought a couple of second-hand silk handkerchiefs, out of civility, no doubt, and then bade the pawnbroker good-night.

It was nearly nine o'clock; but the detective only stopped at his inn long enough to eat about a pound and a quarter of beefsteak, and drink a pint of ale, after which brief refreshment he started for Mellish Park on foot. It was the principle of his life to avoid observation, and he preferred the fatigue of a long and lonely walk to the risks contingent upon hiring a vehicle to convey him to his destination.

Talbot and John had been waiting hopefully all the day for the detective's coming, and welcomed him very heartily when he appeared, between ten and eleven. He was shown into John's own room this evening, for the two gentlemen were sitting there smoking and talking after Aurora and Lucy had gone to bed. Mrs. Mellish had good need of rest, and could sleep peacefully now ; for the dark shadow between her and her husband had gone for ever, and she could not fear any peril, any sorrow, now that she knew herself to be secure of his love. John looked up eagerly as Mr. Grimstone followed the servant into the room; but a warning look from Talbot Bulstrode checked his impetuosity, and he waited till the door was shut before he spoke.

"Now, then, Grimstone," he said, "what news ?"

"Well, sir, I 've had a hard day's work," the detective answered, gravely, "and perhaps neither of you gentlemen—not being professional—would think much of what I 've done. But, for all that, I believe I 'm bring-

in' it home, sir; I believe I 'm bringing of it home."

"Thank God for that !" murmured Talbot Bulstrode, reverently.

He had thrown away his cigar, and was standing by the fireplace, with his arm resting upon the angle of the mantle-piece.

"You 've got a gardener by the name of Dawson in your service, Mr. Mellish ?" said the detective.

"I have," answered John; "but, Lord have mercy upon us! you don't mean to say you think it 's him. Dawson 's as good a fellow as ever breathed."

"I don't say I think it 's any one as yet, sir," Mr. Grimstone answered, sententiously ; "but when a man, as had two thousand pound upon him in bank-notes, is found in a wood shot through the heart, and the notes missin'—the wood bein' free to anybody as chose to walk in it—it 's a pretty open case for suspicion. I should like to see this man Dawson, if it 's convenient."

"To-night?" asked John.

"Yes; the sooner the better. The less delay there is in this sort of business, the more satisfactory for all parties — with the exception of the party that 's wanted," added the detective.

"I 'll send for Dawson, then," answered Mr. Mellish ; "but I expect he 'll have gone to bed by this time."

"Then he can but get up again, if he has, sir," Mr. Grimstone said, politely. "I 've set my heart upon seeing him to-night, if it 's all the same to you."

It is not to be supposed that John Mellish was likely to object to any arrangement which might hasten, if by but a moment's time, the hour of the discovery for which he so ardently prayed. He went straight off to the servants' hall to make inquiries for the gardener, and left Talbot Bulstrode and the detective together.

"There a'n't nothing turned up here, I suppose, sir," said Joseph Grimstone, addressing Mr. Bulstrode, "as will be of any help to us ?"

"Yes," Talbot answered; "we have got the numbers of the notes which Mrs. Mellish gave the murdered man. I telegraphed to Mr. Floyd's country-house, and he arrived here himself only an hour ago, bringing the list of the notes with him."

"And an uncommon plucky thing of the old gentleman to do, beggin' your pardon, sir," exclaimed the detective, with enthusiasm.

Five minutes afterward Mr. Mellish re-entered the room, bringing the gardener with him. The man had been into Doncaster to see his friends, and only returned about half an hour before ; so the master of the house had caught him in the act of making havoc with a formidable cold joint, and a great jar of pickled cabbage, in the servants' hall.

"Now, you 're not to be frightened, Dawson," said the young squire, with friendly indiscretion; "of course nobody for a moment suspects you any more than they suspect me, but this gentleman here wants to see you, and of course you know there 's no reason that he should n t see you, if he wishes it, though what he wants with you—"

Mr Mellish stopped abruptly, arrested by a frown from Talbot Bulstrode, and the gardener, who was innocent of the faintest comprehension of his master's meaning, pulled his hair respectfully, and shuffled nervously upon the slippery Indian matting.

"I only want to ask you a question or two to decide a wager between these two gentlemen and me, Mr Dawson," said the detective, with reassuring familiarity "You bought a second-hand waistcoat of Gogram, in the market-place, did n't you, about a year and a half ago?"

"Ay, sure, sir I bought a weskit at Gogram's," answered the gardener, "but it were n't second-hand—it were bran new "

"A yellow stripe upon a brown ground?"

The man nodded, with his mouth wide open, in the extremity of his surprise at this London stranger's familiarity with the details of his toilet

"I dunno how you come to know about that weskit, sir," he said, with a grin, 'it were wore out full six months ago, for I took to wearin' of 't in t' garden, and garden-work soon spiles anything in the way of clothes, but him as I give it to was glad enough to have it, though it was awful shabby "

"Him as you give it to?" repeated Mr Grimstone, not pausing to amend the sentence in his eagerness. "You gave it away, then?"

"Yees, I gave it to th' softy, and was n't the poor fond chap glad to get it, that 's all '"

"The softy '" exclaimed Mr. Grimstone. "Who 's the softy?"

"The man we spoke of last night," answered Talbot Bulstrode, "the man whom Mrs Mellish found in this room upon the morning before the murder — the man called Stephen Hargraves "

"Ay, ay, to be sure, I thought as much," murmured the detective "That will do, Mr Dawson," he added, addressing the gardener, who had shuffled a good deal nearer to the doorway in his uneasy state of mind "Stay, though, I may as well ask you one more question Were any of the buttons missing off that waistcoat when you gave it away?"

"Not one on 'em," answered the gardener, decisively "My missus is too particular for that She 's a reg'lar toidy one, she is, allers mendin' and patchin' and if one of t' buttons got loose, she was sure to sew it on toight again before it was lost "

"Thank you, Mr Dawson," returned the detective, with the friendly condescension of a superior being "Good-night "

The gardener shuffled off, very glad to be released from the awful presence of his superiors, and to go back to the cold meat and pickles in the servants' hall

"I think I m bringing the business into a nutshell, sir," said Mr Grimstone, when the door had closed upon the gardener "But the less said the better just yet a while I 'll take the list of the numbers of the notes, please, sir, and I believe I shall come upon you for that two hundred pound, Mr Mellish, before either of us is many weeks older "

So, with the list made by cautious Archibald Floyd bestowed safely in his waistcoat-pocket, Mr Joseph Grimstone walked back to Doncaster through the still summer's night, intent upon the business he had undertaken

"It looked uncommon black against the lady about a week ago," he thought, as he walked meditatively across the dewy grass in Mellish Park; "and I fancy the information they got at the Yard would have put a fool upon the wrong scent, and kept him on it till the right one got worn out But it 's clearing up—it 's clearing up beautiful, and I think it 'll turn out one of the neatest cases I ever had the handling of"

CHAPTER XXXVIII.

OFF THE SCENT.

It is scarcely necessary to say that with the button by Crosby in his pocket, and with the information acquired from Dawson, the gardener, stowed away carefully in his mind, Mr Joseph Grimstone looked with an eye of particular interest upon Steeve Hargraves, the softy

The detective had not come to Doncaster alone He had brought with him an humble ally and follower in the shape of the little shabby-looking man who had encountered the softy at the railway station, having received orders to keep a close watch upon Mr. Stephen Hargraves It was, of course, a very easy matter to identify the softy in the Town of Doncaster, where he had been pretty generally known since his childhood.

Mr. Grimstone had called upon a medical practitioner, and had submitted the button to him for inspection The stains upon it were indeed that which the detective had supposed, blood, and the surgeon detected a minute morsel of cartilage adhering to the jagged hasp of the button, but the same surgeon declared that this missile could not have been the only one used by the murderer of James Conyers It had not been through the dead man's body; it had inflicted only a surface wound

The business which now lay before Mr Grimstone was the tracing of one or other of the bank-notes and for this purpose he and his ally set to work upon the track of the softy, with a view of discovering all the places which it was his habit to visit. The haunts affected by Mr. Hargraves turned out to be some half-dozen very obscure public-houses, and to each of these Joseph Grimstone went in person.

But he could discover nothing. All his inquiries only elicited the fact that Stephen Hargraves had not been observed to change, or attempt to change, any bank-note whatever. He had paid for all he had had, and spent more than it was usual for him to spend, drinking a good deal harder than had been his habit theretofore; but he had paid in silver, except on one occasion, when he had changed a sovereign. The detective called at the bank; but no person answering the description of Stephen Hargraves had been observed there. The detective endeavored to discover any friends or companions of the softy; but here again he failed. The half-witted hanger-on of the Mellish stables had never made any friends, being entirely deficient in all social qualities.

There was something almost miraculous in the manner in which Mr. Joseph Grimstone contrived to make himself master of any information which he wished to acquire; and before noon on the day after his interview with Mr. Dawson, the gardener, he had managed to eliminate all the facts set down above, and had also succeeded in ingratiating himself into the confidence of the dirty old proprietress of that humble lodging in which the softy had taken up his abode.

It is scarcely necessary to this story to tell how the detective went to work; but while Stephen Hargraves sat soddening his stupid brain with medicated beer in a low tap-room not far off, and while Mr. Grimstone's ally kept close watch, holding himself in readiness to give warning of any movement on the part of the suspected individual, Mr. Grimstone himself went so cleverly to work in his manipulation of the softy's landlady, that in less than a quarter of an hour he had taken full possession of that weak point in the intellectual citadel which is commonly called the blind side, and was able to do what he pleased with the old woman and her wretched tenement.

His peculiar pleasure was to make a very elaborate examination of the apartment rented by the softy, and any other apartments, cupboards, or hiding-places to which Mr. Hargraves had access. But he found nothing to reward him for his trouble. The old woman was in the habit of receiving casual lodgers, resting for a night or so at Doncaster before tramping further on their vagabond wanderings; and the six-roomed dwelling-place was only furnished with such meagre accommodation as may be expected for fourpence and sixpence a night. There were few hiding-places. No carpets, underneath which fat bundles of bank-notes might be hidden; no picture-frames, behind which the same species of property might be bestowed; no ponderous cornices or heavily-fringed valances shrouding the windows, and affording dusty recesses wherein the title-deeds of half a dozen fortunes might lie and rot. There were two or three cupboards, into which Mr. Grimstone penetrated with a tallow candle; but he discovered nothing of any more importance than crockery-ware, lucifer-matches, firewood, potatoes, bare ropes, on which an onion lingered here and there, and sprouted dismally in its dark loneliness, empty ginger-beer bottles, oyster-shells, old boots and shoes, disabled mouse-traps, black beetles, and humid fungi rising ghost-like from the damp and darkness.

Mr. Grimstone emerged, dirty and discomfited, from one of these dark recesses after a profitless search which had occupied a couple of weary hours.

"Some other chap 'll go in and cut the ground under my feet, if I waste my time this way," thought the detective. "I 'm bless'd if I don't think I 've been a fool for my pains. The man carries the money about him, that 's clear as mud; and if I were to search Doncaster till my hair got gray, I should n't find what I want."

Mr. Grimstone shut the door of the last cupboard which he had examined with an impatient slam, and then turned toward the window. There was no sign of his scout in the little alley before the house, and he had time, therefore, for further business.

He had examined everything in the softy's apartment, and he had paid particular attention to the state of Mr. Hargraves' wardrobe, which consisted of a pile of garments, every one of which bore in its cut and fashion the stamp of a different individuality, and thereby proclaimed itself as having belonged to another master. There was a Newmarket coat of John Mellish's, and a pair of hunting-breeches, which could only have been built by the great Poole himself, split across the knees, but otherwise little the worse for wear. There was a linen jacket, and an old livery waistcoat that had belonged to one of the servants at the Park; odd tops of every shade known in the hunting-field, from the spotless white, or the delicate Champagne-cleaned color of the dandy, to the favorite vinegar hue of the hard-riding country squire; a groom's hat with a tarnished band and a battered crown; hobnailed boots, which might have belonged to Mr. Dawson; corduroy breeches, that could only have fitted a dropsical lodge-keeper long deceased; and there was one garment which bore upon it the ghastly impress of a dreadful deed, that had but lately been done. This was the velveteen shooting-coat worn by James Conyers, the trainer, which, pierced with the murderous bullet, and stiffened by the soaking torrent of blood, had been appropriated by Mr Stephen Hargraves in the confusion of the catastrophe All these things, with sundry rubbish in the way of odd spurs and whip-handles, scraps of broken harness, ends of rope, and such other scrapings as only a miser loves to accumulate, were packed in a lumbering trunk covered with mangy fur, and secured by about a dozen yards of knotted and jagged rope, tied about it in such a manner as the softy had considered sufficient to defy the most artful thief in Christendom

Mr. Grimstone had made very short work of all the elaborate defences in the way of knots and entanglements, and had ransacked the box from one end to the other; nay, had even closely examined the fur covering of the trunk, and had tested each separate brass-headed nail to ascertain if any of them had been removed or altered He may have thought it just possible that two thousand pounds worth of Bank of England paper had been nailed down under the mangy fur. He gave a weary sigh as he concluded his inspection, replaced the garments one by one in the trunk, re-knotted and secured the jagged cord, and turned his back upon the softy's chamber

"It 's no go" he thought "The yellow-striped waistcoat is n't among his clothes, and the money is n't hidden away anywhere Can he be deep enough to have destroyed that waistcoat, I wonder? He 'd got a red wool-len one on this morning perhaps he 's got the yellow-striped one under it'

Mr. Grimstone brushed the dust and cob-webs off his clothes, washed his hands in a greasy wooden bowl of scalding water which the old woman brought him, and then sat down before the fire, picking his teeth thought-fully, and with his eyebrows set in a reflective frown over his small gray eyes

"I don't like to be beat," he thought, "I don't like to be beat" He doubted if any magistrate would grant him a warrant against the softy upon the strength of the evidence in his possession—the blood-stained button by Crosby of Birmingham, and without a war-rant he could not search for the notes upon the person of the man he suspected He had sounded all the out-door servants at Mellish, but had been able to discover nothing that threw any light upon the movements of Ste-phen Hargraves on the night of the murder. No one remembered having seen him, no one had been on the southern side of the wood that night. One of the lads had passed the north lodge on his way from the high-road to the stables about the time at which Aurora had heard the shot fired in the wood, and had seen a light burning in the lower window, but this, of course, proved nothing either one way or the other

"If we could find the money upon him, thought Mr Grimstone, "it would 'be pretty strong proof of the robbery; and if we find

the waistcoat off which that button came in his possession, it would n't be bad evidence of the murder putting the two things together, but we shall have to keep a precious sharp watch upon my friend while we hunt up what we want, or I 'm bless'd if he won't give us the slip, and be off to Liverpool, and out of the country before we know where we are"

Now the truth of the matter is, that Mr Joseph Grimstone was not, perhaps, acting quite so conscientiously in this business as he might have done, had the love of justice in the abstract, and without any relation to sub-lunary reward, been the ruling principle of his life He might have had any help he pleased from the Doncaster constabulary, had he chosen to confide in the members of that force, but as a very knowing individual who owns a three-year old which he has reason to believe "a flyer" is apt to keep the capabili-ties of his horse a secret from his friends and the sporting public while he puts a "pot" of money upon the animal at enormous odds, so Mr Grimstone desired to keep his information to himself until it should have brought him its golden fruit, in the shape of a small reward from government and a large one from John Mellish

The detective had reason to know that the Dogberrys of Doncaster, misled by a duplicate of that very letter which had first aroused the attention of Scotland Yard, were on the wrong scent as he had been at first, and he was very well content to leave them where they were

"No," he thought, 'it 's a critical game, but I 'll play it single-handed, or, at least, with no one better than Tom Chivers to help me through with it; and a ten-pound note will satisfy him, if we win the day"

Pondering thus, Mr Grimstone departed after having recompensed the landlady for her civility by a donation which the old wom-an considered princely

He had entirely deluded her as to the ob-ject of his search, by telling her that he was a lawyer's clerk, commissioned by his employer to hunt for a codicil which had been hidden somewhere in that house by an old man who had lived in it in the year 1788, and he had contrived, in the course of conversation, to draw from the old woman, who was of a gar-rulous turn, all that she had to tell about the softy

It was not much, certainly. Mr Hargraves had never changed a bank-note with her knowledge He had paid for his bit of vict-uals as he had it, but had not spent a shilling a day As to bank-notes, it was n't at all likely that he had any of them; for he was always complaining that he was very poor, and that his little bit of wages scraped together out of his wages would n't last him long.

'The Hargraves is a precious deep 'un, for all they call him soft,' thought Mr. Grimstone.

as he left the lodging-house, and walked slowly toward the sporting-public at which he had left the softy under the watchful eye of Mr. Tom Chivers. "I 've often heard say that these half-witted chaps have more cunning in their little fingers than a better man has in the whole of his composition. Another man would never have been able to stand against the temptation of changing one of those notes; or would have gone about wearing that identical waistcoat; or would have made a bolt of it the day after the murder; or tried on something or another that would have blown the gaff upon him; but not your softy! He hides the notes, and he hides the waistcoat, and then he laughs in his sleeve at those that want him, and sits drinking his beer as comfortably as you please."

Pondering thus, the detective made his way to the public-house in which he had left Mr. Stephen Hargraves. He ordered a glass of brandy and water at the bar, and walked into the tap-room, expecting to see the softy still brooding sullenly over his drink, still guarded by the apparently indifferent eye of Mr. Chivers. But it was not so. The tap-room was empty; and, upon making cautious inquiries, Mr. Grimstone ascertained that the softy and his watcher had been gone for upward of an hour.

Mr. Chivers had been forbidden to let his charge out of sight under any circumstances whatever, except, indeed, if the softy had turned homeward while Mr. Grimstone was employed in ransacking his domicile, in which event Tom was to have slipped on a few paces before him, and given warning to his chief. Wherever Stephen Hargraves went, Mr. Thomas Chivers was to follow him; but he was, above all, to act in such a manner as would effectually prevent any suspicion arising in the softy's mind as to the fact that he was followed.

It will be seen, therefore, that poor Chivers had no very easy task to perform, and it has been seen that he had heretofore contrived to perform it pretty skilfully. If Stephen Hargraves sat boozing in a tap-room half the day, Mr. Chivers was also to booze, or to make a pretence of boozing, for the same length of time. If the softy showed a disposition to be social, and gave his companion any opportunity of getting friendly with him, the detective's underling was to employ his utmost skill and discretion in availing himself of that golden chance. It is a wondrous provision of Providence that the treachery which would be hateful and horrible in any other man, is considered perfectly legitimate in the man who is employed to hunt out a murderer or a thief. The vile instruments which the criminal employed against his unsuspecting victim are in due time used against himself; and the wretch who laughed at the poor unsuspecting dupe who was trapped to his destruction by *his* lies, is caught in his turn by some shallow deceit or pitifully-hackneyed device of the paid spy, who has been bribed to lure him to his doom. For the outlaw of society, the code of honor is null and void. His existence is a perpetual peril to innocent women and honorable men; and the detective who beguiles him to his end does such a service to society as must doubtless counterbalance the treachery of the means by which it is done. The days of Jonathan Wild and his compeers are over, and the thief-taker no longer begins life as a thief. The detective officer is as honest as he is intrepid and astute, and it is not his own fault if the dirty nature of all crime gives him now and then dirty work to do.

But Mr. Stephen Hargraves did not give the opportunity for which Tom Chivers had been bidden to lie in wait; he sat sullen, silent, stupid, unapproachable; and as Tom's orders were not to force himself upon his companion, he was fain to abandon all thought of worming himself into the softy's good graces. This made the task of watching him all the more difficult. It is not such a very easy matter to follow a man without seeming to follow him.

It was market-day too, and the town was crowded with noisy country people. Mr. Grimstone suddenly remembered this, and the recollection by no means added to his peace of mind.

"Chivers never did sell me," he thought, "and surely he won't do it now. I dare say they 're safe enough, for the matter of that, in some other public. I 'll slip out and look after them."

Mr. Grimstone had, as I have said, already made himself acquainted with all the haunts affected by the softy. It did not take him long, therefore, to look in at the three or four public-houses where Steeve Hargraves was likely to be found, and to discover that he was not there.

"He 's slouching about the town somewhere or other, I dare say," thought the detective, "with my mate close upon his heels. I 'll stroll toward the market-place, and see if I can find them anywhere that way."

Mr. Grimstone turned out of the by-street in which he had been walking into a narrow alley leading to the broad open square upon which the market-place stands.

The detective went his way in a leisurely manner, with his hands in his pockets and a cigar in his mouth. He had perfect confidence in Mr. Thomas Chivers, and the crowded state of the market-place and its neighborhood in no way weakened his sense of security.

"Chivers will stick to him through thick and thin," he thought; "he 'd keep an eye upon his man if he had to look after him between Charing Cross and Whitehall when the queen was going to open Parliament. He's not the man to be flummaxed by a crowd in a country market-place."

Serene in this sense of security, Mr. Grimstone amused himself by looking about him, with an expression of somewhat supercilious wonder, at the manners and customs of those indigenæ who, upon market-day, make their inroad into the quiet town. He paused upon the edge of a little sunken flight of worn steps leading down to the stage-door of the theatre, and read the fragments of old bills mouldering upon the door-posts and lintel. There were glowing announcements of dramatic performances that had long ago taken place; and, above the rain and mud-stained relics of the past, in bold black lettering, appeared the record of a drama as terrible as any that had ever been enacted in that provincial theatre. The bill-sticker had posted the announcement of the reward offered by John Mellish for the discovery of the murderer in every available spot, and had not forgotten this position, which commanded one of the entrances to the market-place.

"It's a wonder to me," muttered Mr. Grimstone, "that that blessed bill should n't have opened the eyes of these Doncaster noodles. But I dare say they think it 's a blind; a planned thing to throw 'em off the scent their clever noses are sticking to so determined. If I can get *my* man before they open their eyes, I shall have such a haul as I have n't met with lately."

Musing thus pleasantly, Mr. Grimstone turned his back upon the theatre, and crossed over to the market. Within the building the clamor of buying and selling was at its height: noisy countrymen chaffering in their northern *patois* upon the value and merits of poultry, butter, and eggs; dealers in butchers' meat bewildering themselves in the endeavor to simultaneously satisfy the demands of half a dozen sharp and bargain-loving housekeepers; while from without there came a confused clatter of other merchants and other customers, clamoring and hustling round the stalls of green grocers, and the slimy barrows of blue-jacketed fishmongers. In the midst of all this bustle and confusion, Mr. Grimstone came suddenly upon his trusted ally, pale, terror-stricken, and—ALONE!

The detective's mind was not slow to grasp the full force of the situation.

"You 've lost him!" he whispered fiercely, seizing the unfortunate Mr. Chivers by the collar, and pinning him as securely as if he had serious thoughts of making him a permanent fixture upon the stone flags of the market-place. "You 've lost him, Tom Chivers!" he continued, hoarse with agitation. "You 've lost the party that I told you was worth more to me than any other party I ever gave you the office for. You 've lost me the best chance I 've ever had since I 've been in Scot-

land Yard, and yourself too; for I should have acted liberal by you," added the detective, apparently oblivious of that morning's reverie, in which he had predetermined offering his assistant ten pounds, in satisfaction of all his claims—"I should have acted liberal by you, Tom. But what 's the use of standing jawing here? You come along with me; you can tell me how it happened as we go."

With his powerful grasp still on the underling's collar, Mr. Grimstone walked out of the market-place, neither looking to the right nor the left, though many a pair of rustic eyes opened to their widest as he passed, attracted no doubt by the rapidity of his pace and the obvious determination of his manner. Perhaps those rustic by-standers thought that the stern-looking gentleman in the black frock-coat had arrested the shabby little man in the act of picking his pocket, and was bearing him off to deliver him straight into the hands of justice.

Mr. Grimstone released his grasp when he and his companion had got clear of the market-place.

"Now," he said, breathless, but not slackening his pace, "now I suppose you can tell me how you come to make such an"—inadmissible adjective—"fool of yourself? Never you mind where I 'm goin'. I 'm goin' to the railway station. Never you mind why I 'm goin' there. You 'd guess why if you were n't a fool. Now tell me all about it, can't you?"

"It a'n't much to tell," the humble follower gasped, his respiratory functions sadly tried by the pace at which his superior went over the ground. "It a'n't much. I followed your instructions faithful. I tried, artful and quiet-like, to make acquaintance with him, but that warn't a bit of good. He was as surly as a bull-terrier, so I did n't force him to it, but kept an eye upon him, and let out before him as it was racin' business as had brought me to Doncaster, and as I was here to look after a horse, what was in trainin' a few miles off, for a gent in London; and when he left the public I went after him, but not conspikiwous. But I think from that minute he was fly, for he did n't go three steps without lookin' back, and he led me such a chase as made my legs tremble under me, which they trembles at this moment; and then he gets me into the market-place, and he dodges here, and he dodges there, and wherever the crowd 's thickest he dodges most, till he gets me at last in among a ring of market-people round a couple o' coves a millin' with each other, and there I loses him. And I 've been in and out the market, and here and there, until I 'm fit to drop, but it a'n't no good; and you 've no call to lay the blame on me, for mortal man could n't have done more."

Mr. Chivers wiped the perspiration from his face in testimony of his exertions. Dirty little streams were rolling down his forehead and trickling upon his poor faded cheeks. He mopped up these evidences of his fatigue with a red cotton handkerchief, and gave a deprecatory sigh.

"If there's anybody to lay blame on, it a'n't me," he said, mildly. "I said all along you ought to have had help. A man as is on his own ground, and knows his own ground, is more than a match for one cove, however hard he may work."

The detective turned fiercely upon his meek dependent.

"Who's blaming you?" he cried, impatiently. "I would n't cry out before I was hurt, if I were you."

They had reached the railway station by this time.

"How long is it since you missed him?" asked Mr. Grimstone of the penitent Chivers.

"Three-quarters of an hour, or it may be a hour," Tom added, doubtfully.

"I dare say it *is* an hour," muttered the detective.

He walked straight to one of the chief officials, and asked what trains had left within the last hour.

"Two, both market trains; one eastward, Selby way, the other for Penistone and the intervening stations."

The detective looked at the time-table, running his thumb-nail along the names of the stations.

"That train will reach Penistone in time to catch the Liverpool train, won't it?" he asked.

"Just about."

"What time did it go?"

"The Penistone train?"

"Yes."

"About half an hour ago — at 2.30."

The clocks had struck three as Mr. Grimstone made his way to the station.

"Half an hour ago," muttered the detective. "He'd have had ample time to catch the train after giving Chivers the slip."

He questioned the guards and porters as to whether any of them had seen a man answering to the description of the softy: a white-faced, humpbacked fellow, in corduroys and a fustian jacket; and even penetrated into the ticket-clerk's office to ask the same question.

No; none of them had seen Mr. Stephen Hargraves. Two or three of them recognized him by the detective's description, and asked if it was one of the stable-men from Mellish Park that the gentleman was inquiring after. Mr. Grimstone rather evaded any direct answer to this question. Secrecy was, as we know, the principle upon which he conducted his affairs.

"He may have contrived to give 'em all the slip," he said, confidentially, to his faithful but dispirited ally. "He may have got off without any of 'em seeing him. He's got the money about him, I'm all but certain of that, and his game is to get off to Liverpool. His inquiries after the trains yesterday proves that. Now I might telegraph, and have him stopped at Liverpool — supposing him to have given us all the slip, and gone off there — if I like to let others into the game; but I don't. I'll play to win or lose; but I'll play single-handed. He may try another dodge, and get off Hull way by the canal-boats that the market-people use, and then slip across to Hamborough, or something of that sort; but that a'n't likely — these fellows always go one way. It seems as if the minute a man has taken another man's life, or forged his name, or embezzled his money, his ideas gets fixed in one groove, and never can soar higher than Liverpool and the American packet."

Mr. Chivers listened respectfully to his patron's communications. He was very well pleased to see the serenity of his employer's mind gradually returning.

"Now, I'll tell you what, Tom," said Mr. Grimstone. "If this chap has given us the slip, why he's given us the slip, and he's got a start of us which we shan't be able to pick up till half-past ten o'clock to-night, when there's a train that'll take us to Liverpool. If he *has* n't given us the slip, there's only one way he can leave Doncaster, and that's by this station; so you stay here patient and quiet, till you see me, or hear from me. If he is in Doncaster, I'm jiggered if I don't find him."

With which powerful asseveration Mr. Grimstone walked away, leaving his scout to keep watch for the possible coming of the softy.

CHAPTER XXXIX.

TALBOT BULSTRODE MAKES ATONEMENT FOR THE PAST.

John Mellish and Talbot Bulstrode walked to and fro upon the lawn before the drawing-room windows on that afternoon on which the detective and his underling lost sight of Stephen Hargraves. It was a dreary time, this period of watching and waiting, of uncertainty and apprehension, and poor John Mellish chafed bitterly under the burden which he had to bear.

Now that his friend's common sense had come to his relief, and that a few plain, outspoken sentences had dispersed the terrible cloud of mystery, now that he himself was fully assured of his wife's innocence, he had no patience with the stupid country people who held themselves aloof from the woman he loved. He wanted to go out and do battle for his slandered wife; to hurl back every base suspicion into the faces that had scowled upon his idolized Aurora. How could they dare, these foul-minded slanderers, to harbor one base thought against the purest, the most perfect of women? Mr Mellish, of course, quite forgot that he, the rightful defender of all this perfection, had suffered his mind to be for a time obscured beneath the black shadow of that vile suspicion

He hated the old friends of his youth for their base avoidance of him, the servants of his household for a half-doubtful, half-solemn expression of face, which he knew had relation to that growing suspicion, that horrible suspicion, which seemed to grow stronger with every hour He broke out into a storm of rage with the gray-haired butler, who had carried him pickapack in his infancy, because the faithful retainer tried to hold back certain newspapers which contained dark allusions to the Mellish mystery

'Who told you I did n't want the *Manchester Guardian*, Jarvis?" he cried, fiercely, "who gave you the right to dictate what I 'm to read or what I 'm to leave unread? I do want to-day's *Guardian*, to-day's, and yesterday's, and to-morrow's, and every other newspaper that comes into this house! I won't have them overhauled by you, or any one, to see whether they re pleasant reading or not, before they 're brought to me Do you think *I 'm* afraid of anything these penny-a-liner fellows can write?" roared the young squire, striking his open hand upon the table at which he sat "Let them write then best or their worst of me But let them write one word that can be twisted into an insinuation upon the purest and truest woman in all Christendom, and, by the Heaven above me, I 'll give them such a thrashing — penny-a-liners, printers, publishers, and every man-Jack of them — as shall make them remember the business to the last hour of their lives!"

Mr. Mellish said all this in despite of the restraining presence of Talbot Bulstrode Indeed, the young member for Penruth had by no means a pleasant time of it during those few days of anxiety and suspense A keeper set to watch over a hearty young jungle tiger, and bidden to prevent the noble animal from committing any imprudence, might have found his work little harder than that which Mr Bulstrode did, patiently and uncomplainingly, for pure friendship's sake

John Mellish roamed about in the custody of this friendly keeper, with his short auburn hair tumbled into a feverish-looking mass, like a field of ripening corn that had been beaten by a summer hurricane, his cheeks sunken and haggard, and a bristling yellow stubble upon his chin I dare say he had made a vow neither to shave nor be shaven until the murd͟ .r of Jam͟s C͟ , .l be found He .an͟ .spe͟ra ͟, . . Bulstrode, but .. cl͟v͟ with .f. w͟i͟ .e peration to the det͟.tiv , th. p.d͟ . . .rt

criminal-hunter, who had, in a manner, tacitly pledged himself to the discovery of the real homicide

All through the fitful August day, now hot and still, now overclouded and showery, the master of Mellish Park went hither and thither — now sitting in his study, now roaming out on the lawn, now pacing up and down the drawing-room, displacing, disarranging, and overturning the pretty furniture, now wandering up and down the staircase, lolling on the landing-places, and patrolling the corridor outside the rooms in which Lucy and Aurora sat together, making a show of employing themselves, but only waiting, waiting, waiting for the hoped-for end.

Poor John scarcely cared to meet that dearly-loved wife, for the great earnest eyes that looked in his face always asked the same question so plainly — always appealed so piteously for the answer that could not be given

It was a weary and a bitter time I wonder, as I write of it, when I think of a quiet Somersetshire household in which a dreadful deed was done — the secret of which has never yet been brought to light, and perhaps never will be revealed until the Day of Judgment — what must have been suffered by each member of *that* family? What slow agonies, what ever-increasing tortures, while that cruel mystery was the "sensation" topic of conversation in a thousand happy home circles, in a thousand tavern parlors and pleasant club-rooms — a common and ever-interesting topic, by means of which travellers in first-class railway carriages might break down the ceremonial icebergs which surround each travelling Englishman, and grow friendly and confidential, a safe topic, upon which even tacit enemies might talk pleasantly without fear of wrecking themselves upon hidden rocks of personal insinuation God help that household, or any such household, through the weary time of waiting which it may please Him to appoint, until that day in which it shall be His good pleasure to reveal the truth! God help all patient creatures laboring under the burden of an unjust suspicion, and support them unto the end!

John Mellish chafed and fretted himself ceaselessly all through that August day at the nonappearance of the detective Why did n't he come? He had promised to bring or send them news of his proceedings Talbot in vain assured his friend that Mr Grimstone was no doubt hard at work, that such a discovery as he had to make was not to be made in a day, and that Mr Mellish had nothing to do but to make himself as comfortable as he could, and wait quietly for the event he . . .f .r'

. . . . John," Mr b͟. . . . . l͟, . ͟ it I ͟.d not be-
. . .͟rt ͟ { .. w͟ . m n Gr͟mstone be-

lieves—that we are upon the right track, and are pretty sure to bring the crime home to the wretch who committed it. You can do nothing but be patient, and wait the result of Grimstone's labors."

"Yes," cried John Mellish; "and, in the meantime, all these people are to say cruel things of my darling, and keep aloof from her, and— No, I can't bear it, Talbot, I can't bear it. I 'll turn my back upon this confounded place. I 'll sell it; I 'll burn it down; I 'll—I 'll do anything to get away, and take my precious one from the wretches who have slandered her!"

"That you shall not do, John Mellish," exclaimed Talbot Bulstrode, "until the murderer of James Conyers has been discovered. Go away then as soon as you like, for the associations of this place can not be otherwise than disagreeable to you—for a time, at least. But, until the truth is out, you must remain here. If there is any foul suspicion against Aurora, her presence here will best give the lie to that suspicion. It was her hurried journey to London which first set people talking of her, I dare say," added Mr. Bulstrode, who was, of course, entirely ignorant of the fact that an anonymous letter from Mrs. Powell had originally aroused the suspicions of the Doncaster constabulary.

So through the long summer's day Talbot reasoned with and comforted his friend, never growing weary of his task, never for one moment losing sight of the interests of Aurora Mellish and her husband.

Perhaps this was a self-imposed penalty for the wrong which he had done the banker's daughter long ago in the dim starlit chamber at Felden. If it was so, he did penance very cheerfully.

"Heaven knows how gladly I would do her a service," he thought; "her life has been a troubled one, in spite of her father's thousands. Thank Heaven, my poor little Lucy has never been forced into playing the heroine of a tragedy like this; thank Heaven, my poor little darling's life flows evenly and placidly in a smooth channel."

He could not but reflect with something of a shudder that it might have been his wife whose history was being canvassed throughout the West Riding. He could not be otherwise than pleased to remember that the name of the woman he had chosen had never gone beyond the holy circle of her own home, to be the common talk among strangers.

There are things which are utterly unendurable to some people, but which are not at all terrible in the eyes of others. John Mellish, secure in his own belief in his wife's innocence, would have been content to carry her away with him, after razing the home of his forefathers to the ground, and defying all Yorkshire to find flaw or speck upon her fair fame. But Talbot Bulstrode would have gone

mad with the agony of the thought that common tongues had defiled the name he loved, and would, in no after-triumph of his wife's innocence, have been able to forget or to recover from the torture of that unendurable agony. There are people who can not forget, and Talbot Bulstrode was one of them. He had never forgotten his Christmas agony at Felden Woods, and the after-struggle at Bulstrode Castle; nor did he ever hope to forget it. The happiness of the present, pure and unalloyed though it was, could not annihilate the anguish of the past. That stood alone—so many months, weeks, days, and hours of unutterable misery riven away from the rest of his life, to remain for ever a stony memorial upon the smooth plains of the past.

Archibald Martin Floyd sat with his daughter and Lucy in Mrs. Mellish's morning-room, the pleasantest chamber for many reasons, but chiefly because it was removed from the bustle of the house, and from the chance of unwelcome intrusion. All the troubles of that household had been made light of in the presence of the old man, and no word had been dropped before him which could give him reason to guess that his only child had been suspected of the most fearful crime that man or woman can commit. But Archibald Floyd was not easily to be deceived where his daughter's happiness was in question; he had watched that beautiful face, whose ever-varying expression was its highest charm, so long and earnestly, as to have grown familiar with its every look. No shadow upon the brightness of his daughter's beauty could possibly escape the old man's eyes, dim as they may have grown for the figures in his banking-book. It was Aurora's business, therefore, to sit by her father's side in the pleasant morning-room, to talk to him and amuse him, while John rambled hither and thither, and made himself otherwise tiresome to his patient companion, Talbot Bulstrode. Mrs. Mellish repeated to her father again and again that there was no cause for uneasiness; they were merely anxious—naturally anxious—that the guilty man should be found and brought to justice—nothing more.

The banker accepted this explanation of his daughter's pale face very quietly; but he was not the less anxious—anxious he scarcely knew why, but with the shadow of a dark cloud hanging over him that was not to be driven away.

Thus the long August day wore itself out, and the low sun—blazing a lurid red behind the trees in Mellish Wood, until it made that pool beside which the murdered man had fallen seem a pool of blood—gave warning that one weary day of watching and suspense was nearly done.

John Mellish, far too restless to sit long at dessert, had roamed out upon the lawn, still attended by his indefatigable keeper, Talbot

Bulstrode, and employed himself in pacing up and down the smooth grass amid Mr Dawson's flower-beds, looking always toward the pathway that led to the house, and breathing suppressed anathemas against the dilatory detective

"One day nearly gone, thank Heaven, Talbot!" he said, with an impatient sigh "Will to-morrow bring us no nearer to what we want, I wonder? What if it should go on like this for long? what if it should go on for ever, until Aurora and I go mad with this wretched anxiety and suspense? Yes, I know you think me a fool and a coward, Talbot Bulstrode, but I can't bear it quietly, I tell you I can't. I know there are some people who can shut themselves up with their troubles, and sit down quietly and suffer without a groan; but I can't. I must cry out when I am tortured, or I should dash my brains out against the first wall I came to, and make an end of it. To think that anybody should suspect my darling! to think that they should believe her to be—"

"To think that _you_ should have believed it, John!" said Mr Bulstrode, gravely.

'Ah! there 's the cruelest stab of all,' cried John, "if _I_—I, who know her, and love her, and believe in her as man never yet believed in woman—if _I_ could have been bewildered and maddened by that horrible chain of cruel circumstances, every one of which pointed—Heaven help me!—at her—if _I_ could be deluded by these things until my brain reeled, and I went nearly mad with doubting my own dearest love, what may strangers think—strangers who neither know nor love her, but who are only too ready to believe anything unnaturally infamous? Talbot I _won't_ endure this any longer. I'll ride into Doncaster and see this man Grimstone. He _must_ have done some good to-day. I'll go at once."

Mr. Mellish would have walked straight off to the stables, but Talbot Bulstrode caught him by the arm.

"You may miss the man on the road, John," he said. "He came last night after dark, and may come as late to-night. There's no knowing whether he'll come by the road, or the short cut across the fields. You're as likely to miss him as not."

Mr. Mellish hesitated.

"He may n't come at all to-night," he said, "and I tell you I can't bear this suspense."

"Let _me_ ride into Doncaster, then, John," urged Talbot, "and you stay here to receive Grimstone if he should come."

Mr. Mellish was considerably mollified by this proposition.

"Will you ride into the town, Talbot?" he said. "Upon my word, it's very kind of you to propose it. I should n't like to miss this man upon any account, but, at the same time, I don't feel inclined to wait for the chance of his coming or staying away. I'm afraid I'm a great nuisance to you, Bulstrode."

"Not a bit of it," answered Talbot, with a smile.

Perhaps he smiled involuntarily at the notion of how little John Mellish knew what a nuisance he had been through that weary day.

"I'll go with very great pleasure, John," he said, "if you'll tell them to saddle a horse for me."

"To be sure, you shall have Red Rover, my covert hack. We'll go round to the stables, and see about him at once."

The truth of the matter is, Talbot Bulstrode was very well pleased to hunt up the detective himself, rather than that John Mellish should execute that errand in person, for it would have been about as easy for the young squire to have translated a number of the _Sporting Magazine_ into Porsonian Greek, as to have kept a secret for half an hour, however earnestly entreated, or however conscientiously determined to do so.

Mr Bulstrode had made it his particular business, therefore, during the whole of that day, to keep his friend as much as possible out of the way of every living creature, fully aware that Mr Mellish's manner would most certainly betray him to the least observant eyes that might chance to fall upon him.

Red Rover was saddled, and, after twenty loudly-whispered injunctions from John, Talbot Bulstrode rode away in the evening sunlight. The nearest way from the stables to the high-road took him past the north lodge. It had been shut up since the day of the trainer's funeral, such furniture as it contained left to become a prey to moths and rats, for the Mellish servants were a great deal too superstitiously impressed with the story of the murder to dream of readmitting those goods and chattels which had been selected for Mr. Conyers' accommodation to the garrets whence they had been taken. The door had been locked, therefore, and the key given to Dawson, the gardener, who was to be once more free to use the place as a storehouse for roots and matting, superannuated cucumber-frames, and crippled garden-tools.

The place looked dreary enough, though the low sun made a gorgeous illumination upon one of the latticed windows that faced the crimson west, and though the last leaves of the roses were still lying upon the long grass in the patch of garden before the door, out of which Mr Conyers had gone to his last resting-place. One of the stable-boys had accompanied Mr. Bulstrode to the lodge in order to open the rusty iron gates, which hung loosely on their hinges, and were never locked.

Talbot rode at a brisk pace into Doncaster, never drawing rein until he reached the little inn at which the detective had taken up his quarters. Mr Grimstone had been snatching a hasty refreshment, after a weary and use-less perambulation about the town, and came out with his mouth full to speak to Mr. Bul-strode. But he took very good care not to confess that since three o'clock that day nei-ther he nor his ally had seen or heard of Mr. Stephen Hargraves, or that he was actually no nearer the discovery of the murderer than he had been at eleven o'clock upon the pre-vious night, when he had discovered the orig-inal proprietor of the fancy waistcoat, with buttons by Crosby, Birmingham, in the per-son of Dawson, the gardener.

"I 'm not losing any time, sir," he said, in answer to Talbot's inquiries; "my sort of work 's quiet work, and don't make no show till it 's done. I 've reason to think the man we want is in Doncaster; so I stick in Don-caster, and mean to, till I lay my hand upon him—unless I should get information as would point farther off. Tell Mr. Mellish I 'm doing my duty, sir, and doing it conscientious; and that I shall neither eat, nor drink, nor sleep more than just as much as 'll keep human nat-ure together, until I 've done what I 've set my mind on doing."

"But you 've discovered nothing fresh, then ?" said Talbot; "you 've nothing new to tell me ?"

"Whatever I 've discovered is neither here nor there yet a while, sir," answered the de-tective, vaguely. "You keep your heart up, and tell Mr. Mellish to keep his heart up, and trust in me."

Talbot Bulstrode was obliged to be content with this rather doubtful comfort. It was not much, certainly, but he determined to make the best of it to John Mellish.

He rode out of Doncaster, past the "Rein-deer" and the white-fronted houses of the wealthier citizens of that prosperous borough, and away upon the smooth high-road. The faint shimmer of the pale early moonlight lit up the tree-tops to right and left of him as he left the suburb behind, and made the road ghostly beneath his horse's feet. He was in no very hopeful humor, after his interview with Mr. Grimstone, and he knew that hun-gry-eyed members of the Doncaster constabu-lary were keeping stealthy watch upon every creature in the Mellish household, and that the slanderous tongues of a greedy public were swelling into a loud and ominous mur-mur against the wife John loved. Every hour, every moment, was of vital importance. A hundred perils menaced them on every side. What might they not have to dread from eager busybodies, anxious to distinguish themselves, and proud of being the first to circulate a foul scandal against the lovely daughter of one of the richest men upon the Stock Exchange ? Hayward, the coroner, and Lofthouse, the rector, both knew the se-cret of Aurora's life; and it would be little wonder if, looking at the trainer's death by

the light of that knowledge, they believed her guilty of some share in the ghastly busi-ness which had terminated the trainer's ser-vice at Mellish Park.

What if, by some horrible fatality, the guilty man should escape, and the truth never be revealed. For ever and for ever, until her blighted name should be written upon a tomb-stone, Aurora Mellish must rest under the shadow of this suspicion. Could there be any doubt that the sensitive and highly-strung nature would give way under the unendura-ble burden ? that the proud heart would break beneath the undeserved disgrace ? What misery for her! and not for her alone, but for every one who loved her, or had any share in her history. Heaven pardon the selfishness that prompted the thought, if Talbot Bul-strode remembered that he would have some part in that bitter disgrace; that his name was allied, if only remotely, with that of his wife's cousin; and that the shame which would make the name of Mellish a by-word must also cast some slur upon the escutcheon of the Bulstrodes. Sir Bernard Burke, com-piling the romance of the county families, would tell that cruel story, and, hinting cau-tiously at Aurora's guilt, would scarcely fail to add, that the suspected lady's cousin had married Talbot Raleigh Bulstrode, Esq., el-dest son and heir of Sir John Walter Raleigh Bulstrode, Baronet, of Bulstrode Castle, Corn-wall.

Now, although the detective had affected a hopeful and even mysterious manner in his brief interview with Talbot, he had not suc-ceeded in hoodwinking that gentleman, who had a vague suspicion that all was not quite right, and that Mr. Joseph Grimstone was by no means so certain of success as he pretend-ed to be.

"It 's my firm belief that this man Har-graves has given him the slip," Talbot thought. "He said something about believing him to be in Doncaster, and then the next moment add-ed that he might be farther off. It 's clear, therefore, that Grimstone does n't know where he is; and in that case, it 's as likely as not that the man 's made off with his money, and will get away from England in spite of us. If he does this — "

Mr. Bulstrode did not finish the sentence. He had reached the north lodge, and dis-mounted to open the iron gate. The lights of the house shone hospitably far away be-yond the wood, and the voices of some men about the stable-gates sounded faintly in the distance; but the north lodge and the neg-lected shrubbery around it were as silent as the grave, and had a certain phantom-like air in the dim moonlight.

Talbot led his horse through the gates. He looked up at the windows of the lodge as he passed, half involuntarily; but he stopped with a suppressed exclamation of surprise at the sight of a feeble glimmer, which was not the moonlight, in the window of that upper chamber in which the murdered man had slept. Before that exclamation had wellnigh crossed his lips the light had disappeared.

If any one of the Mellish grooms or stable-boys had beheld that brief apparition, he would have incontinently taken to his heels, and rushed breathless to the stables, with a wild story of some supernatural horror in the north lodge; but Mr Bulstrode, being altogether of another mettle, walked softly on, still leading his horse, until he was well out of earshot of any one within the lodge, when he stopped and tied the Red Rover's bridle to a tree, and turned back toward the north gates, leaving the corn-fed covert hack cropping greedily at dewy hazel-twigs, and any green meat within his reach.

The heir of Sir John Walter Raleigh Bulstrode crept back to the lodge almost as noiselessly as if he had been educated for Mr Grimstone's profession, choosing the grassy pathway beneath the trees for his cautious footsteps. As he approached the wooden paling that shut in the little garden of the lodge, the light which had been so suddenly extinguished reappeared behind the white curtain of the upper window.

'It 's queer!' mused Mr Bulstrode, as he watched the feeble glimmer; "but I dare say there 's nothing in it. The associations of this place are strong enough to make one attach a foolish importance to anything connected with it. I think I heard John say the gardeners keep their tools there, and I suppose it 's one of them. But it 's late, too, for any of them to be at work."

It had struck ten while Mr Bulstrode rode homeward, and it was more than unlikely that any of the Mellish servants would be out at such a time.

Talbot lingered by the wicket-gate, irresolute as to what he should do next, but thoroughly determined to see the last of this late visitor at the north lodge, when the shadow of a man flitted across the white curtain — a shadow even more weird and ungainly than such things are — the shadow of a man with a humpback!

Talbot Bulstrode uttered no cry of surprise; but his heart knocked furiously against his ribs, and the blood rushed hotly to his face. He never remembered having seen the softy, but he had always heard him described as a humpbacked man. There could be no doubt of the shadow's identity; there could be still less doubt that Stephen Hargraves had visited that place for no good purpose. What could bring him there — to that place above all other places, which, if he were indeed guilty, he would surely most desire to avoid? Stolid, semi-idiotic as he was supposed to be, surely the common terrors of the lowest assassin, half brute, half Caliban, would

keep him away from that spot. These thoughts did not occupy more than those few moments in which the violent beating of Talbot Bulstrode's heart held him powerless to move or act; then, pushing open the gate, he rushed across the tiny garden, trampling recklessly upon the neglected flower-beds, and softly tried the door. It was firmly secured with a heavy chain and padlock.

'He has got in at the window, then,' thought Mr Bulstrode. "What, in Heaven's name, could be his motive in coming here?"

Talbot was right. The little lattice-window had been wrenched nearly off its hinges, and hung loosely among the tangled foliage that surrounded it. Mr Bulstrode did not hesitate a moment before he plunged head foremost into the narrow aperture through which the softy must have found his way, and scrambled as he could into the little room. The lattice strained still farther, dropped, with a crashing noise, behind him, but not soon enough to serve as a warning for Stephen Hargraves, who appeared upon the lowest step of the tiny corkscrew staircase at the same moment. He was carrying a tallow candle in a battered tin candlestick in his right hand, and he had a small bundle under his left arm. His white face was no whiter than usual, but he presented an awfully corpse-like appearance to Mr Bulstrode, who had never seen him or noticed him before. The softy recoiled, with a gesture of intense terror, as he saw Talbot; and a box of lucifer-matches, which he had been carrying in the candlestick, rolled to the ground.

'What are you doing here?" asked Mr Bulstrode, sternly, "and why did you come in at the window?"

"I wasn't doin' no wrong," the softy whined, piteously, "and it a'n't your business neither," he added, with a feeble attempt at insolence.

"It is my business. I am Mr Mellish's friend and relation, and I have reason to suspect that you are here for no good purpose," answered Talbot. "I insist upon knowing what you came for."

"I have n't come to steal owght, anyhow," said Mr Hargraves, "there 's nothing here but chairs and tables, and 't a'n't loikely I 've come arter them."

Perhaps not, but you have come after something, and I insist upon knowing what it is. You would n't come to this place unless you 'd a very strong reason for coming. What have you got there?"

Mr Bulstrode pointed to the bundle carried by the softy. Stephen Hargraves' small, red-brown eyes evaded those of his questioner, and made believe to mistake the direction in which Talbot looked.

"What have you got there?" repeated Mr Bulstrode, "you know well enough what I mean. What have you got there, in that bundle under your arm?"

The softy clutched convulsively at the dingy bundle, and glared at his questioner with something of the savage terror of some ugly animal at bay, except that in his brutalized manhood he was more awkward, and perhaps more repulsive, than the ugliest of lower animals.

"It 's nowght to you, nor to anybody else," he muttered sulkily. "I suppose a poor chap may fetch his few bits of clothes without bein' *called* like this ?"

"What clothes ? Let me see the clothes."

"No, I won't; they 're nowght to you. They — it 's only an old weskit as was give me by one o' th' lads in th' steables."

"A waistcoat!" cried Mr. Bulstrode; "let me see it this instant. A waistcoat of yours has been particularly inquired for, Mr. Hargraves. It 's a chocolate waistcoat, with yellow stripes and brass buttons, unless I 'm very much mistaken. Let me see it."

Talbot Bulstrode was almost breathless with excitement. The softy stared aghast at the description of his waistcoat, but he was too stup'd to comprehend instantaneously the reason for which this garment was wanted. He recoiled for a few paces, and then made a rush toward the window; but Talbot's hands closed upon his collar, and held him as if in a vice.

"You 'd better not trifle with me," cried Mr. Bulstrode; "I 've been accustomed to deal with refractory Sepoys in India, and I 've had a struggle with a tiger before now. Show me that waistcoat."

"I won't."

"By the Heaven above us, you shall."

"I won't!"

The two men closed with each other in a hand-to-hand struggle. Powerful as the soldier was, he found himself more than matched by Stephen Hargraves, whose thick-set frame, broad shoulders, and sinewy arms were almost herculean in their build. The struggle lasted for a considerable time — or for a time that seemed considerable to both of the combatants; but at last it drew toward its termination, and the heir of all the Bulstrodes, the commander of squadrons of horse, the man who had done battle with the blood-thirsty Sikhs, and ridden against the black mouths of Russian cannon at Balaklava, felt that he could scarcely hope to hold out much longer against the half-witted hanger-on of the Mellish stables. The horny fingers of the softy were upon his throat, the long arms of the softy were writhing round him, and in another moment Talbot Bulstrode lay upon the floor of the north lodge, with the softy's knee planted upon his heaving chest.

Another moment, and in the dim moonlight —the candle had been thrown down and trampled upon in the beginning of the scuffle — the heir of Bulstrode Castle saw Stephen Hargraves fumbling with his disengaged hand in his breast-pocket.

One moment more, and Mr. Bulstrode heard that sharp metallic noise only associated with the opening of a clasp-knife.

"E'es," hissed the softy, with his hot breath close upon the fallen man's cheek, "you wanted t' see th' weskit, did you ? but you shan't, for I 'll sarve you as I sarved him. 'T a'n't loikely I 'll let you stand between me and two thousand pound."

Talbot Raleigh Bulstrode had a faint notion that a broad Sheffield blade flashed in the silvery moonlight; but at this moment his senses grew confused under the iron grip of the softy's hand, and he knew little, except that there was a sudden crashing of glass behind him, a quick trampling of feet, and a strange voice roaring some seafaring oath above his head. The suffocating pressure was suddenly removed from his throat; some one or something was hurled into a corner of the little room; and Mr. Bulstrode sprang to his feet, a trifle dazed and bewildered, but quite ready to do battle again.

"Who is it ?" he cried.

"It 's me, Samuel Prodder!" answered the voice that had uttered that dreadful seafaring oath. "You were pretty nigh done for, mate, when I came aboard. It a'n't the first time I 've been up here after dark, takin' a quiet stroll and a pipe, before turning in over yonder" — Mr. Prodder indicated Doncaster by a backward jerk of his thumb. "I 'd been watchin' the light from a distance, till it went out suddenly five minutes ago, and then I came up close to see what was the matter. I don't know who you are, or what you are, or why you 've been quarrelling; but I know you 've been pretty near as nigh your death to-night as ever that chap was in the wood."

"The waistcoat!" gasped Mr. Bulstrode; "let me see the waistcoat!"

He sprang once more upon the softy, who had rushed toward the door, and was trying to beat out the panel with his iron-bound clog; but this time Mr. Bulstrode had a stalwart ally in the merchant-captain.

"A bit of rope comes uncommon handy in these cases," said Samuel Prodder, "for which reason I always make a point of carrying it somewhere about me."

He plunged up to his elbow in one of the capacious pockets of his tourist peg-tops, and produced a short coil of tarry rope. As he might have lashed a seaman to a mast in the last crisis of a wreck, so he lashed Mr. Stephen Hargraves now, binding him right and left, until the struggling arms and legs, and writhing trunk, were fain to be still.

"Now, if you want to ask him any questions, I make no doubt he 'll answer 'em," said Mr. Prodder, politely. "You 'll find him a deal quieter after that."

"I can't thank you now," Talbot answered, hurriedly; "there 'll be time enough for that by and by."

"Ay, ay, to be sure, mate," growled the captain; "no thanks is needed where no thanks is due. Is there anything else I can do for you?"

"Yes, a good deal presently; but I must find this waistcoat first. Where did he put it, I wonder? Stay, I'd better try and get a light. Keep your eye upon that man while I look for it."

Captain Prodder only nodded. He looked upon his scientific lashing of the softy as the triumph of art; but he hovered near his prisoner in compliance with Talbot's request, ready to fall upon him if he should make any attempt to stir.

There was enough moonlight to enable Mr. Bulstrode to find the lucifers and candlestick after a few minutes search. The candle was not improved by having been trodden upon; but Talbot contrived to light it, and then set to work to look for the waistcoat.

The bundle had rolled into a corner. It was tightly bound with a quantity of whipcord, and was harder than it could have been had it consisted solely of the waistcoat.

"Hold the light for me while I undo this," Talbot cried, thrusting the candlestick into Mr. Prodder's hand. He was so impatient that he could scarcely wait while he cut the whip-cord about the bundle with the softy's huge clasp-knife, which he had picked up while searching for the candle.

"I thought so," he said, as he unrolled the waistcoat; "the money's here."

The money was there, in a small Russian-leather pocket-book, in which Aurora had given it to the murdered man. If there had been any confirmation needed for this fact, the savage yell of rage which broke from Stephen's lips would have afforded that confirmation.

"It's the money," cried Talbot Bulstrode. "I call upon you, sir, to bear witness, whoever you may be, that I find this waistcoat and this pocket-book in the possession of this man, and that I take them from him after a struggle, in which he attempts my life."

"Ay, ay, I know him well enough," muttered the sailor; "he's a bad 'un; and him and me have had a stand further, before this."

"And I call upon you to bear witness that this man is the murderer of James Conyers!"

"WHAT?" roared Samuel Prodder; "him! Why, the double-dyed villain, it was him that put it into my head that it was my sister Eliza's chi—that it was Mrs. Mellish—"

"Yes, yes, I know. But we've got him now. Will you run to the house, and send some of the men to fetch a constable, while I stop here?"

Mr. Prodder assented willingly. He had assisted Talbot in the first instance without any idea of what the business was to lead to. Now he was quite as much excited as Mr. Bulstrode. He scrambled through the lattice, and ran off to the stables, guided by the lighted windows of the grooms' dormitories.

Talbot waited very quietly while he was gone. He stood at a few paces from the softy, watching Mr. Hargraves as he gnawed savagely at his bonds, in the hope, perhaps, of setting himself free.

"I shall be ready for you," the young Cornishman said, quietly, "whenever you're ready for me."

A crowd of grooms and hangers-on came with lanterns before the constable could arrive; and foremost among them came Mr. John Mellish, very noisy and very unintelligible. The door of the lodge was opened, and they all burst into the little chamber, where, heedless of grooms, gardeners, stable-boys, hangers-on, and rabble, John Mellish fell on his friend's breast and wept aloud.

L'ENVOI.

What more have I to tell of this simple drama of domestic life? The end has come. The element of tragedy which has been so intermingled in the history of a homely Yorkshire squire and his wife is henceforth to be banished from the record of their lives. The dark story which began in Aurora Floyd's folly, and culminated in the crime of a half-witted serving-man, has been told from the beginning to the end. It would be worse than useless to linger upon the description of a trial which took place at York at the Michaelmas Assizes. The evidence against Stephen Hargraves was conclusive; and the gallows outside York Castle ended the life of a man who had never been either help or comfort to any one of his fellow-creatures. There was an attempt made to set up a plea of irresponsibility upon the part of the softy, and the sobriquet which had been given him was urged in his defence; but a set of matter-of-fact jurymen, looking at the circumstances of the murder, saw nothing in it but a most cold-blooded assassination, perpetrated by a wretch whose sole motive was gain; and the verdict which found Stephen Hargraves guilty was tempered by no recommendation to mercy. The condemned murderer protested his innocence up to the night before his execution, and upon that night made a full confession of his crime, as is generally the custom of his kind. He related how he had followed James Conyers into the wood upon the night of his assignation with Aurora, and how he had watched and listened during the interview. He had shot the trainer in the back while Mr. Conyers sat by the water's-edge looking over the notes in the pocket-book, and he had used a button off his waistcoat instead of wadding, not finding anything else suitable for the purpose. He had hidden the waistcoat and pocket-book in a rat-hole in the wainscot of the murdered man's chamber, and, being dismissed from the lodge suddenly, had been compelled to leave his booty behind him rather than excite suspicion. It was thus that he had returned upon the night on which Talbot found him, meaning to secure his prize and start for Liverpool at six o'clock the following morning.

Aurora and her husband left Mellish Park immediately after the committal of the softy to York prison. They went to the south of France, accompanied by Archibald Floyd, and once more travelled together through scenes which were overshadowed by no sorrowful association. They lingered long at Nice; and here Talbot and Lucy joined them, with an impedimental train of luggage and servants, and a Normandy nurse with a blue-eyed girl-baby. It was at Nice that another baby was born, a black-eyed child — a boy, I believe — but wonderfully like that solemn-faced infant which Mrs. Alexander Floyd carried to the widowed banker two-and-twenty years before at Felden Woods.

It is almost supererogatory to say that Samuel Prodder, the sea-captain, was cordially received by hearty John Mellish and his wife.

He is to be a welcome visitor at the Park whenever he pleases to come; indeed, he is homeward bound from Barbadoes at this very time, his cabin-presses filled to overflowing with presents which he is carrying to Aurora, in the way of chilis preserved in vinegar, guava jelly, the strongest Jamaica rum, and other trifles suitable for a lady's acceptance. It may be some comfort to the gentlemen in Scotland Yard to know that John Mellish acted liberally to the detective, and gave him, the full reward, although Talbot Bulstrode had been the captor of the softy.

So we leave Aurora, a little changed, a shade less defiantly bright, perhaps, but unspeakably beautiful and tender, bending over the cradle of her first-born; and though there are alterations being made at Mellish, and loose boxes for broodmares building upon the site of the north lodge, and a subscription tan-gallop being laid across Harper's Common, I doubt if my heroine will care so much for horseflesh, or take quite so keen an interest in weight-for-age races as compared to handicaps, as she has done in the days that are gone.

THE END.

7
1.0

Ingram Content Group UK Ltd.
Milton Keynes UK
UKHW022333260723
425847UK00005B/81